OFFICIAL REPORT

OF THE

TWENTY-NINETH INTERNATIONAL

CHRISTIAN ENDEAVOR CONVENTION

HELD IN THE COLISEUM, THE FAIR-
GROUNDS, AND IN MANY CHURCHES

DES MOINES, IOWA

JULY 4 - 9, 1923.

First Fruits Press
Wilmore, Kentucky
c2015

First Fruits Press
The Academic Open Press of Asbury Theological Seminary
204 N. Lexington Ave., Wilmore, KY 40390
859-858-2236
first.fruits@asburyseminary.edu
asbury.to/firstfruits

Rev. Francis E. Clark, D.D., LL.D.

The Story of the Des Moines Convention

The Official Report

of

The Twenty-Ninth International

Christian Endeavor Convention

Held in the Coliseum, the Fair-Grounds
and in Many Churches

Des Moines, Iowa
July 4 to 9, 1923

Boston.	United Society of Christian Endeavor	Chicago.

Copyright, 1923, by the United Society of Christian Endeavor

CONTENTS

		Page
The Convention Committee		5
We Thank You		7
Des Moines		9

Chapter
- I. Corporation and Trustees Meeting ... 11
- II. Patriotic Opening Session ... 20
- III. The Quiet Hour ... 37
- IV. Christian Endeavor and Education ... 63
- V. The Choral of the Ways ... 78
- VI. Christian Endeavor in Conference ... 87
- VII. Principles and Practice ... 97
- VIII. The Alumni Banquet and Luncheons ... 106
- IX. The Junior Convention and Conference ... 111
- X. Pageant of the New Life ... 122
- XI. Christian Endeavor and World Peace ... 124
- XII. Denominational Rallies ... 139
- XIII. The Parade ... 151
- XIV. The League of Nations ... 154
- XV. Sunday Afternoon Meeting at the Fair-Grounds ... 164
- XVI. Sunday Evening at the Fair-Grounds ... 176
- XVII. Christian Endeavor Field-Secretaries ... 184
- XVIII. Practical Endeavor Problems ... 195
- XIX. A Chapter of Addresses ... 215
- XX. Religious Education ... 230
- XXI. Resolutions ... 256
- XXII. On the Mountain-Top ... 261
- Gleanings ... 267

ILLUSTRATIONS

	Page
Rev. Francis E. Clark, D. D., LL. D.	Frontispiece
Officers United Society of Christian Endeavor	12
Secretaries United Society of Christian Endeavor	14
Looking Down From The Galleries	24
Judge Hubert Utterback	26
Dr. William Hiram Foulkes Rev. William Ralph Hall Frank D. Getty Walter D. Howell	40
Dr. Henry H. Sweets Hugh S. Magill, LL.D. Dr. R. W. Gammon Rev. Royal J. Montgomery	64
The Thursday Night Coliseum Audience	80
Rev. James Kelly Rev. Lionel Fletcher Dr. and Mrs. Francis E. Clark	84
New York Delegation	88
The Winners for the Next Convention 1925	104
The Alumni Banquet, Fort Des Moines Hotel	106
A Maryland Group	108
Convention Pageant, "The New Life"	122
The Coliseum	122
Dr. John Timothy Stone Wayne B. Wheeler, LL. D. Rev. S. R. Harlow of Smyrna Frederick J. Libby	128
Des Moines Group	144
United Society Officers in the Lead	152
Christian Endeavor Parade	152
Minnesota Delegation	152
Illinois Approaching	152
A Feature in the Parade	152
Dr. O. T. Deever Rev. Lionel B. Fletcher Dr. H. L. Pickerill Dr. A. B. Bowman	156
Rev. W. A. MacTaggart Dr. A. B. Kendall Hon. Simeon D. Fess, LL. D.	160
A Portion of the Sunday Afternoon Meeting at the Fair Grounds	168
The Pennsylvania Delegation	184
A Group of Endeavorers on the Banks of the Des Moines River	200
Dr. O. F. Gilliom Rev. Dirk Lay, D.D. Duncan B. Curry	216
They are From Texas	232
On the Banks of the Des Moines River	264

DES MOINES CONVENTION COMMITTEE

JUDGE HUBERT UTTERBACK
Chairman

E. PAUL JONES
1st Vice Chairman

R. J. CORNELL
2nd Vice Chairman

ROY M. SMITH
3rd Vice Chairman

CORA I. UPP
Secretary

ALFRED HAMMARSTEDT
Treasurer

MEMBERS OF DES MOINES CONVENTION COMMITTEE

Herbert N. Brockway,
Chairman Ushers Com.

R. Mabel Bristol,
R. J. Cornell,
Chairmen of Publicity Com.

R. G. Davis,
Chairman Supplies Com.

L. Bruce DeHart,
Chairman Exhibits Com.

Rev. G. W. Emerson,
Chairman Pulpit Supply Com.

Alma L. Garber,
Chairman Music Com.

Mate Goodell,
Chairman Baptist Young People's Com.

E. C. Graves,
Chairman Volunteer Com.

Glen Hatfield,
Chairman Information Com.

Alfred Hammarstedt,
Treasurer.

Geo. E. Hamilton,
Chairman Hotel and Lodging Com.

Wm. W. Hammond,
Chairman Street Meetings Com.

E. Paul Jones,
Chairman of Finance Com.

O. E. Kellogg,
Rev. R. E. Kinsell,
Chairmen Pageant Com.

Marcellus Kirtley,
John B. Machin,
Chairmen Reception Com.

Rev. S. J. Mathieson,
Mrs. Anna Mae Morris,
Rev. A. Newbom,
Chairmen Luther League Com.

Grace M. Pierce,
Chairman Pages Com.

Theo. Rehmann,
E. C. Robinson,
Dr. Herbert Scott,
Alfred Severson,
Chairmen Convention Camp Com.

Rev. R. M. Shipman,
Chairman Epworth League Com.

Rev. W. A. Shullenberger,
Chairman Banquets Com.

Roy M. Smith
Chairman of Four Minute Speakers Com.

Prof. Alfred Smith,
Director of Chorus.

H. T. Steeper,
Chairman Halls and Platform Com.

Merle Scott,
Chairman Parade Com.

Clara Talbot.
Jno. L. Thompson,
Chairmen Colored Welfare Com.

Lynne P. Townsend,
Chairman Program Com.

Cora I. Upp,
Chairman Junior C. E. Com.

Rev. S. C. Wadding,
Chairman Badges Com.

Paul W. Wilderson,
Chairman Decorations Com.

Lelia Wilson,
Chairman Fine Arts Com.

J. B. Weeds,
Chairman Registration Com.

John V. Wicklund,
Chairman Entertainment Com.

W. E. Youtz,
Chairman Official Photographs Com.

WE THANK YOU

The Twenty-Ninth International Convention of Christian Endeavor held in Des Moines, Iowa, July 4-9, 1923, is history. What was said and done at the mid-west convention is compiled in this volume.

For the first time in the history of the United Society of Christian Endeavor nearly all the addresses and conferences were taken down verbatim by stenotype operators, while others covering either conferences or rallies were reported in shorthand at the meeting. Otherwise a report of such proportions covering many simultaneous meetings held in different places would be impossible. We also are deeply indebted to the editor and assistant-editors of "The Christian Endeavor World" and the field-secretaries for much of the matter here published. With this method of gathering data, the compiler feels confident that this report gives a true presentation of the wonderful Des Moines Convention.

It is, therefore, our firm belief that this report will prove a lasting stimulus to the work of Christian Endeavor everywhere, and radiate the spirit of enthusiasm, the helpful purpose, and the deep devotional life manifest in the many meetings here reported. For the privilege of participation in gathering and compilation of this report we are thankful, and submit it for your consideration.

ALVIN J. SHARTLE,
Treasurer and Publication Manager,
United Society of Christian Endeavor,
Boston, Massachusetts.

DES MOINES

By A. J. Shartle

The twenty-ninth migration of Christian Endeavor to its International Convention was an event worthy of note. In this instance these migratory Christian Endeavorers and friends, impelled by the spirit of the occasion, and with an enthusiasm unbounded because of its unquenchable love for Christian Endeavor, converged on the mid-west, the city of Des Moines, the capital of a State "where the tall corn grows."

The Near East sent its delegation, as did England, Ireland, Australia, Canada, and other countries. Our neighbor, Mexico, the land of turmoil for many years, yet productive of Christian Endeavor, was well represented. From the shores of the beautiful and prosperous Pacific to the alluring, rock-bound coast of New England with its hum of industry, and from the productive Gulf States to the Great Lakes they came by train and automobile, or walked, a mighty, singing, shouting, praying host representing the youth of America. They came with all the fire of youth and with an enthusiasm born of a conviction that in Christian Endeavor youth will be taught, trained, and prepared to meet the stern realities of life. In this convention the forty-eight States vied with each other as to which should have the largest proportionate representation, with the result that many, many thousands were registered and in attendance.

Des Moines gave us a warm reception in two episodes. The first episode was presented by "Old Sol" who produced a temperature of from 94 to 96 degrees. Each succeeding evening as he disappeared back of the western horizon he seemed to grin and say, "I'll make it hotter for you tomorrow," and he did, calling the effort "Iowa corn weather." However, Christian Endeavor was compensated by a second episode presented by the Des Moines Convention Committee representing many units of a well-constructed and splendidly balanced organization. This committee received us with hospitality far above 100 degrees of warmth, made our assignments efficiently, and entertained its guests in a manner that will always remain a pleasant memory. The engineer of this well-managed, smooth-running dynamo of Christian Endeavor energy was a man big of body, mind, and heart; a man of genial countenance, good judgment, and love for his fellows. He is a Judge of a Court; a man who stepped from his judicial throne for a time in order to correlate the law with Christian Endeavor to produce a convention,—and what a convention it was! How splendid!

A Des Moines delegation came to Buffalo in 1919 and invited us to hold our Twenty-Eighth International Convention in that fair city. On that occasion it sent its fair young women to plead the cause, and how well it was done! Just as well as on the occasion when all the male officers of the magnificent union resigned in order to enlist in the service of the United States during the great war, and the fairest and best of the gentler sex stepped into the offices made vacant, and kept the Christian Endeavor fires burning efficiently and brightly until the boys returned.

However, we then had obligations in New York City, and the invitation could not be accepted. Undaunted, they came to New York in 1921, extended an invitation for the Twenty-Ninth International Convention which was unanimously accepted. Today the Des Moines Convention is history. It was a wonderful convention, held in a city that is worth-while, backed by a Chamber of Commerce and a Convention Committee that met every obligation, financial or otherwise, according to contract.

Des Moines, we salute you! We thank you! Your work was done so well that we shall always love you. The experiment of amplifying the meetings was such a success that we congratulate you. We know that the thousands who thronged the banks of your beautiful river, and still more beautiful nearby bridges, because they could not gain admission to the crowded auditorium, will always bless you. Therefore, may the convention programme, amplified so successfully in the auditorium and on the fairgrounds that everyone heard and understood, thereby awakening a public conscience to a spiritual need, be amplified again and yet again a million times in the hearts of men through all the years until every knee shall bend and acknowledge Him as "King of Kings and Lord of Lords," and He shall reign forever.

CHAPTER I.

CORPORATION AND TRUSTEES MEETING

It was in the great ballroom of Hotel Fort Des Moines that the first meeting of the Convention was held, a meeting, largely attended, of the officers and trustees of the United Society.

The first speaker, after prayer had been offered by Chaplain Ramsden, was very fitly Rev. Francis E. Clark, D. D., president and founder of the organization. His speech was a telling brief survey of the society history during its forty-two years, which will be printed in a later number.

Treasurer Shartle reported a year of increased sales and income, including a number of sums given to the United Society on the annuity plan. Associate President Poling then told of the new work he is taking up as associate pastor of the Marble Collegiate Church, New York City, a work which will not in any way curtail his Christian Endeavor interests. The trustees voted to send a message of greeting to Dr. David James Burrell, pastor of the Marble Collegiate Church, and another to the officers of that church, for the way in which they are helping Dr. Poling to maintain his Christian Endeavor activities.

General Secretary Gates's report was a thrilling one, telling of wonderful growth. Since July 1, 1921, no fewer than 10,971 new societies have been added to our lists. A round dozen States have made a net gain of ten per cent in the number of their societies. More than 250,000 young people have enrolled in one or several of our leadership-training courses.

The trustees voted to authorize the formation of three commissions to study the needs of Senior, Intermediate, and Junior programmes of work, and to report a year hence.

Alumni Superintendent Vandersall reported achievement in the Alumni department, and intense work connecting funds from many sources for Christian Endeavor at home and abroad.

C. C. Hamilton, field-secretary of the United Society and field-manager of THE CHRISTIAN ENDEAVOR WORLD, briefly related the story of journeyings oft and long, and independently verified Mr. Gates's statement of advancement.

Editorial Secretary Anderson made his report of work done, books written, and literature revised in the past year.

Southern Secretary Evans pointed out that nine out of the ten Dixie State presidents are in the Convention, together with leaders in the All-South Committee. The State conventions have been unusually large.

Dr. Ira Landrith, extension secretary, forcefully and wittily recounted the facts connected with the Fifty-fifty campaign, and the work of placing Christian Endeavor before many communities. People are willing to pay for a thing they come to believe in.

Chaplain Ramsden, army and navy secretary, described his method in his army posts to get local Endeavorers interested in Christian Endeavor work among the soldiers.

Dr. Clark introduced Rev. James Kelly, of Scotland, president last year of the British Christian Endeavor Union, who briefly told of the amazing vitality of Christian Endeavor in Europe in spite of very difficult economic conditions. Even in harassed Ireland Christian Endeavor has advanced by fifty per cent in the past year.

Dr. William Hiram Foulkes, chairman of the finance and budget committee, related steps that have been taken to put the financing of Christian Endeavor on an adequate basis. The Fifty-fifty plan was the result of their deliberations, a plan which gives fifty per cent of sums collected to the State Christian Endeavor work, and fifty per cent to the United Society. The committee also set up a budget for the coming year, carefully analyzing every figure. A permanent budget and finance committee of five was approved, and the members of the committee were later named.

New Jersey, looking to 1927, made an earnest plea through Ex-president John T. Sproull to have the International Convention held in Atlantic City, N. J. The trustees listened sympathetically to this eloquent statement.

Through Secretary Freet, Ohio formally presented Cleveland's invitation for the Convention of 1929, and awoke a hearty response from the trustees.

A YEAR IN FINANCIAL ENDEAVOR

By Alvin J. Shartle

Treasurer and Publication Manager of the United Society of Christian Endeavor

Facts and figures will portray results achieved since last we met. To present such facts and figures is our privilege.

Executive Department

Balance on hand June 1, 1922, $2,587.38. Receipts from all sources for the year ending May 31, 1923 were $69,016.97; expenditures, $62,636.97, leaving a balance of $8,967.38. In this balance are included the financial resources necessary to meet a part of the expenses of this convention. Liabilities, like the

OFFICERS
UNITED SOCIETY OF CHRISTIAN ENDEAVOR

Daniel A. Poling

E. P. Gates

A. J. Shartle

Stanley B. Vandersall

Francis E. Clark

Robert P. Anderson

Amos R. Wells

poor, we always have with us; as of May 31, 1923, they amount to $97,890.11. However, by deducting these obligations from the assets of the organization, which are $330,526.80, we find that the net assets and surplus of the United Society of Christian Endeavor Corporation, as of May 31, 1923, are $232,636.69.

The United Society of Christian Endeavor owned two splendid parcels of real estate. In October, 1922, we sold the second of the two parcels, receiving for both $150,000. After deducting expenses of sale and transfer we attacked that menacing real-estate mortgage and note of $200,000, and went over the top October 1, 1922, with the result that to-day the mortgage on the World's Christian Endeavor Building is $53,000, and we are happy to report that, provided success attends our efforts, we anticipate burning this mortgage on the fiftieth anniversary of the birth of Christian Endeavor, which we may celebrate in Boston in 1931.

The newest trio in Christian Endeavor at Boston Headquarters are *Annuities, Wills,* and *Insurance,* three splendid suggestions for the building up of a *World's Christian Endeavor Foundation,* a foundation that will perpetuate the work of Christian Endeavor for all time. Already friends have purchased some of our Life Annuity Bonds, in denominations of $100, $500, $1,000, $5,000 and $10,000. One lady made a will the other day, devising and bequeathing to the United Society real estate and personal property amounting to $15,000. Others are thinking of Insurance as an investment. Have you ever thought of it? Christian Endeavorers are good risks.

Publishing Department

As Publication Manager I would report a good year and a steady growth.

The cash receipts as of May 31, 1923, are $92,138.61; disbursements, $90,766.74; balance, cash on hand, $1,371.93; net profit, $3,383.34; contributions to the Executive Department, $2,208.96; net sales for the year, $80,217.72.

Our operating expenses for 1923 are $3,084.85 less than for 1922. The sales in the Boston office are $2,264.64 higher than in 1922, while the sales in the Chicago office are $3,628.39 less than a year ago, all of which may be due to a fluctuation of trade.

Assets of the Publishing Department, as of May 31, 1923, are $71,700.41. The sale of literature and supplies yielding $80,217.72 net during a period of twelve months.

Our chief production during the past year is Dr. Clark's Autobiography entitled "Memories of Many Men in Many Lands." The first edition of this wonderful book of a great man is nearly exhausted.

Another production just off the press and published at this convention is "Studies in Stewardship," by our Editorial Secretary, Rev. Robert P. Anderson.

Of the smaller publications, such as leaflets, booklets, and the "Endeavorer's Daily Companion," tens of thousands of copies have been published and sold, while our new designs in Christian Endeavor jewelry and novelties introduced at this convention will prove an enterprise worthy of a department here to serve.

In addition, 40,000 copies of our seventy-two page catalogue have been published and distributed, together with thousands of pieces of attractive advertising so necessary in the promotion of our work.

We desire to commend Mr. R. A. Walker, the genial manager of our Western office at Chicago. His faithfulness and loyalty, qualifications so necessary in the management of a business requiring close attention, are worthy of commendation.

My work in the field during the year was in many States, and in Canada, and covered rallies, conventions, conferences, summer schools, colleges, and Bible classes. The miles travelled number 30,000. In addition, as a representative of the United Society of Christian Endeavor in the work of Americanization and temperance as it relates to law-enforcement, I am serving as chairman of the publicity committee and treasurer of the Allied Organizations Committee for law-enforcement in Massachusetts.

EDITORIAL SECRETARY'S REPORT

Rev. Robert P. Anderson

The work of an editorial secretary is very largely routine work, with nothing spectacular about it, and therefore any account of it must be more or less arid.

Just twelve months ago I was putting through the press two booklets which I had written as part of the routine work, the Daily Readings for 1923 for use in Senior societies, and the Junior Portion or daily readings for use in Junior societies, and also the Endeavorer's Daily Companion for this year.

An important piece of work was the preparation of the manuscript of Dr. Clark's book, "Memories of Many Men in Many Lands," which I also read in proof later. Quite recently I have gone over this work again and made some necessary corrections with a view to the publication of a second edition.

Last fall I prepared a set of topics for Senior societies for 1924, and another for Junior societies for the same year. These were adopted by the Interdenominational Young People's Commission at its meeting last December in Nashville, Tenn. I have since put them through the press in card form, and have also written the Daily Readings for 1924 and the Junior booklet, the Daily Portion for 1924. I have also written the Endeavorer's Daily Companion for 1924, and all these are in the hands of the publication manager ready for the printer.

I have also written a book on Stewardship. It is entitled, "Studies in Stewardship," and is designed for use in study classes.

SECRETARIES
UNITED SOCIETY OF CHRISTIAN ENDEAVOR

It is the first book on this subject ever published by the United Society.

Among minor tasks I revised Dr. Clark's thirty-two page booklet, "C. E. Unions; wrote a four-page leaflet on Evangelism; prepared for the printer Dr. Clark's leaflet, "Making a Will"; and put through the press Mr. Shartle's leaflet, "Life Annuity Bonds." It was also my privilege to prepare for the printer the "Service of Worship" prepared by Dr. Augustine Smith, a service which will be used in this convention.

As chairman of the topics committee of the Interdenominational Young People's Commission I attended a meeting in Buffalo in April where I presented a set of C. E. topics for Senior societies for 1925. The committee also adopted a set of Junior topics, and is at work on a set of Intermediate topics. These topics will all be presented to the Commission at its annual meeting which will be held in Buffalo in December.

Besides this I have read many manuscripts submitted to the United Society for publication, and we have begun the revision of our literature. A great deal of this literature is excellent, but old. It has served its generation well; indeed some of it has served more than one generation, and much of it I hope will serve generations to come. But the garments of literature get worn by many years of pilgrimage, and they need renewing. We believe that with some sartorial embellishment this literature is good for many years to come. Already we have gone over some of our early publications, bringing them up to date, and this work will proceed as rapidly as possible.

Our publication possibilities are limited only by our funds to carry out plans. Various works are in contemplation, notably a booklet on the Pledge, which has been begun, and which will probably be ready in the fall.

ALUMNI SUPERINTENDENT'S REPORT

Stanley B. Vandersall

The Des Moines Convention marks the fourth anniversary of the establishment of the Alumni Department. Four years ago at Buffalo, it was decided to recognize the Alumni work to the extent of having a superintendent to look after its interest and to promote and encourage the Alumni idea in this country and in other parts of the world. From comparatively small beginnings, which date back a little more than five years, the Alumni part in Christian Endeavor has grown until it is definitely established.

Alumni Fellowships to the number of 240 are found from Maine to California. While much of the emphasis in the Fellowships has centred around the annual contributions of the members, a great many other features, such as social gathering, help to local unions and to society work have been of great benefit to the cause.

A little more than two years ago the Alumni Council, designed for the local church, had its beginning. This feature, which is usually not financial, has had a great record of usefulness in many churches. The Alumni Council idea, making as it does a special place for the older people of the church in Christian Endeavor, and relating them to the direct interests of the young people, has a great future in our movement. The seeds of education which have been sown are ripening into the fruit of organization. We now count on the records of the United Society 141 Alumni Councils in many States, with a great many more that have not definitely reported, and have therefore not been given charters. It is safe to predict that within a very few years there will be many hundreds of these Alumni groups in the local churches.

The work of the Alumni superintendent has been varied, including the promotion of the finances, and the collection of the annual pledges, partly through the Fellowship treasurers, and partly by direct mail appeal, writing of literature describing the details of the Alumni work, and field-work of a general nature, as time and opportunity would allow.

There are seventeen different pieces of Alumni literature, all of which are provided without cost to the workers in the field in order that the Alumni idea may prosper.

During the past year the gross returns from the Alumni Department have been $12,019.20. Of this amount, by agreement with the states, there has been turned over to the state unions the sum of $4,370.69. A part of this was on the twenty-five per cent basis, established four years ago and a part of it on the fifty per cent basis beginning in January, 1922. The United Society's share of the Alumni returns during the past year amounted to $7,648.51.

In addition to direct duties in connection with Alumni work, the superintendent has been responsible since November 15, 1922, for all the financial collections of the United Society, including the 50-50 pledges, the direct gifts by mail, and miscellaneous pledge items. The collection department has been systematized so that notifications are regularly made, and complete reports are available, showing the relationship of all the States to the total financial plan of the United Society. Since November 15, the collection department has been responsible for the receipt and handling of more than $30,000. It has likewise made the proper refunds to the State unions, and has kept the field secretaries and other officers informed as to the progress of their respective States. We believe this unification of collections has been a distinct step in advance for the United Society.

In line with financial duties, the superintendent has served as treasurer of the World's Union, handling several thousands of dollars received from friends of the work and expended for Christian Endeavor in foreign lands.

The past year has been a pleasant year of service and it has witnessed marked advances in the program of Christian Endeavor. We believe still more in the future, and are willing to do our share toward greater success.

FIELD SECRETARY'S REPORT

C. C. Hamilton

The field-secretary of the United Society has traveled approximately 100,000 miles during the past two years, and has touched almost every State. In some instances only a few points were visited in a State, and at other times a full month was given to an intensive State tour.

General-secretary Gates, in his characteristic fashion, makes facts and figures tell a thrilling story of organization development and increased number of societies. Certainly one finds much over which to rejoice. After almost continual contact with the field during the past years, I am convinced that our young people were never more willing to give enthusiastic and unselfish service to the work.

Southern-secretary Charles F. Evans, Southwestern-secretary W. Roy Breg, and Pacific Coast Secretary Paul Brown, loom large when a survey of the field is made. The monumental service rendered by these sectional secretaries of the United Society of Christian Endeavor is certainly one of the most stabilizing influences now at work.

The work of Paul Brown during the past year has been little short of miraculous. Everywhere in Washington, Oregon and Idaho new societies have been organized and district organizations developed. Secretary Breg's leadership has been especially helpful in New Mexico, Arizona, Utah, and Wyoming, where the work has made remarkable advance. Under the able direction of Secretary Evans the Dixie States increase in favor with pastors and denominational leaders and challenge a greater number of young people each year.

The state field-secretaries are the hardest working group of folks in the country. No organization has more unselfishly loyal and devoted workers. They are truly rendering a heroic service.

During these past months, I have traveled, worked, and lived with many of them, and my testimony is that the better we know them and the more we learn of their lives and their constant labors for the movement we all love, the greater will be our appreciation of what they are doing for the young people of America.

During the past year, I have done most of my field-work in the Southwest and in the far West. In September I spent three weeks in New Jersey, then followed State conventions in Connecticut, New Jersey, and Tennessee, two weeks in October in Oklahoma, and the month of November in Texas. In early December,

I attended the New Mexico State convention. After the holidays I had ten days in Indiana and an engagement in Detroit.

Leaving Boston in the middle of February, 1923, I jumped to the Arizona State convention, and then spent March in California; April in Oregon, Washington, and Idaho, and early May in Utah and Wyoming.

Without one cent of expense to the United Society 15,790 miles were traveled in the three months' tour. In the three months we had only two nights off, but it was one of the happiest and most successful tours I have ever made. In virtually all these meetings we told the story of the plans and programme of the United Society, and urged attendance at Des Moines Convention, the State objectives were emphasized and "The Christian Endeavor World" subscription campaign was presented.

With a heart full of gratitude to Almighty God for the privilege of service, with sincere appreciation of the sympathetic interest and splendid co-operation of my associates at headquarters, and with a prayer that Christian Endeavor may continue with ever enlarging usefulness to serve for Christ and the Church, this report is respectfully submitted.

The following were elected officers of the United Society of Christian Endeavor Corporations:

Officers of the Corporation

President.............................Rev. Francis E. Clark
Associate President........................Daniel A. Poling
Vice-President............................Howard B. Grose
Clerk...................................Clarence C. Hamilton
Treasurer......................................A. J. Shartle
Auditor.....................................J. J. Arakelyan

The following officers, secretaries, and superintendents were elected:

Officers

General Secretary..........................Edward P. Gates
Publication Manager............................A. J. Shartle
Financial Secretary....................Stanley B. Vandersall
Editorial Secretary........................Robert P. Anderson
Extension Secretary...............................Ira Landrith
Southern Secretary.........................Charles F. Evans
Pacific Coast Secretary.........................Paul C. Brown
Southwestern Secretary.........................W. Roy Breg

Superintendents

Alumni................................Stanley B. Vandersall
Citizenship................................Daniel A. Poling
Army and Navy..............................S. C. Ramsden

Members of the Executive Committee
of the
United Society of Christian Endeavor

Rev. Francis E. Clark, D.D.
Rev. Daniel A. Poling, D.D.
Mr. A. J. Shartle
Mr. E. P. Gates
William Shaw, LL.D.
Amos R. Wells, Litt.D.
Rev. R. P. Anderson
Rev. Stanley B. Vandersall
Mr. C. C. Hamilton
Mr. Erle S. Bacon
Mr. J. J. Arakelyan
Rev. James L. Hill, D.D.
Mr. Charles H. Jones
Rev. William Hiram Foulkes, D.D.
Mr. Fred L. Ball
Rev. E. L. Reiner

Chapter II.

A PATRIOTIC OPENING SESSION

Wednesday Evening, July 4

The great Coliseum was crowded long before time for the opening session on Wednesday evening. It was a brilliant company, gay with many colors, with bright caps of bizarre forms designating the different States. It was a hilarious company, the different delegations, under vociferous leaders, practising in all parts of the hall their diverse cheers and State songs. It was a happy company anticipatory of great things, many of them athrill with the consciousness of such a Christian throng as they had never seen or imagined before.

As Dr. Clark came forward he received a wonderful spontaneous greeting, the vast audience rising and saluting him with handclaps, with the waving of handkerchiefs and banners, and continuing the greeting until he bade them be seated.

As President of the United Society of Christian Endeavor, I declare the Twenty-Ninth International Convention of Christian Endeavor of the United Society of Christian Endeavor open.

The first word should be a word of prayer to Almighty God. Let us pray.—

The convention this evening will be presided over by our dear friend of the United Society, Dr. Daniel A. Poling, and the first exercise is the patriotic musical programme, presided over and arranged by Dr. H. Augustine Smith.

FRIENDS OF CHRIST CAMPAIGN

By Rev. Francis E. Clark, DD. LL.D.

As we come to another hilltop outlook, such as these biennial conventions always afford, we should look in two directions: *backward*, to thank God for His numberless mercies in the past; *forward*, to see what is yet to be done, and how best with His help we may do it.

First, the *Backward View*. While we humbly confess that we have left undone many things which we ought to have done, we can rejoice and be glad in the way God has used the poor efforts, the hesitating faith, the imperfect consecration, we have given Him.

Never, in the more than forty-two years of Christian Endeavor history, has the society been so large in numbers, so resourceful and abundant in its plans and methods of service, so close to the heart of the churches; in a word, never before has it been so pre-eminently blessed of the Master. The more detailed story of the last two years, when told by our general secretary, will confirm these generalities.

It is not with unholy pride that we contemplate our far-flung spiritual battle-line, and that we thank God for our millions of comrades who march under the banner of Christian Endeavor. I recently heard an honored pastor of one of our largest churches, on an anniversary occasion, reckon up the number of persons who had entered his church and chapels during the year at all the services, morning, evening, Sunday school, and weekdays; and he found it was the astonishing number of 175,000.

Reckon up the numbers in all the world who must have attended Endeavor prayer meetings in North and South America, Europe, Asia, Africa, Australasia, the East and West Indies, and Polynesia, since last we met in such a convention as this; and you will find it reaches the enormous total of at least three hundred millions of young men and women, boys and girls. Discount all you will for youthful thoughtlessness and carelessness, and you will have left a mighty residuum of spiritual zeal and earnestness there gained.

Careful consideration shows that at least three millions have also met together in union gatherings of a hundred denominations, races, and languages. Again discount all you will for "mere enthusiasm" and for the inexperience of youth, and yet another vast residuum is left, of fellowship, Christian good will and friendship, the friendship for lack of which the war-torn world to-day is dying.

To five hundred thousand Christian Endeavor committees and ten thousand union-work committees some religious work has been committed for every week of the past two years. Let the pessimist talk as he will of "lame and lazy committees"; yet I can assure him that millions of worth-while deeds for the Master are the result of their efforts.

In our backward look another cause of thanksgiving is the unbroken unity in our ranks. Some organizations within the first four decades of their existence have lost their early zeal, soft-pedalled their Christian purpose, and divided into two or more factions. Not so Christian Endeavor. Its activities and methods have multiplied tenfold; but its fundamental purpose, to train the young for Christian service in the church and for the church, has never been altered or overshadowed.

Do you ask the reason? It is because it is founded not on controversial matters of belief, but upon a broad personal covenant with Jesus Christ. Let it never be forgotten that the belief of a society is and must be the belief of its church. It has no life separate from its church. It has no doctrinal matters to settle. Doctrine is the affair of the mother church, not of the child, which as compared with its mother is but an infant of days.

To sum up our backward look in a sentence, we thank God to-day for continued growth, for enlarged strength, for undiminished unity, for worldwide fellowship.

Now right about face for the *Forward Look*. Encouraged by the past, the past of God's right hand, we will go forward undauntedly. What have we, as Endeavorers, before us? Much land to be possessed. Many souls to be won for the Master. Tens of thousands of churches to be strengthened through the conversion and training of their youth. We have a fellowship to be enlarged, which opens wide its doors to all in every land who adopt its covenant of love and loyalty, love to the Master and loyalty to His church.

A hopelessly big programme, do you say? Ah, no, not hopeless or impossible if it is, as we believe, not our programme alone, but God's programme for us.

In seeking to carry out this programme I propose, with the advice and consent of leading Endeavorers, representing officially all denominations, that we adopt for the next two years a *Friends-of-Christ Campaign*.

We have had many campaigns within the last two and forty years, all of which, in large measure, have been successful. Does not this one express by its very name the pith, the inmost purpose, of Christian Endeavor? Friends *of* Christ. Friends *for* Christ. Friends *in* Christ. This is the *summum bonum*, the highest good for which we can strive.

The noblest title the Bible confers on any man is the designation of

Abraham as "the friend of God." The friend of Jesus Christ carries the same title, an unspeakably noble one.

But as friends of Christ our endeavor shall not be for ourselves alone, but for all our friends as well. "Our friends *for* Christ," then, shall be one of our chief watchwords. Recently our most noted American psychologist said to me: "If we would save civilization, we must get back to the old-fashioned word, 'conversion.' I formerly scoffed at it; the World War has taught me that there is no other word so absolutely necessary. I say it as a psychologist."

Yet many are hurried into our churches to-day who never profess to be converted, who have never made an out-and-out decision for Christ. "Conversion is a lost art," say some. In carrying out our new campaign, "Our friends *for* Christ," let us prove that such a dreadful, fatal confession is false.

There is another important preposition which in our new campaign we must consider. Friends *in* Christ also shall be our aim for ourselves and others. Friends *in* Christ, a personal indwelling in Him and He in us. Consider His words, "He that abideth in me, and I in him, the same beareth much fruit." No fruitful endeavors are promised to those who are not *in* Him.

Do not omit from our campaign any one of these prepositions. Friends *of, in,* and *for,* Jesus Christ will, if you agree, be our specific endeavor, object, aim, and ambition for the two years to come. Translated into three words, they read, *Personal Devotion, Fellowship,* and *Evangelism.*

For a motto what better one can we choose than Jesus' own words, "Ye are my friends if ye do whatsoever I command you"? For our slogan the one tremendous word "WHATSOEVER" has been suggested. I know none better. The Christian Endeavor pledge is an epitome of our whole campaign for 1923-25. *"Trusting in the Lord Jesus Christ for strength, I promise Him that I will strive to do* WHATEVER *He would like to have me do."*

It is interesting to note that the constitution of the first society, adopted by the Williston young people, February 2, 1881, defined the object of the society as follows: "To increase their mutual acquaintance, and make them more useful in the service of God."

What does this original definition of Christian Endeavor embody but the great thought of this coming two years' programme: Friendship, friends of God, friends of one another, our friends for God?

How to carry out this great campaign for Personal Devotion, worldwide Christian Fellowship, and Evangelism will be outlined by our general secretary, aided by denominational leaders, and I need not go into its details at this time. I would suggest that the Quiet Hour and all it stands for, of prayer, Bible-reading, and meditation, the hour which has already enlisted 220,716 Comrades, has much to do with the cultivation of Personal Devotion. It will go far to promote the spirit of Evangelism and Fellowship.

Endeavorers in the past have never been satisfied with vague generalities, however glittering. They have not shot their arrows into the air, to fall to earth they know not where. They have demanded a target to aim at, a goal definite and concrete; and the remarkable success of past campaigns has been due to the fact that something definite has been the object of our endeavor.

So I would suggest for our evangelistic goal that we strive within the next two years to bring to a knowledge of Jesus Christ and into His church a number equal to fifty per cent of the present active membership of our societies. This will indeed mean "Our friends for Chist." If we have one hundred active members, our lowest goal will be fifty; if we have fifty, we will strive to bring to Him at least twenty-five; if we have but twenty, our opportunities will be less, but we will seek for the ten.

In thus seeking friends for Christ do not forget the Juniors. The psychologists now tell us that the peak of the age of conversion is not sixteen, as they used to say, but twelve.

In order to accomplish our great programme, relying on the Lord Jesus Christ for strength, we must put especial stress on decision-days, making them more frequent and effective than in the past. Let us make Christian Endeavor Week a great Decision-Week, to be led up to by much prayer and previous preparation. "Our friends for Christ" will be more than ever the motto of this week.

But this should not be our only season, for decisions. Every consecration meeting may well be a decision-day, with an invitation given to all to become out-and-out friends of Christ. Oh, what may not the record of these two years to come, a record as yet unwritten and unblotted, mean for our Master's cause the continent over? How it may translate our universal motto, *"Pro Christo et Ecclesia,"* "For Christ and the Church," into glorious realities!

Before we meet in an International or World's Convention again, twenty-four months, one hundred and four weeks, seven hundred and thirty days, will have passed, each day bringing with it opportunities to become ourselves closer friends *of* Jesus Christ, and to make more and more friends *for* Jesus Christ.

This campaign carried out will mean hundreds of thousands, yes, millions, of new friends for Christ, new members and workers for the church.

Think, too, of the by-products of such a campaign. Do not let any one sneer at it as merely an effort to save some individual souls, as some moderns are inclined to do. A man must be saved as an individual. But salvation does not end with the individual. Such a campaign means better men and women and better communities. It affects our recreations as well as our work; it means the social gospel in industry and in the affairs of town and State; it means temperance and good citizenship; it means nobler, sweeter, more peaceful nations; it means death to the hatred, jealousy, and revenge which are ravaging the world.

Friends, if you think this campaign is not of God, ignore it. If you think He approves it, stand up and cheer not for the speaker, but for our new campaign: Friends *of* Christ, friends *for* Christ, friends *in* Christ, and for our slogan, *"Whatsoever." Whatsoever He would have us do.*

It was the evening of the glorious Fourth, and surely our national Independence Day was never more beautifully and suitably celebrated than in the Patriotic Pageant conducted by Professor H. Augustine Smith, of Boston University. It was a fine procession that marched upon the platform, led by two lovely girls and a manly young fellow in scholar's cap and gown. One of the girls was dressed as Columbia, the other as Poetry, while the young man was the Voice of the People. Behind them came a file of Boy Scouts and Campfire Girls, ranged across the platform.

In spirited dialogue the three speakers reminded us of the Pilgrims and the other pioneers, then of three great Americans, Washington, Lincoln, and Roosevelt. Next the audience took up the word, singing "America the Beautiful" with appropriate gestures: a salute of the flag for the first stanza, hands shading the eyes in forward look for the second stanza, hands clasped for the third stanza, hands raised to heaven for the closing stanza. Our hero dead were then sweetly remembered with the Salute of the Drooping Lilies. A Boy Scout sounded taps on his bugle, and then, as the piano was played softly, every one slowly lifted a handkerchief allowed to hang loosely, and after they had been raised as high as possible they were as slowly lowered in like fashion,—the most impressive salute we ever saw. The wonderful exercise closed with the singing of the "Battle-Hymn of the Republic," illuminated by Professor Smith's inspiring comments.

Dr. Poling, the presiding officer of the evening, next introduced four prominent Iowans, who welcomed the Convention in a splendid way. The civic welcome was finely given by the city attorney, Hon. Chauncey A. Weaver.

I appear at this hour under a commission from His Honor, Mayor Carl M. Garver, to extend to the delegates and visitors to this Convention an official greeting and welcome to the City of Des Moines.

In the contemplation of this magnificent, this inspirational audience, I am moved to take you into my confidence and confess that I am almost glad the mayor couldn't come. It is the most wonderful Fourth of July audience I ever had. To have even a humble part in an occasion like this, might be classified, it seems to me, among the thrills which come once in a lifetime.

In looking into the faces of you who have come from the North, East, South, and West it would be quite an easy matter to launch into a rhapsody concerning the glories of Iowa and the distinction which Des Moines enjoys in being the capitol and metropolis of such a Commonwealth. I shall not yield to that temptation. You know enough, or had heard enough about Des Moines and Iowa to want to come, and now our chief concern is that your visit shall be so pleasant and profitable you will carry away minds so richly stored with happy memories you will hope to come again.

Des Moines entertains a good many conventions in the course of a year. They meet to consider a wide diversity of themes. With some it is agriculture, some education, some politics, some banking—all the various activities are sooner or later represented—but the people of Des Moines are peculiarly interested in you, because of that for which you stand; for what you represent in the field of moral conquest; for the faith which impels you to surge forward toward the victories which lie just ahead.

The ecclesiastical waters are somewhat troubled in certain sections of our common country just now concerning what should and should not be believed. We are not worried concerning you. Looking upon the banners which head your majestic columns, we see reflected there the unfading radiance of the Star of Bethlehem; the sacrificial love which glorified the Cross of Calvary; and the White Flowers of Immortal Hope which blossomed in the hearts of men when in the pure light of that first Easter morning it was discovered that "the stone had been rolled away."

Delegates to the Convention, you are a part of one of the most wonderful crusades which ever moved across the page of human history.

Des Moines considers it a privilege, not easily measured in words, to have been so highly favored with a place along the line of march.

Dr. Charles S. Medbury spoke for the Des Moines churches, welcoming the Endeavorers not because of what Iowa and Des Moines are, but because of what Endeavorers are.

REV. CHARLES S. MEDBURY for the Churches: We are trying very hard to build a really worth-while city out here in our beautiful central west. You have come to help us, and we are glad. I think without disparaging any city of all our proud America, I may say to you young people tonight that I do not believe there is a city anywhere that would welcome such a gathering as this with more intelligent sympathy than does our own home city of Des Moines.

Your message will not be taken lightly here; your pronouncements will not be viewed lightly; you will be taken seriously, as you deserve to be taken, and the city is ready to profit by your word.

In speaking for the churches, I want you to understand first of all that it is my very great privilege and honor to speak for all the churches of our common evangelical faith, not only those more predominantly or dominantly related to our endeavor movement, but those who have rela-

Looking Down from the Galleries

tionship to common pathways of service, whose young people are under banners a little different from Christian Endeavor; they have all co-operated with the city Endeavor hosts to make ready the welcome that is in the heart of all of us this glad evening hour.

Those of us who are residents here could say much about the beauty of our city, and the glory of our commonwealth, but as Mr. Weaver has intimated,—and that isn't in our mind at all to-night,—we are welcoming you, and glad to welcome you, not because of what *we* are, but because of what *you* are, and that is our particular joy just now.

We are anxious as a body of church people here in Des Moines to have some questions answered that you will most superbly answer. Men and women are asking all the while whether or not the church and its voice, the ministries of the church, are coming to have less power than in the days gone by. You are answering that question in a better way than we alone could answer it. The people are asking these days, young men are asking, "Does the message of the church make an effeminate man, or a weak man? Does it mean that to be good a man must be a sissy or a prude?" In the virile lines of your life you are rebuking that also. In the world to-day there is the question as to the purpose of the young people of our time. Some of the papers and magazines are intimating that the young men and women of America haven't much of a purpose these days, and the lines of faith that marked our fathers and our mothers have largely died out. You, representing other millions whom we can see in spirit, are going to give an answer to boyhood and girlhood and manhood and womanhood in Des Moines that will never, never be forgotten.

I want you to know that we think just this way about it all to-night: it is a very, very little thing for us to try to serve you while you are here within the narrow limits of your stay among us, for you will serve us through long, long years to come, as the standards which you lift high, standards of love and service and faith and human brotherhood, a human brotherhood that takes in every creature for whom Christ died, these standards lifted again by you will not be forgotten in generations to come here in our city of Des Moines. Because, therefore, you stand for God, because you stand for our Father's faith, because your songs are songs of Zion and your tread the tread of victors through Jesus Christ, our Lord, the churches of Des Moines salute and welcome you this hour.

The Chamber of Commerce and other civic organizations were represented by the veteran statesman, Senator A. B. Cummins, known to the nation and the world for his services of a quarter of a century.

HONORABLE A. B. CUMMINS, United Senator for Iowa, Representing the Civic and Industrial interests:

Ladies and Gentlemen:

Organized government has a deep and abiding interest in this great and notable gathering, and it has been fitly expressed in the greeting extended by the official head of the city of Des Moines. It is my mission to speak in behalf of the voluntary civic organizations, commercial in their character, although purely altruistic in their purposes, whose development has been the marked characteristic of modern times.

These institutions, with a membership embracing a very large part of what may be called the business life of this community, join most heartily their worthy mayor and the eloquent representative of the churches in bidding you a sincere welcome to the homes and hearts of the people of Des Moines.

The commerce of America, and of every other country, depends for its permanent success and continuing profit upon honesty and fair dealing; upon faithful co-operation in all righteous undertakings; upon peace in the world, obedience to the law; upon the brotherhood of man and the fatherhood of God.

It ought to be recognized by everybody everywhere that the teachings of the church and the training of the school are the two mighty influences which bind humanity to a common purpose, and make the civilization of which we are all so justly proud possible, your meeting, which has for its object the promotion and advancement of Christian Endeavor in every field of human activity, ought to enlist, and does enlist, the helpful sympathy of all right thinking men and women.

In this spirit I bid you all Godspeed in the work before you.

Judge Hubert Utterback, big of body and of heart, a Christian Endeavorer in high position, the chairman of the Des Moines Convention committee, spoke the greeting of the Des Moines Endeavorers.

JUDGE HUBERT UTTERBACK, for the Convention Committee:

Dear Friends: I assure you that I deem it an honor, a pleasure, and a high privilege to extend, on behalf of the Convention Committee, on behalf of the Christian Endeavor Union of the city of Des Moines, and the Endeavorers of the city of Des Moines, a most cordial and hearty welcome on this occasion.

We are met here, coming from many, many different portions of our land, coming from different nations of America, yes, of the world; all races, all colors, and all creeds are represented here, and yet we have one faith, we have one Christ and one Savior, and we are all children of that same Father.

Friends, it is an inspiration to us here in Des Moines to have you with us. It is a challenge to us. We believe here this evening, and we have in our presence not only young men and young women between eighteen and thirty years of age, that we have the choice young men and young women, the very best young men and young women of the United States, Canada, America, and the world, and I say to you it is a challenge to us in Des Moines to entertain you. We are proud of the privilege of having you among us.

We believe that the biggest business in the world to-day is that of seeing to it that the young men and the young women of America and of the world grow up to be the right kind of men and women, physically, morally, and spiritually. We believe that the Christian Endeavorers of the world are helping to transact that most important business, and because we are privileged to entertain the representatives of that great organization helping to transact the greatest business in the world, we want to do our very best. Your presence challenges the best that there is in us.

The Endeavor societies of Des Moines worked for a long, long time to get this great International Convention here to Des Moines, and for weeks, yea, for months, forty-three of us who have been members of the General Convention Committee, thirty-three who have been chairmen of sub-committees, something over five hundred who have served on those sub-committees, a great chorus of six hundred and forty, over five hundred who shall participate in one of the pageants to be presented here during the programme, have worked hard in order that we might entertain you while you are here, with honor and credit to ourselves and to your pleasure. We have enjoyed every moment of that time. We have enjoyed the doing of everything that we have done, and if we can only pass on to you some of that enjoyment and that pleasure, some of the blessings that we have had out of our work in preparing for your coming, and if we can only be assured that your stay here will be happy, will be a pleasure and in addition to that it will be extremely profitable, I assure you that we shall feel many, many times repaid for anything that we may have done in preparing for your pleasure.

In conclusion, on behalf of almost, if not more than two thousand

JUDGE HUBERT UTTERBACK

Endeavorers in Des Moines who worked hard for this convention and the preparation for it, I want to extend to you our greetings and a most hearty and most cordial welcome during the week that you shall be with us.

The Convention gavel was eloquently presented by Chaplain Berton L. Hoffman, of the Kentucky Penitentiary. It was given by the large Endeavor societies, both white and colored, of that institution. They sent their chaplain to the Convention.

BURTON L. HOFFMAN, Chaplain of the Kentucky State Penitentiary:

I count it a great honor to-night to represent a Christian Endeavor society which for twenty-seven years has been the instrument in bringing sunshine into the lives of men who are shut away from their friends in the world, and of leading them back to God.

The society I represent represents a life investment of one woman, Mrs. Mary B. R. Day, who has given her whole life for thirty years to the service of the men in our institution.

Our Society is carefully nurtured by the Kentucky Christian Endeavor Union, led most notably by Miss Georgia Dunn, our efficient State Christian Endeavor secretary.

You will be interested to know that this group of Christian Endeavorers, both white and colored, during the last twelve months have brought seventy-five men to Jesus Christ, and during that time have reclaimed over sixty men who formerly knew God, but fell away, and now have come back and rededicated their lives to the service of their Lord and Master. We have at the present time three men getting ready to go to Moody Institute when they get out.

One of our former Christian Endeavor workers had charge last summer of the leading Methodist Church in the city of Louisville. They are taking those ignorant, untrained, unlettered men from the mountains, winning them to Jesus Christ, and training them for real Christian service.

You will be interested to know that our men earn ten cents a day. They sent their chaplain to this convention at their expense, and during the last twelve months these men have given more than half of their income to benevolence and charity. I challenge you to produce any Christian Endeavor society anywhere else in the world that equals, in big heartedness, in the giving of the very little they have, the society which I represent.

The officers of our society are practically all men who have taken human life; the membership is composed of murderers, highway men, petty thieves, and men guilty of all crimes, yet these men, because they have found their need of God, have really found it in their Christian lives, are offering a challenge not only to those who come to visit us, but to the Chaplain who tries to lead them in Christian work, and those men have gladly sent this gavel to this convention, this gavel which stands for law and order. The wood in this gavel is historic. The handle is made from a piece of wood taken from the old State Capitol of Frankfort which was built in 1872 with convict labor. The gavel end is made from wood taken from the old cell-house, the oldest west of the Alleghanies, the third oldest in the country, used as a military prison during the war of 1812, and still being used as a cell-house for our colored prisoners. So on behalf of the Christian Endeavorers of the Kentucky State Reformatory, I present this gavel to this convention.

CHAIRMAN POLING: On behalf of Dr. Clark, the officers and trustees of the United Society of Christian Endeavor, and the delegates in attendance at this convention, I accept this gavel and say to you, sir, carry back to your Christian Endeavorers the assurance of our interests, tell them that we thank them from the bottom of our hearts, and say to them that we pray for them and with them. God bless you and them.

We have reached now one of the great moments of our convention. I present to you the Christian statesman, the prophet of the new era of brotherhood, the world-ambassador of peace, who is first in the heart of Christian youth, the President, the founder of the Christian Endeavor movement, Francis E. Clark. Another stupendous greeting received Dr. Clark as he came forward to deliver his biennial presidential message and inaugurate the new "Friends-of-Christ Campaign."

Dr. Clark: Fellow Christian Endeavorers: I had some doubt when I was assigned to this place on the programme whether it would be particularly appropriate on this Independence Day when the fire-crackers are sounding around us and our hearts are keyed to a patriotic tune, to introduce a serious religious message, and yet when I thought of that I was ashamed of myself, for patriotism and religion should always go together.

I believe, as has already been said eloquently by preceding speakers, that the foundation of this country of ours, whose natal day we celebrate to-day, is the religion of Jesus Christ, and so I do not hesitate to give to you my annual message tonight.

I speak not for myself; this is not my speech; I speak for the trustees of the United Society, for the denominational leaders of Christian Endeavor throughout the country, and many denominations. I give to you this message and this proposal for the coming two years, not, as I say, from my own heart simply, but as a representative of some three million Endeavorers in this country, and if I may also say it, in some measure, though this is not a world convention, I believe I am expressing the thought and the heart of Endeavorers throughout the world.

We have upon our platform distinguished representatives from Great Britain, the President of a British Union, the former President of the British Union, who is also the secretary of the Scottish Sunday School Union, men who have come across the water to greet us. Dr. Fletcher and his wife have recently come to us from Australia, where they were great influences in the advancement of Christian Endeavor in that island continent. We have not time to-night to hear from them, but before the convention is over you will hear from them.

We rejoice that though this is particularly the Independence Day of the United States that our Canadian friends can join with us. You will see around the hall the flag of every nation in the world, so the Chairman of the Convention Committee tells me. This is an international convention, it is an all-American convention, it is a meeting that represents the youth of every State in the United States, every province in Canada, and the great Republic of Mexico. We rejoice that we are all here in this North American convention, and now allow me to bring you this message.

Dr. Clark illustrated his address with a gavel given him at

the first New York Convention thirty-one years ago, the handle made of wood from Williston Church where the society was formed, a piece of granite from the corner-stone set in the head, and the inscription engraved on a gold plate. The granite is the strength given by our pledge, the gold is the motive of love to Christ which glorifies all our work, and the wood stands for our committee activities and all our little Christian endeavors.

DR. CLARK continued: I have the privilege of introducing now the field marshal of our great advance. He was born and is equipped to promote causes, he is resourceful, he is full of labors, he is eloquent, he carries in his heart and in his brain the genius of superorganization, Edward P. Gates, General Secretary of the United Society of Christian Endeavor.

General Secretary Edward P. Gates

My report is two years long. It isn't my report anyhow. I am going to ask the fellows that are responsible for this report to stand and come very, very quickly to the platform. Will every Christian Endeavor field-secretary in the house please come up here just as quickly as he can? (The field-secretaries came to the platform and were introduced to the convention by Secretary Gates.)

That is all the report I have. These are the folks that did the work. It is just my job to take the credit.

You will find in black and white what these folks did, with my name signed to it. Read it after the convention is over. Mr. Gates' report follows:

Two years ago at the great World's Christian Endeavor Convention in New York City, our beloved president, Dr. Francis E. Clark presented to Christian Endeavor the Foursquare Campaign. The four fundamental principles of Christian Endeavor were to be emphasized: Confession of Christ, Service for Christ, Loyalty to Christ's church, the Fellowship with Christ's people. Four grades of Christian Endeavor were recommended: Junior, intermediate, senior, and alumni. Four fields of action were outlined: The home, the church, the community, and the world. Four definite goals were suggested as objectives until the next international convention: Graded Christian Endeavor, Religion in the Home, Loyalty to the Church, and Personal Stewardship.

No campaign in the history of Christian Endeavor has met with a more enthusiastic response. As a result of co-operation in the Foursquare Campaign by all friends of Christian Endeavor, these two years have seen a marvelous growth in the number and efficiency of Christian Endeavor societies.

10,971 new Christian Endeavor societies have been added to our rolls since July 1, 1921. This is the largest number organized in a two year period for many years. The exceptional increase is in a measure due to the spread of Christian Endeavor in the more newly settled sections of the country, to the growing recognition of the importance of graded Christian Endeavor, and to the addition of new denominations to the Christian Endeavor fellowship.

The following states report a net gain of 10% or more in the number of their societies: Arkansas, Arizona, California, Connecticut, Delaware, Florida, Georgia, Idaho, Illinois, Indiana, Kansas, Kentucky, Louisiana, Maryland, Mississippi, Missouri, Nebraska, New Jersey, New Mexico,

New York, North Carolina, North Dakota, Oklahoma, Oregon, Texas, Utah and Wyoming.

Not less than two hundred and fifty thousand young people have completed one or more Leadership Training Courses in the study of missions, church history, methods of church work or similar subjects. California leads with a reported enrollment in study classes of 12,183.

California leads the country in all-round promotion of the Foursquare Campaign with 619 Honor Societies, but many other states follow close behind. The roll of states that made exceptional achievements would include nearly all of the forty-eight.

Nearly every denomination reports increased interest in Christian Endeavor. Around the world the Methodist church continues to lead in the total number of Christian Endeavor societies. The union of the Evangelical Association and the United Evangelical Church, followed by the adoption of Christian Endeavor as the official young people's society of the new denomination has added hundreds of societies to our fellowship.

While we rejoice over the achievements of the past, we are more concerned at this convention with the future of Christian Endeavor. Dr. Clark has proposed for the next two years the "Friends of Christ Campaign."

The details of this campaign have been outlined by the officers of the United Society of Christian Endeavor in consultation with denominational young people's leaders. No hard and fast standards are set. Suggestions for definite work are given, but each Christian Endeavor society is urged to consider these as suggestions only, and to plan its work in the light of the needs and program of its own church.

Authority in Christian Endeavor rests not with the United Society, but with the pastor of the local church. The activities in our new campaign are suggested with that principle in mind. The pastor is the final authority in adapting these suggestions to the work of his young people.

Naturally, therefore, the first main division in the new campaign is service in the church. Christian Endeavorers are urged to work to increase church attendance, to help the pastor in such ways as he may suggest, to fit the society program into that of the church, and to support by money and service the enterprises of the church and denomination.

The hope of America is not in national organizations but in the self-sacrificing pastors of local churches who are preaching the gospel and training their young people for efficient Christian service. Christian Endeavor, therefore, seeks, not to tell the pastor what to do, but to follow and serve him in his work. It was Christian Endeavor that launched and promoted the "Help our Church" campaign. It was Christian Endeavor that nine years ago coined the slogan "Go to Church Sunday" and started the campaign which on Christian Endeavor's birthday, February 2, 1914, filled nearly every church in America.

Our new campaign proposes that every Sunday shall be "Go to church Sunday," and that every Christian Endeavor society shall accept as its definite responsibility the bringing of people where they may hear the message of the gospel. "Help our church" is the tocsin for every society all the time.

The new campaign emphasizes graded Christian Endeavor, and urges that enough societies be maintained to reach young people of all ages. In most churches, this will mean three societies, a junior society for boys and girls under twelve, an intermediate society for those of seventeen and younger, and a third group for older young people. Some churches will not find it possible to have three societies. It will not always be possible or desirable to insist on hard and fast age limits. An increasing number of churches are finding four, five and even more societies desirable, corresponding in age limits to the divisions of the Sunday School. Again the decision must rest with the leadership of the individual church. Local needs should determine the number of societies as well as the nature of their program.

We believe that every church will profit from the service of an alumni council. These groups of graduates and friends of Christian Endeavor are marching behind pastors everywhere in a wonderful way and are proving themselves sources of great strength and encouragement to the young people of the church.

The second main group of suggested activities calls for service in the society itself. Christian Endeavor seeks to build societies that will win and train young people for Jesus Christ. Prayer meetings should be planned that will attract young people and help them in Christian expression. The devotional life must be developed.

Christian Endeavor trains its members for Christian leadership. Therefore instruction in missions, stewardship, methods of church work, and other important subjects, should be part of every year's program. Opportunities for life service should be presented. Young people should be given information about the ministry, the mission field, and other forms of full-time Christian work. The opportunities of the Christian in secular occupations should be explained and guidance given in the right choice of a life calling. All of these are definite suggestions in the new campaign.

The broadest service program in the church for young people is that offered by the Christian Endeavor society. To every member should be given progressive tasks to develop skill and initiative in Christian service.

While seeking in every way to add to its numbers, no Christian Endeavor society can afford to lower the standards of active membership. The pledge is still the backbone of Christian Endeavor. The exact form of words is not important—the United Society publishes several forms, and every church is free to write its own—but the principle of definite standards is fundamental.

Just as the first great emphasis of the new campaign is upon loyalty of young people to the church and the second is upon training for service through the activities of the society, so the third purpose is to send these young people into world and community service. The campaign challenges us to win friends for Christ near home, to reach the young people of the community and the world with the Master's message and with Christian Endeavor fellowship. It emphasizes the importance of increased support of home and foreign missions by money, prayer, and service. It proposes a program of community recreation. It suggests practical service for the neglected and unfortunate groups of the community.

Christian Citizenship, respect for law and order, Christian standards in business and industry, international, inter-racial and interdenominational friendship are suggested ideals. Let us learn more of our constitution and seek to encourage obedience to it. Let us put into every Christian Endeavor convention program and frequently into our local Christian Endeavor prayer meetings a frank discussion of the Golden Rule in business and industry.

Since this is a Friends of Christ campaign, let us seek also to make friends with those who are His friends in other lands. Why may we not have world friendship clubs through which Endeavorers in America may exchange greetings with the Endeavorers across the sea!

For His glory, and at His command, let us as friends of Christ, strive to make these coming years a time of great victory in winning friends for Him.

CHAIRMAN POLING: We have with us tonight the General Counsel of the Anti-Saloon League of America, a great orator and an eminent lawyer. In the humble judgment of your presiding officer, he is the most essential figure in the whole field of prohibition law enforcement. I present to you Wayne B. Wheeler.

THE DUTIES OF MAJORITIES AND MINORITIES UNDER THE CONSTITUTION

By Wayne B. Wheeler, LL.D.

It is always a pleasure to speak in behalf of the Constitution of our country before any group of patriotic citizens; it is a double pleasure to do so before Christian Endeavorers.

This is the day when every one of us rejoice that he is a citizen of the United States of America. The Britisher may boast that the sun never sets on the possessions of the Empire. God bless England. May the ties of friendship between England and our country constantly grow stronger. The Frenchman may sing the Marseillaise with new meaning since the close of the last war. We shall never forget the debt of gratitude we owe to France. In America there is no one with soul so dead who never to himself has said on the fourth of July—"This is my own, my native land—Sweet Land of Liberty and opportunity."

The most severe test that our democracy has faced is being made today. In other years, whatever the point at issue, the conflict practically ceased when we had written into the law the will of the majority. When the Constitution was under consideration, Patrick Henry, with his fiery eloquence, denounced it as "consolidated tyranny." Gerry, Randolph, Mason and twelve others walked out of the convention to show their contempt for that great instrument which has gone down in history as the greatest charter of human liberty ever conceived in the mind of man. We must not be disturbed, therefore, when highly intelligent people differ with reference to the adoption of a constitution or law. We have a right, however, to be anxious for the welfare of our country when a minority refuses to obey a constitutional provision which has been adopted by the legal processes of government. The example set by Patrick Henry and those other opponents of the Federal Constitution in declaring their allegiance to the Constitution and their obedience to it when it was adopted should be emulated today by the opponents of the Eighteenth Amendment.

The recognition of the right of majorities to rule and the duty of minorities to obey the law adopted by the majority is essential to the perpetuity of the republic.

In our game of democracy, when the wets were at the bat and knocked the ball over the fence with the bases full it was a home run and four scores were marked up. Now the drys have knocked the ball over the fence and they claim it should be scored as a single. They will tally the anti-whisky man we had on third, but the anti-wine man on second and the anti-beer man on first and the anti-home brew man who batted the ball clear out of the lot must remain on the bases or they declare that they will protest the whole game and ask that it be played over.

The situation we face in this nation is a challenge to every friend of the Constitution and of orderly government. The Eighteenth Amendment was adopted after more education on the part of the people and more of preparation for it and by a larger majority than any other part of our organic law. It was not "put over" or forced over by a minority. Our Constitution cannot be changed in that way. It takes 72 state legislative bodies and two Federal legislative bodies to amend the Constitution. It takes only 13 state legislative bodies to defeat an amendment. Prohibition was supported by 93 out of a possible 96 state legislative bodies. If its enemies could not muster 13 state legislative bodies to defeat its adoption they will never rally 72 to repeal it. It is here to stay as long as Old Glory floats over the best nation there is in the world.

Our enemy frankly and defiantly declares in favor of the repeal of the National Prohibition Act and for the right of the states alone to control the liquor traffic.

This doctrine of nullification of the laws of the nation never has had respect of patriotic citizens. At one time it was honestly believed by a part of our country that it could secede from the Union when it felt that the Federal laws were unduly burdensome. But the right of any state to secede was settled at the close of the great Civil War. The leaders of that struggle themselves denounced this nullification doctrine. Jefferson Davis, in his farewell speech in the United States Senate, said that nullification was indefensible as long as a state was a part of the Union. Andrew Jackson, the patron saint of democracy, told the people of one of the southern states that if there was one drop of blood shed by those who attempted to nullify the laws of the United States he would hang the man responsible for it to the first tree he could reach. In order that he might lay upon their minds the danger of the course they were following, he later said of those who were heading the nullification movement: "They will be remembered only to be held up to scorn by those who love our glorious Constitution and government of laws."

This is an inseparable union. The United States Constitution and the Federals law are supreme. We owe to them our first allegiance. When we must choose between loyalty and Uncle Sam and our state, the Star Spangled Banner comes first.

When the states of the Union entered into a mutual agreement to adopt prohibition they accepted it as our national policy and as an obligation on themselves to adopt the necessary legislation to enforce it. How can we carry out the purpose of the Constitution, to form and sustain a more perfect Union and allow the outlawed liquor interest to separate the states into law-abiding and lawless states? When the law was wet the drys obeyed the whole law. Now the law is dry and turn about is fair play. For a Congressman to take an oath of office to support the Constitution without mental reservation or purpose of evasion, and then to vote to repeal the law to enforce the Constitution, or for a beer and wine amendment that would make the amendment non-enforceable is worse than being a hyphenated American.

If the brewers can nullify the Eighteenth Amendment by the methods they propose, taking away the laws by which we are to enforce it, it will stand as a precedent for the overthrow of the government itself.

No sooner did the Supreme Court declare that foreign ships entering into our jurisdiction should obey the laws of the United States than the liquor interests of several foreign nations declared that the prohibition law should not be enforced against their ships; that reprisals would be made; that international laws would be jeopardized in the interests of a mug of beer or a flagon of wine. It is unbelievable that a rum fleet may hover on our border and shoot holes in our Constitution, and that we are without a remedy. There are legal methods to stop it. If necessary, Congress can extend the three-mile limit far enough to protect our shores from these rum pirates. The government should use every diplomatic means to influence foreign nations to prevent their ships from violating our fundamental law. If they refuse co-operation, then we should do as England and France did when the expedition was planned in Louisiana to invade Cuba—say to the nation that harbors those who violate the laws of other nations—"If you do not stop it, we will. No nation can afford to give encouragement to lawlessness at home or abroad. Liquors are now being consigned from foreign nations to the United States, clearly for use in violation of our laws. This raises again the question whether any nation can hold itself blameless when it allows its citizens to use its territory as a base of supply for violating the laws of another country. We appeal to the delegates from every nation here represented to use their influnce to establish the just principle of legislation within their own countries that no nation shall allow its territory to be used as a base for defying the laws of another nation. We have applied it with reference to counterfeit money to be used in defrauding the people of other nations. Why should not the same principle be applied with reference to the beverage liquor traffic?

The Eighteenth Amendment, even under handicap, has proven the greatest public welfare measure ever adopted by a self-governing people. America was never as rich, strong, healthy, law-abiding and ambitious as today. When she closed the door of the saloon, she opened the way to greater wealth, health and power. She saved the lives of 500,000 people in the last three years largely through prohibition. That is the difference between the number of deaths since the Eighteenth Amendment when into effect and the number who would have died had the death rate of the wet years continued. By that single result, she added a billion dollars to the nation's value if a human life is worth no more than $2,000.

The money that once went into the bartender's till goes into honest business now. We have added two billion dollars to our savings accounts in spite of hard times since prohibition. We are writing over a million new life insurance policies each month, totalling not far from a billion dollars. Much of this new business comes from the group who formerly furnished the patrons of the saloon.

Home life reflects the change, and many of the 6,000 new homes we are building each month would not have been built if the saloon had not been closed. Each day sees nearly 3,000 persons join the church and seven new church organizations are being formed for each day in the year.

Crime has decreased in the degree that prohibition has been enforced. The drier the community is, the lower its crime rate. Not only is there less than half the number of arrests for drunkenness and crimes related to drink but crimes of violence are far less in proportion than ever before. We shut the breeding places of crime when we closed the saloon doors.

Attendance at moving picture shows, the consumption of ice creams and soft drinks, the increased demand for athletic supplies and camping equipment, the records being broken monthly by the automobile trade, which plans to deliver 3,000,000 machines this year, all tell of wholesome pleasures replacing the demoralizing saloon.

Even the poorest enforcement of the prohibition law has proved a thousand times better for a community than license ever was.

Mr. Ernest Bohm, author of the "No beer, no work" strike propaganda, was shown to have been closely associated with the secretary of the United States Brewers' Association. The liquor traffic, throughout its whole history, has been a lawless traffic, breeding contempt for law and encouraging lawlessness in others. It is natural that it is today seeking to nullify the Constitution of the United States and to defy the laws enacted to enforce it. The literature distributed by the forces opposed to our government is a menace to the nation. No good purpose can be served by literature which advocates "Throw away your shovel, get a gun and be rich before night"; or "The Right to be Lazy," or ridiculing marriage through such propaganda as "Women as Sex Vendors," and other stuff which is in direct conflict with everything that real Americans stand for.

The citizens of the United States have come to the parting of the ways. We have to choose between orderly government and disorderly government; between law and lawlessness; between civilization and chaos; between loyalty to the Constitution and anarchy.

The Constitution of the United States is the greatest bulwark of the human peace, property and safety that has ever blessed a self-governing people. Lincoln was right when he said "Let every man remember that to violate the law is to trample on the blood of his fathers and to tear the charter of his own and his children's liberty." Law and its enforcement are the foundations of orderly government. Without them every guarantee of life, liberty and the pursuit of happiness are insecure. Without them civilization goes back to chaos and to anarchy. Were it not for the law, the only guarantee we would have in the enjoyment of our homes, property or personal rights would be the brute force that we could exert against the invader.

Those who dynamite the Eighteenth Amendment because it conflicts with their thirst set a dangerous precedent to the anarchists who would dynamite a factory because he does not believe in our system of property rights. There is only one consistent attitude for red-blooded Americans and Christian citizens to take: obey the laws of our country. If they are bad they will be repealed or amended. The measure of our citizenship is not in obedience to laws which we personally favor, but in obedience to laws enacted for the public good which may even hurt when we conform to them. The solution of liquor lawlessness is not beer in private homes—but "punch" in official places, and there will be "punch" in official places *whenever private citizens insist that it be there.* That means you and me. Let Christian Endeavor set the pace.

CHAIRMAN POLING: Now all of you who wish to give back to this man who goes out with others to lead us in this war to mark a great new moral epoch, give to him your declaration of faith, give to President Harding, to Roy Haynes, your declaration of unyielding loyalty and support. All of you who would so declare stand to your feet. (Audience arose and pledged loyalty to prohibition.)

CHAPTER III.

THE QUIET HOUR

Quiet-Hour services were held morning by morning in three churches, great crowds attending. The following are partial reports:

The Sword or the Cup

Dr. William H. Foulkes put in sharp contrast Peter's use of the sword, which Christ forbade, with the Saviour's prayer in the garden, accepting the cup according to His Father's will. To every one there comes a time for full surrender. In a minister's home visited by Dr. Foulkes was an only son, a fine, promising young man. Just after graduation from the high school he was suddenly stricken with illness. The father, who had baptized him and received him into the church, preached his funeral sermon, and could say, "The will of the Lord be done." Near the end the boy had said to the father, "I gladly surrender my career to the will of God." To those not on a dying bed, but in the fulness of power, comes the question, Can you say, "I gladly surrender my career, my life, my friends, my hopes, my ambitions—I surrender all to the will of my God"? Will it be a sword for you or a cup?

A season of brief, earnest prayers was summed up by the subdued singing of "Where He leads me, I will follow," with bowed heads. While heads were still bowed, those wishing to renew the full surrender of their lives raised their hands and Dr. Foulkes led in a closing prayer.

Friends of Jesus

The watchword for the campaign of the next two years, "Friends of Jesus," was the key-note of the convention Quiet Hour on Sunday morning. Rev. James Kelly touched on four phases of the topic. There is given an assurance of the enriching friendship of Jesus. All that we can use Jesus Christ conveys to us because we are His friends. Jesus Christ has chosen us and intrusted us with the work of His kingdom. Never suffer a doubt that the love lasts; it will bring forth fruit, and the fruit will abide. I believe not only that a man is immortal until his work is done, but that his work is immortal as well. In order completely to furnish us to every good work Jesus assures us that whatever petition we present to the Father in His name God will answer as He sees best. In prayer is strength; in prayer is tenacity of purpose; in prayer is victory over trouble.

Christ the Saviour of the World

At the Quiet Hour at the Central Presbyterian Church on Saturday morning, with the theme "Christ the Saviour of the World," a series of brief prayers followed the repeating of many Bible verses.

Rev. Ralph Harlow, of Smyrna, Turkey, the speaker, adapting a saying of William James that greatly impressed him in undergraduate days, declared, "If you go away from Des Moines without the pain of a new vision that you follow out in action, you will leave weaker than when you came." He enforced the command "Be ye doers of the word and not hearers only" by the results of observation of conditions in nineteen countries. A club of Chinese students in the University of Michigan is collecting and sending to Chinese educational centres clippings from papers showing what Christian America is like. The returning Chinese student is the greatest menace or the greatest asset to the cause of Christ in China according to the influences he received while in America.

REV. ROYAL J. MONTGOMERY

CENTRAL PRESBYTERIAN CHURCH

Friday Morning, July 6

You will recall that in the Sermon on the Mount Jesus is outlining the meaning of true righteousness. He is talking to a group of people who consider themselves experts in the field of righteousness, and he is seeking to show that in many ways they are merely on the borderland of spiritual development and attainment, that they have become so involved in the letter of their religious life that they have overlooked the spirit.

Our relationship to God is a matter of spirit, a spirit of reverence, of righteousness, the spirit of love or good will. These spirits, working together in us and through us, directing us, motivating our life, give us joy and gladness in our religious experience that makes for contentment and progress. I believe that is one of the things we all, as Christian people, need to learn, even in our day. A great many people in Christian life are handicapped, for they are interpreting Christianity from the standpoint of precept rather than principle. They are living in the childhood stage of religion. When the child is small, mother says, "John, keep away from the stove." She does not stop to explain. He acts on precept. Later on he goes to high school and college and studies the principles of combustion.

In religion, we ought to advance from this stage of precept in which we are told to do things and follow that broader platform. Dr. Thatcher says a precept is a direction respecting a given action. It is definite, precise, specific, fitting, and belonging to particular cases. The principle is comprehensive and fundamental. It prescribes no particular action but a course of conduct. A precept bids one to do. A principle trains him to be and so begets that inwardness and continuity which are essential to character.

I want to illustrate the idea, and perhaps the most effective point I can take from this discourse to illustrate the idea are the words found in the forty-first verse of this chapter: "And whosoever shall compel thee to go a mile, go with him twain." That phrase has never meant much to many of us, for in our system we do not speak much of the first mile, but the Jews in that audience got that idea right away, for they had a law of the first mile to the effect that if one were lost in passing through the country he could stop at the door of any householder and request the householder to show him a mile on his way. It was incumbent on that householder, no matter how inconvenient it might be, to show the traveler a mile on his journey.

Now, Jesus is saying to these Jewish people, "When somebody comes along some stormy night and you are nicely tucked away in bed at one or two in the morning, comfortable and happy, in a sound sleep, and the traveler says 'I am lost. Come on and show me the way,' when you find yourself in that situation and you have shown them that mile, instead of being grouchy about it, try going the second mile, another mile down the road for good measure." I believe in this phrase we have one of the secrets to a happy Christian experience, a guide toward the spirit of the gospel. And I want to go on briefly to emphasize the practical nature of this thing.

A good many of you said in your minds, "That is all very beautiful to think about; that is a fine piece of idealism." A great many have that attitude with reference to the Sermon on the Mount. I want to try, if I may, to show you that it is eminently practical, one of the most magnificent utterances ever spoken on the idea of good will or love; in other words, of always going the second mile. Take it in the life of our homes, those of you who have been married as long as I have realize that if you have any sort of a happy home life it must be governed on the basis of the second mile. There must be the recognition that always there needs to be certain give and take, if like is to be happy. Father comes home in the summer time from work. It has been a hot day, just like we are having now. Everything has gone wrong in the business. Everything has been going to aggravate him, and he comes home in an awful temper, all out of sorts. Now, if mother wants to she can stand on her dignity and get hold of the rolling pin, walk up to father, shake it in his face and say, "Here, you old rascal, get out of it. You can't put any cave-man stuff over on this house." She can treat him severely, and you know what may happen to mother. Mother is a sensible woman. She does not handle the situation that way at all. She knows he is not his natural self, and so she fixes him a nice strawberry shortcake, puts it before the old fellow. The wrinkles come out of his brow, and he softens up, and in a few minutes he is all happiness and radiance and says: "I think we ought to take a few days off and go to the lake. Let's go and have a good time," and everything is beautiful, because mother knows how to play the game on the basis of the second mile.

So it is in our church work. You find a church that is running on the basis of the first mile and you find a church always in difficulty, always having spats and troubles, this person criticizing the other and complaining about the other, Mrs. Jones afraid she will bake one more cake for Ladies' Aid than Mrs. Smith.

That cripples a lot of our Christian Endeavor societies. We have so many first milers, just figuring how easily they can get off in a situation. If we are to get anywhere in our co-operative activity in the church, we must organize on the basis of the second mile. So it is with our business life. One of the places where this principle of the second mile is coming into its vindication is in the business world today. There is not a business enterprise in this community that is not operated on the basis of the second mile. Business men are learning that it pays in cold cash to work on that principle.

A friend of mine was in a big store of this State the other day. A lady came in with a dress. The clerk came up with it and said to the manager, "This lady says it is not what she wants." He could have said: "That is just exactly as it was represented. She can take it and do as she pleases." He was a wise business man, and he said: "You arrange with the lady as she wishes. If she wants it, give her back the money." So the clerk gave back the money. The lady was happy, and she thinks well of that store. She will come back and she will spend hundreds of dollars there. While the merchant lost a few dollars on that single sale, he will get hundreds out of that customer before he is through with her, for he had the good sense to co-operate on the basis of the second mile.

So it is with out industrial problems. We realize that if we are to get anywhere in their solution we must operate on the basis of the second mile. Henry Ford has shaken up the world a great deal with his little car, but one of the things he has done is to vindicate this idea of the second mile. It pays to do more than the situation requires. He has a minimum wage. You remember when he took over the iron mines in Winconsin or Michigan instead of putting in the current wage scale he put in his higher minimum wage scale, put in some lockers and shower baths so the men could get cleaned up and go home with more self respect to their families.

It is one of the things we need to learn. We cannot get along on the basis of the employee of whom it was said a little while

Dr. William Hiram Foulkes

Rev. William Ralph Hall

Frank D. Getty

Walter D. Howell

ago that if the whistle happened to blow while he had his hammer in the air, he left it there and went home to dinner. We will never get anywhere on that basis at all—if we work by the clock and see how little we can do.

So it is in our judicial life. There was a time when we operated on the basis of "an eye for an eye", the thing to which Jesus refers in this Sermon on the Mount. I have had experience in the juvenile court as probation officer in these last years, and one of the things that impresses me is how far you can get with this principle of the second mile. In seminary days we used to visit the juvenile court of Chicago. There we saw Judge Julian Mack, not seated behind a desk with all kinds of dignity, but behind a table. The boy would come in, and the judge would say: "Come up here, son, and tell me how it all happened. What is the trouble anyway? Let's find out all about it." The little fellow would unburden his soul and tell the old judge just how it happened, and because there was confidence established he would lay on the old judge the burden of his heart. Tears would trickle down the little lad's face, and the old judge would say: "We believe in you. There is a fine possibility for your life. We are going to help you." With a word of encouragement he would turn the lad over to the probation officers and he would go out on his second mile, hopeful and radiant because some one had confidence in him.

So it is in the field of our international relationships. America ought to be impressed with the idea that it does pay. Some twenty years ago or more China, after the boxer uprising, was required to pay over to the United States twelve million dollars as an indemnity. We had a good Christian for a leader, and with the advice of other Christians, he turned back this money to China and said: "We are not here for any sort of revenge. We don't want your money. We want to help you." The Chinese were so impressed by that unusual action that they took those twelve million dollars, invested them in an educational fund, adding millions to them, and to-day there are hundreds and thousands of Chinese boys and girls who are studying on that indemnity fund in the spirit of good will. That did more for the establishment of happy relationships between this country and China than a thousand battleships would do.

America is not a first-mile nation, but a generous-spirited, wholehearted helper of the earth. By the blessing of God we will take our place and do our part as valiantly and splendidly in the spirit of the second mile as those boys did across the sea in the days of the struggle.

And so it is with reference to these racial problems that trouble us. The problem that seems so perplexing at times with reference to the colored race in our midst will never be solved on the basis of the Ku Klux Klan, which is the spirit of the first mile. It will be solved rather in the spirit of that great cartoon of Darling's in the "Des Moines Register" the morning after the death of Booker T. Washington, picturing that great soul climbing towards the light of a new day, towards his second mile. That is the spirit that is going to win out in the solution of our racial problems, whatever they may be.

And so it runs through the whole gamut of our lives. Everywhere we find that when we work in the spirit of good will and helpfulness we find enlargement of our own lives. For the joy of living, my friends, is in the second mile. Just look over the first milers. See what a grouchy lot they are! The people who always stand on their dignity for their rights, wanting everything to come to them, remind me of a preacher friend who had a wedding.

I wish we might move now in our thought from the mountain on which this sermon was given to that other great mountain on which it was exemplified, where, without a city wall, high and lifted up, our Lord Jesus Christ, gave His life for the redemption of mankind. As the world has looked upon that figure lifted up there, it has been driven to say again and again, "He is none other than the son of God," as He in his last moments said, "Father forgive them, for they know not what they do." We all realize that to-day each and all of us are challenged to live generously, graciously, and helpfully in the spirit of the second mile.

Let us pray: Our dear Heavenly Father, we look to thee this morning for thy help, for it is easier to talk about the spirit of the second mile than it is to exemplify it in our lives, and we realize that if we are to be effective in Thy service in the development of Christian character and the doing of Christian service we must keep close to Him who so beautifully and powerfully exemplified Thy spirit in His own life and ministry. And so help us to live close to Christ, to do his bidding to-day. We ask it in His name, who is able to keep us from falling and to present us faultless before the presence of His glory with exceeding joy. To Him, the only wise God, our Savior, be glory and majesty, dominion and power both now and forever.

REV. EDWARD LAWRENCE REINER

Thursday Morning, July 5

Central Presbyterian Church

Your Call and Mine

A few years ago in "The Christian Endeavor World," Dr. Cowan used a pat phrase. The phrase is this. "Gyroscoping a Wobbly World." A gyroscope is a stabilizer when something is proposed to be kept in perfect equilibrium. That's a funny word, "balance!" When things are to be kept in balance and there is some question about how to do it, the engineer comes along and says: "That is simple. Just gyroscope it, that is all, and it will keep its poise and run in the track as it should." Dr. Cowan said, "We are gyroscoping a wobbly world." You know that things are unstable. You know that. Look about you and see. We talk about the eternal hills. They are not eternal. They are crumbling in the dust and those from the West know something about it as well as we do who live in this central part. The hills are not eternal. We talk about the sun, yet they tell me the sun is shrinking at the rate of an inch a year, and in forty million years the sun won't have much power. I wish the sun would shrink to-day just a little bit for the blessing of everybody here.

When I use the word morality I think of the finest part of a man's spirituality, and you know yourself as you look back that the old world is certainly wobbling morally. Men are evading law, winking at it. They care nothing about the law. This old world is just moving from side to side, and some of us wonder how long it can go and not take us into some chaotic condition.

Now it is a great task to gyroscope a morally wobbly world. Think of the young people in your church, your community, your centre, and think of the immorality everywhere, and then your church, functioning in that centre. Half the time the congregation is at home or some other place, the Sunday-school teacher absent, the Christian Endeavor Society caring little, the deacons not deaconing, the trustees not trusting, and the old church is trying to gyroscope a community like that.

We are the great missionary nation of the world, not just projecting into the world's great industrial scheme, not taking sin and running across the waters with it. We have done enough of that, and it has not helped the world so much, but I believe that in gyroscoping and steadying the old world America must be the moral impact. She must go over there and beat the old world into that place where the old world can run as it ought to run Some of you are whispering in my ear and saying, "Yes, but America must learn to run her own world first." I know that and admit it, but I want to say this: All things considered, with the lawless running riot, America is still moving on much finer than any other nation in all the world at this time, and so the task of gyroscoping a wobbly world means that each one of us must do our task. Are you getting that? Not a little task, not an insignificant something, not going to church and praying when you please and when it is convenient, but doing these things at all times because of the Herculean task that faces the world.

If we are to do a great task, we must have a great faith. The French nation tried to build the Panama Canal for how many years? The French nation tried it and failed, but Uncle Sam said, "I believe we can do it." Then we went out and got a genius, an engineer by the name of Geothals. He said, "Certainly it can be done, and if it must be done I am willing to assume the responsibility." I could mention the names, and so could you, or two or three others who were in that great scheme. When the thing had to be done America went out and made a survey and said, "It is a great task." Only one man stood up like a Lincoln in his day and said, "If it must be done, I will have faith in America to believe it can be done," and you know that it was done, and largely because one man believed in the project and the enterprise.

Some one has said that man is a recurring decimal. "You can't keep a good man down" is saying the same thing. The Salvation Army says this, too: "A man may be down, but he is never out." In other words, a man of faith is always dominant. The man of faith always rises above his difficulties, and I believe God is looking with longing heart for some man worth while who believes strongly enough in Him and His almighty power to proclaim a gospel of universal brotherhood in Him, laying aside all the arguments and all the quarrels of the ecclesiastical councils everywhere, going forth in majesty preaching Jesus Christ, the greatest lover of man that ever lived. When that man rises, America will stand by him, and we will go forth doing the things worth while.

Do you know the trouble with the church to-day? Wise men and foolish men are preaching their doubts to young people and filling their minds with doubt. What care I about the story of evolution when it comes to the salvation of a soul? I know the man is here, whether his ancestors were monkeys or men. The man is here. His moral soul is gone and I believe, verily believe, because I have proved it, that Jesus Christ can make it over.

I came out of the Roman Catholic Church. My mother gathered her little brood of children together. It was European in size. I am my youngest brother's distant relative. I was the first. He was the thirteenth. But every night that Roman Catholic mother did what few in my parish do. She gathered her brood around her, and while the sun set every night, whether we were listening, praying, kicking each other, or sticking pins in each other, my mother took her beads and said her rosary to her God for us, and I think out of that prayer came my new faith. I do not criticize the Protestant church. I don't find fault with it. I like its programme, but there are men who criticize the Protestant Church who have been reared in it from infancy, and those men criticizing it could not run a peanut stand on the corner without a whistle.

There is a great task before us. If you get that point, the rest of the talk may be forgotten. The task is big. The world must be steadied. We must gyroscope it. A great task takes a great faith. A great faith takes a great programme, and a great programme takes a great leadership. Mortenson, of the Chicago Public Schools, said, "Two per cent of America leads, and ninety-eight per cent toddles along behind." This, the church of Jesus Christ, will find a good deal of its leadership will be due to Christian Endeavor, for it is an organization that trains for leadership.

Some of you will go to foreign fields. Some of you will become workers at home. Some of you will have fit preparation for a real leadership, will stay at home and be leaders, clergymen, workers in settlements, but you can't go out of this church to your home tasks, to sit at your typewriter, to the shop, the factory, or the store, and be the same. I am challenging you now. You will be less than you were or you will be more than you were when you came in, and that is the work of that Divine Spirit. The message, what is it? Let me illustrate. I use the language of the missionary who wrote the story. "A few years ago a missionary and his bride went to India to serve under one of the Denominational Boards. They stayed in that country for eighteen months when a smallpox epidemic broke out and that whole country was blighted and devastated. The natives were dying on the streets as flies die in summer. The roads were filled with the dead. They were picking them up, carrying them away, putting them into ditches as fast as they could. This discouraged missionary, who for eighteen months had pleaded with the people of his community to believe in Christ, was walking from the compound, the place where he and his wife lived, to the village nearby, and I use his language when he said: "I saw a thing lying in the roadway. I noticed that it was breathing. I went to a nearby stream and took a little of the dirty water from it and poured it into the mouth of that breathing, vile, foul thing. I went to the village and returned in the evening. The thing was still alive, and I poured into the foul mouth more water. Then I went home and brought emollients and medicine, and for weeks I ministered to that thing which lay in the shadow of the trees to which I pulled it the first morning when I found it.'

" 'Day after day I ministered to it. One day I came to the tree, and it was gone. The great man to whom I had ministered and brought through the terrible epidemic had gone. I went back to the compound instead of to the village with my heart under my heel, and I said, 'Wife, you know the man that I have been helping all these weeks has gone, and he didn't say "thank you." He just walked away.'

"In womanly fashion, and with womanly faith and grace she said, 'My good husband, we did not come to India for thank you's. We came here for the soul of India'."

The man trundled off down to the village and back. Eighteen months after that India was again in her livery of green, beautiful verdure everywhere, when one day there came a knock at the door of the compound. The missionary went to the door, and there standing in the sun was a great giant with his sweaty body shining like a piece of mahogany in the sun. For a moment the missionary did not recognize him, for now he had come to his full stature. He was a real, physical, Indian giant. He laid at the missionary's feet two of the finest tusks of ivory that ever had been seen in that part of India. Then he loosened two bags filled with gold and said: "I go get more. I go get more."

The missionary said, "Just a moment," and the humiliation of his soul was like that that comes to every pastor occasionally.

The misionary said: "Wait a moment. You are the man I pulled into the shadow of a tree. You are the man I helped."

"Yes, yes," he said, "I go get more."

"Wait a minute. The things I did for you, I did not do for ivory or gold, or for any other material thing."

The man said, "Why did you do it?"

The missionary said, "Many years ago God saw that the old world in which we live was lost, and He sent His Son, Jesus Christ, into this world to save man and woman. One day this Jesus saved me and my wife, and I came out here and poured water into your mouth and ministered to you, because Jesus Christ, the Savior of men, saved me for time and for eternity."

The giant looked up into the face of the missionary and then flung himself at his feet, gripping his ankles. He said, "Show me him. I love him too."

HOW TO WIN FRIENDS FOR CHRIST

By Rev. Lionel Fletcher

Central Church of Christ

Thursday Morning, July 5

This morning I intended just to have a talk with you about our own relationship to Jesus Christ, because unless we ourselves are friends of Christ, we cannot hope to win friends for Christ. Then to-morrow morning I am going to speak on personal work, and the following morning I will speak on the difficulties that have to be overcome, and how to overcome them.

There is a passage in the fourteenth chapter of the gospel of St. John, the 21st verse, that I am very anxious for you to lay hold of and to remember in the days that are to come. We think we know the Fourteenth Chapter of John. There are some of us who can recite it from beginning to end, and yet we may know the chapter and know not what is in it. In the 21st verse it says this: "He that loveth me shall be loved of my Father, and I will love him."

I would like to say to you this morning that in Great Britain there is a wonderful spiritual revival being experienced, and many of the great religious leaders say that there has been nothing like it in this generation.

I went to Great Britain seven years ago during the war and have stayed there practically ever since, and now my dear wife and I have given up our great church—the greatest church of its kind in the British Empire, a great Congregational Church — that we might go out on this special work, because of the mighty harvest that is being reaped in our country and the fewness of the reapers that are there to gather in the golden grain, and we are sure it is the result of the prayers of God's people throughout the earth.

As I was leaving Great Britain to come here, one of the editors of one of the largest religious journals in the world said to me, "Fletcher, when you get to America see if there is anything akin to this in America, and if there is, write and tell us about it," because the British people are just looking to you here, hoping that the blessing is coming to you, too. Now my time is too short this morning to tell you about it; it may be that I will have more chances as I go along, day by day, but only this I can tell you: it began in a little town in what we call East Anglian Heights. Down in the Southeast corner is Suffolk, and in Suffolk there is a little town of Lowestoft, and in Lowestoft the Baptist minister, Douglas Brown, went two years ago to have a four days' convention with the Baptist folk, to have a quiet time waiting upon God; but instead of staying four days, he stayed fourteen weeks, and that work has never stopped; there was no organization, there was no advertisement, there was nothing at all. It simply seemed as if the Spirit of God fell on them while they were gathered there together. By God's wonderful providence the fishing fleet from Scotland was there on the herring fisheries, with the men catching the fish and the women preparing them for market. These fisher folk crammed into the churches, and they got on fire for God, and when they went away to the north of Scotland they set Scotland on fire. My wife and I have been up in Scotland helping for a little while with that work which is still going on, and in all denominations in some way or other there is a great ingathering of men and women into the communion of the church. That work now is marching down through England from north to south. Remember, it began in the south, but it went to the extreme north, and it is coming south like a flame of fire, and I think I can safely say that in this winter that has just gone we have had in our country of Great Britain more than a hundred thousand men and women who have professed conversion, and the work is going on this summer.

I have come straight from a great seaside resort where the place is packed with people going for pleasure. We took the pavilion out on the end of the pier, the last place on earth you would think people would go to worship God, yet night after night that great pavilion was packed with these people who had come for pleasure and who stayed for worship.

There are places, of course, in Great Britain to-day that are as dead as they ever were, but, nevertheless, there is the movement of the Spirit of God in our nation.

I met Gipsy Smith, the evangelist of whom you have all heard, in a town the other day and he put his hand on my shoulder and said, "Fletcher, how do you find the work of God?" I told him what I thought of it and he said: "I am going to tell you how I feel. I have been an evangelist for forty-two years; I have been leading men and women to Christ all over the world. I am getting to be an old man now, but never in my life have folks so turned to God as they are turning to-day wherever I go to proclaim the gospel of Jesus Christ.

Now I think I ought to tell you that because there are many of you who have been hanging on in your Christian Endeavor societies, longing, looking, praying for the coming of the blessing of God. How is it going to come with you? That is the great concern. How are you going to win friends for Jesus Christ? In this Fourteenth Chapter of John that I was reading it says, "He that loveth me shall be loved of my Father, and I will love him." Well, do you love Jesus Christ? I ask you as one man asking another, as one Christian speaking to the soul of another; I have got a right to ask, and you have got a right to answer.

I think one of the bitterest experiences of my life was one time in Australia — my own native country, which is akin to yours, very much like it to look at, and in climate too — when there we heard news, my wife and I, of a little woman who was dying. They told us she was starving. We went into her house and we found her there practically starving to death; and no one has any right to starve to death in our country. She was a proud little woman, and it took my wife a long time to drag her story from her. We found that she had been married and she had borne seven or eight children, and all those years her husband had never given her a penny. She had to fight for her children's lives and work for their living, and now at last she was broken in body and broken in soul, and she was practically dying from starvation. We took hold of her and nourished her and looked after her for a year or a little more, then she crumpled up and and died. I will never forget the night she died if I live to be a thousand years old.

I went into that house where the poor woman was dying; the film of death was already over her eyes. (I know her husband very well. He was a big silver miner, a great big strong sort of man.) I took her by the hand and was speaking to her. — I knew she was slipping over the valley — and she beckoned me down. When I bent over her she said, "Mr. Fletcher, will you let me see Jack before I die?" Jack was her husband; he was lying out in the yard in the rear in the tall grass, drunk, and I didn't want to tell her that,. I thought perhaps that her mind would wander and she wouldn't ask me again. I said, "Oh, yes, you shall see Jack presently." By and by she seemed to feel that I was putting her off; she gripped my hand, and although death was on her face, she said, "Mr. Fletcher, you won't let me die until I see Jack." So I promised that I would let her see him. He had a big strong relative there, and I said to him, "Whatever we do we have got to take this man in." We practically carried him through the house, and when we got him into that little bedroom we had to kneel him down by the bed and we had to kneel down on each side of him to hold him up. That poor woman was so near death that she couldn't see him, but she put her hand up and felt his face and she went back to the days when that man had courted her and she had married him. You could see the love in her face and hear the tenderness in her voice. She felt his face with her fingers and she said "Oh, Jack, that is you; kiss me." When the big fellow leaned over to kiss her she put her arms around his neck and said, "Promise me you will give up drink and meet me in heaven." He promised her, and she died just like that. When I buried that little woman out in the forest that big fellow stood by the grave, and in all my life I have never heard such a cry of pain from any human lips as came from that man's lips. When the funeral was all over and everybody was going away he simply flung himself face downward on that heap of earth by that open grave, and his cries rang through that bush like the cries of a wounded animal. He cried out, "Oh, my God, my God, how I loved her, how I loved her!" We took him home, and we have had him at our house off and on for six months helping him put up a terrible fight against that cursed drink.

As he lay on that earth and I heard him crying there, I thought, yes, but what was the use of his love. God knows it was real enough, but what was the use of a love that let that little woman die? The doctor told me she died because she hadn't been nourished, she died because her heart was broken for want of love and a little attention. She might have lived on and been the happiest of mothers, and he might have been the happiest of men, but his love stopped with emotion. It didn't issue in deeds, and he let the one he loved slip away into the grace.

You see what a lovely and what a tender chapter this Fourteenth Chapter of John is, but do you know it is one of the sternest chapters in the Bible? It is the sternest chapter in the Bible, because the stern side of tenderness is the sternest thing in the world, and when Jesus Christ was stern, His sternness made men tremble. Jesus talked of the mansions of glory, He talked of the Father's love, but in that wonderful way of His He defined those that loved Him and those that didn't, "He that hath my commandments and keepeth them, he it is that loveth Me."

I heard a quotation from Ruskin the other day that helped me tremendously. He said that the Scriptural injunction is what you must do with your might what your hand finds to do, not what your eyes see needs doing, not what your mind tells you ought to be done, — you will never reach that, — but what you must do is do with your might what your hand finds to do. The circumference that can be reached by your outside hand is the circumference of your responsibility to Almighty God. If every one will do his best within that limited sphere with his heart for Jesus Christ, then the world will soon turn to know and to love Him.

And what does this old Book say? It says, "He that loveth me shall be loved of my Father." Oh you tell me that God loves everybody! I know He does. I sometimes wonder how He can, but He does. Then you know if you take the Greek words in the New Testament, you will find that there are three distinct words for love, and one is a word which means a deep, special, spiritual passionate love. As you take that New Testament you will see it is said that Jesus loved one disciple, and that was John, but He loved all the others nevertheless. What He means is that there was a special spiritual quality in the love that Christ had for John, and I am satisfied as I stand on this platform this morning that God has a special love for those that love His Son.

My first little church was away out in what you might call the backwoods, and the great city of Sydney was miles away from us with its population of nearly a million people. For three or four years we had a terrible drought, and it seemed as if that great city was going to perish for want of water. The gardens were all dying off. We got from America some of the best machinery and the best engineers that you had, as well as men and machinery from other parts of the world. They put across from one mountain to another just near where I had my church a marvelous wall of concrete and stone, across the bed of a little tiny river. They did it because they felt that they could conserve water there in a wonderful way. When that wall was built, God in His wonderful providence just sent the rain and filled that valley with water. I went out under that wall when it was officially opened, and on it were two hundred of the leading engineers of the world who had come to see this extraordinary engineering feat. I remember as well as if it were yesterday a man coming along with a great key under his arm and he said, "Gentlemen, watch!" He didn't want them to watch him, but the river bed. On the other side of the wall was the river bed as dry as the floor of this church, but there on this side of the great wall were seven miles of water, and in some places it was 250 feet deep. It was wonderful to look at it. Away down at the bottom of the wall were gates. I watched him go down a spiral staircase and I looked down to see what he would do, and I saw him fit a key into a place, and he turned that key once, then he turned it twice, and as he turned it the second time, the whole wall began to tremble as under an earthquake; when he turned it thrice, it was like letting loose a hundred pieces of artillery; the whole valley was filled with a sound, and the mountain peaks took it up and flung it from peak to peak until it echoed away with a roar in the distance. Any of you men who have knowledge of hydraulics can imagine the pressure behind that water — seven miles of it, 250 feet deep — when those gates were opened. The whole river-bed was filled with a rolling, tumbling, roaring mass of water, and it seemed with a shout of triumph it rushed down the mountain side and disappeared on its errand of mercy.

I stood there on that wall and I thought I could see the water going right through those canals and through those pipes in the prepared reservoirs, and I could hear the engines pumping it away to that city, and I watched the women in imagination turning the taps and filling their kettles and putting them on the fire; then I saw the men going into their gardens and fitting on their sprinklers, and watering their flowers, and I watched the petals opening and drinking it in; I saw the water gurgling in the troughs in the streets, and I watched the tired horses burying their nostrils into it and drinking of the liquid flow. I said to myself, "It is just the same water," and then answered, "No, it is not. Up here it is a water-conservation scheme; down there it is cleansing and salvation and life. So long as it stayed here the city might die for want of it."

The world is filled with the love of God, don't make any mistake about it. The whole world 'round us with its beauty of hill and dale and flower and field and gushing stream and singing waterfall tells of the love of God. You stand out in the night and watch the star-spangled sky like a dome of a great temple and it tells you of the love of God, and yet millions are dying for need of it. Why is it? It is because they haven't got some one with a key in their hand to open those gates and let the love of God flow into their soul. What is that key? It is love for Jesus Christ.

Oh, my dear Fellow-Endeavorer, that is my message to you this morning, it is the love of Jesus Christ, the personal love of your heart for the personal Christ who comes from God's heart, and when your heart is filled with love of Jesus Christ, when you have seen Him afresh, when you have loved Him with a new passion of love, when you have given your life to Him, when you say, "It doesn't matter about social status or anything else, my first and chief concern is that He shall be my Savior, my love, my God, the centre of my life, I give Him my life," do you know what happens? You have got in your hand the key of His love and it opens those gates of His sacrifice which He put into that dam of sin, and as they open, there comes into your very soul the love of God gushing up within you, a well of water, and a life everlasting, bringing life and joy and salvation.

REV. LIONEL FLETCHER

Central Church of Christ

Friday Morning, July 6

This morning we are going to see how to win friends for Christ, and then to-morrow morning we shall see how to overcome difficulties in the way.

I began my own Christian life, my own Christian work, in a Christian Endeavor society when I was less than twenty years of age, and it was in a Christian Endeavor society in a dead church with an antagonistic minister who wouldn't come near us or have anything to do with us. It was one of the finest things that ever happened to me, I am sure. Sometimes we complain in some of our churches that our ministers won't have much to do with our Christian Endeavor work; but don't complain. If the minister is dead, then you get on fire yourself. If the church doesn't welcome you, then you make yourself a place in your church by the eagerness and the completeness of your consecration to Jesus Christ. I look back now and I thank God that in His providence he gave us a minister who was so dead and so antagonistic that he wouldn't come near the Christian Endeavor society at all. He fought my father for years and resolved that there should never be a Christian Endeavor society in the church. My father was the head master of the great college there, and he was just as determined there should be as the minister was that there shouldn't, and finally, my father, with his influence and with the backing of men in the church, after a couple of years' fight, got the Christian Endeavor society established.

Then we had a little branch church, and it was there that we began a second Christian Endeavor society. My father persuaded me to become its secretary. I know now it was for my sake that he put me there because he wanted me to get into Christian service. We had just a little handful of people. The minister was very antagonistic. If he did come to the meeting we would wish he hadn't. When he did come it was like a chunk of ice with all the fog and the coldness.

We got to our knees, these young men and young women, and prayed for the Holy Spirit, and there came a revival into our little church, and in not more than a month there were more than a hundred young men and young women, and to-day they are in China and in Australia and one or two of us in Great Britain preaching the glorious gospel of Jesus Christ. But we had no help from our minister at all; he, as well as many of the leading officials of the church, thought we had gone mad.

Now I just wanted to give you that chapter out of my early history, because I am going to show you that often man's obstacles are God's great opportunities. You may, of course, say to me, "Well, my church doesn't welcome a Christian Endeavor Society." That is the very church that needs a Christian Endeavor society, and you are the ones that ought to show that church that a Christian Endeavor society is an essential part of the organization of a good church.

How are you going to become personal workers? If you turn over in your New Testament to the first chapter of John, which is always the chapter every one takes when he wants to study personal work, you will find the statement about Andrew who, after he had found Christ, first brought his own brother Simon to Jesus Christ. That is in the fourteenth verse; but before that, don't forget the twelfth verse. I always feel that that is one of the greatest verses in the Bible. We are always quoting John 3; 16; it is a magnificent verse, but to my mind an equally magnificent verse is the twelfth verse of the first chapter of John. You have got it in the old translation, and you have it in your own revised version; you can take it which ever way you like, but there it is, "But as many as receive him, to them gave he power to become the sons of God, even to them that believe on his name." That is the first essential of personal work, that you shall have claimed your right as a child of God.

Oh, you young men, you young women, religion isn't just a passing emotion. Do you know what religion is? An American writer's statement (I have forgotten who he is) lodged into my heart many years ago. He said: "Religion is relationship, and the life that results from this relationship. It is the relationship between a personal being called man and a personal being called God, and the life that results from that relationship is religion." And do you know, that is true. It isn't just our external worship, it isn't just our meeting in conventions and crying hallelujah and singing hymns. Religion is life, it is the life which results from the relationship betwixt you and God through Jesus Christ our Lord and that life is the life of a child of God, and the life of the child of God ought to be filled with dignity, fiilled with power, filled with the Holy Ghost.

Some folk think the greatest thing in life is to have plenty of money and plenty of motor cars and plenty of comfort and plenty of ice water, and all that sort of thing. Some people think the greatest thing in life is to have comforts. It isn't at all, and if you are not careful, in a rich country like this, with all its wonderful possibilities, you will put those comforts first instead of putting Jesus Christ first. What you want to do is to realize that the finest and the greatest thing in your life is that you are a child of God, that your first concern isn't the business that you are in —the business that you are in is only the way you earn your living —but serving God, and serving God is your vocation, and as a child of God that is the great thing in your life. You may never have the ordaining hands of a man on your head, but you have always got the ordaining Spirit in your heart, and if God fills you with the Holy Spirit, you are ministers or high priests of God, children of the King going to do his business.

I have seen a family split in half by a terrible family fued. There was a young man who married a girl that his people wouldn't receive, and this family was rent in twain. A little baby was born in that house, and you know I went around to the mother of the girl — the young people had been cast right out from both families — in a taxicab, and I went into her house and said, "I have come to tell you that your daughter is very ill." She jumped from her chair and said, "Where is she?" I said, "You come with me," and she came with me in the taxicab, and we went around into that room. I put her in that front room and made her wait there, and then I ran into the bedroom and the nurse put the baby into my arms; I simply went out into the room and put that little bundle of clothes into the woman's arms, and when she looked at it her heart just broke, and she said, "Where is my daughter?" I took her into the bedroom and left her there. That little baby with its little pink fists and chubby face and dimpled mouth simply bridged the gulf between those two families.

Directly a human personality is born into the world it brings into the world some power that you can't define, but it is there. Sometimes you, perhaps, in your supersensitiveness — it may be in your supermodesty — imagine that you have got no power; you have, my dear friend. Just because we didn't discover the power of electricity or the power of steam in the days gone by didn't make power non-existent; that power was always there. And so I want to help you find your power this morning.

My dear friends, do you know I have had a bitter experience of it in my own life, and I never like to forget it. I never like to talk about it, but sometimes I feel constrained of God just to speak of it that it may help others. When I was sixteen years of age I went to sea and before I was eighteen I had gone around the world on a big old sailing ship. While I was away a mighty man of God came from England to Australia and conducted a great many missions through Australia, and he came to the church that I had been brought up in as a boy. It was a very aristocratic church; in those days there used to be around that church in the morning many carriages with their footmen and coachmen in livery, and I was reared in that church from a boy. It was a college church.

While I was away this great preacher came to this church and the power of God swept that place, and there were two hundred and fifty of the young men and young women who professed Christ. When I sailed into Sydney harbor on the old sailing ship my chief chum came out in the boat at four o'clock in the morning to meet me, and I remember the first words he shouted to me from his little boat. I was up on the side of the ship and he called out to me, "There has been a revival in our church." You know my heart jumped for joy. I thought to myself, "He is going to tell me he is converted, and if he is, I will start with him." I rowed over and I said, "Who was converted?" Then he said, "Very nearly all the boys and girls." I said, "Were you?" And his answer was this: "No, So-and-so and I" (they were my chums) "would have been but for you; we didn't want to leave you out by yourself, so we decided to wait until you got back," and they are not converted to-day. I was eighteen years of age then; I am forty-six years of age now, and those two lads are my age, middle-aged men like me; and they are not inside the Kingdom of God. I don't know that they ever darken a church door. I am not going to tell you that their life is immoral or bad, but I do know that religion as we know it has no place in their life, and I have never been able to lead them into the Kingdom of God since. You know, all my life, to some extent, that shadow has been over my soul. Men say to me, "But Fletcher, you couldn't help it." Yes, but I could have helped it.

I make this earnest plea with you this morning that you shall get that power and line it up with the power of God, so that like Andrew, you may go out and lead your loved ones and your friends into the Kingdom of God. Oh, it is marvelous how that power can be used. It is sometimes a power which can be used in public utterance, and sometimes in private speech, and sometimes through writing letters.

Some of you won't agree with what I am going to say, but I am going to say it, nevertheless. I have been working for Christ now for twenty-seven years and in the whole of that time I have tried to save souls. I do say that I am not a believer in the promiscuous approach of men and women with a glib utterance about their religious life. You say to me, "But I have led men to Christ that way." Then thank God for that, but look out! *You may have driven more men away from Christ that way.* When I was a young fellow the thing that nearly made me an infidel when I was in the most delicate state of development was that men should come to me and with glib utterance talk about my soul and my salvation; and I didn't know who the men were, or the women, either; it wasn't that I minded their approach, but it was the way of their approach, a sanctimonious, pietistic breathing of the thing through their nose with an intonation which isn't natural. If you are going to talk about religion, talk about it as naturally as you talk about anything else in the world. If the Lord Jesus Christ is our Saviour and our King, why should we whine about it or put on a false sort of piety and use certain set phrases which the world doesn't understand?

You young fellows, be as manly about your religion as you are about your sport; stand on your feet and talk as a man ought to talk, and you young women do the same. Let those with whom you come in contact see that religion hasn't made you into a soft, sappy, sentimental person.

Religion is something which is noble and beautiful and glorious and as free as the open air, and as full of majesty as a great towering mountain which God has crowned with snow.

You know my wife and I have traveled a great deal; we have been from Australia to England and from England to Australia and back again to England, and then across here to you, and in the twenty-four years we have been married we have been all over the place on board ship, and I am going to tell you this: never have I approached a stranger on board ship about his religious life until I get a point of contact, and my dear wife the same; we never approach any one about religion until we get a point of contact, but we have never been on board a ship yet without some one or many coming to us, or in some way giving us an opening which we have been able to help them and lead men and women to Christ. You know once you get a point of contact and establish a friendship, the door begins to open and you have got the right of approach.

It is wonderful how you get the right of approach. Right deep down in the human heart is really the longing for God. There is no use saying it isn't; I know it is.

I was among the Australian soldiers in the war; I was among your boys who came over. I had hundreds of your sailors coming to my church, and I used to go to the Y. M. C. A. and speak to them, and in your great country, as in my great country, you have got some of the best in the world, and you have got some of the roughest in the world; but do you know I never got in touch with any group of men in any part of the army of the allies but that I found deep down in the heart of every man of them there was a longing for God. The first thing when I would talk to them, their hand would go into their pocket and bring out a pocket-book and they would open it up; and generally the first photograph was the photograph of a woman, generally of their mother, and if it wasn't of their mother it was of their wife, or if it wasn't of their wife it was of their sister or sweetheart; they would bring it out directly they knew you were in sympathy with them. I would go in dressed as a minister and they would look and wonder what I was going to do. If I started to preach, they would say, "Pass on." But I didn't, I used to go in and sit down alongside them and talk about their country. If they were from Australia, I could talk about every State. If they were from America, I could talk about my friends in America, and I would start to talk and get a point of contact, and get home with them, and it isn't far from a man's love for his home to his love for God. I used to get a point of contact, and then by and by I would find that deep down in every man's heart there was something that could be touched by his love of God.

Oh, it is worth a lot of trouble to find out how to get contact and just to be able to touch human souls. But don't forget those of your own household. Simon was led by his own brother to Christ, and you know it is always hardest to lead your own folk to Christ, and I'll tell you why: because your own people know you for what you are, that is why it is hardest. There are lots of people who appear like angels of light when they are out in the world, but they are angels of Godliness in their own house. I have seen plenty of men who were so polite in the world that you would think they were glorious, and they tell me they are just like great big bouncing bears in their home. What is the use of all your pietistic talk with people that know you, if your religion won't stand the test of living with you and knowing you as you really are?

I do make this plea to you this morning in God's dear name: if there have been mistakes in your domestic relationships, unloving qualities in your own life, then be outspoken of your acknowledgment of that with those you love, if you are determined by God's grace that you are going to start all over again. You know if your religion is worth anything it is worth this: that it will show you where you have been wrong, and you will be as willing to start right as you were to be originally converted. This morning if you know there has been a weakness in your life, then let me plead with you this way: in this gathering right here and now, you lift your heart to God and say, "God helping me it shall be different from to-day," and then if it is so, if there is any one affected, you go to them and tell them with candor how that thing has happened.

In Australia I had been preaching about family prayer and I started a crusade to get family altars put up in the house. I had a deacon who came to me and said: "Mr. Fletcher, I will be very candid with you. My boys know me for what I am, and if I want to open the Bible on my breakfast table they wouldn't stay to worship. I wouldn't dare do it, although I know I ought to do it." I looked at him and I said: "You will forgive me, but if I were in your place I'll tell you what I would do. I know your boys as well as I know you. Your oldest boy has an influence over all your other sons. Now suppose when you go home you go into his bedroom and put your arms around his neck and tell him straight that you have been doing things that a Christian ought not to do, and that you are ashamed and are going to begin all over again and set up your family altar, and claim his loyalty to Christ. You try it and see what happens. It is an awful thing for a father to have to humiliate himself like that, but if you have humiliated Jesus Christ in front of your sons, you go now and humiliate yourself."

The following Sunday he came to me with the tears rolling down his cheeks. He said: "You never saw such a thing in your life. I got my boy in his bedroom and when I got half way through my confession to him he began to realize what I was saying and he flung his arms around my neck and kissed me and burst into tears and put his hand over my mouth. He said, 'Dad, I don't want to hear any more.' I tried to go on but he wouldn't listen, and when I told him I was going to put up the family altar, he said, 'We will all start.' And we all did start."

I am going to tell you that was the first step in that family; his sons and daughters began to join my church, and just as I was leaving to go to another church he presented me with a row of books that I have in my library to-day; that row of books was his and his family's thanksgiving offering that the family had been united in Christ Jesus, and that union began with a humiliation of the father himself to one of his sons who knew he had been living a life that wasn't a Christian life.

You must get right with God; you must get right with those whom you have hurt; you must get that point of spiritual contact in life, and you will lead your pater to Jesus Christ, and as a result it will go on and on and on and on to all eternity.

I am just finishing now so that I may let you go, but will you hear me in this moment? If the life of one man or one woman or one boy or one girl is wrong, and they through their influence lead somebody else wrong, that one may lead two, and those two are sure to influence four, and those four will influence eight, and those eight will influence a hundred, and that hundred will influence a thousand, and God knows how far it will go on. This old Book says, "Better were it for a man that he were never born that he should cause one of Christ's little ones to stumble."

Another text, "Let him know that he that converteth a sinner from the error of his way shall save a soul from death, and shall hide a multitude of sins."

Oh, let your life be lived with Christ in God. Cultivate your own personal piety; read God's word every day; pray to Him every day; make Christ King. Oh, I wish you had that in your singing at this convention—"Make Christ King;" follow Him as His loyal subject.

THE SWORD AND THE CUP
EXCERPT OF ADDRESS BY DR. WILLIAM HIRAM FOULKES
Plymouth Congregational Church, New York
THURSDAY MORNING, JULY 5

"It is little wonder that the world misunderstands the spirit and programme of Jesus when His own disciples fail to grasp their meaning. Rome was a past-mistress in the art of the Sword. Poor, blundering Peter was no match for her, with his draw sword and his impulses to fight when he had forgotten to watch and pray. The rebuke Jesus gave him was severe and unexpected: 'Put thy sword into the sheath! The cup which the Father hath given me to drink, shall I not drink it?'

"Ever since that day the followers of Jesus have been confronted by the dilemma of the sword and the cup. On the one hand are all the human instincts that bid men to grasp and get, to seize and take, to have and to hold. Force is the keynote of the philosopher. It does not matter, either, whether it is the force of a nation that tries to win the world by conquering it, or the brute force of men like those who on yesterday turned our national holiday into bloody shambles, contending for physical supremacy and a large lot of lucre, by the spectacle of a brutal prize fight. It is the same spirit that moves employers to regard their employes as serfs to be driven, and that impels workers to sabotage and others forms of industrial wickedness.

"The Church, being human as well as divine, does not escape the temptation to which Peter succumbed. It it prone to put its trust in its driving power, its corporate wealth and prestige, its capacity to move men by the force of its externals. On the other hand, the true symbol of a conquering Church is not the sword but the cup. It is in unselfish surrender to the will of God, in devoted service of the many who are estranged, in willingness to bear the cross as a living reality, rather than as a wooden badge, that the Church may find its power. The world's remedy for the sword is another one, a bigger, brighter, sharper, and inevitably bloodier. Christ's remedy for the sword is a sheath and a cup. His Spirit calls to individuals and nations, but most of all to His own disciples, to put the sword forever into the sheath and to take the cup of sacrifice and suffering, without flinching. Four million Endeavorers with glistening swords might fight on the right side of a war for justice; but in the long run, in the words of Luther, such 'striving would be losing.' If this great host were to take Christ's weapon, the cup, and use it as He used it, they could conquer the world."

BROKEN CISTERNS AND THE LIVING FOUNTAIN

There is no human agency deeper than the anguish of thirst. It becomes properly the symbol for all the surging and pent-up longings of humanity. To-day, as always, men are athirst for life. They desire to know its meaning and its purpose. We seek an explanation for its ills and the secret of its blessings. They thirst for life.

In the Orient there is a conceit that heavenly water is that which comes from the sky, while that which wells up from some hillside spring is only earthly. Under the influence of this superstition the ancients frequently builded huge cisterns to catch and hold the water that fell from heaven. Under the furious heat of the eastern sun, even well-built cisterns would soon crack and crumble, and even the stagnant water which once had been held would disappear.

The old prophet denounced the people of God for two evils. One was then hewing out cisterns, with toil and trouble, cisterns that could only hold stagnant water, and could not hold even that long. The other was their turning away from the living fountain which never ceased to flow, full and free.

The Oriental superstition and the sin which the prophet denounced have their modern counterpart. The world to-day is just as thirsty for life as during any past age. Men are still hewing out cisterns instead of turning to the fountain.

There is the great earthly cistern of paganism, erected by the toil of generations, and cemented by the life-blood of millions of unsatisfied souls. The philosophies and religions of the pagan world do not satisfy even those who have erected them. The intolerable economics, political and moral conditions of the pagan world are a clear testimony to the fact that the philosophy of life taught by pagan faiths is a broken cistern. Deluded globe trotters who spend their money like water in the great treaty ports of the world and then come home saying that "their religion is good enough for them," are colossal in their ignorance. What they see is the gilded paganism of a few centres that have borrowed the lustre of Christian ideals and practices. Let the men who have lived for generations or years in the Orient testify and they will tell of poverty, disease, immoralities, and vices that beggar description. In it all, however, is the ineradicable thirst of the human soul for life.

What President Nicholas Murray Butler, of Columbia, calls neo-paganism is sweeping like a tidal wave over our own country. Neo-paganism is the broken cistern that deluded people who profess to be civilized, hewn out of the rock to hold the water of life, while they contemptuously turn their backs upon the living fountain. Jungle music and jungle motions, murderous clothing and shameless countenances, souls that jazz themselves to a moral desuetude that is akin to spiritual death, all of these are the portion of those who drink at the broken cistern of Neo-paganism. Psycho-analysis, Eudarmonism are the philosophy of unadulterated happiness, mediumship, spiritualism, and a hundred other broken cisterns litter the modern roadside with the wreckage of their blasted hopes and ill-spent lives.

What a day in which to call men and women to the living fountain! The Christian Endeavor movement has never broken with the Christ who satisfies thirst. It knows the way to its cooling springs. It has a wonderful opportunity to-day through the voice of the millions of young men and women who have found the water of life, to call others to the fountain. This is the hour for the greatest revival of real religion that a war-weary, sin-cursed world has known in a hundred years. This is the golden opportunity for Christian young people all over America to lead the host of American youth to the true source of happiness and joy, which they themselves have found in the teaching and the spirit of Jesus Christ who said, "I am the water of life."

"WHY THIS WASTE?"
Quiet Hour Address
SATURDAY MORNING, JULY 7, 1923
BY WILLIAM HIRAM FOULKES

God gives liberally, but he abhors waste. Extravagance and waste are cardinal sins of a prosperous people. When money is earned easily it is spent freely. Babson has pointed out that economic prosperity moves in cycles. First there is one of great prosperity. Then carelessness and extravagance set in and moral fibres are weakened. Hard times and even panics follow. Then people become repentant and begin to save and prosperity once more is established.

The American people are the richest and the most wasteful in the world. They throw away what would fully support other peoples. Their habits of excessive eating and of pandering to bodily demands have made the name of America synonymous with selfishness, to many of the nations of the earth. Underneath it all America is idealistic and unselfish.

There is no nation that carries on a more widespread and self-denying ministry of helpfulness all over the world than the United States of America. Her philanthropic and missionary enterprise girdles the globe. Her noblest sons and daughters are engaged in gainless, humanitarian pursuits. Whether it is America or the Dominion of Canada, Europe, or Asia, the world must face anew to-day the question of waste. The waste of war and the causes and policies leading to war stagger the imagination. Industry has its widespread waste, not only of substance but of life.

In particular, the youth of the world are allured to-day as they have never been before, by the fascination of life with its creations, comforts, and its sensuous pleasures. Every nation has its "great white ways," with their wanton pouring out of life upon fleeting things. It is a false conclusion, however, that the youth of the world, and notably of Christian lands, are dead to the motives of service and sacrifice. While youth seems to be out of joint to many of the older generation, and actually seems to have given itself over to an orgy of spending and waste, down underneath it all young people to-day are as much concerned as ever with the meaning of life, and want to get as much as possible out of it.

One reason why modern young people repudiate the philosophy and the faith of the elders is that the former know that the latter do not always or largely live by their own professions. Young people growing up in prayerless, selfish, ambitious homes, are going to discount the religious professions of the older members of the family circle who say one thing and do another. "Like parents, like the chilren!"

The remedy for the intolerable waste of youthful energy and enthusiasm is not scolding strictures, but unselfish challenges and consistent examples. The Christian Endeavor host has an opportunity seldom if ever equalled. It has the chance of so living its Christian ideals in the midst of the larger group of non-Christian youth, that the latter may be won from its waste to fruitful service. The most powerful argument against the wanton, pleasure-mad life of modern youth, is the simple example of young people in every community living joyous, contented and useful lives without the extravagances which characterize the temper of the day, Christian Endeavorers could not do no more far-reaching thing than to dedicate their bodies, minds and spirits to a new understanding and interpretation of their own Christian ideals. The only way to call back lives that are being wasted is by the example of others who are living unselfishly.

The spirit of conservation of life and its real values is nowhere more clearly seen than in the missionary enterprise of the Church. Literally thousands of young men and women have heard the call of the economic, intellectual and moral waste of the pagan world and have gone "overseas" to watch the wastage of life there by the laying down of their own lives in devoted service. The most notable thing one may see in all the world is that band of unselfish souls who have left home and native land and are living and dying out in the wastes of the world's filth and sorrow. They walk and work in the midst of blindness and insanity; of men and women who are like beasts driven by perpetual fear. They have begun the process of relieving the world's suffering by suffering for it and with it. They are matching the waste of human life and human souls all over the world by what the world calls the waste of their own lives, yet a glorious waste. They are following the example of many who broke her treasure upon the feet of Jesus and wiped them with the hair of her head. These noble youth see the feet of Jesus in the dirty, disagreeable feet of lepers and plague-stricken men and women, and in the feet of little children all over the world. Whenever they find tired and wayward feet they see the feet of the Lord, for His feet are still on earth.

The missionary enterprise which cold-blooded business men often charge with extravagant waste of life and money, is really the one great remedy for the world's appalling waste. The cost of one battleship invested in heroic and unselfish lives overseas, would do more to promote the peace and welfare of the nations than a hundred times as much spent in destructive enterprises and schemes.

THE GREAT CRUSADE

QUIET HOUR, MONDAY NOON, JULY 9, 1923

BY WILLIAM HIRAM FOULKES

(EXCERPTS OF ADDRESS)

It is easy to lose sight of the fourth horseman of the Apocalypse. The other three are vivid and picturesque. War, famine, and death stalk their unchallenged way through the world and men all hit despair of staying their bloody march through the ages. They forget the figure of the horseman whom God has appointed to go forth, conquering and to conquer—the rider upon the white horse.

In His name and Spirit the Christian Endeavorers of the world, four millions strong, are called to the great crusade. They are summoned to enroll anew under the banner of the White King. They are to be mobilized and disciplined. They are to be equipped with arms and supplies. They are to be marshaled in such manner as may best permit them to serve on the whole long battle front. They are not called for dress parade, but for war. Their first enemy is war itself.

There need be no reflection upon the heroism of the men who hitherto have fought in the wars of the world. Christian Endeavor furnished its full quota in the recent World War. Their record is as glorious and unsullied as the record of any. The hour has now struck when war must be made upon war itself. War-lords and war-properties, war-causes and war-inheritances, war-hatreds and war-sorrows, must be resolutely faced and to the last ditch. There are enough Christian Endeavorers in the world and their patriotic zeal is so importuned that if they were to throw themselves solidly behind a movement against war, they could lead the greatest crusade in all history to a glorious triumph. We have been skirmishing around the edges long enough. We must train our guns upon the centre. The rider of the red horse must be put forever hors de combat. Sentiment will not carry us far enough. It will require convictions born of conscience, courage that arises out of a supreme faith in God, and a covenant together that we will fight war morning, noon and night, until this arch enemy of human progress has been destroyed.

The great crusade is also to be against the rider of the black horse. Half the world is perpetually starving to death. The pagan world is practically destitute of medical and surgical relief. Economic bondage worse than that of ancient Egypt is the lot of over half the human race. There can be no peace on earth and good will among men so long as men and women and little children are deprived of bread. The twelve-hour day and the seven-day week, wherever they still stand in industry, are a violation of the law of God and the rights of men. The Orient that does not have Christian ideals is apt in its imitation of western ways. I saw in Shanghai a silk factory where little girls as well as grown women stand on their feet twelve hours a day, seven days in the week, plunging their hands into vats of hot water and earning "as much as ten cents a day," as the foreman proudly told me. It does behoove America to point its finger at China for such cruel and sordid practices, so long as there are great industrial enterprises in a Christian land controlled by men who profess to be Christians, who still perpetuate and to that extent defend the iniquitous grind of toil without rest. It is fine to hear from the lips of a great industrial leader that the great need of the world is a revival of religion. It is distressing to hear from the same lips on the same day a justification of the twelve-hour day on the pagan ground of its expediency, this, too, in the face of other voices from other industrial leaders who have already put an end to such tyranny. It should not be overlooked, however, that a great crusade against economic imposture will not go far merely by attracting leaders of industry. Those whom they employ are in many cases even more deserving of rebuke, for their greed and sordidness, for their sabotage and the un-American and un-Christian tyranny over their own fellows. The Church and its organized youth must take sides neither for or against employers or employee, but for and against both. The Christian attitude toward the economic order of the world is supremely ethical. It knows that nothing can be finally good for people that is not eternally right. Men who are fighting against a day of rest, against reasonable hours and wages in return for honest toil and faithful production, against constitutional and statutory law that protects the nation against devastating economic and moral traffic in poisons that kill the body and the soul, are fighting against the stars in their causes.

The great crusade must also marshal its forces against the rider on the pale horse. The eternal issue is between death and life. On one hand are all those forces that tend to the disintegration of the bodies and souls of men. On the other, the energies that give strength to the soul and welfare to the body. The rider on the white horse came that men "might have life and might have it abundantly." Nothing that concerns the welfare of men, temporal, or eternal, is beyond His care. The enlightenment of the human mind, the enriching of human emotions by elevating stimulation, the challenging of the human will by setting forth the Kingdom of God as the end of all human energy and choice, all of these are the mission of the great crusade.

The crusaders must carry a sword and a shield, a helmet and a breastplate, a girdle for the loins, and sandals for the feet. Their sword is the authoritative, unchanging word of God which has survived blatant radicalism and pessimistic reactionism for nearly two thousand years, and which despite the fury of theological controversy, is the only infallible rule of faith and practice, the only aggressive weapon given to the crusader. His shield is a living faith in God and in his task and its ultimate triumph. His helmet is salvation through a divine Saviour. His girdle and his sandals are truth and peace. With such an armor the crusader who follows the fourth horseman of the Apocalypse may face shrapnel and shell, devastating submarines and destructive aeroplanes, tear-bombs, and poison gas. They all came from the pit into which they shall all be cast. His weapons are the instruments of another world. He is facing a defeated foe. His leader has already overcome the world. "Who follows in His train?"

Chapter IV.

CHRISTIAN ENDEAVOR AND EDUCATION

The Coliseum

Rev. Stanley B. Vandersall, Presiding

Thursday Afternoon, July 5

On Thursday afternoon by 1.45 hosts of delegates flowed into the Coliseum to hear expert talks on practical Christian Endeavor principles and ideals. Professor H. Augustine Smith led the devotional service, pointing out the place of proper song in worship. Seldom, we venture to say, has the Coliseum been filled in the afternoon by an audience like this, an audience of youth, ardent, purposeful, melodious, enthusiastic, invincible, the hope of America's life. It was as large an afternoon audience as we remember seeing in Christian Endeavor.

Stanley B. Vandersall was the leader, presiding tactfully, graciously, and efficiently over an audience of thousands.

*Rev. William Ralph Hall, director of young people's work in the Presbyterian church, dealt with the tremendous theme, "The Right Foundation for the Individual Endeavorer." This was the first of three afternoon lectures by Mr. Hall. It was a new experience for a Christian Endeavor Convention, a lecture, like a classroom lecture. It was a lecture full of information and suggestive thoughts. The aim was to impart information about the essentials of Christian Endeavor, and in this Mr. Hall was eminently successful. He laid weight on seven essentials in Christian Endeavor, the first of them being a definite purpose, expressed in the Christian Endeavor pledge. The second is a deeper spiritual life, without which Christian Endeavor can never have the power it should have. To enrich the life of the church we must have spiritual sustenance. The third is training in devotional leadership — the leading of meetings, prayer and testimony. It is by *doing things* that Endeavorers develop their talents; Christian Endeavor is a training-school of leadership, the expression of our individual ideals.

The fourth essential in Christian Endeavor is that of execu-

---

*For Rev. Mr. Hall's three lectures see chapter XIX.

tive training and leadership in organizing and carrying out plans of religious work. Here the opportunity comes through committee work, through being an officer, and through private study of leadership methods. The pastors need multitudes of such volunteer leaders trained in Christian Endeavor to do efficient work in the church. Ninety per cent of efficiency in leadership can be learned, and it *is* learned in Christian Endeavor if we do not shirk responsibility.

A fifth essential is a larger vision of the Christian church's programme, and this is attained through study-classes of all kinds. Information! Without it we shall never hear the call of the world's need. Endeavorers must study and study more and more.

The sixth essential is soul-winning, personal service, and the seventh, eloquently described by Mr. Hall, is the Endeavorer's example in the home, school, office, workshop, or mart. These seven elements enter into the very vitals of Christian Endeavor. Without any one of them we are weak. To grow we must serve.

An interesting item was a ten minutes' demonstration, staged by Publication Manager A. J. Shartle, of Boston, who not only showed the audience some of Dr. Clark's books published by the United Society, but accompanied the presentation of each book by a racy, anecdotal talk about the books and their author.

"Christian Endeavor and the Home" was the theme to which Rev. A. E. Praetorius, director of young people's work in the Evangelical Church, devoted careful analysis and thought.

CHRISTIAN ENDEAVOR AND THE HOME

Rev. A. E. Praetorius

Director of Young People's Work in the Evangelical Church

The easiest and yet most difficult place in all the world for Christian Endeavor to function is in the home. Here is where the folks know us. All pretence, and all sham, and all mere bluffing on the surface will not go in the home, because the folks will detect that at once, and are very frank to tell us about it, too; yet there is no place in which an honest attempt and earnest endeavor to do something that is lifting and worth while will be more truly appreciated and evaluated than just in the home.

If Christian Endeavor can succeed in the home it can succeed anywhere, but if Christian Endeavor can not succeed in the home it can not succeed anywhere. The home offers the largest return for any effort we put forth in lines of Christian Endeavor. It is like working virgin soil, for the home is the fundamental institution; out of this institution come all other institutions that go to make up both the state and the church, and whatever we put into the home we are ultimately putting into every other institution that goes to make up both state and church. Therefore, he who builds largely in the home is building most largely in both state and church. But the worth of the home as a builder of both the state and the church is in exact proportion as religion is vital in that home. Wherever religion is weak and insipid and has no real vital grasp upon the home, there we shall find less of the building power of that home as it goes out in the state and in the church; but where that religion is deep and

Dr. Henry H. Sweets

Hugh S. Magill, LL.D.

Dr. R. W. Gammon

Rev. Royal J. Montgomery

strong, sincere and vital, there we will discover that that home is a real, strong builder of the church and of the state.

There are four essentials which must be found in every true home. They are: Affection, mutual understanding, appreciation, and confidence. Where affection, the outward manifestation of love, where mutual understanding, where appreciation, the saying of a kind word in response to a goodly deed or an honest effort and work, where confidence and trust are lacking there can be no true home. Where cold reservedness and where fault-finding and misunderstanding and distrust are found, there a true home can never be builded. We discover in the modern tendency that we are attempting to build a whole house in the church, and I have no fault to find with that; but if I read the New Testament correctly, it seems to me that the effort there is to build the church in the house. How often do we meet with this phrase in the New Testament, "The church that is in thy house," the church which meets in thy house, but how seldom do we find it to-day in the annals of modern church activity! The church once more must be builded back into the house if the church is to do in the house and in the home what God intended it should do? But one may ask how will all of this fall within the scope of the work of Christian Endeavor? It seems to me upon the surface that it is the province of Christian Endeavor, if Christian Endeavor has any province at all, to work in the home, for is it not the very idea of Christian Endeavor itself to discover, to lift up and to train leadership in the great sacrificial callings of the world and of the church?

One said to me one time: "I am against it all. I am against all your young people's societies."

I said, "Well, why?"

"Well, because it seems as though it is a match-making affair."

Well, that is a terrible thing if some of our Christian Endeavorers should happen to get married some of these days and set up homes!

Christian Endeavorers do set up homes and begin that most marvelous thing in the world—a true Christian home. Is it not the purpose, is it not the intent of Christian Endeavor to build that affection in homes and in relationships one with another where love does not fall back silent and dead upon itself but goes out in expression and in appreciation? And is not Christian Endeavor here to build up mutual understanding among nations, among folks in their home city, in their home church, and fundamentally in their own homes?

But how can we build up a home religion that is vital?

First of all, by building up home prayers, the family altar a centre of them. It is said that Abraham, the great home-builder, built an altar while he pitched his tent, but I fear too many of us to-day are willing to build the tent and forget the altar. But is it not within the province of Christian Endeavor to see that that little altar is built and maintained in the home, that the fire shall never go out upon that altar?

In the second place Christian Endeavor can build in the home by building home music. It would do some of us good if we should just take a careful walk up and down the avenues of music in our home and censor some of the piano pieces and go through the records of the graphaphone and break a few of them.

Shall not Christian Endeavor attempt to build back in the home once more the gathering of the family around the organ or the piano for an evening song or season of song together? Or at least once a week the family can gather to sing the great songs of Zion? Some of the most precious memories of my life are of those days when as a family we gathered together.

Then in the third place, attend to home literature for the elimination or displacing of that which is salacious and objectionable. Remove some of the yellow-backed novels that are now bound in nice green and red and blue and white cloth and sold at a dollar and a half to three dollars apiece, replacing them with books that are uplifting and helpful. See that the Bible is in evidence, and see that good Christian literature, magazines and periodicals, are found upon the tables of the home.

And then may not Christian Endeavor add more than that, attend to the home conversation? It has got to such a sorry pass that in many homes they can not carry on conversation for a single minute without some hurtful gossip about some one. Can not Christian Endeavor in the home help to introduce good uplifting, valuable conversation and displace much of this hurtful gossip that tends only to destroy and has never yet been a building factor?

Christian Endeavor can do much in the home by encouraging home discipline, good old-fashioned, rugged discipline that teaches a family to obey the law of the house, that teaches childhood and youth to come beneath the judgments of their parents and guardians. Can we not by example as well as by word encourage old family discipline of that lad and lassie who will not obey father and mother, will not obey the law of the house, will neither obey God nor the state when they get out?

Last of all, can not Christian Endeavor do much toward building a home atmosphere, that undefinable something, that glorious something that must be found in every household to make it a true home, that does not rest in furniture, that does not rest in meals or in programme or equipment, but that something that grows out of good will and good cheer? Can not Christian Endeavor build that?

America is one great peril as I see it, and that is the peril of losing her own homes. Yes, we are growing rich, we are growing world famous, we are attaining world leadership, we are at the head and top of it all, it seems, but the danger is that we may lose our homes. You have seen the cartoon that depicted the home, a place in which to grab a bite to eat and to powder the nose and then to run. What shall it profit America if she shall gain the whole world of wealth and of fame and of leadership and of prestige and of power and lose her homes?

It was a pleasure to hear Rev. Henry H. Sweets, D.D., secretary of the Board of Education of the Southern Presbyterian Church, whose theme was "Choosing a Life-Work."

CHOOSING A LIFE WORK

Rev. Henry H. Sweets, D.D.

Secretary of the Board of Education of the Southern Presbyterian Church

When one has chosen Jesus Christ as his Savior and friend there remains one other supreme choice, a life work that shall engage his purposes and the energies of his being. No one can truly estimate the importance of these supreme choices, as back of the tree is the tiny seed, and back of the river the rivulet, so back of our life and its destiny lie our choices of good or of evil. You who are here this afternoon have yielded your hearts to the Lord Jesus Christ as the Master of your life; as Christian Endeavorers you have taken this solemn pledge in his sight, "Trusting in the Lord Jesus Christ for strength, I promise Him that I will strive to do what he would have me do." I want to tell you, friends, that you can have a clear perception of what God's will for your life is. God has a plan for every man. It will be the joy of His heart to reveal to you day by day and hour by hour the parts of His plan for you.

> We are not here to play, to dream, to drift;
> We have had work to do and loads to lift.
> Shun not the struggle, face it; 'tis God's gift.

Possibly I am talking here this afternoon to some young men and young women who are running before God, who are making plans for their own lives, who have marked out their career without reference to the plan of the great architect of the universe. Let me plead with you with all my heart to pause, to listen for His voice, to cry from a heart willing to obey, "Lord, what wilt Thou have me to do?"

Many years ago at Cornell College, a young man coming down the stairway heard the sound of music through an open door. He entered and found himself in a student-association meeting. He said afterward: "I don't remember anything that the speaker said that day except the words of his text; he was speaking from those words of the prophet, 'Seekest thou not great things for thyself?' This message of God to the heart of that young man. He was seeking great things for himself. He was planning a life, like so many lawyers he was probably dreaming of that time when he might have a seat on the bench of the Supreme Court of our great nation, but this came as the turning point of his life —"Seekest thou great things for thyself? Seek them not."

That young man, John R. Mott, went out of that room that day saying, "By the help of God, I will seek great things, but I will seek great things for God." He gave his life to be used of Him and how marvelously has God used it!

When I returned to my home in Louisville, Kentucky, some time ago my little eleven year old boy said, "Daddy, if you will give me seventy cents I can go down to the five-and-ten-cent store and I can get enough parts to make us a radio set, and then we can all hear everything that is sent out from our broadcasting station here in Louisville." I gave him the money and he did that job, and then he went out to fix his aerial; his mother and his little brother were there by his side, interested in him, and he commenced talking about grounding the wire; and then he dug a hole and put a piece of iron there and wrapped a wire around it and sunk it down and covered it over, and while he was in that process his little brother, just seven years old, looked up into his face with a twinkle in his eyes and said, "Henry, I wouldn't put that wire down into the ground, you will just be hearing what the devil is saying all the time."

You don't have to ground the wires to-day. If you pick up the papers, if you look at the magazines, if you examine the books, you will find the noise that comes to us from the evil one. Be still and listen for the voice of God. You will ofttimes hear this as you pray to him: Pray to Almighty God. All the men and women who have done things in this life that have blessed their fellowmen have been men and women whose years have been marked by prayer. Think of Spurgeon, Moody, Frances Willard, and all the host of those who in their generation have sought to do the will of God and have succeeded. Hudson Taylor had studied very carefully the needs of the whole world, and one day as he prayed he said: "There seemed to come to my heart this whisper from my risen Lord and Friend: 'Hudson Taylor, I am going to evangelize China, if you will walk with me I will do it through you,'" and being not disobedient to the heavenly vision, Hudson Taylor went out and established that great China Inland Mission, and there at the time of his death he had with him not fifty or a hundred or five hundred devoted men and women, but more than seven hundred who had no agency to furnish them funds, but whose support was coming in answer to prayer to Almighty God.

Jesus Christ in John 7:17 said this: "If any man wills to do the will of God, he shall know the teaching, whether it be of God, or whether I speak of myself." What does God mean by this? Well, just simply and practically this: He means that if you want to do what God wants you to do, He will lead you on, day by day and hour by hour, into the fullness of His plan. I don't mean by that that he will say to some of these boys here to-day, "I want you to be a minister," or to some of these girls, "I want you to go to China." He may not make known the aim from the beginning, but day by day as you trust Him He will lead you on and on until you come into the fullness of his plan. Many of us may learn just what life's work to choose as we look at the life of Jesus Christ our Savior. He is our great example. He says, "I am the light of the world;

he that followeth me shall not walk in darkness, but shall have the light of life." He plans within him something that will illuminate the way before him, each step made clearer and clearer as he proceeds to follow Him. We know something of the purposes that drove Jesus on. He exclaimed, "Lo, I come, in the volume of a book it is written of me, I delight to do Thy will, O my God."

Many of us, as we are seeking what choice we shall make as our life work, may be conscious that Jesus Christ Himself is leading us on. It is possible for every one of us to start out on the adventure of life as a personally conducted tour. He Himself has said, "Lo, I am with you always, even to the end of the world."

It is possible for us to go forth under his personal leadership, accomplishing through his name what God, would have us do, although no earthly eye may see the source of our power. When Chinese Gordon was going down on his last fateful expedition he was heard to exclaim, "I go down, but Jehovah of Hosts is with me."

Adam McAll, a student of one of the universities, heard of the sickness and sorrow and death and superstition and anguish in Africa, and he said, "I can't stay here while men and women and children are dying like that over there." He sailed over the seas and he began promising work, and then he was smitten with the awful fever, and as he lay dying one heard him in communion with this unseen friend as he exclaimed, "Oh, Lord Jesus, Thou knowest that I dedicated my life to Thee and to Africa, but if it pleases Thee better to take my life than to accept my service, what is that to me? Thy will be done."

There is just one incident in the life of Jesus, friends, that may shed light upon this problem you are facing—what life's work shall I choose? How shall I find God's plan for my life? We were told that Jesus was out on the mountain side, the great multitudes were gathered before Him. and this is the record that when He saw the multitudes He was moved with compassion upon them, for they fainted as sheep having no shepherd. Turning to his disciples He said, "Truly the harvest is plentiful, but the laborers are few." Think of Jesus there on the slope of the mountain. He saw multitudes before him. They were hungry, and He had fed them; they were sick, and He had restored them. Some of them were blind and He gave them back their sight; some of them were deaf and He restored their hearing; some of them were outcast lepers and He healed them. He ministered to their bodily needs. But, oh, as Jesus saw that multitude He saw the sin-sick soul for which He had come to die and He gave His life and ministry to that. He saw the multitudes. Friends, have your eyes ever looked out upon the great multitudes of men that are feeling about, if haply they may find God, who are distressed and driven and fainting, sheep without any shepherd, scattered abroad?

I had a friend who was spending a summer two years ago in the Ozark Mountains in Arkansas. He found a little boy that had been on a bed of languish and pain for years. His spine was broken. His parents were ignorant and poor. He said: "I want that boy. I am going to take him over to my city to a Christian physician. I believe he can restore him." He took him over to Memphis, and they put him there in a plaster cast so that the poor little fellow couldn't move at all, and while he was there on his bed my friend, his benefactor, visited him week by week. He said, "Every time I went into that room that little fellow looked up with great hungry eyes, and there came an awful shriek from his soul as he said, 'Take this off, let me out!' "

Oh, I thought of that little boy and then my thought turned to these poor ignorant superstitious men and women and little children bound in their ignorance and superstition, fearing some awful, dreadful thing, who, not knowing it, are calling to us, "Let me out, take this off, break these bounds that hold me and bind me."

One-half of this old world has no doctor and no nurse. Do you know, friends, that men who have investigated very carefully say that in the country of India alone five million men and women and little boys and girls and tiny babies die every year from preventable diseases. They have no physicians, there is no hygiene, there is no sanitation, there is no nurse, there is nobody that cares for their bodies.

Jesus went about preaching in their villages. Do you know that one-half of the old world to-day nearly two thousand years after Christ died, have never heard that name that is above every name? What a privilege to go forth, to enlist unto the banner erected by Dr. Clark last night, win these, friends, to Jesus Christ, and to make Jesus Christ a dominant power in their lives.

I have a book in my office that lists fourteen hundred separate and distinct vocations. I believe that in every one of them a man might serve Jesus Christ and his fellowman to-day. But, oh, in this hour of need, as the old world is sick and tottering, and the foundations of its religions and philosophies have tumbled beneath it, can we not give our lives to those things that will directly affect their souls and lead them to the Lord Jesus Christ?

King Saul who lived for himself died as a suicide, and you remember the wail of his heart as it cried, "I have played the fool." Later Saul of Tarsus gave his life that those who had never heard the name of Jesus might know of His love and His grace and His power, and he said, "There is laid up for me a crown of righteousness which the Lord, the righteous judge, shall give to me in that day."

Governor Taylor of Tennessee said: "The most pathetic thing that ever came to me in my administration as Governor of Tennessee happened just before I went out of office. Over in East Tennessee a man in a fit of anger had taken an axe handle and killed a fellowman. The jury that sat upon the case said he must spend the rest of his life in the penitentiary. He had been there a few months when the door of my office opened and a woman and little child were ushered in. The woman came to me and said, 'Governor, I came to ask you to pardon my husband. He did it in anger. He was a good father and good husband. You must let him go.'

"The Governor shook his head and said, 'No, I know that case, I can't pardon him.'

"In a little while the little child came up and said, 'Oh, Governor, 'as you dot a little dirl in your home? Won't you let papa come home to mama and to me?'"

"Governor Taylor said, 'I may not have been right to do it but that child touched my heart.'

He said, "I will look up the record and if there is any way that I can conscientiously pardon him, I will do it."

In a little while he sent a messenger over to the penitentiary and said, "Give that man his liberty."

In an hour or two after that, the man, his wife, and child came to the door of his office and knocked and came in and said, "Governor, I can never thank you for this."

He said, "You go on home and make a good citizen and provide for your wife and your child. That is all the thanks I want."

But the man fell down on the floor before him and said, "Oh, Governor, I can't leave you. Just give me a little place here by you, and I will stay here with my wife and little child and we will serve you all the days of our lives. You have done so much for us."

"Were the whole realm of nature mine,
  That were a present far too small;
Love so amazing, so divine,
  Demands my soul, my life, my all."

"Christian Endeavor and the Churches" was the theme selected by Rev. R. W. Gammon, D.D., secretary of the Congregational Society. He said:

RELATIONSHIP OF THE CHRISTIAN ENDEAVOR ORGANIZATION TO THE DENOMINATIONS

By Rev. R. W. Gammon, D. D.
District Secretary Congregational Education Society

Fifty years ago the churches of America were doing very little to bring their young people into the programme of the church. Young people's conferences, a parish house with a gymnasium, social, and dining-rooms for their use, and a director of their work who gave his whole time to them were unheard of and unthinkable in that far-away day. In those days young people were to be seen and not heard—the admonition of Paul to the Corinthians that their women were to keep silence in the churches was applicable to the young people in the churches of America fifty years ago.

Gradually our viewpoint has changed and our practice until it has come about that every denomination which expects to have a future, and in fact every movement that hopes to have a future, is training its young people to take up its tasks. One of the most significant developments in this regard in the last few years is the organization of the youth by the Masonic order. This is characteristic of the thinking of adults to-day. In the dearth of work for young people a half century ago a few men of clear vision like our own Dr. Clark began these movements which have meant so much not only to the young people but to the church and to the Kingdom at large. Christian Endeavor, the Epworth League, the Baptist Young People's Union, and a number of smaller organizations came into being and have waxed strong in their service for the young people.

The only one founded upon a purely interdenominational basis was the Christian Endeavor. My memory covers its whole history. I recall the days when nearly all the denominations regarded it as their young people's society. I attended its great conventions when the leading ministers of the denominations were present as members of its executive committee and in those days its conventions were by far the largest held in the country. My mind goes back to those large gatherings at Cleveland, Chicago, Boston, Denver, and other places. At Cleveland, in '94 perhaps it was, the convention registered 100,000 people. Those were the days of unbounded enthusiasm and loyalty in personal service and in money to the Christian Endeavor movement.

In the phrase of the newspaper cartoonist, "Them days is gone forever." We have come to a very different situation. In the twenty-five or thirty years intervening practically every one of the large denominations has organized under one name or another a department of religious education and young people's work and these departments are under the leadership of secretaries and a field force of trained men and women who give their whole time to this service. In a number of the denominations an elaborate organization has been built up which conducts young people's conferences for the denomination, which carries no recruiting for leadership at home and abroad; it makes programmes of study and service for its young people's groups and plans for the entire religious life of the young people of its denomination, save that which is interdenominational.

This denominational organization makes first claim to the allegiance of the young people on the ground that it is representative of the denomination and has a right to expect that it will have first call upon the loyalty of the denominational youth. So strong has the demand become for this work that denominational seminaries and colleges are offering courses in religious education and young people's work to train not only workers in the local church but also to train men and women for the field-force and for executive secretaryships in this field. This is true not only of denominations such as the Methodists and Baptists, both of which have their own young people's organization, but it is also true of Presbyterians and Congregationalists which continue to co-operate with the United Society of Christian Endeavor.

It was one of our own poets who said, "New occasions teach new duties, Time makes ancient good uncouth." This new day to which we have come with the work with the young people demands certain adjustments if we are to make the most of it. The denominations that clear their interdenominational work through Christian Endeavor, and the leaders of the latter organization, must understand each other and work together or else they both lose. We can afford to have no division in our Protestant forces anywhere. The forces of evil are so powerful and often so united that we shall go down to defeat before them if we are divided. We must find a way to get together so that denominational leaders having first claim upon the young people of their respective denominations shall gladly give proper place to the interdenominational work, and shall help it in every possible way, and on the other hand bring it about that the leaders of the interdenominational organization shall recognize the primacy of the organization set by each denomination to do its own particular work, and shall adjust the interdenominational machinery so that it shall co-operate and not compete.

On this feeling as a basis for our co-operative movement, we may confidently expect that we shall get together completely upon what we shall teach our young people. We may expect that not only will the denominational leaders be called in by Christian Endeavor to help make the policy which shall hold in the teaching, but shall help plan the topics furnished the societies, and shall find Christian Endeavor leaders ready to leave large place for the introduction of topics by the leaders of the respective denominations. My impression is that this plan is largely in effect now. If it is not, we shall undoubtedly go forward to make it effective as soon as it can be done. This will give each denomination opportunity to bring its own missionary work and other denominational plans to bear upon its young people. Plans allowing much of this have been in effect for many years.

So far as appears we shall do our missionary work for a long time to come, both at home and abroad, through the medium of denominations. I trust that this does not mean that we shall retain the secretarianism that we now have. With many others I am hoping and praying for the day when we shall have a united church of Christ in America that shall include all the evangelical denominations and as many others as are willing to come in. I do not see that it is possible for us to arrive at this much desired haven in five years or ten years. It will take a long period to bring enough of our people to believe in this ideal to make it a fact. This being true and taking into account that the allegiance of our young people, when they are past the Christian Endeavor age, if they remain Christian, will be to the church. We believe that most of the emphasis in their missionary teaching should be placed upon the missions that they will support. Anyway this should be true so far as their giving is concerned. Their studies in missionary text-books will be entirely, or almost so, undenominational. If their loyalty to missions is to be kept it will have to be centered upon a definite task. This means that it is better to attach the young people to that to which they will give their allegiance in maturity rather than to a task which will be of passing interest only. We may confidently expect therefore that denominational leaders of young people, and the leaders of the United Society, will get together regarding missions and the giving to missions and will see eye to eye in this important task.

The theological world is greatly disturbed at the present time. Not only are denominations in some measure set over the one against the other regarding important doctrines, but there is very marked division in some of the larger denominations between the conservatives and the liberals. A year ago it looked as if the great Baptist denomination might be rent asunder by this controversy, and our Presbyterian brethren had a struggle at Indianapolis a few weeks ago which caused much bitterness. There are certain schools of theology which many denominational leaders regard as antagonistic not only to the denominational life, but to the very structure of the Christian church. This condition creates delicate situations and puts not only denominational leaders but those who are responsible for interdenominational organizations in a very embarrassing position.

We are expecting that Christian Endeavor leaders will play this game throughout the country with absolute fairness, and continue to place the emphasis in the future as they have in the past upon Christian Endeavor without regard to theological technicalities. They have in the past been evangelical and constructive, and we are trusting them to be so in the future. In the Chicago district where Moody's Institute is strong we shall expect them to be alike friendly to the Institute and to the most liberal leaders of the co-operating denominations. In California, where the Los Angeles Bible Institute is strong, we shall expect that the organization will be just as friendly to Dr. Carl Patton, the modernist in the First Congregational Church, as it is to Dr. Torrey. If there are forces that cannot work with the Christian Endeavor with this emphasis upon a constructive evangelical attitude, then Christian Endeavor must pursue its way without the help of those forces. We shall expect that Harry Emerson Fosdick will be just as welcome on the platform of the conventions of the organization as is William Jennings Bryan, and that the organization will recognize the former as as great a force for evangelical religion as is the latter. Christian Endeavor in the past has not tried to be a judge of heresy, and we are trusting it in the future to be a practical leader of righteousness for the whole body of the churches which it represents.

Our new day means that the Christian Endeavor and the denominational leaders will arrive at an understanding concerning their claim upon the young people for the activities of the latter. It was once possible for the former organization to make its dates, set up its conventions and carry forward its programmes without fear of conflict with anything that the denomination might be doing for its young people. This is no longer possible. Practically all the denominations clearing through Christian Endeavor are now holding week-end conferences in the winter, summer conferences, recruiting meetings, schools of methods, camping trips, and many such gatherings for their young people. They confidentially expect that Christian Endeavor leaders will recognize their first claim, and that the latter will seek to co-operate with the former to the end that there shall be no conflict. The other day a district Christian Endeavor Union conducted a large excursion on the very day that one of its co-operating denominations began a young people's conference for the young people of that district. This made in the lives of a number of young people a conflict. The dates of the Young People's Conference had been advertised for at least six months, and had been in the hands of the Christian Endeavor organization for several months.

This indicates that the programme of the Christian Endeavor will be cut down to cover the interdenominational aspects of the work. Our young people, many of them, have all their dates taken for weeks ahead. If both organizations attempt to appeal to them for the entire round of activities, missionary, conference, summer camp, excursion, and all the rest, our young people will constantly be a strait betwixt two. We are confidently expecting that Christian Endeavor leaders in every district and State will take this into account, and bring their work to conform to the new situation in which we find ourselves.

For some years most of the denominations have failed to recruit enough young people to take care of their leadership at home and abroad. My own denomination, the Congregational, has been one of the worst sinners in this regard. We have been constantly stealing ministers from the Methodists and Presbyterians, and then were hardly able to keep our ranks full. Fifteen or twenty years ago we were doing little in the way of recruiting. Now almost all the denominations have student-life or recruiting secretaries who give their time in part or in whole to this task. They know the life of the denomination, the type of missionary work to be done, and can best make the appeal of the denomination for life service. They are looking to Christian Endeavor to leave this field untouched, feeling that it is a denominational rather than an interdenominational task.

We are confidently expecting that the Christian Endeavor organization will become more and more representative of the denominations that it serves. It will undoubtedly do this in two particulars. First, in the making of its convention and conference programmes. We are looking to the Christian Endeavor leaders to call in the men and women responsible for the leadership of young people in the denominations, and to treat them as consulting engineers in the making of every programme, and this to be done from its very inception. Second, we are expecting the Endeavor movement to keep its emphasis upon Christ and the church. This will mean that it will magnify the work of the church, and say no more about its own machinery than is necessary to make the machinery function for the church. We are expecting that the leaders of Christian Endeavor will along with ourselves recognize that the permanent religious relationship of the young people will not be to the Christian Endeavor society but to the church. We are sadly in need of a revival of the exaltation of the church. It has been discounted in too many circles, and we are sure that Christian Endeavor leaders would be the last to allow their organization which is making a most important contribution to the church to become a competitor with the church for the loyalty of the young people.

We are looking to Christian Endeavor to so conduct itself that it will in the future, as it has in the past, be a tremendous force for breaking down sectarianism. Apparently there has been a revival of this since the War. The era of good feeling among the denominations which was so noticeable while we were under the stress and strain of war has largely passed. We cannot believe that we shall remain permanently in this slump. To the Christian Endeavor, and to one or two other organizations, large credit is due for the great advances made in the last thirty years in denominational co-operation. The leaders in Presbyterian, Disciple, Congregational, and other churches who now control the situation were trained in Christian Endeavor. We shall never be able to break down sectarianism by an appeal to the older people. We say upon the street, that you cannot teach an old dog new tricks. Christian Endeavor is teaching the young people of a number of denominations to work and to worship together while they are in the formative period of life, and the organization is thus making an invaluable contribution to the solution of one of the most critical phases of American church life.

This organization in the past has in its great conventions introduced to the young people the finest leaders not only of their own denomination but of other denominations and of the world. No one denomination has all the spiritual and intellectual excellences in its leaders. Denominations large, and denominations small, have a contribution to make to leadership. Some of the men who are heard most gladly by our young people come from our smallest denominations. As a rule there is little chance for the leaders of other denominations to be heard in our denominational gatherings. A convention such as this commands the attention and the service of the best leaders that the world affords not only to inspire our young people to the noblest living but also to broaden their intelligence so that they will be sympathetic with and tolerant toward those who may differ from them in modes of worship and theological attitudes.

In some quarters it has become a habit of those dealing with young people to feel that they must approach the latter upon a level of jazz and pep if they are to reach them. The songs, address and recreation used with the young people are upon a low level. Christian Endeavor began with one of our saintliest and finest Christian ministers and it has continued by having the direction and help of the best men that the denominations afford. We are expecting that in its appeal to the young people it shall expect the best of them, and shall approach them on the high levels that shall challenge them to their best. This does not mean that we are against humor and fun and happy rollicking songs and high-grade pep, but we believe that the Christian Endeavor will keep its appeal on the higher level rather than on the lower that prevails among some.

As indicated above, the denominational leadership of young people is a trained leadership. In most of the denominations those who are accepted for this service are college and seminary trained, and many of them have had special courses in religious education and young people's work. The Christian Endeavor movement began with high-grade leadership, and we are confidently expecting that it will so continue, and that it will give attention of securing for State and district leadership men who will not suffer in comparison with the leaders doing a like work in the denominations. Only as it keeps up its high-grade leadership can it hope to have the respect and confidence of the ministers of the churches and the denominational leaders in like work. We are sure that this great organization will not disappoint its constituency in this regard.

The Christian Endeavor organization has an opportunity with the young people which comes to no one of the co-operating denominations. No one of us, not even the Presbyterians or Disciples, each with a membership running well over a million, can hope to bring together such an aggregation of young people as Christian Endeavor secures. Every such aggregation of people has its own psychology and offers certain great opportunities for leadership. In this convention we have a group sensitive, emotional, idealistic, and ready to serve. In these three days at Des Moines the life destiny of many a young man and young woman will be settled. Christian Endeavor has always made a great appeal on these occasions. We denominational leaders are committing our young people to you for these three days to let you do what you will with them under these unusual circumstances. We are depending upon you to see that no appeal is made that is small, mean, technical or sectarian. We trust you to do what you have done in the past, to appeal to our young people to follow Jesus in all His love, His sympathy, His tolerance, His brotherliness and His compassion. We are trusting you to put speakers upon this platform who will exalt what we all deem essential and who will forget the things that any considerable body deems non-essential. We rejoice in this great opportunity that you have, and as members of the Christian Endeavor we seek to bear with you the responsibility of this opportunity.

Another important theme on the programme was Dr. Hugh S. Magill's splendid and thoughtful address on "A Comprehensive Programme of Religious Education." Dr. Magill is general secretary of the International Sunday-School Council of Religious Education.

A COMPREHENSIVE PROGRAM OF RELIGIOUS EDUCATION

Hugh S. Magill, LL.D.

General Secretary of the International Sunday School Council of Religious Education

I am to speak on the subject, "A Comprehensive Program of Religious Education." Now this thought of religious education is a very vital one to-day. If I were to ask you how many of you are directly interested in or working in the field of religious education in the Sunday school, or in daily vacation Bible-school work, or in some form of week-day religious instruction, I am sure that a very large proportion of the audience would hold up their hands. I know you are interested. Every one of the leading

Protestant Christian denominations is putting greater emphasis on the programme of religious education.

Up to a year ago or a little more, there was the International Sunday School Association which existed for many, many years, and in all the different States, or nearly all, there were State Sunday School Associations, and down into the counties and cities and local communities there were Sunday school organizations, all a part of the great organized Sunday-school work of the nation. Then the great denominations recognized the importance of this ministry of teaching, and they, too, began the development of their Sunday-school work. They organized their Sunday-school boards and they formed the machinery and the organization and the plans for carrying forward this great programme of religious education.

Now, as they developed in this, feeling the co-operative idea, too, they formed the Sunday School Council of Evangelical Denominations, and twenty-eight of the leading Protestant Christian Evangelical Denominations united in this great Sunday School Council. They began to have a part in the selection of the Sunday-school lessons and the old International Sunday School Committee was re-organized, and every one of these twenty-eight denominations was granted a representative on that committee that selects the passages of Scripture that form the basis of the Sunday-school work.

As the International Sunday School Association and the Sunday School Council of Evangelical Denominations went on with their work, there was an overlapping, and it began to be seen that this work could best be done if united in one organization, this one organization to represent the co-operative work of all these different denominations. So a year ago last February the Sunday School Council of Evangelical Denominations voted to merge with the International Sunday School Association on an agreement that had previously been arrived at. The plan was unanimously ratified by a great convention in Kansas City, made up of more than seven thousand delegates. So to-day there is no International Sunday School Association; there is no Sunday School Council of Evangelical Denominations. There is in the place of both of them the International Sunday School Council of Religious Education, and as a result of this merger there should be no competing programmes on the part of Sunday-school forces with the denominations, but each denomination will carry forward its own programme. The main thought was to do away with competing programmes and make co-operative programmes, to do away with overlapping and make one great interdenominational forward movement in this great field.

In the International Sunday School Council of Religious Education there are two outstanding committees—the one is the International Lesson Committee. This committee goes on selecting the passages of the Bible to be studied, but always keep in mind, please, that when these different selections are made they are given back to the different denominations, and each denomination makes its own lesson helps, determines its own interpretation of these selections of the Scripture, publishes its own Sunday-school literature, and its own text-books dealing with these questions, so there is no interference with the autonomy or individual initiative of the several denominations.

Then there is the other committee, the Committee on Education. This Committee of fifty-five meets together and determines the policies, the programme, the outlines for teacher-training, for leadership-training, for organization, and all of that; then they make their report to the International Council. The International Council is made up of approximately one hundred and sixty members. One-half of these are appointed directly by the denominations and officially represent the different co-operating denominations. The other half are elected by the State Sunday School conventions and represent what is commonly called the territorial group in the field of religious education; and this Council finally determines the interdenominational standards, the community standards, and the general programme of the work.

Briefly I want to call your attention to some very basic facts. Some of them I will not need to argue, they are accepted. One of them is this: That the future of civilization, the future of society is determined in a very large measure by the education of the childhood and youth of to-day. What you are teaching the children of to-day, the training that you give them to-day will motivate their lives, discipline their character and determine the civilization and the citizenship of to-morrow.

A second thought that I want to leave with you as a basic principle is this: That no system of education is complete that leaves out the spiritual nurture and training of childhood and youth.

If we leave out the spiritual nurture and training, I do not believe that we can hope to attain, yea, more than that, experience has shown that we can not attain the objectives which we seek to attain. Well, the public school is a wonderful institution. It is to organize primarily the training of the mind, but we have come to recognize long ago that that is not sufficient. Theodore Roosevelt said well and truthfully that he who is educated in intellect and not educated in morals and religion will become a menace to the nation, and so the public school which seeks to develop the finest type of citizenry must go farther than mere training in intellect. So we find the public school reaching out in an ever-broadening, expanding programme of education. It seeks to develop the physical as well as the mental, it seeks to develop the social, that is the ability to work together, it seeks to develop these youth vocationally that they shall be prepared to do their work in life, and the public schools to-day are seeking to develop sound morality. Obedience to law, obedience to constituted authority, honesty, integrity, uprightness, purity of life and purity of character, all these things are essential if we are to develop in America the noblest, loftiest type of American citizenry, but the public school will find, yea, I know from experience that the public school does find its strongest support in the development of morality, in the teaching of the great basic principles of religion. Religion is the greatest bulwark of good morals.

Now we find historically that when the public schools began in America, the religious motive was very dominant. You know the old New England primer out of which the boys and girls were taught in the early days back in New England set out as the objective or the incentive to the youth that they should learn to read that they might read their Bibles, and so we find the public schools of the early day stressing religion; we find the fathers of our country when they set up our Constitution gave very clearly expression to the thought that religion is essential to the life of our nation. We find in the ordinance of 1787 which was set out to rule the great Northwest Territory of Ohio, Indiana, Illinois, Michigan, and Wisconsin, which was then a great wilderness, that they, the very men who made the Constitution of the United States in part, declared that religion, morality, and knowledge are necessary to free government and to the happiness of mankind. We find Washington saying that of all the dispositions and habits which lead to political prosperity, religion and morality are indispensable supports.

Now as time passed there was debate as to what should be taught about religion in the public schools. A movement began to separate the public schools from any ecclesiastical or church control. The idea arose that religious liberty is a priceless heritage, that every man in America may worship God according to the dictates of his conscience.

Now, I am one of those who from experience believe that we can not efficiently and sufficiently teach religion in tax-supported schools. I do not agree with those who say that our public schools are Godless. I believe the public schools of America are just as Godly as the teachers in those schools. I know from experience that if we could put into the public schools the kind of Christian men and women that you in this great society exalt, men and women of Christian ideals, you would exert a tremendous influence over the pupils. But I do not believe that that is sufficient. I began teaching school at nineteen years of age; I talked it over with my mother the night before, who was the grandest teacher that I have ever had, and I told her that I would open my school in that little country school house with the reading of the Bible. I shall never forget that first morning, just a boy, twenty-six pupils in that little country school. I opened with the word of God, and we bowed our heads and repeated the Lord's prayer, and in all my schools after that I followed that example, and when I became a principal of the high school in audiences as large as this, I never opened an assembly that I didn't read the Bible and repeat the Lord's prayer. That was in Illinois where the Supreme Court holds that the reading of the King James' version can not be carried on in public schools if there is objection; but there never was objection.

I think that the church of God must be responsible for the teaching of God's word, and that the church must develop along with general education, a comprehensive system of religious education that shall bring to all the childhood and youth of America those teachings that shall make them see the great spiritual value in life.

Now, while I have emphasized this material side of it, I don't want you to think that I overlook or fail to appreciate religious education from its evangelistic side. I believe deep in my heart that there is no means better calculated to bring childhood and youth to a knowledge of Jesus Christ as a personal Savior than through Christian education, and I believe the statistics show clearly that the largest source of membership in the Christian church to-day through the Sunday school and through these organizations like yours that are devoted to the teaching of the Christian religion.

Paul said that Godliness is profitable unto all things, both the life that now is and the life that is to come. I have come to be deeply convinced that Godliness is the only thing that will save us in the life that now is, in society and civilization and government.

When Dr. Sweets was talking this afternoon about a life work, I thought, "Oh, what a call there is to-day in the field of religious education, the ministry of teaching, that we should have teachers in our Sunday school who shall be trained and prepared to go out and do this great work consecratedly, devotedly, effectively, thoroughly, efficiently." That is the challenge of to-day.

I spoke in St. Louis night before last in a great hall to an audience larger than this, held by one of our great denominations, to emphasize the importance of religious education in that denomination, and all around the hall were those two impressive words in large letters, the words of Jesus, "Go teach"; "Go teach"; "Go teach." That was the message of that convention, and I think it is a message which comes to all of us to-day as we love the great cause of Jesus Christ, that we shall exalt all efforts that shall bring to the childhood and youth of America a konwledge of the commandments of the Lord, as exemplified and taught by Jesus Christ, the Son of God and the Savior of men, and only in following in the pathway that he has outlined shall we be able to save ourselves in this world, and in the world that is to come. It is the compelling, gripping conviction of that thought that is leading many persons to-day to throw their whole energies back of this great movement for Christian Endeavor.

CHAPTER V.

THE CHORAL OF THE WAYS

Before the opening of the session Thursday evening the Coliseum rang with the songs and cheers in which State delegation vied with State delegation or the whole assembly joined in "The Little Brown Church in the Vale" or some other song that was called for. Conspicuous were the red fezes worn by those from "Dixie," the yellow caps and sunflowers that marked their wearers as from the Sunflower State, the broad red collar bearing the word "Illinois" and the symbols telling the home of other groups.

At the fall of the gavel in the hand of Dr. Clark, who presided, the demonstration gave place to silence, and the choral service in charge of Professor H. Augustine Smith began. He presented the chorus of five hundred seated on the platform and their leader Professor Alfred Smith, the director of music in the city schools, who were welcomed by the assembly.

The first part of the service, entitled "The Way of Green Pastures," began with a verse of "Saviour, like a shepherd lead us," followed by the repeating of the twenty-third Psalm and then Nathaniel Dett's spiritual song, "Listen to the Lambs" effectively given by the choir.

The second part, "The Way of the Water of Life," started with the congregational singing of "Break Thou the bread of life," after which the choir gave Macfarlane's "Ho, every one that thirsteth."

These led up to "The Way of the Cross," the third part. The thousands that filled the building joined in the reverent repeating of part of Isaiah 53. "Calvary" was fittingly rendered on the piano; and this part of the service found it climax in the striking "Fling wide the gates" from Stainer's "Crucifixion," excellently interpreted by the chorus.

"Coronation" had more than its usual power when sung by the whole audience as the crown of the service, the triumph contrasting with the sadness of what had just preceded.

As the next division of the evening's programme opened, Professor Augustine Smith called out a beautiful "snow-storm" of waving handkerchiefs all over the hall, answered by a similar demonstration on the part of the choir under the lead of Professor Alfred Smith.

Dr. Clark then led the assembly in repeating the "traveller's

Psalm," which was followed by prayer by Rev. James Kelly, of Scotland.

A series of announcements given in Secretary Gates's usual felicitous style contained one received with special enthusiasm, to the effect that the trustees had unanimously chosen Portland, Or., as the place for the Convention of 1925.

Associate President Poling presented a telling resolution on prohibition and law-enforcement, which was enthusiastically passed by a resounding and repeated "Ay," after being interrupted by applause as it was read.

Bishop S. C. Breyfogel, bishop of the Evangelical Church, a church which is one of the latest fruits of church union, was then presented to speak on "The Supreme Choice and the Master Motive."

THE MASTER MOTIVE

By Rev. S. C. Breyfogel, D. D.

Bishop of the Evangelical Church

If it is true that every age creates its own philosophy, then we may well inquire what theories of life this virile and restless age will produce. In the heart of the twentieth century lie hidden the growing conceptions of a future philosophy of life. From it will be born a new age.

Will it be a crippled birth, mis-shapen by the effects of a crass materialism, or will it come forth in the comely proportions and vigorous spirit of a triumphant Christianity?

The sea of humanity has been profoundly moved. The tides of the world are running fast and furious. The nations are tossed to and fro. Transitions in thought are so swift as to be in danger of losing their anchorage in fundamental thought.

Where amid all the uncertainties of present-day thinking can be found the ultimate reality? What should become the governing motive in the thought-life of today? A supreme end in life implies a comparison of objects for the purpose of selection upon due reflection and under the driving influence of motive.

Thus do men and women select, wisely or unwisely, their calling in life. A young man at the threshold of life's career is confronted by the various avocations. The ministry, medicine, law, education, commerce, industry, the farm, all offer their appeal. Finally he selects one from among them, and identifies himself with the one chosen, while the rest recede from his vision. So also man chooses in the moral realm. The broad road of self-seeking that endeth in destruction, and the narrow way that leadeth unto life everlasting, both lie before him. The ways of sin entice him. A life of character and influence appeals to him. He chooses the evil and drifts towards the abyss, or he chooses God and, turning from sin, runs with eagerness the heavenly race.

A master motive is a necessity of man's nature in order to unify and uplift all of life. Many subordinate motives enter into the sum total of life, such as the need of food, shelter, education, the comforts and conveniences of home and recreation, but these all need to be fused into unity by some great master motive, or they will break up into unrelated fragments.

Some golden cord is needed upon which to string the pearls of daily thought and desire, of purpose and deed, lest all of life be scattered around our feet. There is a graduation of motive. A man may work merely for his wages or he may be prompted by the desire to contribute something to the wellbeing of humanity.

There exists also a series of motives the urge of each lying back of the other and in seemingly endless regression, but in reality arriving again at the starting point and forming a circle closing in upon itself.

Will you on this hot summer evening imagine a man going to a clothing store on a cold winter day. What is his immediate motive in so doing? In order to buy an overcoat. But back of this surface motive lies a series of others. Why should he want to buy an overcoat? In order to protect his body against the inclemency of the weather. But why should he desire so to protect himself? In order to retain his health. But the series does not end here, for why should he want to keep well? In order to be able to work. And why work? In order to earn money. And what does he want with money? TO BUY AN OVERCOAT. The series of motives has now closed in upon itself and arrived at the starting point. I admit that this is a very elementary illustration of the point under consideration. Life, however, abounds with these circles. The multitudes rush in the morning from their homes to office and workshop, driven by the motive of daily need and ambition, and, in the evening they plod their weary way homeward, repeating the round through the ceaseless days; or, rushing into crowded cars and suburban trains they are hurled back and forth by the swinging pendulum which marks the daily heart-throbs of a city.

Early in life men are sustained by the motive of wealth and ambition, but later they become disillusioned by the exhaustion of their ideals and whether successful or not, they still go swinging through the same monotonous round.

Ah the bitterness, the utter weariness of doing the same thing over and over again in treadmill movement, with no perceptible progress.

It is well to remember at this point that this whole routine is essential to life, and therefore possesses a real dignity and nobility. But life is too great, too sublime, it too quickly exhausts the range of subordinate motives and leaves the soul unsatisfied.

What we need is something higher, something divine to interpenetrate and uplift the sphere of life to a higher level, and sustain its weight, in order that whether we eat or drink, whether we work or play, we do it all under the drive of some great master motive.

We need a great governing choice, some clear bugle note to which every activity of life keeps step. Then the centrifugal force of daily need and motive will still drive us forward, while at the same time the master motive presses upward. We will be still moving in the circle of daily life, but it is no longer a closed circle. It is now a spiral, for while you are going around, the master motive is uplifting you, and each return to the starting point finds you a little higher up.—The converse of this is also true, that is, if the controlling choice of your life is ignoble, each return will find you further down. A right master motive therefore not only gives unity to the whole series of lesser motives, but lifts the entire level of life to higher altitudes, invests the commonplace with significance and dignity, and projects all the elements of personality forward in mass formation.

A MASTER MOTIVE always requires as its supreme end a person to be loved and served. That truth has been upheld by Christian thinkers. Christ taught it. Paul found it to be true in his experience.

All the facts of life may roughly speaking be divided into two classes—Being and Non-being, Nouma and phenomena, or in plain speech, persons and things. A person is a self-conscious spirit endowed with reason, conscience, the power of self-determination, and with an abiding identity in spite of change. A thing is an object without these endowments. Objects of nature, money, and other material possessions, fall into this category.

A thing is an object to be possessed; a person is the possessor. A thing is a means to an end; a person is the one who selects the end and employes the means. A thing may be the product of transcendant genius. A transatlantic steamship, to the construction of which every art and every science has brought its contribution for the safety and comfort of its passengers is a wonderful creation, but only a thing. But the captain

The Thursday Night Coliseum Audience

who stands on the bridge, who in spite of tempest shock and the siren song of the deep controls the whole astounding mechanism, is a man, a personality. A thing may take on enormous proportions and almost unconquerable difficulties, but in the last analysis it is only a thing. I would remind you of the Panama Canal as an instance. A sliding mountain overhanging a projected waterway, resistless tides of unmeasured weight, feversmitten districts filled with death, things; yes, but things titanic in their defiance, and yet,

> "A man went down to Panama
> Where many a one had died,
> To slit the sliding mountains
> And lift the eternal tide;
> A man went down to Panama,
> And the mountains stood aside."

Now the supreme end in life can never be any other than a person and that person must always be either self or some one other than self. With some men the accumulation of wealth seems to be the master motive in life. But this is impossible, for even a miser is still a person, while money is only a thing. His real object is to enrich himself or his heirs.

The ambitious man seeks public office with absorbing eagerness. Men say of him that office is his supreme choice in life. But this too is impossible, for office is only an opportunity in which he intends either to advance his own personal interests or in which he hopes to serve his constituents. A master motive therefore demands for its supreme end a person, and that person is either self or some one other than self.

A generation ago the slogan in certain circles was the word "self-centred." It became a popular ideal. But alas we soon discovered that when a man is too self-centred, he will also soon become self-circumferenced, that is his centre and his circumference will coincide and he will be a mere mathematical point, having a real existence but no dimensions.

Into that most exalted of human relations, marriage, there enter motives which are at once permissible and laudable, but in themselves not adequate or altogether worthy, such as the comforts of a home, an assured support, and the enjoyment of an agreeable and attractive companionship.

A young man confides to his friend the announcement of his coming marriage. He dwells upon the excellencies of his intended, particularly her house-keeping qualities. He waxes eloquent as he portrays his ideal of a home in which he himself is the centre of all living solicitude. In touching terms he delineates the home to which he expects to return on the evening of each day to find the table decked with the kind of food which he particularly relishes, the home in which the children will all be tucked away in their beds in order that he may be able to read his evening paper under his own vine and fig-tree, where no one can molest him or make him afraid.

Now that particular young man is in love, indeed his state of mind amounts to an infatuation, and he is in love with a person, but the lassie who deludes herself with the thought that she is the object of his affection will some day be cruelly disillusioned. The only person who he loves is himself. What is the real motive in this tender, sacred relation. It is some one other than self to love and to serve, and thus in mutual self-surrender and ministrations of affection fulfill the law of Christ, and thus make home the gateway to heaven.

Why am I a Christian? Here also there runs a range of lesser motives. It is that I may escape future punishment? This is an important consideration. Fear is a genuine instinct, final retribution, a reality. When, however, the only motive is fear, then religion degenerates into superstition. Is it the desire for heaven and its final rewards, the enjoyment of its intellectual and spiritual delights; to meet loved ones?

> "Once more to touch the hand now vanished,
> Hear again the voice now still."

A high motive is this, but still inadequate.

Up above the fear of hell, up above the desire for heaven, above self, our ultimate choice must rise until it reaches the Supreme Person.

The greatest fact in the world is the personality of man, the supreme reality in the universe is the personality of God.

The final word in philosophy is personality. But this is nothing new. The first and last word in Holy Writ is personality. St. Augustine, realizing this, cried: "My soul is made for Thee, and my soul is restless until it rests in Thee." We cry for things, we grasp for things, we even pray for things. What we really need is God. This modern Vesuvius of materialism is threatening to bury under clouds of golden dust our nobler ideals of the ethical and religious life, and stifle with its abnormal heat the spiritual breath of earth's inhabitants. One of old caught the secret when he cried, "Whom have I in heaven but Thee, and there is none on earth that I desire beside Thee?"

The prodigal said to his father, "Give me the portion of thy substance that falleth to me"; things, money. Then he found other things lower down, husks, rags, swine. Later he began to think of the better things at home, soft raiment, plenty to eat, a comfortable mansion; *things*. All this brought him nowhere. But finally when he came to himself he thought of his father. The image of the old man rose up before him. Above the things he loathed, and above the things he longed for, his spirit rose and said, "I will arise and go unto my father." What mattered things in comparison with the reconciliation with him?

This husk-feeding age must arise and go back to spiritual realities, the greatest of which is God. And this God is personal.

He is not an "Emersonian ideal which lets him evaporate into abstraction;" not "a vague floating fire-mist evolving an ethical system." But GOD. He is the absolute self-existent Being, infinite in wisdom, glorious in might, energizing in love and mercy, the Everlasting Father revealing himself in Christ as "God manifest in the flesh," who gathers up into his high-priestly heart the tortured, suffering souls of men. Paul understood this when he cried out, "I count all things but refuse that I may gain Christ." Having chosen God as the supreme end of life, mere things find their relative value and place in the scheme of life. Things are essential to the superstructure of character, but they do not constitute the foundation. It means that God's love is shed abroad in our hearts by redemption, and that this love in turn is shed abroad by us into the lives of others by service. If we had more love for men, men would have more faith in us.

This great master motive imparts to us courage and strength to stand against the forces of evil now at work in society. May I call your attention especially to the peril that threatens the Christian home. The worst, the most atrocious war the world has ever seen is now being waged against the sanctity of the home and the purity of the marriage altar.

Home, its portals the gateway of life, its memory a shrine; its experiences an imperishable rememberance; its teachings a guiding star in all subsequent life; its prayers a legacy laid up in heaven; its songs a music that with seraphs' hymns might blend; the image of familiar faces hung in the gallery of an immortal love! Home! Father's House! Mother!

And this shrine, this dwelling place of light and love, this bond of the social nexus, this key to Christian citizenship, community welfare, and the spiritual life, is threatened to-day by the diabolical forces of evil.

Tragedy broods over it. Its sacred precincts are being invaded by the polluted feet of those who exalt a sinful passion above a hallowed love.

Movie stars, corrupt social leaders, men and women with a passion for publicity, who would burn down this temple of humanity in order to see their names in print, are parading their vices through the newspapers and divorce courts. The columns of the daily press are besmirched by the record of infidelities on the part of the rich and the once influential. To the youth of the land is fed this witches' broth of hell. How long will the church tolerate this invasion of the home by the forces of evil? The first and last line of defence in the nation is the home. It is the inner sanctuary of the church, and she is responsible for its integrity. Modern wealth, luxury, and indulgence are poor substitutes for the simplicity, the thrift and the purity of the old-fashioned Christian home.

This great choice and governing motive in life includes all men, in all lands. The sea of humanity, whether it flows in frigid zones or under tropical skies, speaks always with the same deep voice of unfathomable woe, or the thunderous shout of conscious power and progress. The sob that breaks from its heaving heart, the angry roar of its contending billows, the musical rhythm of its sun-crested waves is everywhere the same. The same sun shines upon it, the same winds caress it. It rolls and heaves in the hollow of the one omnipotent hand, and only the Man of Galilee can speak peace to the troubled waters.

The responsibilty involved in this relation to God and to humanity is correspondingly high and imperative. As a closing word I will venture a definition of responsibility. In the republic of Christian virtues, responsibility is a state of moral obligation bounded on the north by authority, on the east by intelligence, on the south by ability, and on the west by opportunity. Its Capitol City is conscience, located on the river Truth. It is traversed by mountain chains of difficulty and made fruitful by streams of intelligence. Its natural resources are brains and hearts and hands and feet. Its products are deeds, and its inhabitants are called Doers. It carries on an interstate commerce with neighboring States. Its builder and ruler is GOD.

At the close of the address Dr. Clark referred to the report that the young men are deserting the churches. In answer to that he asked the men in the audience to rise, and the number that stood was an effective object-lesson.

The closing address was by Rev. Lionel Fletcher, the new president of the British Christian Endeavor Union. As he came forward to salute the audience, wearing the gold chain, one link for each president, the insignia of his office, the company greeted him by standing and applauding with tremendous energy.

THE CHALLENGE OF THE TIMES

By Rev. Lionel Fletcher

President of the British Christian Endeavor Union

THURSDAY EVENING

I just want to say that this surely is the proudest moment in my life. Out in Australia I used to think it would be a marvelous thing if I could ever come to America to see a Christian Endeavor convention. That hour has now come, and I stand before you, proud to think that I can be here to represent not only Great Britain and Ireland, but to represent my own land of Australia.

We had our great British national convention in Cardiff last May, in my own great church, with its thousands of delegates from all over Great Britain, and when I asked them would they send you a message of love and of sympathy, every man and every woman arose, and with cheers waved their handkerchiefs and sent to you that greeting across the sea; I bring it to you tonight.

Australia sends through me its greeting of love and kinship, too, and I am glad to be here in that capacity. One of my own lads whom I ordained to the ministry is their President this year, and he sends to you from Australia their greeting and their love and the assurance of their kinship and their desire that you may be blessed of God in the days that are yet to be.

Christian Endeavor; it is a word which, if we take it and look at it, does not denote something soft or sentimental, but is a challenge that you and I shall go out in the name of God to fight sin and to build the glorious kingdom of Jesus Christ.

I am old-fashioned enough to want to bring God's word and leave it with you. The passage that I want to leave with you as my note to you from Britain and Australia, in the second book of Samuel, Chapter ten, verse twelve: "Be of good courage, and let us play the man for our people, and for the cities of our God, and the Lord do that which seemeth him good."

Do you remember the joy of the great Jewish general when he issued that challenge to his young General Abishai, took that youth and showed him the enemies of God's people in a mighty enveloping movement which threatened to cut off his army from Jerusalem? In all probability, as he outlined to him the plan of campaign, he showed the danger of the situation, and looking at Abishai he saw in his eye something of fear. So taking him by the arm in a grip of iron he said to him, "Abishai, let us be of good courage, let us play the man for our people, and for the cities of our God; and let the Lord do that which seemeth him good."

He called on him to be brave, he adjured him to be patriotic, and then he pointed at him and told him that he must trust God with an implicit confidence, and trust after he had done his best to serve God according to his word.

Young men and young women, as a young man myself tonight I come to you with that challenge; it is the supreme challenge. The eyes of the world are upon you just now, the eyes of Great Britain are upon you, the eyes of Australia and of Africa and of New Zealand and of the nations of the earth, they are upon you as they are upon no other nation in the world today.

Europe to-day is a seething pot of anger and jealousy and blood-lust, and God only knows how we are going to come out of the terrible crisis. I want to face you with that situation, I want to let you see the full danger of it, and I want to say that though there may be fear in your heart, be of good courage, be brave, be patriotic, put your trust in God.

But then you yourselves have been raising up enemies, you yourselves have dared in the name of God a mighty and tremendous experience. You have said what no other nation in the world has dared say, you have said to the liquor traffic, "Be gone from our coasts," and what have you done? You have raised up enemies within your own nation, and you have raised up enemies in other nations. I am here to-night representing hundreds of thousands of Christian Endeavorers in Great Britain and tens of thousands of Christian Endeavorers in Australia, and I go farther than that, I am here to-night representing millions of Christians throughout the world who speak your tongue, though they may not be citizens of your nation, and I am going to tell you this: *that all through those millions of people there is a great big heart full of love for you, and prayers for your behalf.* They don't agree with that fleet of ships outside your three-mile limit waiting to violate your Constitution and your law. Don't believe they do! Remember this: the liquor interests with millions of dollars and millions of pounds sterling are using this money to exploit the press of the world, and their money is so tremendous that they have been able to fill the press of the world with lying reports concerning you. One of the greatest papers in Great Britain had a column one time which I read, and as I read it I challenged the statment from the platform of the City Temple in the heart of London. It was a statement concerning your prohibition, showing how absolutely futile the whole thing was. When I read that statement I took it to one of your leading men who was over in our country from America and said, "Is that true?" He took that thing and sent back here to America and he brought back a letter and showed it to me, and it was this: "That report which appeared in that British paper was sent by the liquor interests of America to England to be published and *was a statement of something which had happened five years before prohibition ever took place.*" It was

Left to Right: Rev. James Kelly, Rev. Lionel Fletcher
Seated: Dr. and Mrs. Francis E. Clark

being published in Britain to show that prohibition wasn't working in America!

How are we to know the truth when your own enemies within your own gates are pouring out their millions of dollars to lie to our people across the sea. When I think of the liars they are, I realize that the traffic is from hell and I am thankful to God you have cast it out.

But I want to tell you this: if you go down the street and see a mob of dogs and you pick up a stone and fling it into the mob, every dog in the pack won't howl; the dog that will yell is the dog that is hit, or the cur that is afraid he is going to be hit. When you hear the yells coming across the sea from Britain, remember they are only the echo of the yells from your own country; there are some dogs in your own country that are being hit by the stone that you have thrown. Their pockets have been emptied, and they have to earn an honest living for once in their life, and they howl. But then there are some curs across the sea, and they see the stone coming their way, and they are howling before they are hit because they are afraid of what they are going to lose when they do get hit. Remember that for every dog in the pack that howls, there are ten that never say a word.

In Great Britain behind all those yells and howls there are millions of people who are wishing you well and praying God to give you blessing, and oh, you Americans, I have asked God to grant that America will never go back on the great thing that she has set her hand to. I have asked God to grant that that flag of mine and that flag of my fathers there, and that flag of Canada yonder, and the flags of the British Empire shall some day float with your Old Glory over the lands that have cast out the devil's masterpiece from their midst as you have done.

Hear me to-night, young man and young woman, the world of tomorrow is going to be what you make it, and if you in the sight of God, having set your hand to this tremendous ideal ever permit your land to go back from the great pinacle of daring courage and patriotism that you have climbed to, then you are going to put the clock of progress of the world back a century, and there will be millions thrown into misery and heartbreak because you failed to accomplish what you set your hand to do.

When the war was on I went across to England from Australia. I went down amongst the soldiers at Salisbury. Hundreds of soldiers were camped in there. I was in a railway carriage and a door opened and a Tommy got in. He flung in his kit bag and I took it from him and pitched it upon the rack. I watched the people around the door bidding him farewell. Every one of them was crying except one, and she was a tall woman, holding a golden-haired girl by the hand. I guess she was his wife, and I'll tell you why, because every time her eyes would brim with tears she would turn her back and wipe them away for fear he would see her. She wanted to do her part. He had a wound stripe on his arm. He had been nearly killed. Now he was going back, and she wanted him to go with a brave heart. Presently she could bear it no longer; she stepped forward and kissed him, and he kissed her, and he kissed the little girl; she stepped back again and then presently the conductor blew his whistle and waved his flag for that train to start. That woman picked up the little girl and put her into his arms, and she put her arms around his neck. I don't know whether she had been taught to say it, but she laid her baby cheek against her father's rough brown cheek and said to him, "Daddy, promise me you will come back!" The big fellow's voice broke and he said, "Yes, I will come back darling." And the little child took her other cheek and put it against the side of his other cheek and said to him, "Daddy, promise me you will come back!"

"My God," he said "yes I will promise you I will come back," and he tried to kiss her but the little child dodged back and she took his big brown face down which the tears were trickling into her little hands and looked at him and she laughed at him; she didn't understand, and she said, "Daddy, but promise me you will come back." The big fellow could stand it no longer. The train was beginning to move. He just crushed her to him and then the train pulled out. I told my little girl about it and she would lay her golden head against my cheek and pray that prayer, "Oh, God, let that little girl's father come back."

You know when I thought of it I thought that was what the men went out for, they went out for the people, for the wives, for the children, for the nation, for the cities of our God. They went out to do and to dare and to die, if need be, that there might be liberty, and oh young man and young woman, the war drums aren't rolling, thank God, the war flags aren't flying, but the Christ is calling and He is calling you to live, calling you to act, calling you to suffer, even though you may be sneered at or looked upon as a pussyfoot, He is calling upon you to go and bear His reproach for the cities of our God, and when you have done your part, you can turn your face to heaven unashamed and you can say to him, "My God, I have done my part; now Thou Great King, do Thy part," and surely He will.

Chapter VI.

CHRISTIAN ENDEAVOR IN CONFERENCE

Expert Endeavor

Southern Secretary Evans is an Expert of Experts. He not only knows all about Christian Endeavor methods, but he is exceedingly skilful in presenting them, and his personality is so pleasing that he wins and holds his students. The group of earnest workers that came to him for instruction in the "Expert Endeavor" text-book closed with an examination for the C. E. E. degree received wise directions and inspiring suggestions. He took the book chapter by chapter in a very thorough way, providing capital outlines, answering questions, and telling about tested and proved methods. The Endeavorers of his class got from the work a far better equipment for Christian Endeavor than they had before.

A Programme of Religious Education

An ideal church programme of religious education with Christian Endeavor's place in it was presented in the conferences conducted by Mr. Walter D. Howell. The need for a stronger programme was made clear by some of the present conditions affecting religious education. The conference was especially for leaders of young people, especially pastors and directors of religious education. The sense of the gathering was that only between ten and fifteen per cent of the homes are giving definite instruction in religious education. The Bible as a practical guide in all departments of life is largely neglected. The various organizations and methods that have been introduced have not relieved the home of responsibility, and cannot do the work without the co-operation of parents.

Recreation Methods

Mrs. E. P. Gates had a large room in the Central Church of Christ for her conference on recreation and social methods, and the room was crammed in every corner, with every available inch utilized as standing-room. Mrs. Gates is a charming speaker, and practically effective. She handled her important subject in a vital way, drawing largely from her own thorough experience in planning and conducting Christian Endeavor socials. She advocated the most thorough and painstaking planning for socials, and she gave an outline of attractive socials for all parts of the year. Most societies, though they greatly enjoy socials, are careless in their social plans, do not reach out and draw the best from Christian Endeavor social literature, and so fail of the good times which they might easily enjoy.

MISSIONARY EDUCATION

Miss Faye A. Steinmetz, Leader

1 THE MISSIONARY ADVENTURE

There is no greater adventure than that of giving the message of Jesus Christ to the world. The romance of the unknown, the lure of the seemingly impossible and the challenge of the hard task have drawn men and women of dauntless courage to achievement in the missionary enterprise.

The Modern missionary movement began about one hundred years ago. William Carey was sent to India, Moffat to Africa, Morrison to China, Henry Martya to Mohammedans.

Christianity has to-day penetrated all continents. There are perhaps 20,000 Protestant missionaries, but only one-third of the world's population can be counted Christian.

Missionaries are those sent out. Administrators are those who make the going possible. Revenue must be obtained from the constituency, literature prepared to keep interest aroused, new candidates secured so the denominations organize boards to make policies and administer the work.

2 THE MISSIONARY MEETING

The most familiar method of giving missionary information to the group is through the missionary meeting. Its purpose is to awaken interest, break down indifference, overcome prejudice, create enthusiasm for the work of the Kingdom. The missionary Committee finds it is essential to success to have definite meetings, definite prayer for its own work, a clear aim, a carefully made plan, early preparation, the participation of several, and much enthusiasm.

Advertise the meeting. Create atmosphere by appropriate decorations. Use various methods of presentation such as stories, dramatizations, dialogues, impersonations, stereopticon slides, debates, forum discussions. Use novel settings, plans such as: An Indian camp fire, an African Pelaver, a Japanese tea party, a radio meeting, a missionary newspaper, around the world via aëroplane, a missionary World's Fair.

Material for such meetings is found in current magazines, musician text-books, in reports and leaflets to be secured from missionary boards.

3 MISSIONARY READING

The reading of missionary books is an important part of missionary education. Use the late Sunday afternoon hour to gather the groups around a fire-place, if possible, and read a stirring tale of missionary adventure. Frank Higgins, Trail Blazer, Ann of Ava, the moffats, Livingstone, the Pathfinder. Serve apples or sandwiches and chocolate in the social half-hour before the Endeavor meeting.

Use fifteen or twenty minutes of each Christian Endeavor meeting for a given number of weeks in reading a mission story book.

Plan a reading-contest—deciding definitely upon all rules for the contest

New York Delegation

such as: what constitutes a "point" or credit, length of contest, how pass on books, length of time contestant is allowed to keep book, awards, etc. Select books suited to age and interest of the group. Borrow books from the library, the women of the missionary society, the pastor, if suitable ones can be secured. If not ask individuals each to pay for one book, or earn money to purchase them. Establish a mission library and add to it each year. Close the contest with a story or hour meeting in which each tells the most impressive incident in the reading.

Interesting facts, figures, and statements on charts or posters have real educational value. Make use of talent in the society in preparing these. Have them simple but challenging.

4 MISSIONARY DRAMATICS

Though the dramatic presentation the experiences of other people are made real. The church uses this method for two reasons:
1. The development of the young people.

The person seeking to portray the life and experiences of another "loses" himself in the presentation. Makes careful study not only of the characters, but of the conditions which have contributed to his present state—customs, living condition, surroundings, even costumes.
2. Presenting the message in a vivid way.

This is more compelling than the usual address, the talk, or even the story, it is the reproduction of the incident or situation in dramatic form. Care and discrimination should mark the use of the dramatic method in the church.

Choose drama, carefully keeping in mind the age of the persons who give the production, and the *message* which they are capable of giving. Assign the characters carefully. Encourage a study which will make possible a sympathetic and authentic interpretation. Use no unnecessary time in rehearsals. Do all work prayerfully.

Plays: "The Pill Bottle," "Two Masters," "Hanging the Sign," "Broken China," "Cindy's Chance," "Robert and Mary."

Better than the use of the prepared play is to build a drama from the study of a book or story.

The pageant form is descended from the ancient festivals and is different from the play in that it has no hero, but celebrates the progress of many. Pageants are particularly united to presentation in churches. Some Pageants are: "The Striking of America's Hour," "The Lamp," "Voices That Call," "The Way" (Japanese).

Helpful books are: "Following the Dramatic Instinct," by Anita Ferris, "Pageantry and Dramatics in Religious Education," by Meredith.

Parties or socials with a missionary purpose and message have a part in the programme of missionary education. Mission Movies, Mingling Nations; Jungle Party; All-Nations Festival; Eating in Foreign Languages, etc., offer opportunities for a study of the life, customs, and work of other peoples.

"Joy from Japan," by Catherine Miller, will greatly add to the fun of this year's study of Japan.

5 THE MISSION STUDY CLASS

A group of people meeting regularly for the study of a course or book is a study class.

When shall it meet? Late on Sunday afternoon leaving time for supper and social hour before the Christian Endeavor meeting. Use part of the regular meeting time for six weeks. Have supper and class on any week night. Have it as part of the church school of missions.

Who shall lead? One interested and willing to learn how to lead. Not necessarily the pastor or a woman from the missionary society, but one of the members of the group. Send prospective leader to a summer camp for training.

What to study? The young people's books following the theme of the year. "Japan in the Upward Trail," by William Arling, and "The Child and America's Future," by Jay S. Stowell.

Helps. Write to your denominational boards for helps in teaching the study books.

What methods in Teaching? Use the discussion method with assignments, map-talks, impersonations, and dramatic presentation.

Have a Climax. Pass on the message to others by having an exhibit, play, or pageant.

Service follows knowledge. Let study lead to action. Do something practical to meet need such as sending materials to help with work. Pray. Give money. Consider life service.

6 HOW SHARE IN THE MISSIONARY ENTERPRISE?

Each denomination has a specific part in establishing the Kingdom of God on earth and needs the active participation of all its young people. They may serve *by interesting others* through active and enthusiastic participation in missionary activities such as the meetings, study classes, reading groups, and service plans, such as work in the community, or for home and foreign stations and missionaries.

By personal gifts of prayer, time, money, and life. Definitely consider the whole problem of stewardship of time, money, and life.

Write to your own denominational mission boards for information about *your* share in the great task.

Citizenship and Community Service

The conference on citizenship and community service in charge of Dr. Poling was addressed by Dr. Wayne B. Wheeler on law-enforcement. He said that a large percentage of men not in favor of prohibition could be won to uphold the enforcement of law, and that a smile will go farther than bitter words. He was just on the point of leaving for Europe to help Scotland and other countries by telling what has been done in the United States. He went with a hearty God-speed from the conference expressed in a prayer by Dr. Poling.

PRAYER-MEETING METHODS

By F. D. G. Walker

Field Secretary of the Illinois Union

Three headings have been assigned for our discussion, the first being, "Planning and Conducting Christian Endeavor Prayer Meetings." One of the first things to remember is that it is not a "Christian Endeavor meeting," or an "Endeavor Meeting," but as the name implies, a Christian Endeavor prayer meeting. It might be likened to a "filling station," where we take on fuel that will enable us to carry on across the highway of life until we come to the "filling station" again the next Sunday evening. It is the heart of the whole society, and must never be given a subordinate place.

Two people should be at every meeting to insure the best results. They are "Mr. X. Pect Ation, and his twin brother, Mr. Prep R. Ation." Plans should be made well in advance. As to the exact length of time, this can be well left to the individual society. As the leader looks forward to the time of his meeting, he will find much in his daily activities that bears on the topic. Of course the topic Scripture, and daily readings, will be read by him, and studied. The spirit of prayer must not be given a secondary place, in either the preparation or conducting of the meeting. Success or failure depends largely on the leader.

The ideal meeting is one in which all have some part. The Word of God is the Sword of the Spirit. Learn it. Use it. Practice it. Learn the Bible prayers, and see how they fit into your needs. Never, say, "Let us repeat the Lord's Prayer." A phonograph can do that. When you use the Lord's prayer, PRAY IT. Pray as though all depended on God, and work as though all depended on you.

Do not neglect the preprayer service. It is the dynamo behind of your society.

Vary the meetings enough to make them interesting, but never let them degenerate into a lecture by some outsider. Do not hesitate to talk because you can not do as well as some one else. God never rewards success, but He does reward honest effort put forth, even though the world may call it failure. Keep a wall pledge in sight at all times.

The duties of the prayer-meeting committee may be briefly summed up as follows:

First decide to do something. Otherwise, it is very likely that nothing worth while will be done.

Second, decide definitely, what things you are going to do, or make an honest effort to do. Good intentions do not insure success, while decisions good are a long step in the right direction.

Third, is to make these decisions IN TIME. At the first committee meeting agree as to what the main efforts of the term of office are to be focused on.

Fourth, FORMULATE THESE PLANS, into a committee policy, and have all members of the committee sign it.

Fifth, ORGANIZE THE COMMITTEE, that every member will have some specific job for which to be responsible. "The unorganized indifference of the individual Christian, is more to be feared than the organized, unrighteousness of the world." There is a job for every Christian Endeavorer worthy of the best mettle in them. Challenge it. Use it.

Sixth, MAKE GOOD, by careful planning, and persistent work.

Seventh, PRAY, the last merely for sake of emphasis. Prayer should precede and accompany all others.

We must not forget to "advertise the prayer meeting." If we have something worth while in our church, why not tell the world about it? See that there are items about your society in the church bulletin. Your local paper will be glad to take items if they are written as news. Posters can be made by anyone, and a special poster committee might well be named, to keep the society before the church and community. Special emphasis should be made on the announcements through the church and Sunday school. Don't allow a Christian Endeavor society to be conducted week in and week out and not be sure that every member of the congregation knows of it. The real success of a society depends on the individual. Yes, *you* not some one else. God will make good on His part if you will let Him.

RELIGIOUS VOCATIONS

Rev. Frank Lowe, Jr., Ph.D.

The conference on religious vocation, held Thursday and Friday mornings in the auditorium of St. Paul's Episcopal Church under the leadership of Dr. Frank Lowe, Jr., enrolled about two hundred. The attendance was twice as large as at the same conference under the same leadership two years before at the New York convention. Perhaps this increase indicates the growing interest in general in the modern approach to the problem of the application of vocational guidance to the Life-Work-Recruit movement.

For the underlying purpose of this conference was to discuss questions pertaining to recruits; to locate the place of religious vocations in the work of the world; and to study first hand, as far as time would allow, the United Society's text-book, "Religious Vocations," an outstanding book in this field, produced recently by Dr. Lowe, the conference leader.

Several special features developed during the two-day programme deserve mention. The first was the place of the personal private conference in connection with life-work problems. It was felt that the perplexities here are largely personal. To a certain extent it was felt that each individual presents a unique case, and to be most serviceable counsel and advice must be personal, too. To this end the leader offered to meet individuals for private conference during the afternoons in the study of the conference church. The response was such that both afternoons were completely engaged.

Another interesting item was afforded from the information gained on the enrollment cards. From these data it was possible to describe the make up of the conference as follows: Of the 180 who turned in enrollment cards, 75 were Christian Endeavor Life-Work Recruits; 105 were not. 61 were men; 112 were women. Although ages ranged from 15 to 67, 124 persons or 68 of these enrolled were less than 25. A total of 28 different occupations were listed by the group, ranging all the way from a machinist to a college president, the largest single group being students to the number of 64, and the second largest occupational group being teachers to the number of 35. The scholastic acquirements of those attending the conference was no less varied. They ranged from grammar school to those holding as many as three degrees. The largest single group, 46 in number, were high-school graduates. Those who had graduated from college or had taken from one to three years in college, or were at present attending college numbered 48. Aside from indicating the predominant tendencies of the group, these figures show the great diversity of interest and outlook of those who are attracted to a conference on religious vocations.

A more ambitious attempt to arrive at the qualifications of the men and women in attendance was made by giving a short general intelligence-test to the Life-Work Recruits. Use was made of the "Otis Self-Administering Test of Mental Ability; Higher Examination; Form A," by Arthur S. Otis, published by the World Book Co., Yonkers, N. Y. In giving the test it was especially explained and emphasized that no undue importance was to be placed in the result; or that any "general intelligence" test whatever could finally or ultimately or conclusively determine any person's ability or chance for success in any calling, especially in any religious calling. The highest possible score was 75. The scores of 71 recruits ranged from 27 to 74, the average grade being 50. A normal of 60 or better is suggested by Otis as indicating in general the ability required for success in college or in the profession. A large percentage of the Recruits made a grade of 59 or better.

For purposes of comparison the same test was given to a small group of professional workers in attendance at the convention. Twelve pastors and four Christian Endeavor field-men took the test. The average score for the 16 was 45. Only one of the number reached a score of 59 or better. The number taking the test in the second case was far too few to furnish any basis for generalization. As far as it goes, however, it indicates that the calibre of the Life-Work Recruits measures up to the professional demands of the religious vocations.

Lest the foregoing report indicate that the entire time of the conference was taken up with the dry bones of statistical method, a word should be said about two inspiring addresses. The first was "The Value of a College Training" by Rev. Glenn McRae, Field Representative of the United Christian Missionary Society of St. Louis. The speaker brought out well the practical value to a religious worker of the scientific, sociological, and philosophical courses of the college. The second address was on the theme, "Religious Journalism on a Life Work," by Rev. H. F.

Shupe, D.D. The message was one which answered squarely and forcefully for this one calling many of the questions which were being raised in a general way all through the conference. Both speakers made big splendid contributions to the programme.

Throughout the six hours of conference time Christian work had been viewed in a perfectly sane, sober, and practical way. Each period had opened and closed with seasons of silent prayer. The closing ten minutes was devoted to audible sentence prayers. There was a flood of prayer. Quietly those who cared to become Recruits were invited to step into the study as the conference closed. 16 responded.

In conclusion, the results of the religious-vocations conference indicated the desirability of emphasis upon the following steps:

1. An even greater use of the text-book, "Religious Vocations," as a study book for Christian Endeavor societies in general, and especially in connection with conventions and young people's institutes.

2. The organization throughout all the states of Life-Work Recruit Bands along lines so splendidly developed in Wisconsin under the able leadership of Miss Gevennola E. Lucas, State Supt., Peshtigo, Wisconsin.

3. The recognition within the Life-Work Recruit Movement of an enrollment of Recruits for volunteer service for those who share the spirit of Recruits but who can never hope to become full-time workers.

4. The need for a preliminary vocational-guidance pledge to be taken before the present Life-Work Recruit pledge is signed. For a suggestion along this line refer to the address of the leader of this conference at the Monday afternoon session of the convention.

Teaching Missions

Dr. W. M. Cleaveland is the field-secretary for Presbyterian foreign missions. If any one doubts the zeal of Christian Endeavorers for mission study, he should have attended Dr. Cleaveland's enthusiastic conference on the best way of teaching the new mission-study text-books. Dr. Cleaveland is so stimulating that he speedily got the Endeavorers to talking. Every chair was occupied, and all were evidently intending to teach one or more of the remarkable set of home and foreign mission textbooks provided for the present year, books far more varied and numerous than ever before. The questions of the Endeavorers came from life, and Dr. Cleaveland met all their problems wisely. It is certain that his conference will result in many mission-study classes, and in the use of the best methods of teaching missions.

UNION WORK CONFERENCE

By Clarence C. Hamilton

Field-Secretary of the United Society of Christian Endeavor and Field Manager of "The Christian Endeavor World"

A lively interest in the subject of "Union Work" was demonstrated by the live-wire group of young men and young women attending this conference. Full freedom in discussion was allowed, and union leaders from almost every State had opportunity to ask questions and to tell of plans and promotion methods used by them.

An interesting feature at all times was the conflict of ideas between the East and the West—or rather between the leaders from sparsely settled regions and those from congested centres. Different conditions suggested different methods of procedure.

The practical suggestions and adaptation of the Friends of Christ Campaign made by General Secretary E. P. Gates, were given full discussion.

Mr. L. H. Brownell, president of the Pennsylvania Union, gave a spirited and informing talk on "Planning and Promoting a City Union Mass Meeting."

The general outline followed by the conference covered the following subjects:
1. Why, Who, and How of Union Work?
2. Officers.
    a. President.
    b. Vice-President.
    c. Secretary.
    d. Treasurer.
3. Committees.
    a. Lookout.
    b. Missionary.
    c. Social.
    d. Music.
    e. Publicity.
    f. Finance.
    g. Citizenship.
4. Meetings.
    a. Executive.
    b. Congress.
    c. Mass Meetings and Rallies.
    d. Conventions.
5. Union Help to Churches.
6. Union Community Helps.
7. Friends of Christ Campaign.

The Fine Arts in Religion

Professor H. Augustine Smith rendered fine service in his "Temple of Fine Arts," set up in Plymouth Congregational Church. In a semicircle of Sunday-school rooms were displayed a large number of beautiful and varied religious pictures which guides explained to a constant stream of interested visitors. The "temple" was open all day Thursday, Friday and Saturday, special addresses on a great variety of themes being given each hour of each day by Professor Smith and others.

Professor Smith is seeking to arouse the church to the possibilities of developing the emotional life of young people through eye-gate — the presentation of pictures, drama, and pageantry — and through ear-gate — the use of music in worship and in connection with pageantry.

Masterpieces of religious art were shown and explained, travelogues illustrated with streopticon slides were given, adult and Junior choir problems were discussed, and the beauty of climax in worship. The use of religious drama was clearly outlined, and helpful talks were given on how to study a picture, how to find new meanings in old hymns, how to build up programmes of music, and how to put through an art programme that will greatly benefit the young people and the church. These talks were valuable, full of material new to the listeners, and rich in practical suggestions.

INTERMEDIATE CONFERENCE

Rev. Frank Getty

The attendance varied from 125 to 200. It was lowest when the roll was called.

The work covered varied somewhat from the usual material found in such conferences, in that the time was about equally divided between a discussion of things to do in an Intermediate society and a study of the Intermediate boy and girl. In this study attention was given to the outstanding characteristics of the early and middle adolescent periods covering the years twelve to eighteen. The thoroughness of this work was limited by the shortness of time.

It was the decision of the class that the principle characteristics of the Intermediate are, activity or depression, formation of ideals, hero worship, unusual physical growth, beginning of independent thinking, definite shaping of habits, and so forth. Since most of the members of this conference were adult leaders of Intermediates, the time was well spent on a discussion of these characteristics.

Next came listing and study of the essentials of leadership. Each member of the class, thinking from the standpoint of a minister in a church, expressed the qualities which would be looked for in the selection of a leader for the Intermediate society. A few of the qualifications named were consecration, patience, sympathy, tact, perseverance, fairness in judgment, positiveness, as opposed to negative elements, courage, breadth of vision, broad thinking, adequate preparation and training, etc. The details of several of these received careful consideration.

Further time was given to a study of the relationship of boys and girls to the principal institutions of life such as the home, school, church, other boys and other girls. Special attention was given to the contacts and relationships of boys with girls, boys with boys, girls with girls, and girls with boys. It was quite evident that many members of the class had failed to see and realize that in the problems of these relationships may be found numerous opportunities for the society to be of service to the individual.

On the second day the time was given to the more mechanical methods. First it was decided that each society should have a definite purpose to justify its existence, and the leader might well have in mind those things, which should be accomplished in as long a time as three years. Consideration was given to the necessity of organization with an effort to keep this at a minimum. Duties of officers and communities were briefly discussed. In connection with the necessity for a programme the essential elements such as devotional activities, missions, leadership-training, social activities, evangelism, service, and finances were talked about. How these elements may be put in a programme in proper proportions was also considered.

Problems of the individuals in their own fields were heard and discussions intended to help to solve these problems followed.

Before the conference closed it became evident that some things which must be considered in the future are: definite age limits for Intermediates with a possible promotion of one society for the ages 12 to 14 or 15, and another for the group 15 to 17 or 18; additional literature and separate topics for Intermediates, and the training of a large number of leaders for this age group.

CHRISTIAN LEADERSHIP

One of the most important conferences for the spiritual life of the individual, as well as for his or her service of leadership, was Rev. H. L. Pickerill's course on "Principles of Christian Leadership." The leader used the Socratic method of drawing forth information by means of questions.

Mr. Pickerill took Jesus Himself as the master-leader of men, and sought to bring out the essentials of His leadership as a model for us: first, the purpose of His life, to bring to men the abundant life, and then His growth in wisdom, in stature, and in favor with God and man. The picture of Christ drawn by the leader was that of a young man, strong, virile, filled with buoyant and enthusiastic idealism.

From this initial study of Jesus as a leader, Mr. Pickerill passed to a consideration of four fundamental desires in youth to which we may make appeal with assurance of response: (a) the mating instinct, or companionship; (b) the desire for leadership; (c) for service; and (d) for knowledge. Then followed a study of the nature of Christianity and of the religious programme of the church, and the part Christian Endeavor has in it. The course opened up a vision of opportunity and suggested lines along which we may prepare to lead the youth of the church into ways of service.

CHAPTER VII

PRINCIPLES AND PRACTICE
Friday Afternoon, July 6

Coliseum

Rev. R. P. Anderson, Presiding

The weather man screwed it up hotter and ever hotter, but the indefatigable Endeavorers made a great Coliseum audience on Friday afternoon. The praise service was very impressive, being entitled "The Cry of the World for a Saviour." It voiced the appeals of the most needy parts of the world, the response of the Christian church, and the great invitation to Jesus Christ. Thousands will go away from these services of Professor Smith with a new and very precious conception of the possibilities of such exercises in religious gatherings, whether great or small.

The presiding officer, Rev. R. P. Anderson, opened the session with an uplifting prayer, after which we had beautiful singing by the male quartette of Buena Vista College, which was heartily encored. Then Mr. Fegert read for the trustees a resolution favoring the eight-hour day, supporting it with an illustrative anecdote of much point. The resolution, was adopted by the audience.

Rev. William Ralph Hall's second lecture on the formulation principles of Christian Endeavor continued the logical method of the first lecture, its clearness of statement, and its evident interest for the Endeavorers. His theme was the work of Christian Endeavor as a training-school for Kingdom leadership. He showed how our society is held together by its constitution and pledge; how it is centered upon Christ and the church; how it is of, for and by young people; how its work depends on its regular prayer meetings, study classes, thoughtful committee meetings and business meetings; how it supports the local church and the denominations' plans, and how it meets wholesomely the social needs of youth.*

Mr. Shartle then introduced to the audience some of Mr. Well's books which he had on sale. He was followed by the male quartette once more, and that by a series of strong and attractive addresses, the first being by Rev. Dirk Lay, a long-time worker

*(Address in Chapter XIX.)

among the Pima Indians of Arizona and the president of the Arizona Christian Endeavor Union.

AMONG THE PIMA INDIANS

By Rev. Dirk Lay

The Pima Indians live on the Gila River between Phoenix and Tuscon, Arizona. They were there when Columbus discovered America. They have a ditch there seventeen miles long, in places fifteen feet deep and twelve feet wide. The bottom they dug with sticks and carried the dirt out in baskets. The ditch is still being used, and when the white man permits his water to pass his dams on the river above us we get a little to put into that ditch. The Pima Indians are known to-day as a God-fearing tribe. They love the principles of Jesus Christ for which Christian Endeavor stands. It was in the late sixties that their chief saw a cloud in the eastern sky that was in the shape of a hand. The hand seemed to be pointing upwards. The chief called his counselors together, and after they had talked the matter over they decided that this meant there was some one in the East who could show them a better way. General Alexander, who was then in charge of that part of the country with headquarters at Ft. McDowell, was the man to whom they came. General Alexander, being a Christian, sent the word to some ladies in New York City. They published the appeal in a little paper that fell into the hands of Charles H. Cook. Dr. Cook told me when he had read that appeal he started to pray that God would send some young men out into that country to preach the gospel to the Pima Indians, and as he started his praying the thought came to him that perhaps he was the man. He offered his services to the Methodist Church; he offered his services to the Congregational Church: and they told him they had no money. He came to the Presbyterians and they gave him the same answer.

The American people were willing to reach into their pockets to get money to pay taxes to buy bullets to send out there to kill Indians, but there was no money to send a missionary.

Dr. Cook said, "I will go anyway. God wants me to go and He will see that I get there."

So that man of God started out without means of support, only his faith in God. Dr. Cook traveled overland, walked most of the way, and reached Albuquerque broke. He sold his army rifle there, and a man who bought it asked him where he was going. He said, "I am going down below Tuscon to the Pima Indians."

He said, "How are you going? Are you going with some one else?"

"No, I am going out alone on the trail. There is a train going to start out from Albuquerque in a day or two, and they will overtake me on the trail."

Dr. Cook had served seven years in the regular army. This man asked him what kind of a gun he was going to buy. He said, "I am not going to take any gun with me."

The man looked at him and said, "You don't mean you are going outside of Albuquerque without a gun?"

"Yes, I am. God has called me to be a missionary to the Indians, and I am going out there in the name of my Christ to preach his salvation to them."

"My friend, let me tell you something: I am a Christian too, but you can't handle Indians that way. You will not be two days out of Albuquerque before you will encounter these Red Men, and the only thing they talk with or listen to is the crack of a rifle."

As Dr. Cook was camping by the roadside, he saw a cloud of dust coming towards him, and then he made out the ponies and the forms of Indians on the ponies, riding upon him.

They started in that peculiar way they had of circling around their prey, coming in a little closer and a little closer. They didn't fire, though several had rifles. Finally one of them who was the chief got off his horse and came towards Dr. Cook. He went through his pockets and not finding what he wanted, he unrolled his blankets, and not finding what he wanted he turned to Dr. Cook and said (he had learned a little English, and I guess he wanted to show off): "No gun! No good! Let go!"

Dr. Cook landed on the Pima Reservation on December 23, 1870. Mrs. Grossman told me the story of his landing there. She is the widow of Captain Grossman who was in charge of the Reservation at that time.

That night Captain Grossman and Dr. Cook talked over a lot of experiences in the army, and the next morning when the captain awakened, he said to Mrs. Grossman: "I know what I am going to do with him. He is just the man these Indians need. I will make him a teacher for the Indians."

Charles H. Cook landed there on December 23, 1870, with $2.70 in his pocket and his faith in God. As far as Christian Endeavor is concerned this is a whole lot. January 1, 1871, he started drawing from the United States treasury at the rate of a thousand dollars a year and expenses paid. When God asks you to do something, He will see to it that you will be able to do it.

He worked on, and after nine years of work won one convert. Out on that desert he lived. He came back, after he had been out there two years, to marry his sweetheart. Ten more years went by before he had sixteen members out of which he could organize the first church.

Then Mrs. Cook died. The faithful sixteen members seemed to have some way of communication, and these sixteen, though they were scattered over a district thirty-five or forty miles long (some of them ran to church as far as thirty miles), those Indians came together and helped as best they could. One of those who was present at the services told me that they carried Mrs. Cook's body into the little chapel and Doctor Cook spoke of the glorious hope that the Christian has of meeting his loved ones with Jesus, the tears rolling down his cheeks. They buried her back of the chapel, just in front of our new church, and there that woman of God lies to-day.

The Indians are coming into the church and the Christian Endeavor society to-day. That is the best society in Arizona as far as the Efficiency Campaign is concerned.

At my right are three full-blooded Indians. Johnson M'Afee is the man who has done a good deal to put across efficiency in that society. Next is David Nelson, President of the Blackwater society; and the next is Alfred Jackson, president of the Sacaton society. The Pimas have sacrificed to send them here. The last one I mentioned is the efficient treasurer of the Arizona State union. He is the son of an elder of the Presbyterian church, the first policeman there who had the nerve to break up the terrible drinking going on.

My friends, these Indians stand out and out for Jesus Christ. They do their very best.

The Pima Indians live on the Gila River. That is now dry. When their forefathers were there they fought for that country and kept the Apaches from running over it. A lot of your ancestors could tell you stories of how these men stood by them and helped them. Here is what we are asking you to do on *December 9th.* It is a long way ahead, but if you have a good memory you will remember December 9th, and will pray for these Indians in your meeting that evening. It is a Sunday evening. It is shortly after Congress has opened again. After you pray for them do this, as well: take the telegram which has been handed to you here, or just about the substance of it, and wire it to your Congressman, so that the wrongs committed against these, the original Americans, may be rectified, and the water taken from them may be given back to them. The government as far as the Interior Department is concerned is back of us, but Congress must do its part.

[A resolution was unanimously passed asking Congress to take steps to see that the Pima Indians get the water which is justly theirs.]

Dr. O. T. Deever, young people's secretary of the United Brethren, made a strong presentation on the value of the pledge, which he called "the backbone of Christian Endeavor."

THE PLEDGE, THE BACKBONE OF CHRISTIAN ENDEAVOR

By Rev. O. T. Deever, D.D.

Young People's Secretary of the United Brethren Church

I am to speak on "The Pledge, the Backbone of Christian Endeavor." I think we might understand at the beginning that as we speak of the pledge we are not thinking of any particular form of pledge, but of the pledge idea, the principle. And having this in mind, we would agree, no doubt, that the Christian Endeavor pledge is at the very heart of this movement, that without it probably the movement would have disintegrated long ago. The pledge is a *sine qua non* of the Christian Endeavor movement, giving it backbone, giving it stability, giving it unity, giving it life. I wish to give a number of reasons why it seems that the pledge is essential.

The first reason is that without a pledge an Endeavor society or an Endeavorer is without this opportunity of giving definite announcement of his open committal to the will and strength of Jesus Christ. There is an advantage in an open committal, a definite announcement, and the pledge gives the Endeavorer an opportunity to make it. Most of us are so constituted that after we have committed ourselves we are then in a position to more earnestly and more enthusiastically carry out a given purpose.

That word "trusting," with which our pledge begins, is one of the richest words in our Christian vocabulary. "Trusting in the Lord Jesus Christ for strength." I stood one day on a corner of the sidewalk in a city when the traffic was going rapidly by. The vehicles were moving here and there rapidly; automobiles were rushing down the street, and I saw a little girl standing there on the corner wishing to get across. She seemed timid, afraid, to undertake the trip across the street, and as I stood there I looked at her and said, "My little girl, don't you wish me to help you across?" She looked at me a moment studying my face and seeming then to have trust in me she put her hand up and I led her across.

Now the pledge is that act of faith by which we put our hands in the hands of Jesus Christ and he leads us across the highway of life.

The Endeavorer taking the pledge is like a blind man taking the hand of one who has two good eyes to direct him; taking the pledge is like a crippled soldier, accepting the proffered arm of a well and strong comrade to help him along.

Another reason, while the pledge is essential to the strength and life of the Endeavorer, is that without the pledge the Endeavorer would be without a spiritual programme. In this spiritual programme the Endeavorer emphasizes the word "do." Christian Endeavor stands for service. "Trusting in the Lord, Jesus Christ for strength I promise Him that *I will do.*" It is a programme of action, of service, a spiritual programme. Some time ago I figured out that my mother or my wife or some other person's mother or wife had cooked about forty thousand meals for me since I appeared on the scene of action in this world. It is a good deal of effort to live; there are certain details in the process of living that some of us sometimes do not think much about; and in the process of carrying on God's work, in building the church, in building the Kingdom, there is service to render and work to do, and the Christian Endeavorer recognizes this fact and he undertakes a spiritual programme which involves definite activity.

The programme is comprehensive. It is a seven-day-a-week programme. It is not comprehended in what he does on Sunday evening.

"Trusting in the Lord, Jesus Christ for strength, I promise Him that I will strive to do whatever He would have me do," and thus he is led to Bible reading, for it is only in the Bible that he can discover God's will, and the Endeavorer goes to read his Bible much like a lover goes to the post office for a letter. This word of God becomes a message of life to the Endeavorer.

He also undertakes in this spiritual programme outlined in his pledge to support the work and worship of a church; he recognizes that the two aspects—faith and work—are necessary, that character and conduct are always like the Siamese twins, they are always united together, or are two aspects of one thing.

The Endeavorer thinks of the truth as Ruth thought of Naoma when she said, "Intreat me not to leave thee, or to return from following after thee: for whither thou goest, I will go; and where thou lodgest, I will lodge: thy people shall be my people, and thy God my God: where thou diest, will I die, and there will I be buried: the Lord do so to me, and more also, if ought but death part thee and me."

Another reason why the pledge is essential is because without the pledge the Endeavorer would be without a definite covenant openly and clearly defined, a definite covenant with God. The Endeavorer realizes that it is only through co-operative effort with Jesus Christ that spiritual attainments are to be realized, that as God says to the farmer, "Co-operate with me, you till the soil, you plant the seed, and together we will raise a crop of corn."

The Endeavorer in taking the pledge does not involve upon himself new obligations. These obligations already exist. They exist because he is a follower of Jesus Christ and in taking the pledge he simply acknowledges that he is under certain duties, that he has upon him certain responsibilities and obligations.

Without the pledge the Endeavorer would be without such a helpful standard of character and conduct, one that helps to cultivate good habits. Here is a constant reminder, here is a constant prompter to the acquiring of certain habits of spiritual conduct, daily reading of the Bible, taking part in the meetings. The Endeavorer in doing this remembers that life is made up of habits, that character is made up of habits, that habits are the things that constitute character. Some time ago I found that I was winding my watch every night upon retiring. I said to myself, "I am not going to be bound by that habit, I am going to change it, I am going to wind my watch in the morning." I undertook that morning to wind my watch, but at night I found myself winding my watch again, and I am still winding my watch at night—force of habit. One day in going along the public road I saw an old blind horse in a pasture and it was going in a circle. I discovered that this old horse had been formerly used on a sweep of an old sorghum mill, and in response to a habit that became fixed in its life it went round and round in a circle, eating that way even while free in the pasture.

Young people need this pledge in acquiring the habits of daily prayer and testimony and speaking and the other elements that enter into our lives.

I have thought of the pledge as a spiritual act of faith by which the young man, or young woman, who is hounded and pursued by the enemies of his spiritual life, throws himself at the feet of Jesus Christ and says, "I trust in Christ for strength," and Christ then becomes not only his source of strength to gain him courage for the fight, but also becomes his helper in the conflict.

Let us stick to our pledge, let us make more of it, let us be more careful in using it in taking new members into the society, and let us constantly have a promotional campaign on for its careful and earnest and enthusiastic use in the life and work of the society.

CHAIRMAN ANDERSON: The last address of the afternoon is by Rev. W. A. MacTaggart. Mr. MacTaggart is President of the All-Canada Christian Endeavor Union. He has been actively engaged in Christian Endeavor work in Canada for a number of years, although he is a busy pastor with a large congregation on his hands. For sixteen years he has been a member of the General Assembly Board of Sabbath School and Young People's Association, and since the union of the three great Canadian denominations is practically assured, there has been set up a new Board of Religious Education to work out a young people's programme for the new All-Canadian Church to be, and Mr. MacTaggart is a member of that Religious Education Board, too. He knows Christian Endeavor from the ground up; he knows Canadian conditions from the ground up; and he is going to speak to us this afternoon about "Substitutes," speaking out of his own experience in Canada, substitutes that have been proposed for Christian Endeavor societies in his home land.

The concluding speaker, Rev. W. A. MacTaggart, is president of the All-Canada Christian Endeavor Union. He is a vigorous speaker, and a firm friend of our society. His subject, "Substitutes," gave him a chance to describe the various attempts which have been made to form other types of young people's religious society.

SUBSTITUTES FOR CHRISTIAN ENDEAVOR

By Rev. W. A. MacTaggart, D.D.

President of the Christian Endeavor Union of Canada

Christian Endeavor has long since passed the experimental stage. Although for many years there have been those in various denominations who have been trying their hand at new experiments, in our experience we have found that in every case what has been proposed has made no step in advance at all.

For the first ten or fifteen years Christian Endeavor had the field to itself, and it swept around the world, commended itself to every denomination, and it was found to be really indigenous to every land where the gospel of Jesus Christ was preached.

Most of the confusion has come in the minds of those who have been trying to propose substitutes for Christian Endeavor, because they have failed to distinguish clearly three of the main functions in connection with the work of any Christian congregation. We have the *preaching* function, we have the *teaching* function, and the *training* function. The preaching function is predominantly associated with the service on Sunday morning and Sunday evening, and our Sabbath school work has been suffering greatly and has been seriously handicapped, because the preaching function has been overshadowing the teaching function, and the teachers in our churches and our schools have been struggling for many years to emancipate themselves from the preaching.

I once went to a certain man and asked if he would take a class in Sunday school. He said he would rather preach than teach. That was enough. I knew he wouldn't be a teacher, and I didn't want a preacher just then.

We have many in our Sunday-school classes who select some verse in the lesson that will lend itself to easy division, and then begin an exhortation of the class, and we wonder why the boys and girls begin to leave them when they come to be thirteen or fourteen or fifteen years of age. These boys and girls don't dislike preaching, but they don't want that sort of preaching. But where they get teaching—the right kind of teaching—they stay with the school and do not leave it. Sometimes a superintendent feels that he has to preach a sermon on Sunday afternoon, and our Sunday-school work has been crippled and handicapped. To-day we are getting a new type of buildings, where each department has a room of its own, but if we are being emancipated in our Sunday-school work from the preaching function, we have a long way to go before we find our freedom in our training work from the teaching department.

I remember a time when the Sabbath School Committee and the Young People's Committee of the Canadian Presbyterian Church were put together under one board. The first remark I heard was by the former chairman of the Sabbath School Committee: "Now we are going to get somewhere; these folks have been meeting together in their societies; they have been picking a little here and a little there, discussing this topic, and that topic, and the other topic. Now we are going to get somewhere. We will begin in the fall with a course, we will go right through with it, and then we will feel we have accomplished something."

I said, "What have you to suggest?"

There was then a new missionary book by a very estimable man in our denomination on "The History of the Missions of our Church," and instantly he suggested that this should be used as a text-book and that we should take a chapter each night until we went through it.

I said, "It will kill any young people's society in the whole country."

He was going to exploit the Christian Endeavor society for the teaching function of the church. He had Sunday-school classes and Sunday-school goggles, and he saw everything through them, and when he saw a group of young people he immediately thought of a Sunday-school class and of the great opportunity there was there to exploit that group for teaching. Now we must emancipate our young people's society from that conception. They may be a part of the great religious education programme of the church, but we must realize that the primary function of our Christian Endeavor societies is that our young people are to be given expressional training for service.

I believe that Dr. Clark, who was inspired of God to organize the first Christian Endeavor society, was equally inspired of God as he wrote the Christian Endeavor pledge, and the Societies that have swung true to that pledge, and to the high ideals contained in it, have been societies that were imbued with spiritual power and they have accomplished something, and they have got somewhere, and they have grown.

Is that too difficult a pledge? I hope I shall never be guilty of receiving, as a Christian minister, any man or woman into the membership of my church that will do less than that, that will trust in Jesus Christ as their Savior and will promise to do their best to love Him and to serve Him, and everything else in the pledge is implied in that. That is the whole pledge. The rest simply unfolds it a little and makes it a little clearer and a little plainer. But when we see folks trying to organize something else, what do they do? They do what a green golf player generally does; he gets his eye off the ball; and when he swings around he draws back a little bit, and if you draw back half an inch while making your drive you will slice the ball. You may call it shinny, but it isn't golf. If we as young people draw back in the least from the high ideals and the high principles that are contained in out-and-out loyalty to Jesus Christ, uncompromising service for Him, we shall slice the whole business and make a mess of all that we are trying to do. The folks that have gone back on the pledge, that have weighted it down, have been pulling back, and missing their drive. Sometimes they have one meeting that they call the Christian Endeavor meeting, another meeting a literary meeting, another meeting a social meeting, until the month is all sliced up and there is only one real religious meeting left, I know one denomination in my country that has honored Christian Endeavor by still calling that one solitary meeting the Christian Endeavor meeting although they haven't any Christian Endeavor societies. It reminds me of the porter whom the man asked if he would change a $100 bill, and he looked rather astonished at him and said, "No, boss, I haven't any hundred dollars, but thanks for the compliment just the same."

We are grateful to those who call the only religious meeting they have in their churches a Christian Endeavor meeting. What has been the result? In the Presbyterian Church the guild that was organized on that basis passed away years ago. This year at the last meeting of the General Conference of the Methodist Church in Canada the Epworth League was decapitated; there isn't any longer officially an Epworth League in Canada. They are swinging back now to something else, swinging back to the Young People's Department, the Sunday-school idea again. We remember the time when they told us that the adult Bible class was all we needed, that the activity in connection with the committees of the adult Bible class was all that is necessary, but we realize that as long as it is a Bible class the teacher is more or less the centre of it, the teaching function is more or less the predominant function, and the special training that is received is very often and became more and more a negligible quantity.

No one tells you to-day that you can do your expressional work through the committees of the organized Bible class, but there is a brand new suggestion that they are bringing to us, and that is the Young People's Department of the Sunday school, gathering all the young folks in the congregation together as we have in the junior department and the primary department and the intermediate department and the senior department of the Sunday-school, with their own superintendents and in their own rooms, and then having another meeting for expressional purposes.

Now I have just one or two difficulties in connection with that proposal, and the first difficulty is this: the best young people in my church are not in that department. They are the folks who have got the spirit of service, who have been trained in Christian Endeavor, and when an appeal has been made for Sunday-school teachers, they are the ones that have responded. So the best young people are in the primary department and the junior department and the intermediate department as workers, and what is left for a Young People's Department are only those that will not serve, only those that will not respond to that appeal, and I don't want a young people's society in my church that hasn't the opportunity of having the best folks in the congregation in it.

Another difficulty in connection with it is this: of course, it hasn't any pledge. If you are going to have everybody there you must have a standard that will suit them. It reminds me somewhat of the old parish idea that perhaps still predominates in some parts of the old land, where the parish minister feels that everybody in his parish is a member of the church.

If we began a congregation in any town in this country, and had only one church in the town, and wrote down on its membership roll in that congregation the name of every man and woman in the town, and then tried *to put on a programme of Christian service that would please them, what sort of standard would it be?* I am sure it would not be the standard of Christian Endeavor. "Trusting in the Lord, Jesus Christ for strength I promise Him that I will strive to do whatever He would like to have me do."

Just one word about the Sabbath school. Two years ago last October when I came back from my vacation, on rally day I went to the superintendent of the junior department of the school who required about thirty-five teachers to man that department, and I asked her how many teachers she needed, how many vacancies she had. She said, "I have eight or nine vacancies." I made the suggestion that she put every one of her teachers in the second and third years and clear out the first year; and then I went to the superintendent of the Intermediate Christian Endeavor society and said, "I want you to choose for me the best eight or nine young men and young women you have in that society." He named them and he said to them, "The minister wants to see you in the vestry." They came and I told them I wanted every one of them for first year junior teachers and I asked them how many were willing to do it. *Every one was,* and for three months I taught them the graded lesson for the first-year department. They went down and taught their classes. They are teaching yet. *They*

The Winners for the Next Convention 1925

are the best teachers in the department; they are always on the job and are never absent. Why? They had three or four years as Junior Endeavorers, they had three or four years as Intermediate Endeavorers, and they were ready for the job and ready for work, ready for the challenge when it came.

Our teaching will not suffer if Christian Endeavor gets a chance. The stronger Christian Endeavor becomes, the more efficiently will our Sunday schools be, and we still have a greater need than ever for good Christian Endeavor teachers.

Perhaps twenty-five years ago the chief appeal that was made to any man or woman to teach Sunday school was the appeal of piety. If a man didn't have a genuine religious interest and conviction he wouldn't do it. Then we began to realize that the teaching qualities of our schools would have to be elevated, that we were not measuring up to the standards that were set by our splendid public schools and our high schools. We adopted more educational methods, graded lessons, and when we began to look for Sunday school teachers we were not putting the emphasis so much upon piety as on a good education. Now when we are hunting for a young man to teach a class of boys, what do we want? We want a fellow who is a good sport, the emphasis being shifted again. It was shifted first from the heart to the head, and now it seems to be getting to the heels. Well, it is a good thing to have it there, but we don't want it all there; we want the heart interest still; I want educated teachers, I want athletic teachers, but, above all, I want *Christian* teachers, and I want *Christian-Endeavor-trained teachers.* Will our pulpit suffer from this? I remember a very striking incident that happened at the Synod of Manitoba a few years ago. One man was given the undertaking to make a list of volunteers for the ministry and for active service in our church each year for the last fifty years. After a great deal of research, looking up all the records, he produced a chart, and he drew it on the blackboard; and the chart showed that the supply of men for the ministry began to rise about forty years ago and began to rise rapidly; until about twenty or twenty-two years ago it was at the top, then it began to fall and to fall gradually until it was down almost at the bottom again.

The general secretary of the church who was in the audience rose up and said: "Mr. Moderator, I wonder how many of those who are present at this meeting can see the full significance of the chart that this man has drawn, that gives us a picture of the supply of men for the ministry for the last fifty years? I notice that the supply began to rise about the time the Christian Endeavor movement was born, and it rose steadily and gradually until the time that the denominations thought they could produce something better and began to pull away and organize leagues and guilds and all sorts of things. "And it is falling, falling, falling; but I believe it will rise again." In these last two years since the New York convention we have had a wonderful increase in membership in Canada, and we had a summer school for the training of our leaders. Three years ago it had forty-five members, one year ago it had eighty-nine members, and this year it has a hundred and forty paid registrations, and the end is not yet. The supply is rising again, and as it rises, we will get good Sunday-school teachers, we will get the best ministers, and the best of missionaries, and the work of Christ and His kingdom will go forward again by leaps and bounds. Let us stand fast for Christian Endeavor.

Chapter VIII.

THE ALUMNI BANQUET AND LUNCHEONS

No fewer than seven hundred lively Endeavorers gathered around the tables in the beautiful banquet hall of the headquarters hotel, Fort Des Moines. They paid their respects heartily to the viands provided, but hilarity was their chief employment and feast. Every year adds dozens to the already copious supply of merry little songs, vigorous and melodious cheers, and ridiculous "catches" and "stunts." For much of this the jubilant bunch of field-secretaries was responsible. Did ever the four walls of one room hold two dozen Christian Endeavor field-secretaries-on-their-high-horses before? Under the inventive leadership of President Freet, head of the Field-Secretaries' Union, the talented and sportive double dozen entertained the crowd that had already entertained itself most satisfactorily for the past hour.

The Buena Vista male quartette delighted us with jovial songs, and then Alumni Superintendent Vandersall introduced as the presiding officer "the best-beloved man in Christian Endeavor," who could be no other than Dr. Clark. The evening speeches began with an exhibition by Mr. Vandersall of the large and exquisite silver loving-cup, which has been presented to the United Society by those most helpful friends of the Alumni cause and of all Christian Endeavor, Mr. and Mrs. Fred L. Ball, of Cleveland. The cup is to be awarded each year to the State union that has done the best Alumni work, and the name of each State receiving it will be engraved upon the cup.

Dr. Foulkes was then called upon, and made a bright and exceedingly effective speech, picturing the scene when Christ spoke of the man who brought out of his treasure "things new and old." And the Master put the new things first. So let us put the new things first. Let us herald the dawn of the new day. Let us plan for new things and larger things for Christian Endeavor. He told of the way Dr. Lowrie, of China, translated for his visiting-card Dr. Foulkes's title, "Secretary of the New Era Movement of the Presbyterian Church," which Dr. Lowrie rendered, "Secretary of the New Day Going Forward Together of the Company of Growing Old Believers in Jesus." Dr. Foulkes proposed this as a name for Christian Endeavor, as happily combining the new and the old in our society and its plans.

President MacTaggart, of the All-Canada union, told how dear

The Alumni Banquet, Fort Des Moines Hotel

Christian Endeavor always had been to him, and it is growing dearer as the days go by. Christian Endeavor's international fellowship is one cause of his joy in the society. Canada and the United States, with four thousand miles of common boundary, have for more than a century been at peace, and much of the present friendship between the two countries is due to Christian Endeavor. The society's interdenominational fellowship is another joy. Canada's recently completed union of the Methodists, Presbyterians, and Congregationalists has certainly been greatly aided by the union work of Christian Endeavor.

Mr. Sproull spoke of the great debt of gratitude which many years president of the New Jersey Christian Endeavor Union, was introduced in a justly complimentary way by Dr. Clark, but responded by telling the story of an old maid whose engagement to be married was spread abroad. On the street a friend rushed up to her and told her how glad she was to hear the news. "There ain't a word of truth in it, Julia," she replied, "but thank God for the rumor."

Mr. Sproull spoke of the great debt of gratitude which many of us owe to Christian Endeavor, and of how, in partial payment of this debt, we should take a large share of the financial burdens of Christian Endeavor. He also urged that Christian Endeavor Alumni should let our churches and communities know what Christian Endeavor has done for us, and should become the exponents of Christian Endeavor as far as we can reach with our words and our influence.

Mr. Duncan Curry, of Jacksonville, Fla., a well-known insurance man, testified that he had got more out of Christian Endeavor than from any other organization to which he had belonged. He outlined the new plan which he has conceived of a census of old-time Endeavorers in Florida, asking each to give in his name, his old church and society, the Christian Endeavor positions he has held, a renewal of his pledge applying it to the church prayer meeting, and an adhesion to the Florida Alumni Association with annual gifts to the work. Also as an insurance man he urged that every Endeavorer should have himself insured for the benefit of Christian Endeavor. Dr. Clark in this connection introduced Mrs. Carrie Conrad, of Florida, who has just given $10,000 to Christian Endeavor on the annuity plan. She was most warmly greeted by the Alumni.

Dr. James Kelly, of Scotland, told us of the Scottish Christian Endeavor Alumni, who now entirely finance the field-secretary of the Scottish Christian Endeavor Union,— and his office and travelling-expenses. He also gave us glimpses of his recent travels through Europe as president of the European Christian Endeavor Union, with pathetic and moving stories of the destitution there and of the fidelity in many lands to Christian Endeavor.

Dr. Poling opened his speech by quoting the testimonial once written for Dr. Liverpill: "Dear Doctor: The mother-in-law of my uncle's nephew was tottering at the very gate of Paradise. Your medicine pulled her through." The associate president of Christian Endeavor was confident that the Alumni movement will pull Christian Endeavor through all its financial difficulties. Poling told in a most interesting way of his recent stay in Arizona and of how everywhere he went in that State he met old-time Christian Endeavorers, still with their old-time enthusiasm warm in their hearts. He told also of a splendid Endeavorer who gave up his life for liberty during the World War, and he made a stirring appeal for the dedication of life for Christian Endeavor through the gifts of money. At the afternoon trustee meeting a group of trustees gave two thousand dollars, and the count, when made up, will show that the Alumni were equally generous.

The Junior Workers' Luncheon

An hour of delightful fellowship was enjoyed by the Junior workers at their luncheon Thursday noon. Applause greeted the representatives of different States and Provinces as they rose in response to the calling of their names by Miss Mildred Haggard, who presided. Mrs. Fletcher, the wife of the president of the British Christian Endeavor Union, was especially warmly welcomed.

The announcement of Mrs. Francis E. Clark to give the address brought the company to their feet to receive her with hearty applause.

There never was a time, she said, when work like that of the Junior superintendents was more needed. Times have changed. There is call for a great deal of patience and tact and loving-kindness, and a great deal of prayer and planning, if the boys and girls are really to be helped to do things for Christ's sake. Many more things are done for children in these days, but it sometimes seems as if their souls, the most important part of all, were neglected. So it is a great joy to know what the young men and women are doing to teach the boys and girls to love Christ and to work for Him.

The Intermediate Superintendents' Luncheon

The goodly company of Intermediate superintendents at their luncheon were happily introduced to one another before the speaking began. Rev. Paul C. Brown, who presided, first called on the State superintendents to rise, give their names and States, and in a sentence tell of conditions in their States. Then came the district and county superintendents in like manner. Last, the society superintendents stood and gave the names and locations of their churches. Those that remained were classed by Paul Brown with himself as not superintendents but "boosters."

Miss Adeline Goddard, field-representative of the United Christian Missionary Society, who gave the address, declared it

A Maryland Group

to be the duty of every church to offer its youth an opportunity to grow in the four ways in which Luke says that Jesus grew. She sketched the leading characteristics of youth between twelve and fourteen; between fourteen and sixteen, the emotional age; between eighteen and twenty, the intellectual age; and emphasized the kinds of effort especially needed at each of these periods. Attention must be given to the time of development of the social instinct, of spiritual awakening, of tendencies to crime and suicide, of doubt and perplexity. It is a duty and privilege to be a friend of the youth of one's church.

The Luncheon for Experts

The spacious dining-rooms of the great Y. M. C. A. building furnished a most enjoyable luncheon on Friday noon for fully 250 Endeavorers interested in Christian Endeavor Expert work. The meal was enlivened by many jolly cheers and every one was in good humor. Southern Secretary Evans was the organizing spirit and the presiding officer. The speaker of the happy occasion was Dr. R. F. Kirkpatrick, the vice-chairman of the All-South Extension Committee. In an earnest and pointed address he urged the Endeavorers to know Christian Endeavor, to put their own thought into their Christian Endeavor efforts, to base their planning on the fundamentals of Christian Endeavor, and especially the Christian Endeavor pledge, the most inspiring and at the same time the most searching test of character he had ever seen. Above all he urged that the Experts should know Jesus Christ, for this knowledge is the source of power and the secret of success.

The Life-Work Recruits' Luncheon

Fully 150 young people gathered for the Life-Work Recruit luncheon, the presiding officer being Ohio's popular Field-Secretary Freet. It was a gathering of youth, full-blooded, ebullient youth, filled with the keenest joy of life, yet ready to devote their enthusiasm and their energies to speeding the gospel of Jesus. They proved their "pep" — the Wisconsin delegation leading with unfaltering vigor — by their yells and songs and happy witicisms.

It was a testimony luncheon, Recruit after Recruit telling of decision and study. Miss Grace McNutt, Oxford, Wis., was the first speaker introduced by Mr. Freet. She is getting ready for work among the Indians in Arizona. Anita Gregson, of Cincinnati, who took the Recruit pledge at the Buffalo Convention, spoke of her prospective field in the Punjab, India. James Wray, former Christian Endeavor field-secretary, now a missionary in Mexico, said that the last two and a half years spent in the Master's work were the happiest in his life. He urged consecration heartfelt and complete.

Mr. Freet brought the after-dinner period to a close with a

fervid and helpful talk on consecration and preparation and devotion to the high ideals that Recruits have set before them. The company trooped to the street — or most of them did — where a picture of the group was taken.

Chapter IX

JUNIOR CONVENTION AND CONFERENCE

Friday, July 6

A wealth of varied entertainment and instruction was packed into the two crowded hours of the Junior convention in the Central Church of Christ on Friday afternoon.

The Juniors were divided into groups assigned to rooms where conferences were held for presidents and vice presidents, lookout, prayer-meeting, and missionary committees. Under skilled leaders the half-hour was used to good purpose, and the Juniors were alert to answer questions and to report methods used in their own societies.

When they assembled again in the auditorium, Wendell Shullenberger, the pastor's son, was introduced as the presiding officer, who voiced the Juniors' pleasure at having a part in the Convention, and announced as the first speaker Miss Mamie Gene Cole, the national Junior superintendent, who had the oversight of the programme.

Miss Cole briefly stated the goal of Junior workers to train the boys and girls for service in their own churches, to have a Junior society in every Christian Endeavor church, and to bring every boy and girl to acceptance of Christ as a personal Saviour before leaving the Junior society.

Several hymns were sung with much expression, with Mr. R. A. Walker as leader.

Southern Secretary Charles F. Evans complained of the unfairness of his introduction because his name was given, but the names of the Juniors had not been given. So he asked all the Juniors to give their first names when he had counted three, and the introduction was completed. By telling of the way in which he spent three days in a visit to the Mammoth Cave under the direction of a guide he illustrated capitally the motto of the meeting, "Be ye therefore followers of Christ," making the point that we must follow closely in order to hear His voice. Junior Endeavor, he showed, means following Christ closely, being brave, and helping others live purer lives.

Some of the Juniors had been winners in a contest involving quickly finding Bible passages that had been memorized. Three of these girls and two boys took seats on the platform with Bibles in their hands. Bible verses were read, not arranged in any order known to the Juniors. As quickly as any one recognized the verse and could find it in the Bible, he rose, gave the reference, and read or repeated the verse.

About a dozen verses were thus given out, and the responses were marvellously prompt, in some cases nearly the whole five being on their feet reading the verse before it had been finished by the one giving them out.

A telling incident of the loyalty of three Mexican Juniors and their superintendent was given by Mr. James Wray. Captured by some Catholics, with their hands bound behind them, they were beaten severely and stoned because they refused to worship the picture of a saint, and were kept prisoners until soldiers went to their rescue the next day.

A solo by a Junior, Richard Hyde, was so excellently given that he was enthusiastically recalled.

With a reference to the debt that great men have owed to good mothers Mrs. Francis E. Clark was introduced as the mother of Christian Endeavor, and while the Juniors rose to honor her, a beautiful basket of flowers was handed to her by a Junior girl.

Mrs. Clark spoke of the Christian Endeavorers that she had seen in many lands. In China the missionaries said they could tell the Endeavorers because they behaved so much better than others. In Budapest the Endeavor boys and girls were helped by frequently looking at a motto meaning, "What would Jesus say to that?" In China she had seen a peace-making committee. She asked all the Juniors to imitate her in giving a Chinese salute by clasping their own hands and pronouncing the Chinese phrase. Then they all joined her in repeating the first promise of the pledge.

She told a story illustrating the Bible saying that a merry heart doeth good like a medicine, and urged all the Juniors when they had to do something hard in order to please Jesus to be like the little engine that said, "I think I can."

Rev. James Kelly, of Scotland, was called to the front for a word, and he and the Juniors clapped their hands by way of greeting. He told of being a Junior twenty-six or twenty-seven years ago, and charged the Juniors to be loyal to their pledge.

JUNIOR METHODS

CENTRAL CHURCH OF CHRIST, FRIDAY MORNING, JULY 6

Miss Mildreth Haggard Presiding

Our first subject this morning is, "The Challenge of Our Boys." Mr. Winship, the editor of "The Journal of Education," who is known across the country as "The Boys Winship" has written a little article in which he gives a new designation of boy life. He gives the designations of three years each, and this is the way he gives them.

NOTE.—Conferences on Junior methods were held also on Thursday and Saturday, but we have space to report only one day's conference.

A leafing time—from infancy to three years.
A pruning time—from four to six years.
A budding time—from seven to nine years.
A blossoming time—from ten to twelve years.
A fruiting time—from thirteen to fifteen years.
A harvest time—from sixteen to eighteen years.
A marketing time—from nineteen to twenty-one years.

The real object of this designation, these seven periods of three years each, according to Mr. Winship, is to magnify two specific facts:—first, that the right home guidance of each of these seven periods radically differ each from the other; second, the public should accept responsibility for the education of mothers in skilful guidance of their children, so far as the home life is concerned, in the leafing, the pruning, and the budding time, and the education of the fathers, especially in the guidance of their sons, in the blossoming, the fruiting, the harvest, and the marketing time.

I give you this outline from Mr. Winship because he is a specialist in boys' work, and it seemed an appropriate introduction to Miss Cole's first address this morning on "The Challenge of our Boys."

If there is time later in the morning, I want to say something more with regard to the training of the parents as far as our own particular responsibility is concerned.

MISS MAMIE GENE COLE: If there is one subject that should be before the minds of Junior superintendents to-day, it is this subject, "The Challenge of Our Boys." We need to think of that subject because in many cases our programmes are planned too much from the point of view of the girl.

First, we want to know what the boy is interested in, and how to hold his interest. What are boys naturally interested in? First, I think that boys are interested in sports of various kinds. Most boys like to play all kinds of running games—ball, and that sort of games. I wonder how many superintendents here have ever used the game "Bible Baseball" in your Junior Christian Endeavor societies. If you haven't, I hope you will, because I don't think there is a better Bible drill anywhere than Bible Baseball. You may play it with the questions for the regular game, or play it with Bible verses. I think boys are interested in those things.

A boy may be interested in music (many of our boys are studying piano or violin), or he may have a beautiful voice. You want to show him that he may use his talents for the Lord, and let us use those talents in our Junior Christian Endeavor societies.

Many of our boys to-day are interested in radio. I know one boy in my home town that has built a number of radio outfits, and I think if we told those boys we were going to have a radio meeting in Junior Christian Endeavor, they would come and they would become interested.

Boys love heroes, and we can show our boys that there are heroes in the Bible, that there are heroes in the mission field, as wonderful heroes as they will read about anywhere. We want to make them love and honor the heroes in the Bible history.

Then we want to show our boys that we need their brains, that the church needs them, that the church needs leaders, and that if they are going to be approved unto God they must study.

If I were a boy and I went to a Junior society where they had four girls up for officers, I would go home and stay there. If they were going to have all-girl leaders in that society, I wouldn't be interested. Girls will follow boys, but many times boys will not follow girls, especially in the Junior age, and so I would say that in ninety cases out of a hundred a boy should be president of the Junior society, even if some girl may have more talents. It seems to me that we want to train our boys to be leaders, too, so let us have two of our officers boys, and the other two girls.

Now I do not say that we should not consider our girls, because we should, but it seems to me that we have been giving the girls the preference, and that is the reason we are losing our boys.

Boys want responsibility, and if they are going to be interested in this society, we must give them this responsibility. Make them officers, chairmen of committees, ushers, ask them to come and do things for you, show them that you can't get along without them and that you are expecting them to help you.

Usually the boy who gives trouble in the Junior society is the bright boy. I think you will find that in public school work, and if we use that accomplished. I believe that in the churches where the women are doing most of the work it is because in the Junior years the boys were not given a chance, and when they wanted anything done they asked the women and the girls to do it.

CHAIRMAN HAGGARD: Miss Cole has told you many things to do for your boys. Now what we want to know is, what are you folks doing for your boys? May we have very briefly from a number of you just some of the things that you are doing for your boys?

MRS. MARTIN: For our boys we organized what we call Junior knights, and for the girls Junior princesses. We took the things that they were just a little bit slack on in our societies to make the goal for those Junior knights and Junior princesses, especially emphasizing reverence in church and attendance at church, Bible memory work, and good order in the Junior meetings. The boys were so interested in that that they just responded nobly. These Junior knights really captured. We got blocks of tin and cut out tin shields in the shape of the Junior shield, and then for the things they did we painted on those tin shields first the "C. E." and then "J-u-n-i-o-r," and by the time they had done all of those things, they had learned a lot of Bible memory work, they had been reverent in the meeting for seven months, and they had attended church for seven months; for they couldn't earn any of those letters until they had been reverent in church for a month; that meant no whispering, laughing, or talking in church, and they had to take part in the responsive reading and in the singing, and also attendance at Junior meetings and good order in the Junior meetings.

MRS. ALLAN (California): We had one boy that we wanted to reach who was very much interested in radio, so we told him two Sabbaths before that Archie Stanton would be responsible for the radio meeting. He came on the Sabbath day with his radio, the foundation of which was a shoe box, and the rest the very simplest apparatus he could get, and it is needless to say that he was intensely interested in the radio meeting.

MRS. HOLLOWAY (Nebraska): I let my boys whistle instead of sing; they don't seem to like to sing very well, so I let them whistle the accompaniment to all the songs, and they want to know if they can't whistle for special music some Sunday. I don't know what the effect would be on the community.

MR. McINTYRE: I organized my boys into a baseball team, and we hadn't much more than organized until they began to commercialize the game and bring boys in from the other towns. I immediately got them to playing their pas and grandpas, and now the whole bunch is interested, and the boys can just barely beat them, and they are winning their pas and grandpas for the church. They are very enthusiastic.

MRS. HUGHES (Iowa): We have special music for our Juniors every Sunday. We have never been late beginning our meetings except once, and then we ran overtime a couple of minutes. Somebody that they don't know about goes to the piano and furnishes the music. Then they are interested in the baseball game, also.

MRS. HAGAR (Illinois): We have a Junior church service in our church just after Sunday school, and preceding Junior Endeavor; one Sunday we had quite a number of girls, and, of course, the girls are on the front seats. The pastor thought it would be a fine idea if we could get more of the boys out to our Junior church service, so I just whispered to the boys on the quiet that we would have a surprise for our pastor and see if we couldn't push the girls back and get the boys on the front seats. So we had just a little friendly contest for a few weeks and each one of the boys worked very hard in his own Sunday school class to get all the boys out that he could, and we drove the girls back three seats. We kept that up until we closed our Junior church service for the summer season. We have a boy usher for our Junior church service, and we have our own collection plate, and as our ushers go to the front to receive the morning offering, this little Junior boy usher goes forward with them and then passes the collection plate to the Juniors; that gives your boys another job in the church, and it is a better way to collect your money than just promiscuously.

MISS TOCHTERMANN (Wisconsin): We have an odds-and-ends committee, as I call it. I have them try to think up different ways of arranging the chairs, putting the chairs back and putting the room to order after the meeting is over.

MISS BROWN (California): We have a leaflet that is called the Junior Christian Endeavor Conference. It is a ritual based on the way the lodges are run, and there are different stations according to the work the children do; at each station they have to learn so many books of the Bible and the stories of the Bible, and then they present them, then they go to the next station. That especially appeals to the boys, so if you have trouble with your boys and care for a copy of that, we can furnish it.

MRS. HOWELL (N. C.): For six years we have had early morning Christmas service. The first Christmas we had it in the Sunday-school room, and then all voted they wanted it at my house, so we had it with the Christmas tree; heretofore I really felt like I was doing more of the work than the Juniors, so I put it in charge of our boys this last year. I was wondering about the automobiles for the early morning. Those boys had everything in detail. I only gave them suggestions of the hours, how to arrange to call for them, and they went ahead and got the people with the machines. I feel that the greatest need for the boy is to let him know that he has responsibility and let him know that you are counting on him and if you do that he will not fall down on his job.

MISS COLTRAIN (Nebraska): I am in charge of a meeting of all nations in Omaha; we have no church, it is just Bible study and Junior Endeavor work. We have each one of the boys and girls be responsible for two chairs, and if they can't get any one to fill the other chair, they have to fill it themselves, so it is rather a hard problem for them. When I took charge of it three years ago we had nineteen members, and at the present time we have forty-three. There is hardly a nationality or a color that you can mention that isn't there. Once a month we give a banquet to our fathers and mothers, and the children do all the work, with the exception of two helpers.

MRS. W. H. BROWN (N. Y.): I have great success in training the children through the church by having a Junior choir; our pastor is very good and lets us have ten minutes, so we prepare the pieces for the Junior meeting, and then march in church to the front seats and sing.

QUESTION: I want to hear about Miss Cole's Bible baseball.

MISS COLE: This is the plan: You have teams just like you are playing baseball. You have your pitcher and your catcher and your fielders and your basemen. You can use as many as you have. The best way to start is to have the pitcher state a Bible verse, and then if the batter can quote one before the catcher does, he goes to the first base. It has to come back to the pitcher every time. Then the pitcher quotes another verse, and if the catcher quotes one before the batter does, the batter is out, and three outs is half an inning and the other side comes in. You count just runs. If the pitcher wants to run around and say to this man who is getting from second to third base, "Quote a verse," and if the man can not quote a verse before the fielders or the baseman out here can quote a verse, he goes out; if he can, he goes on. A better way, after the boys and girls have learned the references for their verses, the pitcher might say, "John III, 16," and if the batter can quote that before the catcher, he goes to first base, and so on. Of course, you have to have an umpire, and the superintendent or one of the helpers may be the umpire. It seems to me that a man might take that job.

The boys and girls love it. I never will forget when we tried it in our church. One of the boys made a poster and we put it up in the church. It said, "Baseball Sunday afternoon at three o'clock." Some of the teachers came and asked me what we were going to do. I told them to come down and find out. They came and they were very much impressed, and I don't think anything ever helped our society quite so much, because they are required to learn the verses before they can play. It makes them alert, and it seems that they remember them bcause they have used them.

There is a game called Bible baseball that you can buy from the United Society; it is questions on the Bible, and it is splendid. It costs fifty cents. The superintendent may ask the questions, and if the child trying to make the home run can answer all four questions, he makes a home run. If he can answer one, he goes to first base, two to second base, and so on.

CHAIRMAN HAGGARD: Tell them about the radio meeting that you planned.

MISS COLE: I think the plan that has worked out best in Dixie for special meetings this year, at least the plan that I have heard most about, has been a plan for radio meetings. I say to them, "How many of you have ever listened over a radio?" and of course they all have.

"But if you are listening to a radio programme, do you see anybody?"

"No."

"Well, if you are going to have a radio programme in Junior Christian Endeavor would you see anybody on the special radio programme?"

"No."

We have a curtain up in front for the people to stand behind. Of course, this is a special part of the programme, and not the devotional programme at all. I say to them, "Most radio stations have three initials in their name. If the Junior Christian Endeavor society is going to have a radio station, what do you think would be a good name?"

"JCE," so we will call our station "JCE." Then we have a boy with a big voice to be the announcer, and he will go back of the curtain and say, "This is JCE, the radio broadcasting station of the Junior Christian Endeavor society. Kindly stand by for a few seconds for the first number on JCE, the radio broadcasting station of the Junior Christian Endeavor society." Then if Mary Jane is going to sing a solo, she comes and stands behind the curtain, and he says, "The first number on JCE, the radio broadcasting station of the Junior Christian Endeavor society will be a vocal solo by Mary Jane." When she gets through he comes back and says, "Kindly stand by for a few seconds for the next number of JCE," and so on. Then instead of your United Press Dispatch notes you might have a story or something along that line. Of course, go ahead and have your Bible lessons and your Bible drills and your special programme and after that is over have your radio programme.

CHAIRMAN HAGGARD: The Bible for the Juniors is our next topic.

Mrs. R. E. Kinsell of Iowa has a very splendid plan on Bible drills which she is going to present to us now.

MRS. R. E. KINSELL (Iowa): The Junior has a mind, and he also has a body, and you know as well as I know that activity is the keyword to all of their lives.

First, we have got to get the Bible into their minds, and second, we have to use the Bible for their activity. Sometimes we wonder how we can use the Bible when the Juniors do not have Bibles. I am going to give you three ways to get the Bibles: when we graduate our primary pupils into the Junior department in our Sunday school, our church buys a Bible for every primary pupil that has done the work and receives a certificate. We make so much use of that Bible that the boys and girls who did not graduate will buy Bibles. Those are two ways. Another way, our Senior society has bought a number of Bibles and they keep them at the church in the library and they lend them to the Juniors for our work in Junior Christian Endeavor.

There are several ways that we might teach the Bible. The first is the teaching of the Bible books. There are two or three ways we might use. This is a hand, and it represents the Old Testament, and we divide the Old Testament, as you know, into different divisions. The thumb is law, the forefinger history, the big finger devotion, the ring finger major prophets, and the little finger minor prophets. I have another hand for the New Testament, and that is divided also into five groups—biography, history, special letters, general letters, prophecy, just something that the children can see; that is the only advantage of that.

And then the contests. The Juniors love contests, and I brought these three Juniors along with me just to show you what we do in our contest. I am going to ask you three little girls to turn your chairs around. I am going to ask them to find some references. We do this every Sunday almost and we keep track of those who find them first and give the announcement. They have no idea what I am going to ask them to find. I just want to give you an idea how quickly they can find the verses.

Mrs. Kinsell called off a list of references and the little girls located them and read them.

Then we have the biographies of characters found in the Bible. They say, "I am thinking of a character," and they go on and tell the story, and they are to guess who this character is.

Then we have the different characters and they are to find the place in the Bible where these stories are found. We take the book of Mark and name some one story in that book, like the transfiguration or feeding the five thousand, and the children are to know where that story is in the Bible, and they find it and see which can find it the quickest, and when they find it, they stand, and we keep track of that kind of thing.

We had in our Junior Department a Bible library. One of our parents made the Bibles out of wood. They are just about five by six, and they have the names on the back. We mix them all up and see how quickly the children can place them in the right place.

Then we have what we call a Bible town. In learning the books of the Bible, we have this Bible town. You can get this from the Presbyterian Board. This is the Old Testament on this side of the river, and this is the New. We have the Law Street, the History Street, the Poetry Street (we called it Devotion before we got the map), Major Prophets and Minor Prophets; then over in the New Testament, we have Gospel Street, History Street, Paulina Street, General Letters, and Prophecy, and then we let the boys and girls find these pictures or houses. We put the Genesis house on Law Street, and all the girls stand up and name the books of law. We have the houses to represent each book. Then we say, "Now who lives in the Genesis house?" And they tell the characters in the Genesis house. You can do a wonderful amount of memory work in this way. The price of this map is five dollars. You can make it yourself if you are an artist.

CHAIRMAN HAGGARD: Now will you tell me what other devices for Bible drill work you have been using?

MISS TYSON (Alabama): Every child brings a Bible every Sunday to Christian Endeavor. We call "Mass," and they sit up straight in their chair; "Attention," and they stand up perfectly straight with the Bible in the right hand; "Salute," they hold the Bible over their head with the right hand; "Charge," and they hold the Bible in the left hand on top; "Draw swords," and they open it as quick as they can to any reference you call. It is a wonderful way to get the children to look up references in a hurry.

MRS. ALLEN: In our Bible drill work we do very much as the lady did, except we give headmarks; we have a regular spelling match; we give a reference and the one who finds it the quickest moves up.

MRS. ORT (Cedar Falls): My plan is very much the same, only I put the children in a circle and then go around and see who can stand up the longest.

MISS TENNIS (Ohio): We have used the spelling bee instead of the spelling match; it is conducted about the same as the spell-down. The class is divided into two divisions, and you can have your pastor see that your verses are quoted correctly, and see which side stands up the longest. They enjoy it and they really ask for it each Sunday. No verse is repeated, and if they quote it wrong, they have to sit down.

MRS. MARTIN (Illinois): We have tried it in a different way, giving out a set of fifty questions, and we have used it very successfully. We ask for the longest verse in the Bible, the shortest verse, and questions like that; any one missing any of these questions sits down just the same way.

MISS BROWN (California): We mix verses of the Bible with familiar quotations and have intelligence tests, much like they give in school. They must guess whether they call quotations from the Bible or from books.

MISS ALLEN (Arizona): Our children enjoy the inner-circle. We have an immense circle of them, and every one that is turned down steps back, and we keep on until those that can stand the test are really the inner circle.

MRS. ALLEY (White Plains, N. Y.): We have what we call a Bible ballot. We divide the Juniors into two sections and on the platform put rows of straight lines to represent soldiers, about twelve or fifteen in each row, and as each side gives a Bible verse, that kills a man, and we see which line scores first.

MRS. RUSSELL (Nebraska): We have a little game that youngsters enjoy greatly; we call it the popcorn game. First we ask if they like to pop corn, and, of course, they all say they do, and then we tell them that this game is like popcorn, that they must jump up quickly when the finger is snapped and say a Bible verse, or the popcorn is ruined, and then we like to see how much we can make in an afternoon, whether we can have a great lot of popcorn or just a little. They enjoy the game greatly.

CHAIRMAN HAGGARD: We want to think of the Bible now

from a little different angle for Juniors. We have been talking about Bible drills, the public use of the Bible in the meeting. Now may we come to what is perhaps surely the foundation of public Bible drill in the meeting, the personal use of the Bible. I want to think of ways in which we may help the Juniors to own a Bible, to know the Bible, to use the Bible, to mark the Bible, to carry the Bible, and to love the Bible, just as they love an old rag doll.

Perhaps the most concrete way to present that and the briefest way is to present it over the heads of the pocket Testament League, and I want to ask for the sake of presentation that Miss Darnall say a word about that, and will you be thinking about it?

MISS DARNALL: I happened into one of our churches not long ago before an evening service; it was a mid-week service with young people. We were there just a little ahead of time. Down in front was a group of Junior and Intermediate boys. I thought they were getting ready for their Children's Day services, and I sat down to see how their programme was coming along. I was personally interested in that programme that was to be used on that day. It wasn't the Children's Day programme that they were getting ready for at all; they had our little pocket Testament League demonstration, a little dramatization that they were to use on the next Sunday morning in their Bible school, to present this movement to the whole school.

We are following up this year our Easter campaign with very definite promotion of the Pocket Testament League idea, carrying the Testament about you all the time.

Testaments are provided purposely for their plan; in the back of them are some suggestions and some things that will help you find perhaps the quotation or the reference that you are looking for or that you are needing; also the covenant there for the person who has not made the confession. We are finding that it is one of the finest ways to follow up our evangelistic programme at Easter time.

CHAIRMAN HAGGARD: Who of the Junior workers here have used the Pocket Testament League with their children?

MISS FRANCES SMITH (Cincinnati, Ohio): I just had a class of boys and I asked them to join it, and they did. I had nine or ten boys. I just tried it with the Junior class I had several years ago. We used to always sing that song, "Take it wherever you go," by John M. Alexander.

MISS BROWN (California): We have used it this last year; it is the first time that we have incorporated it in our Junior programme. The children are carrying their Testaments and they are using them. The Bakersfield Junior Christian Endeavor society has an enrollment of somewhere around 175 Juniors.

MRS. McNUTE (Wisconsin): We used the pocket Testament league in the society. When we first began the sharpshooting the boys and girls did not have Bibles, and the Bibles in the church were so worn out that oftentimes they wouldn't be able to find the reference, and they seem to think it much nicer to have a little pocket Testament of their own, so we decided the best way to do was to earn our own pocket Testaments and then send for them. That was one method we used of getting the boys and girls in the society. They carried it to school, and when the other boys and girls would see they had pocket Testaments they would say, "Do you read the Bible every day?"

"Yes."

"Every single day?"

"Yes."

They thought if they could do it, they could, too, and in that way we got the boys and girls into the Junior society.

CHAIRMAN HAGGARD: May we leave this subject and consider

another phase of the Bible work? In what ways have you attempted to express your Bible drill or your use of the Bible with the Juniors?

MRS. MARTIN (Illinois): We have had them take Mrs. Clark's Bible autobiographies and tell those stories in a meeting.

MISS HOLLOWAY (Nebraska): Our minister had us to act out and pantomime some of the Bible stories for the first part of the Sunday evening service.

MRS. HOWELL (N. C.): One way that I had was for them to read a Bible story and have a guessing game the next Sunday. After we had had our little devotion we would have this little story.

CHAIRMAN HAGGARD: That is very much like something I heard at the University Church of Christ here in Des Moines. The children were divided in sides for the last few minutes of the meeting, and one child each month would bring a hundred word story, without any name, of some Bible character. The child on the other side who first guessed about whom it was had the privilege of bringing one a month from that Sunday. It was a monthly feature which was rather helpful.

MRS. MURPHY (Newton, Iowa): Our children are especially interested in the object lesson as it is presented in the Endeavor work. I remember one lesson that impressed them very much; we made the cross, and then we made links of a chain with little verses on, and fastened the cross to the crown, the verses that leading up.

CHAIRMAN HAGGARD: In connection with this I want to suggest something of this type of expressional work of a Bible story. The day school children do a great deal of cut-paper work. They express their own personality, the message which is brought to them they put on the paper, cut it out and paste it, expressing what they get out of some particular experience. This is simply an illustration of how a child might listen to a certain story in the Bible and, according to his training in school, put it down on paper.

May I suggest for the use of the superintendents the Modern Reader's Bible, which puts the Old and New Testament stories in individual units; it is very helpful for your use.

We have been looking forward to memory work. I want to abbreviate it as much as we can and yet cover as much as possible. May I first speak with regard to the devices for memory work.

MRS. SPROULL (New Jersey): I take a board like this, and I write, "And Jesus answering said, thou shalt love the Lord thy God with all," and then I leave a blank and write the rest of the verse and then make a heart, and then the children like to write it that way, and whenever they see the heart, they repeat the verse. One week we have the verse on the Bible, and the next week they see a large chart with the symbol on, and each verse is added.

MISS MARTIN (Illinois): I made separate little sheets of the different emblems and had one each Sunday, and they had color work in connection with it.

MISS SMITH (Saline, Mich.): In our society we have the string of pearls and some of my Juniors finished the work in getting the pin.

CHAIRMAN HAGGARD: May I add that in my own society I made a little string of alphabet verses for them for their Christmas remembrance, and the children appreciated that very much.

MRS. HUGHES (Iowa): We put on the top of the blackboard, "Not that which we can remember, but that which we can not forget counts to knowledge." Therefore, if we review the verses over and over again so that the children can not forget them, he has got something of permanent value.

CHAIRMAN HAGGARD: I can see that there are a great many places where perhaps rewards or recognitions are necessary. I want us to be most awfully careful about rewards and recognitions. Oh, let's never say *prizes*. Let's try to put the motive as serving Christ and pleasing Him, the religious motive.

MRS. KINSELL: I want to say one word about the meaning of the verses that you are giving the children. I had a Junior come to me and say, "When I go upstairs to bed I can't go to sleep, I am so scared," and it flashed into her mind, "What time I am afraid, I will trust in thee." She came to me afterwards and said, "When I think of that verse I never get scared."

MRS. CUNNINGHAM (Peoria, Ill.): We are a society just organized a little less than two years and we have used the first and second year Junior memory work. I bought them by the dozen and each child learned their memory work at home and then I would hear them say their verses; we would take a certain part of our society time to hear them.

MISS HOLLOWAY: I have the cards strung on wire, the ones that are finished on one side of the room and the ones that aren't finished on the other side.

CHAIRMAN HAGGARD: How much memory work ought we to give the Junior in the Junior society?

MISS TENNIS (Ohio): I should say it would have to work in with the day school and the Sunday school.

MRS. KINSELL: I don't think we ought to back down and say our children can't learn the Bible because they have so many things to learn in school. I think we ought to correlate our work, though, and I do think we ought to teach them memory work, because that is the ideal.

MISS GERRY: As a suggestion, if in the Sunday School they are learning the Twenty-Third Psalm, then in the Junior meetings have them repeat that until we can correlate the work between Sunday school and Christian Endeavor and all the other activities in such a way that they will not be trying too many different things at the same time, and yet cover the work. I am not at all in favor of dropping memory work in the Junior group.

Chapter X.

PAGEANT OF THE NEW LIFE

The Coliseum
Friday Evening, July 6
A. J. Shartle, Presiding

An immense crowd filled the Coliseum Friday evening for the great pageant demonstration in which more than five hundred persons participated. The pageant was arranged under the direction of Professor H. Augustine Smith.

To the singing of a choir on the floor a great band of Juniors in red blouses, each carrying a blue muslin scarf, marched to the platform, bringing up in a brilliant row on each side of a tall Columbia.

The first scene was *Americanism*. A motley crowd, dressed in the garb of many lands, lifting the flag of the United States, gathered in the front of the hall and asked in unison if there is a place in America for them. Columbia answered, giving welcome, and the choir burst into song, "Three cheers for the Red, White and Blue," while the immigrants marched upon the platform. Here various nations made their appeal to Columbia to open wide her gates and receive the downtrodden peoples of the earth.

This dramatic presentation, with America's responses, made a great impression, calling up as it did feelings of sympathy and visions of a world's need. Many of the responses were in the thrilling words of Scripture and of modern poetry.

The second scene was *Commemoration* of the Flanders dead. To the strains of "Keep the home-fires burning," by the choir, the ranks of Juniors on the platform parted, revealing behind an altar of commemoration. One can imagine the thrill that swept the audience as a troop of United States soldiers, with guns on their shoulders, marched smartly across the stage in front of the altar. "The boys come home! The boys come home!" And then a great crowd of white-clad girls slowly marched up the centre of the platform and laid wreaths upon the altar of their dead in front of three angels standing in the background. What surging and tumultuous thoughts arose as we gazed on the long white rows on each side of the altar, and the soldier boys behind. As a piece of symbolic pageantry it was tremendous; never has anything like it been put on in any Christian Endeavor Convention.

Convention Pageant, "The New Life"

THE COLISEUM

The third scene carried us back to Bethlehem. It was *Consecration*. In front of the altar was a manger in which lay the Christ-child, Mary bending over Him, while the choir sang, "O little town of Bethlehem." Here, too, were the wondering shepherds, and the Wise Men from the East bearing their gifts. "Oh, come, let us adore Him" sang the choir, voicing, surely, the feelings of the great audience.

Then the Spirit of Christianity, clad in heaven's blue and carrying her lighted torch, appeared and threw out a thrilling challenge to the world for lives to be laid at the feet of the Babe of Bethlehem, the Saviour of the world, the bright and morning star. The lighting effects were wonderful, as workers of all kinds, Spirit of Service, of Faith, of Triumph over Ignorance and Disease, of Investigation, of Brotherhood in Industry, of Devotion to Children, of Christian Endeavor, one of the youngest daughters of the church, ranged themselves around the Spirit of Christianity and offered themselves in Christian service.

Dedication was the fourth scene. Here white-robed girls, black-robed students, working men, and others formed a kneeling circle, and sang, each holding a lighted torch, "Come to the light, it shineth for thee." This was the new world marching through the Gate Beautiful. Then came a company of priests singing the words of David, "Lift up your heads." Here, indeed, was the city of the King, as a host of Juniors, bearing palms, marched to the platform, behind the others there arranged, and disappeared at the rear of the stage, into the City of the Redeemed.

Then the climax, a tremendous scene, *Coronation!* Above, behind the platform, in the darkness, flashed a large blue cross. "Silent night" rose from the choir, as all faced the cross, while Mary, now in front, her face illumined, gazed down upon the cradle and the Babe. All knelt, and the song swelled, "When I survey the wondrous cross." The cross flashed white, and, our thought directed by a speaker, we saw in imagination the marching multitudes, out of every nation and tribe, coming to God and home. Yet not wholly in imagination, for here they were, marching, in gayly colored Indian garb, carrying in their hands palms of victory. "They come," sang the choir, and they came "to the light," girls now, black-garbed and white-robed alternately, symbols of the womanhood of nations. "They come," still sang the choir, and again they came pouring down the aisle like a river in full tide, girls robed in beauty—women from the isles of the sunny seas, from dark lands, from north and south, east and west, with palms, palms, palms! This, sang the hearts of the audience, this is what Christ does for the world! Then there, before the cross, they knelt—the audience spontaneously rising and joining in the irresistible song, "All hail the power of Jesus' name." Then, as the great crowd of participants marched off the platform, from the choir came the ringing song of victory, "Onward, Christian soldiers."

Chapter XI

CHRISTIAN ENDEAVOR AND WORLD PEACE
Saturday Afternoon, July 7
C. C. Hamilton, Presiding

The third of Rev. William Ralph Hall's lectures on the foundation principles of Christian Endeavor treated the right foundation for service for others. This calls for a definite programme that shall take in the entire society and cover the full year. There should be practical service for the local church, including some definite personal help to the pastor; service in the community by visiting hospitals, working in missions, etc.; gifts of time and energy and means to extending Christ's kingdom around the world; gifts of life to full-time service; support of the denominational programme; and participation in the fellowship of the different unions, State, county, district, and city.

Resolutions relating to interdenominational and interracial fellowship.

Introduced by Rev. Abram Duryea, a glee club of girls from Central College, Pella, Io., sang a selection that made the audience call for more.

At the call of Mr. Shartle seven girls come upon the platform, all bearing flags that were samples of the different styles to be carried in the parade. Attention was also called to some of the newer publications of the United Society.

Then followed a novel demonstration of The Christian Endeavor World. The district and field-secretaries filed across the platform, each of the twenty-six bearing a banner on which appeared a design and a title representing some department of the paper. As each in turn came forward, speaking as impersonating his department, he told briefly what it offers the readers. The display furnished not a little entertainment and enthusiasm.

"Christian Endeavor and World Peace" was next discussed by Frederick J. Libby, the executive secretary of the National Council for the Prevention of War.

CHRISTIAN ENDEAVOR AND WORLD PEACE
By Frederick J. Libby
Executive Secretary of the National Council for the Prevention of War

On July 28 and 29 there is to be celebrated in all civilized countries of the world the anniversary of the outbreak of the great war under a slogan. In Europe they are going to celebrate under the slogan of "Universal Armament." There could be no better slogan for Europe at the present moment than that. In America we are going to celebrate under the slogan of "Law, not War."

I was much interested in the resolutions that you have just adopted for a warless world, and I wondered as you adopted them if you realized that all well-informed men in Europe and America know that we are drifting toward another war. When Germany and Russia recover their strength, there are questions that will have to be straightened out in Europe, and those questions will be settled in one of two ways, either by war, or through the machinery that we shall have set up in the meantime for dealing with such disputes.

If war comes in Europe in ten, fifteen, or twenty years, our country will be in it; however our politicians may cry aloud, no power on earth can keep America out of the affairs of the world henceforth forevermore.

What kind of war? A war of gas and airplanes. I was in Dayton, Ohio, a little while ago, and when I finished speaking a young man came up to me and said, "Do you know about our bug?" I asked him what kind of a bug. He said, "We have a little airplane here that we call the bug. We sent that airplane down to Xenia and turned it around and brought it back with nobody in it, controlling it by wireless." Airplanes with nobody in them, necessarily, and poison gas, a gas one breath of which is instantaneous death; if it touches the skin only it kills by the poison penetrating the blood. Thomas A. Edison says that with that gas and a fleet of airplanes, London with its seven million and a half of people can be wiped out in three hours. The leading naval expert of England said that France with her present supremacy in the war would be able to wipe out not only London, but half the cities of Southern England. Those best informed say that when the next war comes, if it does come, it will be the twilight of our civilization. Let us face facts as they are. I am an optimist; I believe that we are going to be able to save our civilization, but I recognize this fact: That in the past four years of opportunity neither the Christian Endeavor nor the church nor labor nor our government itself has taken any effective step yet to prevent the occurrence of war.

We must take such steps before Germany and Russia recover; we must have adequate machinery established in the world for the settlement of all disputes that may exist or may arise. There is no other way out. What kind of machinery? I was glad that you included in your resolutions the resolution for the World Court. President Harding's proposal that our country shall join with the fifty-two other countries that are already in that court in recognizing it as a method of settling disputes is a little step in the right direction.

The progress of civilization has been first to extend the law method in place of the war method between individuals. We have done away with carrying pistols in our pockets as a method of settling our disputes, we take our cases to the courts; we have done away with the war method and substituted the law method between communities. We have substituted the law method between States and between groups of States, and now one more step remains only and that is the step that is incumbent upon us to substitute law for war between nations. We have got to build up a world court. If the President's proposal is the minimum possible, what steps will be made? You remember that all human history is step by step.

There are no revolutions in human history; always when they attempted it they have had to go back and go painfully over that which they tried to jump. Step by step we shall have to go forward in making that court more effective. First, accept it, and you must help to bring that about through this "Law, not War," on July 28th and 29th, and then that court must be given more jurisdiction.

Call a crime a crime. Murder is always a crime, and, therefore, we have got to go forward to where murder in war is a recognized crime between nations, just as it is now between individuals and between states.

A friend of mine down in Maine said as I read my morning paper, "It seems to me that I have sinned in bringing a child into this world." Why has he sinned? Because the world is not safe for children. We have got to create a world that is safe for children.

We have got at the same time to hammer down the armaments of the world. No nation has the courage to disarm alone, but all nations together can disarm, and through another international conference we must limit the rest of the armaments.

Still there will remain something yet to do. I just came from the conference in San Francisco of the educators of the world. They are organizing a world association of educators. They are electing an American as its president, and a Chinaman as one of the vice-presidents, and an Englishman the other. They are planning to have a commission to deal with the text-books, the histories, the geographies, the readers of the world, holding up to the light the bad ones and the good ones that promote international understanding and good will. When I was a boy studying the history of the Revolutionary War, I got three things out of it: I got a love for France through Lafayette, that brave Frenchman that came to help us in our time of need. I got a love for Poland through Kosciusko, that brave Poland that came to our help in time of need. And I got a prejudice against Great Britain, those Red-Coats; "we licked them once and we can do it again," was the spirit of that history that I studied, and it stuck, it stuck for more than twenty years; not until I went to England and became acquainted with some of those fine Englishmen did I get over that prejudice that was taught to me when I was a child. Here in our country, the South and North, the same story is being reenacted, handing down hate from generation to generation. Every nation is doing it. and, therefore, this conference of educators is doing a great thing for the world in planning to get hate out of the text-books by making less of the wars and more of the great constructive achievements of peace.

The weakness of the League of Nations in Europe is far more than the absence of America, it is due to the fact that it was established so suddenly that there has been no opportunity to build up a world opinion to give it support. Without educating world opinion no machinery, however good, will work.

Sentiment will not end war. It is not enough to think; thinking will not end war, there must be action, there must be effective action if your resolution is to be true. A resolution implies resolute people, it implies people that resolve to do something.

A warless world! What are you going to do? You can educate, first, yourselves. Study these questions of peace. I just received word of a Christian Endeavor society in the city of Washington where I live which has begun sending out pilgrimages of peace. They are writing to different Christian Endeavor societies in their neighborhood and asking if a little group of five or seven may come and visit their society and hold a peace meeting together. That is beginning to get on; it is that kind of thing that you are personally responsible to do.

Then there is another thing. Here is this "Law, not War" day. I just received word from our office that in Philadelphia they are organizing a great committee of a hundred men and women to help put across a tremendous "Law, not War" demonstration on that day to help the President out, to help put across that world court, and then to go on to construct peace.

I have word here that the Federal Council of Churches in Dayton, Ohio, has ordered 25,000 of those posters, one for every home in Dayton; that out in Palo Alto, California, one of the organizations is arranging for a great demonstration, that Pennsylvania is to be thoroughly covered by another organization, and yet Christian Endeavorers in Pennsylvania will find great gaps there unless they take their posters home. In Virginia there is some work going on, in Rhode Island also; the Colorado W. C. T. U. has sent an order for 5,000 of these posters; down in Louisiana where they did nothing last year they are ordering 500, but the western coast and the northwest and also the southeast need them.

Now there is a specific beginning; there is where you can start. You can buy some of these posters from our office. Write down the address—National Council for Prevention of War, 532 17th Street, Washington, D. C. You can order some of these posters for your community. They should be predominant in the smallest community. There should be a meeting in every church. In Philadelphia they are hoping that every minister in the city is going to preach the necessity of the world court and of other steps in the direction of world peace on July 29.

We haven't more than ten years in which to build up this effective world organization. We are drifting towards war, and when that war comes, if it does come, we shall have no moral right to protest against giving all if we have not done our utmost to prevent it.

"The Negro's Contribution to the Religious Life of America" was the subject of an address of Bishop L. W. Kyles.

THE NEGRO'S CONTRIBUTION TO THE RELIGIOUS LIFE OF AMERICA

By Bishop L. W. Kyles.

I am asked to address you on "The Negro's Contribution to the Religious Life of America." It would be comparatively easy to indicate the economic and industrial contribution to our national life. When we are dealing with material values, stocks and bonds, banks and railroads, factories and stores, houses and lands, gold and silver, iron and steels, wheat and cattle, silk and cotton, and such like, it is not difficult to arrive at a fair appraisal. But when we come to deal with religious values, with spiritual energies and potentialities, with forces that are subtle and intangible, influences that are elusive, the difficulties become well night insuperable.

Some time ago Dr. Newell Dwight Hillis paid a glowing tribute in one of his sermons to the Negro janitor of Plymouth church, who had died a few days before. In the course of this remarkable utterance, he said: "Plymouth church was to him as beautiful as a king's palace, and Charles wore his position as a King wears his crown. His name should have been loyalty. On his tomb I shall inscribe these words: 'He was faithful unto death.' Deserted by his father, orphaned by his mother's death, buffeted by fate and circumstances, a newsboy and bootblack and milk-boy, porter in hotels, lured into the sparring ring thronged by gamblers, drunkards, evil men and women, all trying to destroy him, this colored man rose superior to all temptations, and was fidelity itself. Perhaps you and I will never see Charles again, he will be so near God's throne that there will be no telescope with which you and I can see him. Yet he groaned only while he taught us peace, and with his broken heart died while we were smiling." If you can measure the influences for good released by such a soul through its contracts, and then multiply it by innumerable cases of which this is merely typical, and you may arrive at some approximation of the indirect and unconscious contribution of the Negro to the religious life of America.

I. *The Negro has contributed to the religious life of America a large philanthropic and missionary impulse.*

The Negro here in America for the past three hundred years has been an opportunity and a challenge. Think of the miserable condition of the slaves for the most part. What sore needs were here—many, varied, clamorous. How the institution of slavery itself—which Mr. Wesley characterized as "the sum of all villainies," challenged, evoked and developed the humanitarian and altruistic sentiments of the finer souls in the nation, and set in motion a stream of philanthropy which abides as one of the chief glories of America. With the passing of slavery there came larger opportunities for responding to the still crying needs. There was the need for consecrated teachers and preachers, for schools and churches, for friends and counsellors, for sympathy and understanding, and all the thousand and one things a helpless and mistreated people needed.

So far we have dealt with the purely passive side of this matter. But when we speak of the impulse given to the cause of missions, I would remind you that the Negro has made an active and positive contribution. Perhaps the best illustration of this is to be found in the place of honor given to the memory of a Negro by the name of John Stewart at the Centenary Celebration held the other day at Columbus, Ohio. What is the significance of this remarkable tribute? Just this: that John Stewart, after his conversion, felt constrained to go as a missionary to the Indians. He travelled to the Delawares, on the Muskingum, thence to a tribe near Pipetown on the Sandusky, and among the Wyandottes on the upper Sandusky. Speaking of his work and its effects, a historian of American Methodism says: "And thus went forth from the first settlement in the Northwestern territory the first American Methodist Missionary, John Stewart, and he an African, the founder of that series of aboriginal missions which has since been extended over most of the Indian counties, and which has rescued amid the general decline of the tribes thousands of immortal souls, and opened the whole missionary career of the great Methodist Episcopal Church." The activities of this colored man furnished the inspiration for the organization of the first missionary society of this great denomination, which was approved by its ensuing General Conference.

II. *The Negro makes a valuable contribution to the religious life of America through his remarkable emotional endowment.*

I am aware that there is a tendency to decry emotionalism in religion. There are those who want cold rather than heat; refrigeration rather than incubation. There are others who would not go so far, they would be amicable Laodicians, neither hot nor cold; they believe in moderation.

There is no gainsaying the fact that one of the greatest perils of our religious life to-day is to be found in our tepid, commonplace, Laodician attitude — a thing that is intolerable even to loathing in the eyes of the Master. Professor George Jackson, himself an Englishman, says in this connection: "With multitudes to-day the emotional life is not getting fair play; we are guilty of wanton suppression of its natural and proper manifestations; we are deliberately starving one whole side of our nature; and the cold-blooded pedantry which affects to look down on all religious excitement as vulgar rant is being suffered to inflict the gravest injury upon the whole life and work of the church, and, not least, upon the life and work of the preachers. Therefore, if a preacher has received from God a rich, strong emotional nature, let him give no heed to the silly chatter of those who tell him he has no right to work on men's feelings, as if a religion could do anything for a man whose feelings are not worked on! Let him give it full play and he will find it mighty to the opening of many doors against which his most powerful logic will beat itself in vain."

Speaking of the emotional endowment of the Negro, President Henry Churchill King remarks that "the whites may well be on their guard against that 'certain blindness in human beings' which should keep them from, at least, some imaginative appreciation of the powers of insight, revelation, and enjoyment, involved in such emotional capacities." Dangers this immense emotional endowment certainly has, but let one measure its worth by remembering that the sense of reality roots itself in feeling, and by recalling the difference between the hours in which life seems cold and dead and those in which, in warmth of feeling, his being tingles with the sense of life's meaning.

III. *Perhaps the most important and outstanding contribution of the Negro to the religious life of the nation is made through the remarkable exhibition of certain Christian qualities and graces, which receive so much emphasis and are given so much prominence in their life, that they may be said to be distinctive.*

Dr. John Timothy Stone

Wayne B. Wheeler, LL.D.

Rev. S. R. Harlow of Smyrna

Frederick J. Libby

I refer to the Negroes' native kindness of spirit, their patience and longsuffering, their genial optimism, their lack of resentment, not to mention their fidelity and loyalty.

This is no mere claim which we make for ourselves, for abundant testimony to it is given by many capable judges among the white race. Dr. Frank Crane says: "There are certain qualities of spirit, certain shades of passion and conscience, which the Negro can portray better than any other race. There is a pathos, a tenderness, an edge of sympathy, a beauty of loyalty, and a genuineness of simplicity, wherein the African excels. I think the Negro is by nature the race best suited to Christianity—he has none of that hard and offensive pride which stains the Caucasian."

President Henry Churchill King of Oberlin has this to say: "Both whites and blacks may be reminded also, that as a great philosopher has pointed out, the qualities that have made the Anglo Saxon so often dominant are not always enviable qualities. They have their distinctly ungenerous, hard, selfish, domineering, side that any race may well avoid. The so-called John Bull attitude the Negro need not envy. As contrasted with this, the pure Negro seems to have a temperamental kindness of disposition, a good nature, a readiness to make the most of a situation, and to find none insufferable, that, while it may often be an obstacle to advancement, has a great gift to make to the contentment and happiness of life. It is possible to make life quite too strenuous, to live so completely in the future as never really to live in the present — to take no enjoyment in life as it passes. And this is the certain danger of the American rush. The Negro's tendency to content, while, undoubtedly, is a temptation to laziness, has in it thus a real element of strength and much-needed suggestion for an overenterprising people that has become frantic in its haste. . . . And we may not forget the positive genius which the Negro seems to have for religion. His natural religious endowment is probably unsurpassed by that of any race, unless it be the Jew. And the modern Jew is hardly his rival here."

Among other things, Bishop Quale claims for the Negro that "He is not discontented — He believes in man, in God, in the divine and human governments, he has not grown pessimistic nor misanthropic—he is not bitter."

IV. *Finally, the Negro has contributed to the religious life of America a great opportunity for the practical application of the principles of Christianity as they relate to human brotherhood.*

Christianity clearly touches the doctrine of the universal brotherhood of mankind, and it bases it very properly upon the universal Fatherhood of God.

If Christendom had accepted this idea, not as a beautiful theory, nor as an ideal which might become real at some remote time and in some ideal society, but as something capable of regulation here and now, something to be wrought out and brought to pass even by us, we should have been spared the dreadful world tragedy, through which we lately came, and from the effects of which we shall not soon recover.

But out of the grim sufferings of those calamitous years we have learned some lessons. For one thing we have had the thought of brotherhood forced into the foreground of our consciousness. We are thinking and talking of international brotherhood. We are talking of a United Christendom as a step toward the realization of the larger relationship. America has been assuming a sort of leadership in this direction. Meantime, she has had a wonderful opportunity for giving the world a splendid object-lesson of two races living together as brothers.

But America has failed. Here the Negro meets with prejudice, injustice, hatred, violence, on nearly every hand; he is exploited, victimized and crushed; deprived of his rights and privileges; lynched and burned, and, as if to give a keener edge to the already poignant tragedy, the church, which should be the champion of the oppressed and the down-trodden, has maintained, almost without exception, a consistent and persistent silence in the face of these conditions which seem to mock our Christianity.

Will Christian America rise to its opportunity? Would that it might listen to the voice of Edwin Markham, who said:

> "The crest and crowning of all good,
> Life's final star is Brotherhood;
> For it will bring again to Earth
> Her long-lost Poesy and Mirth;
> Will send new light on every face,
> A kingly power upon the race,
> And 'till it come, we men are slaves,
> And travel downward to the dust of graves."

May I close with these beautiful words of Bishop Quale: "I want to see the heavenly harpists harping on their harps. 'Twill be a famous orchestra. I hope to sit near and see the harpists' what time they play the tune of redemption, called 'The song of Moses and the Lamb'; and if I sit close (being privileged of God), I surely will see fingers glancing like rain down the strings of the harps — red fingers of America's primitive race; yellow fingers of Asia's farthest East, watching the sunrise; brown fingers of India's folk, lifting their eyes for morning on Himalayan crests; black fingers of Africa, schooled to lift loads what time they lifted; white fingers of the race whose joy it is to spread abroad the Gospel of the Son of God — all fingers smiting the harpstrings into rhapsody."

THE WORTH AND MISSION OF CHRISTIAN ENDEAVOR

By Rev. Ira Landrith, D.D.

Extension Secretary of the United Society of Christian Endeavor

Christian Endeavor is called of God for an hour like this, and it is one of the modern miracles of our time. I have said many times in the hearing of some of you that God is never in a hurry and we always are, and God is always ready and we never are, and God is always right and we seldom are. God got ready for 1923 by leading to the beginning of a Christian Endeavor society forty-two years ago. I believe that the world's one need is just one dependable informed generation of young people trained to right thinking and right doing, a single generation of young people that think right and speak right and do right and are right, and that one generation would solve all problems if they vote right and serve right in all other connections.

I believe that the solution of all problems is the Golden Rule, and I believe that in order to have the Golden Rule of conduct for all the world, there must be a single generation of people trained to be fit to live and fit to live with, and I do not know how you are going to get that unless you come back to the shadow of the cross under the influence of the church of Jesus Christ and get that generation trained from its youth up.

I have a good many articles of faith. I believe that God is omnipotent and that no wrong is a mortal wrong, that God is right and no wrong can live, that the church of God is God's organized omnipotence of right, and that the church would do what it would if it would do what it could, and I believe that the church of Jesus Christ is nearer to the accomplishing of the things the Master wants at its hands to-day than it ever was before. I believe in God the Father Almighty, Maker of heaven and earth, in Jesus Christ our Savior, and potential Savior of the whole world. I believe in my neighbor, that my neighbor is worth saving and helping and, therefore, of too great consequence to be hindered or hurt; I even believe in myself as the servant of God, capable of doing God's will, and I believe a lot more things, because I am a Presbyterian, and I have got more creed than I know what to do with.

I said to a company of your citizens in a club at noon to-day that I believe God is not only omnipotent, but I believe that America is God's new Holy Land, and that Americans are God's chosen people, and I believe that America is called of God out of the nations of the world in this great hour to do three things. First of all, to answer affirmatively the commandment, "Go ye unto all the world and preach the gospel to every creature," and secondly to carry the gospel of sobriety and decency to all mankind, and thirdly, to answer the Master's prayer that they might all be one sufficiently to end forever all the cruelties of international warfare.

I believe that somebody must give us a generation of people who do that thing or God will curse America instead of giving her the attitude of the peacemaker and of the pure in heart. I took a look around the other day to see if I could find any other organization, any other aggregation except the church of Christ that would give us that generation. I looked first into the international relations of the world, and I discovered that so far they had not regenerated human society. The best they could do was to plunge a world into a sea of blood and transform brothers into brutes. Internationalism's power is blood and terror. I took a look about me and decided that maybe we might find it in intelligence, that perhaps if we could have the world decently educated we could then depend upon the world to cleanse its own moral life; and then I took a look at the greatest nation on earth intellectually, and discovered the Hun and all that that was involved in world war and world brutality, and I discovered that education wouldn't give us a generation of young people fit to live and fit to live well. And then I glanced at the American public school,—and I am an unqualified, unapologetic, unafraid friend of the most American thing in America, the American public school,—and I discovered that the best the American public school could do was hindered by sectarianism and that the public schools could not even preach the Ten Commandments and the Sermon on the Mount and the Golden Rule in many communities and, therefore, the public school couldn't give us what we need, a generation of young people fit to live and fit to live with.

I heard a man arise in St. Louis, make an elaborate speech in which he said, "If you want the world sober and kind, you must divide the wealth of the world amongst the people who don't have it." There are a great many people in the world who think prosperity will give us integrity; but I looked about me and found that the richest are often the most ignoble, that wealth is often ill-gotten, and that poverty very many times is lacking in virtue; so on general principles I decided I couldn't find it there. I saw labor and capital at each other's throats when they ought to be co-operating for each other's welfare and all mankind's benefit; and I couldn't find it there. Then I decided that maybe human society, that thing that we attend when we put on a full dress suit,—very little dress but very full, —was what would answer the demand, and I looked about me and saw how frivolous and Godless and indifferent and insignificant and unimportant that sort of thing is, to march up and down a receiving line, shake hands with all the dudes and dudines in town to say, "*Delighted*," when you could do it if you were a wax figure with internal speaking machinery, so that you could touch a button and make the figure shake hands and say, "So glad to meet you." So I decided it wasn't worth doing.

Then I looked in every other direction and finally ended by looking at politics, hoping that politics in this Republic would give us one trained generation of young people fit to live and fit to live with, and then I discovered that every time I talked about political integrity, politicians laughed and the rest of the world hissed. I soon discovered that politics in America is not all it ought to be. I discovered two great political parties co-operating in a world war, standing together, even with a President that was elected by a minority of the American people, and by no women at all, I saw us standing by that President and doing our best in war, and then when a really greater movement came in the world's history, the movement of peace, when we might have walked out amongst the warring nations of the world bearing the American flag and saying, "*Peace, be still,*" we played politics with broken-hearted humanity and refused to let America, the called of God, speak peace to a troubled world.

I believe with all solemnity that God called America to give the word peace, sobriety, and salvation, and I would like you to hear me say that one of the greatest events in human history is the destruction in America of the legalized, authorized, publicly lionized, and privately unionized American liquor traffic. I hate it. Yet America used it as its side-partner and Uncle Sam was in the liquor business in America for something like sixty-five ugly years; but one day, about the time we were making the world safe for democracy we made America safe for Democrats and Republicans, and we got rid of the liquor traffic, and that came the next year after peace came. Then in 1919 we enfranchised American motherhood and gave women the right to defend the ballot box and the babies that had been born to them.

America has done three great things that will enable her potentially to save the world. *We are universally self-determining, we have destroyed America's worst iniquity, we have given women the right to vote.* I have no disposition to go into that, I am no prohibitionist, bless your soul; if I got up and talked about being a prohibitionist, I would be just as inconsistent as the fool who gets up and says, "I am wet," and he has no right on earth to say it. I might as well say I am a horse thief or a highwayman. You have no right to be wet, and I have no right to be a prohibitionist. I am a *constitutionalist,* I am an American citizen, and no man has a right to be anything else. If we could ever repeal prohibition you would have to fight for its repeal; but you can't repeal it until the Master repeals the Ten Commandments, and there is no more chance of repealing prohibition than there is of the return of African slavery, and we Southerners don't want that.

I have three good reasons for saying it, and I am not going any farther with it. First, we got prohibition. While the wets were inside we were outside, and now we are inside and they are outside, and they are going to stay outside. In the second place, we got prohibition by a majority of forty-six States to two, and all honor to you Connecticut Yankees and you Rhode Islanders, we could drop both your States into western Iowa and they wouldn't irrigate a dozen farms. And in the third place, we got prohibition before we gave you women the ballot. I said that to-day, I say it to-night because there are more of you here. I want you women forever to remember that it was mankind, *masculine mankind,* that gave you prohibition. It is soon enough after commencement to give a stunt in grammar. We got prohibition before *we* gave *you* the ballot. *We* is a personal pronoun, first person, plural, nominative case, and *masculine* gender.

Some woman said, "Our State had woman suffrage before prohibition." All right, who gave it to you? The men, yes, the men, because you didn't have any ballot and had no more right of the ballot-box than an imbecile, an insane person, or a convict in the penitentiary. All the right you had was a right of taxation without representation, except as your drunken husbands misrepresented you; and one day we gave you the ballot. I said that up in Canada and had trouble with a woman. She had a mouth that looked like a new-made button-hole — you know what I mean — and she was mad. She came at me with some such statement as this: "You said you men gave us women the ballot. *We made you do it.*" And that is a fact. I am a married man myself. We never would have had prohibition but for you women, but we gave it to you because you wanted it, and if you don't vote now that you have it, it wasn't worth our while to give it to you. Now you get that. This is the Christian Endeavor's new citizenship motto, and remember it: *"Every election every enfranchised Endeavorer votes."* Now take that from me by the finger method, *"Every election every enfranchised Endeavorer votes."*

If I could get that into your blood, every political Belshazzar in America would climb upon the water-wagon looking like Melba and singing like Carrie Nation, "This is what I long have sought, and mourned because I found it not."

An then the other thing we did was to guarantee to all the world brotherhood, good will, peace; and I believe Christian Endeavor more than any other organization on earth is responsible for those ideals of twentieth-century American Christians, universal prohibition, universal peace, following universal regeneration through the blood of Jesus Christ our Lord.

I said in the hearing of some of you some time ago that I spent two and a half hours lately with Luther Burbank. Luther Burbank is the greatest scientist of his kind on earth. Luther Burbank is the "onliest" man in the world who can take a sweet potato, cross it with a cactus, and make a jack-rabbit out of it. I said that somewhere lately, and a woman, one of the kind that never sees a point until she blunts it — there are people like that, the folks who have no sense of humor, therefore not much of any other kind — came up to me and said, "I like what you said, but I don't believe that story you told about Mr. Burbank." I have some doubt of it myself!

Mr. Burbank said to me, "There are two things I want you to tell the American people for me, because I am busy and you aren't," and I promised, and I am going to say it to-night and run. He said, "Tell the American boy for me" (that is you, son, you youngster, under twenty-one, you, high-school boy in course of preparation for life, you, boy with a brain that is in process of evolution, you, boy about whom we have some right to hope for the best, intellectually, physically, morally), *"that I never saw a great scientist or a great psychologist that ever used cigarettes when he was a boy."* I didn't say it, Burbank said it. I never say mean things, I quote them. It is safer! I say that every time I lecture to the graduating classes of theological seminaries. Burbank said that. He didn't say that to you grown-ups because your brain is already finished. He didn't say that to you fathers because you have got no additions to make to your intellectuality. He said it to you, son, that you can't grow a brain and smoke it at the same time; if you do it, it won't be a brain, it will be a cranium full of pickled pigs' feet. Don't you imagine that is a guess, and I am not speaking it lightly, I am not here to discuss cigarettes, I haven't any time for the discussion of cigarettes or dudes or flappers. I want to discuss something worth while! I am merely saying that you should not use cigarettes, son. Don't learn. If you do use them, quit! If you do use them and can't quit and you know you would die if you did quit, quit! Quit if it kills you, for blessed are the dead that die in the Lord forevermore; and will bury you with pleasure, all because you are a hero, that is all!

The other thing Burbank said was this: "Tell the American people for me that now we have got rid of the liquor traffic and the baby can have a fair chance and a square deal, so that the baby can be born of honest, clean parents; and now that we have crossed and re-crossed all the blood of the world as I crossed and re-crossed the plants and flowers, we are about to rear a stable race of the greatest people this world ever saw." Oh, I like that. I wonder how you old mothers ever had the courage to be mothers at all. When I remember what it meant twenty-five years ago to bear a baby in America as you did, what it meant of potential drunkenness and disgrace, what it meant of the return of sons, foul-smelling, rotten old drunks, to parental love and fireside, what it meant to throw young girls into the lascivious embrace of drunken husbands, how did you have the courage to be mothers at all? And I do not speak that lightly, I speak it with the blood earnestness of tremendous fervor and profound conviction. Your baby girl may go into her birth chamber now, unafraid, for America has forever banished the liquor traffic, and Americans will henceforth be supermen. All honor to you Canadians who are doing the same thing,—but hear a Britisher, for I am a Britisher (I have got more British blood in me than anything else, and from general appearance I think you will concede that I have some blood in me), and I am speaking for the fatherland. If Great Britain does'nt sober up, the United States of America in competition will sweep her from all the seas of commerce and from every campaign of Christian education on the face of the earth. A sober America will win against any kind of drunken other nation on the face of the earth, and every true Canadian joins us in the fight we are making for universal English speaking sobriety; and when England, Great Britain, and America go dry, the rest of the world will go dry. Now, Christian Endeavorers, stand for that!

Those three things — the salvation of the world through Jesus Christ, the salvation of the world from war to brotherly love and prosperity, the salvation of the world from the liquor traffic — can be brought about more through the Christian Endeavor society than any other organization on earth, and to finish that task we need just one generation of young people, and we have that organization ready at hand, the United Society of Christion Endeavor, and local Endeavor societies to do exactly that job.

For forty-two years Christian Endeavor has been living on crusts of bread to accomplish this will of the Lord, and that is a very broad hint that I have come to ask you to stop that crust-of-bread business and give us at least a loaf of whole wheat from now on, which is one way of saying that we need in the United Society's work, according to the Committee on Finance, representing most of the churches, and there are eighty of them (God pity us that there are that number of denominations!) for its work at home and abroad, not less than $75,000, and I was asked to ask you for it. That is the smallest job I have had for a long time.

Now I am going to say this: Christian Endeavor has done, as my friend Stone said in my ear before I came to this platform, a greater work on a smaller budget than any other organization that ever lived under the cross of Jesus Christ. I know of single congregations of Christians in America that raised almost as much for their own work. I know young people's movements in a single denomination that raised more than that, and we represent eighty denominations, eighty thousand Christian Endeavor societies, four million members, and sixteen million others that have formerly been at the altars of Christian Endeavor and are now leading in the churches, and we never saw seventy-five thousand dollars in a single year for the work of Christian Endeavor. We are asking the American people to give Christian Endeavor seventy-five thousand dollars that it may continue to do the thing God wants done in the American church for American youth, and I am going to ask a lot of youngsters that are all ready to serve to go through this room now, quickly, and put in your hands a little envelope. Now help us out by taking an envelope, and don't decide what you are going to do with it, because you don't know, and I don't want you to do anything with it yet, unless your name is Idlewitz or something like that, in which case write it slowly and print it, for you know it a whole lot better than we do; but don't do anything else except write your name and address, and the church to which you belong.

That card is Christian Endeavor's declaration of independence of paralyzing poverty. That card is printed for the purpose of giving the people who want to do it a chance to help Francis Clark preach Christian Endeavor gospel around the world. He looked proud and pleased at our board meeting yesterday, because he said, "I have had nine thousand dollars for foreign Christian Endeavor this year." Now those of you who are quick in arithmetic divide nine hundred million people into nine thousand dollars and see how much Christian Endeavor believes in the salvation of the world. We gave, last year, nine thousand dollars to carry Christian Endeavor to all the nations overseas, when many of our allied nations in Europe needed Christian Endeavor even more than they needed the bread line. We authorized the United Society to spend twenty thousand dollars next year, and then Dr. Clark said, "Where are we going to get the money?" I decided that you had just as well give it as anybody else, and I suspect you want to do it.

TO LIVE IS CHRIST

By Rev. John Timothy Stone, D.D.

Pastor, Fourth Presbyterian Church, Chicago.

I want to speak from the text, the twenty-first verse of the first chapter of Philippians, "For to me to live is Christ." We have been hearing a good deal to-night about living, and living right, and living right with others, and living right for God. Now in this text, "For me to live is Christ," there are five things. First, *purpose*, for me to live. Why do I live? Opportunity for me. There is *personality* in it. "For me to live." That personality means life. For me to live is. There is *actuality* in it. That single verb with all its meaning means actuality, and last of all is *Christ*.

Now this world asks the question of every Christian, "What is the purpose of your life?" One of the difficulties we are having to face in American life to-day as Christian people is this: that a great share of the criticism of the Christian church is expressed by people who never enter the Christian church. A great many of the editorials that are denouncing Christianity to-day are written by men who never attend church, and who know nothing whatever about the influence of the Christian church personally; and it is all wrong. If my child is sick I do not go to a lawyer to find out what is wrong, and to get a prescription for that child. If my business is complicated, I do not go to a doctor to find out what should be done to satisfy legal obligations in that business, but I seek the physician and I seek the lawyer because the physician knows medicine and the human system, and the lawyer knows law and understands what to do in the regulation of law in business, and it is all wrong for us to take the standard and definition for which the church of God stands from men and women who do not know God. We have done it too long; nine-tenths of those who are criticising the church to-day are those who do not know the church personally and who have no purpose in following the church.

The purpose of a man controls him. Show me what purpose a man or woman has and I will tell you what his life is going to amount to, and for what it stands. Paul always was living under that standard of purpose; he knew not only whom he believed, but he knew he was willing to give all that he had for Jesus Christ. Take that wonderful verse when he wrote to one of the great churches, the church of Ephesus; what did he say? "For this cause I bow my knees unto the Father of our Lord Jesus Christ, of whom the whole family in heaven and earth is named, that he would grant you, according to the riches of his glory to be strengthened with his Spirit in the inner man." What did he say? He said the purpose of a life demonstrates: "for this cause I bow my knees."

Now, men and women, this old world doesn't know God, this old world doesn't know Jesus Christ; tens and hundreds of thousands of children to-day are growing up with no religious instruction and no knowledge of God in their own lives; hence, they do not understand him. If this world is going to know God and is to know Jesus Christ, there must be a purpose in our Christianity for which we sacrifice. A fellow who is a man of the world and cares nothing at all for Christianity said to a group of us the other day, "If I believed what you men say you believe, I would give my last drop of blood to make the world know it; but you are a set of quitters, you live religion as if you had no interest in it at all," and it was a just rebuke.

If you and I are living the Christian life as we ought to, we ought to be interested not only in winning people to Christ, but in tying them up to Christian service after we win them to Christ. You know one of the greatest difficulties we face in the church to-day is this: that the front doors are all lighted with crosses that are brilliant, and there are plenty to invite and to ask others to attend the church, but the back doors of the church, where people are going out, are dark, and there is no illumination, and in many a church it is simply a passage way. People come to the altar, they come into the church, and they go through that church, but they are not tied into active work. A Christian minister who is more interested in the number of people who join his church than he is in setting to work those people who have joined the church and making them soul-winners, and tying them up to Christian activities, is not a minister who will stay long in his parish; and if he does stay he will not be very effective. Something or other is going to affect him. He will be looking for another church, or his wife will lose her health, or something will be the matter just as sure as the world, if he is not tying his people into the work.

The first duty of a Christian minister, in my judgment, is not to win people to Christ. The first duty of a Christian minister is to train his members to be soul-winners. Instead of seeking to do that work himself, his duty is to train them and to train them to do something. We have a motto in our church — "Work for Every One and Every One at Work." You can not make it a hundred per cent, but you can aim toward it. It is tying people into regular activity. You can give a job to every man, you can give certain work to everybody, and you can make that work important. I heard a man say recently, "All I have to do is usher in the church." Usher in the church! Why, do you know our Ushers Association is doing more good work for our church to-day than any other similar organization I know in the church. Forty or fifty men never absent; twenty or twenty-five in the morning, and fifteen in the afternoon, and twenty in the evening, different men, always there. I have known men to come as far as from Eighty-Third Street, on the South Side, and they are always there on time. It is only the people that live near the church that are late. We have a long church in the way of aisles, and it is difficult to get the people up front. One usher will say, "Yes, just come on this way," and he passes the visitor to a second usher, and he is up front before he knows it. Ushering is not an easy job; it is a very difficult job if it is done well, but it is only one among a great many other things in winning men to Christ. This is a city of insurance; it is one of the great insurance centres of the United States and the world. Do you suppose general agents in this city ever write insurance simply by trying to do all the work themselves? There are a lot of ministers who are so versatile that they are practically powerless. A minister who will try to do all the work himself, or a church officer, or a young people's secretary, who will try to do all the work himself is not doing the work which should be done for "Him"; it is not simply your own task, it is a personal task with others. We must put other people to work, and the great difficulty is that so many people do so many things fairly well that they do not do anything very well, and there are too many jack-of-all-trades in the church to-day who are simply willing to do anything, but they do not do any one thing better than anybody else.

Now for me to live this life with its thrill is not only the spirit of the Golden Rule; it is living that Golden Rule. Mr. Wolf tells a wonderful story of the pickets and peasantry before the war in Russia. He says one bleak night in November a peasant was going home with his large wheel vehicle and his heavy fetlock horse, and the sleet was beating in his face and here was a picket out there that bleak day trembling hand and limb, worn out, hating all the peasants. As this peasant came along with his overcoat buttoned up around his neck, he saw that picket shaking and trembling in the wind and in the storm, and before he knew it he jumped off the old cart and pulled off his overcoat, and put it around that picket's shoulders. He said: "Man, I can keep warm, but you are going to be here all night. You take my coat." The man who was filled with hate and bitterness toward the peasantry did not know what had happened, but all he saw was a man beating his arms, in an opposite way from what you and I want to do to-night, and disappearing in the distance. He said to the man as he left, "I can keep warm," but he didn't. A cold set in when he got home, then pneumonia, and he died. He was a Christian man, humble as he was. Just before he died he called his wife and his little children over to his bedside and he said, "Mother, you know I don't have dreams, but I have had a dream to-night. I am going to die, and, mother, I saw Jesus Christ on His throne, and Jesus came down from his throne, and He came to me and He called me by name; He took my hand and He welcomed me, and, mother, He had on my old gray overcoat."

When this world sees Jesus Christ living in the sacrifice of our service, —for me to live is Christ—the world is going to believe in Him, and not until then.

We have a man in Chicago who was converted a good many years ago in the city of Cleveland. Some years ago he was a bowery saloon-keeper. He did not know what Christianity was. I remember the first time I saw him was at Northfield, at one of the student conferences. Mr.

Clay of the Fifth Avenue Church in New York sent him up to that student conference. He wanted him to get some vital religion. It was a hot day. He took off his coat, and he had on a very bright pair of red suspenders. The college boys thought he was peculiar. After a time he got acquainted with the boys, and he had a wonderful knowledge of Scripture, and he learned more and more. He is the chaplain of our jail, the Bridwell, in Chicago, and has been for ten years. I love to hear him speak. His language isn't always the best, but do you know I once heard one of our greatest newspaper men in the United States say that it was Mr. Moody with his poor language that started him; he selected him in an audience one night, and pointing down to him, and, calling him by his first name, said, "My boy, isn't it time that you started for Jesus Christ?" And that newspaper man has said that the thrill of that invitation and that personal suggestion, the actuality of it, the meaning of Christianity got into his soul, and it has made him the great philanthropist that he is to-day.

Every time Baldwin speaks he says something like this: "Men, women, this religion of Jesus Christ is real, it is real; I know; it saved me, it is real."

For me to live is Christ. Yes, but Jesus Christ in this world is the one who will solve every problem. I thought to-night when Dr. Landrith was speaking that if the whole world could see Jesus how the whole problem would be solved. I believe in peace and international peace, but I am here to say there never will be any international peace that will last, no matter what agencies may be at work, until the gospel of Jesus Christ teaches men what peace is. There can be no permanent peace until those of us who know Jesus Christ preach the gospel of peace and reveal the Golden Rule in our daily living, and with this illustration I am through: all the world needs is to see Jesus Christ, and they must see him in your life and see him in my life. The world will never believe the emblem of the cross, wonderful as it is, until it sees Jesus Christ in us, in human flesh and blood.

They were having their fiftieth reunion at Yale. It was the largest fiftieth-year class they had ever had back in their alumni. An old gray-haired man with long beard came in and stood before the table where these fifty-year men were having their class reunion. One nudged another and said, "Who is this man?" And another said, "Who is he, anyway?" Then they said, "We don't know you. We know you are one of the class or you wouldn't be here," and then an intelligent and thoughtful alumnus of Yale said, "Say, friend, tell us who you are. We love every man in the class, and we know you are one of the class. Tell us who you are."

The old man didn't say a word. He just turned around and opened a door and said, "Come in, John." The old man's trousers were baggy, his coat shiny, he wore a little worn-out white tie, and his beard was uncut. When John came in he had a fine, late tailor-made suit, his socks matched his necktie, and everything just as it should be in a modern lad. He stood there, and the old fellow said, "John, smile for the boys, will you?" John smiled and the crowd went wild. They said, "It is old Bill, it is old Bill." Old Bill had been the most popular man in the class; for forty-seven years he had been preaching in a little Congregational church out in Utah. He had never got back to New Haven; they had never seen him since, but when they saw that son John smile, they knew the father, and every one listened to Bill that night; the New York bankers had no influence over that Yale crowd. It was old Bill that held sway.

Young people, this old world doesn't know God, and this old world is longing to know God. The wickedest man and the vilest woman want to know God, and they know him more than we know it, but they don't see him. They don't know Him; they think he hates them. The heathen world have made the most atrocious idols, because they are afraid of God and fear that God is denouncing them. The world doesn't know God, but mark you, when the world sees the smile of the Son they will know God. The world will say, "God, what must I do to be saved?"

MR. SHARTLE: Before we close this meeting there is one

other matter. When I opened the meeting I said this was going to be a Golden Rule meeting, and now we have a Golden Rule resolution to be read by Dr. Frank Lowe, Jr.

The Golden Rule in Industry

We rejoice to see a growing spirit of partnership between employer and employee, and an increasing desire on all hands to follow in business relationships the spirit of the Golden Rule. We rejoice in the development of conscience in industry, and in the fact that to-day less than ever before in history does either employer or employee wish to stand on the opposite side of any labor question than that on which they honestly believe Jesus Christ would stand, were He among us. We believe that the law of brotherhood and love and generous dealing alone contains the solution of labor problems. Christian Endeavor stands for this law. It teaches no economic theory, but seeks to make grow in the hearts of men the kindliness of Jesus Christ. Standing on the Golden Rule it urges generous and full service on the part of the worker, and on the part of the employer a reward that will mean not merely a living-wage, but comfort and the ability to save for the future. We believe that only that specific code of economic programme can live and endure which is fertilized by the laws of Christ, and one of the biggest tasks of the Christian Endeavor movement is to bring the spirit of these laws to the youth of to-day, that the men of to-morrow may translate them into a programme of constructive action.

The resolution was adopted unanimously and this memorable meeting closed by singing "America."

CHAPTER XII

DENOMINATIONAL RALLIES

SATURDAY MORNING, JULY 7

United Brethren (Old Constitution)

In a short discussion by those present at the rally the fact was made known that the endeavor work in the denomination is growing rapidly. Especially is this true in the field of Junior Endeavor, of Life Work Recruits, and of Comrades of the Quiet Hour.

The general secretary has just completed a tour of the Pacific coast district, and reports everything on the increase. Many new societies have recently been organized; a district convention was held, covering the States of California, Oregon, Washington, Idaho, and Utah. This association of conferences will make the holding of this convention an annual feature.

The general supervision committee of the Endeavor work of church has the plans all laid to begin the publication of a new Christian Endeavor paper to be called *The United Brethren Magnet*.

In response to a cordial invitation from the other branch of the United Brethren a part of their programme and a fine luncheon were enjoyed with them.

Friends

The Des Moines Friends' Meeting and Christian Endeavor society were gracious hosts to the Friends in their rally.

About two hundred and seventy-five Friends, representing the New England, New York, Wilmington, Indiana, Iowa, Nebraska, Kansas, Oregon and California, Yearly Meetings, were present. With Helen E. Hawkins, executive secretary of the Board of Young Friends' Activities of the Five Years' Meeting, presiding the meeting was opened by a period of worship, after which Helen Hawkins placed before the delegates for consideration these three thoughts: How can we best play our part in the great Christian Endeavor "Friends-of-Christ" campaign for 1923-1925? Is there a "Quaker message" at the present time? Christ for the youth of to-day and youth as flaming evangels for Christ.

Howard Cope, of Iowa, spoke on "The Challenge of the 1923

Convention," emphasizing depth of spiritual experience and the Christian love and unity in the church universal.

Gladys Smith, of Iowa, a missionary to Jamaica, brought a message concerning the way our nearest territorial neighbors regard "Christian" America, touching such problems as race prejudice and hatred and social morality.

Alfred Smith, of Nebraska, called attention to the vast frontiers of the West where for hundreds of square miles the message of Christ is little known.

There then followed a general discussion of problems, after which Frederick J. Libby, of Washington, D. C., appealed for the whole-hearted devotion and support of Friends' Christian Endeavorers in the cause for the outlawry of war in the next ten years.

Presbyterian Church in the United States

The rally of the Presbyterian Church in the United States was held in the banquet room of the Y. M. C. A., and was led by Dr. R. F. Kirkpatrick, pastor of the Presbyterian church of Anderson, S. C., and Duncan B. Curry, chairman of the young people's work in the synod of Florida.

Practically the whole Southern Presbyterian Church was represented, among those present being the following:

Paul W. Rawlings, president of the North Carolina union; Clyde Underhill, president of the Georgia union; Mrs. Charles S. Long, Texas; James Wray, missionary to Mexico; Huberta Lippard, Texas; Isabel A. McDougall, North Carolina; W. H. Williams, Arkansas; Emma Archer, Arkansas; Florence Collins, Alabama; Henry Meyer, Tennessee; Mrs. Nora G. Myer, Tennessee; Lavinia Shepardson, Tennessee; Henry Meyer, Jr., Tennessee; Clara Beadle, Arkansas State secretary; Gerald Harris, vice-president of the Louisiana union; Mamie Gene Cole, Junior field-secretary; Homer W. Fulwider, president of the Mississippi union; Mrs. W. H. Howell, State Junior superintendent, North Carolina; Mrs. W. W. Crofoot, Texas; Dr. R. F. Kirkpatrick, vice-chairman of the All-South Extension Committee, South Carolina; M. E. Boland, Washington, D. C.; Eunice Long, State secretary of North Carolina; Lulu V. Tatum, South Carolina; A. Clinton Decker, Alabama; Vera Thomas, Alabama; M. Jean Miller, Oklahoma; Marion Pinner, Oklahoma; F. B. Porter; Texas; Mrs. F. B. Porter, Texas; Emma Hutaff, North Carolina; Mary Chitton Tyson, Alabama; J. C. Hall, president of the Arkansas union; J. A. Flanagan, president of the South Carolina union; M. E. Deibert, president of the Virginia union.

Every delegate present was encouraged to bring before the conference any problems or any especially strong features of any work among the young people. Definite responsibility for the Christian Endeavorer's share of the home and foreign missionary programme of the church was emphasized by a number of speakers.

Close co-operation of local societies and all unions with our denominational agencies was emphasized and discussed at considerable length. It was distinctly the sense of the conference that there should be an active and hearty co-operation on the part of the various synods and presbyteries in handling the denominational programmes at State and district conventions. Looking to this end, a resolution was adopted requesting each synod to elect a pastoral counsellor who should be responsible for the presentation of the denominational programme at the denominational rally in the respective State conventions. It is hoped furthermore to have a similar counsellor appointed by each presbytery to plan and direct the denominational rallies in all district conventions. It was the unanimous feeling of the delegates present that the societies represented by them are anxious to comply in every way with the requirements of the denomination and desire a fuller measure of guidance from their denominational leaders.

The Presbyterian progressive programme was discussed, and it was discovered that in the carrying out of this programme the two years' campaign of the United Society, as announced by Dr. Clark, will be covered in a very wonderful way. This was felt to be a most happy coincidence.

United Presbyterians

A very interesting meeting was held in the Central Christian Church, presided over by Rev. James A. Cosby, Ellwood City, Penn., general secretary of young people's work of the denomination.

For the devotional part of the meeting each person present repeated from memory a verse of Scripture; two Psalms were sung without books; and several prayers were offered.

Three missionaries were present: Miss Rose Minteer, of Egypt; and the Misses Josephine Martin and Kate A. Hill, of India. Each gave an interesting talk, the first two telling of Christian Endeavor in their fields.

The chairman gave a few facts from his annual report as general secretary. He told of eleven Senior and six Intermediate societies, one hundred per cent of whose members are pledged to pay the tithe; and 120 societies reported that from fifty to ninety-nine per cent of their members were tithers. A little more than one-half of the total contributions last year of the societies was given to missions.

Miss Edith McDonald, superintendent of Intermediate Christian Endeavor work in California, and Mr. John Purdum, Nampa, Ida., who had won a free trip by securing subscriptions to THE CHRISTIAN ENDEAVOR WORLD, travelled the farthest to attend the Des Moines Convention.

Disciples of Christ

The Disciples of Christ delegation accepted the kind hospitality of the University Place Church of Christ and its minister, Rev. Dr. Charles S. Medbury.

Mr. Matheson, the assistant pastor, called the meeting to order. Professor Alfred Smith, the local director, led the singing.

Heart-searching devotional services were conducted by Rev. W. A. Shullenberger, of the Central Church of Christ.

H. L. Pickerill, superintendent of young people's work under the United Christian Missionary Society, was presented as master of further ceremonies. The entire group was introduced by States, twenty-four different delegations standing.

Southern Secretary, C. F. Evans, general secretary of All-South Christian Endeavor, spoke from the viewpoint of a worker in union ranks.

Miss Adeline Goddard, of Oklahoma, at one time a national Christian Endeavor superintendent, brought a brief message in behalf of the field force and a programme for young people's work.

Mr. Vance, the new office man in the promotional department of the United Christian Missionary Society, and Miss Clark, of Des Moines, who will enter the missionary education department August 1, were presented to the young people.

An explanation of the plan and purposes of the Pocket Testament League was given by Mrs. Mary E. Furbish, superintendent of religious education in Kansas.

Various Disciple leaders of young people's work were requested to stand and be introduced.

Five simultaneous conferences were held: Junior, Miss Nora Darnall leading; Intermediate leaders, Mr. H. L. Pickerill, leader; Intermediates, led by Miss Adeline Goddard; Seniors and Young People, led by Mrs. Mary E. Furbish; and one for leaders of Seniors, in charge of Glenn McRae. After re-assembling Miss Miller rendered a solo.

Donald McGavran, under appointment for service in India, in an address on "The Challenge of Christ" brought a tremendous appeal to his listeners.

Dr. C. S. Medbury, a member of the executive committee of the United Christian Missionary Society, made a plea for loyalty to God, and urged each Christian Endeavorer "to live everywhere each day."

The young people of the Des Moines churches were hosts for a delightful picnic lunch on the campus of Drake University.

The Christian Church

The rally of the Christian Church was held at the Central Church of Christ, Dr. A. B. Kendall, of Springfield; O., presiding. About 150 were in attendance. Dr. F. T. Coffin spoke on the theme, "Our Part in the New Christian Education Programme of Our Church"; Dr. L. E. Follansbee on "Building the Young Life into the Church"; Rev. J. M. Kauffman, of Iowa, on "Vital Evangelism"; and Dr. Kendall on "A Look Ahead."

One of the very interesting features of the conference was the singing of a song, "Endeavorers for Jesus," composed by Dr. Kendall. It was adopted as the Christian Endeavor song for the Christian Endeavorers of the Christian Church.

The addresses were all of a high type, and the fellowship of the after-meeting was a means of getting the delegates from the various States acquainted.

This was pronounced by many the best rally ever held by the Christian Church at an interdenominational conference.

The Mennonites

The Mennonite conference was led by O. F. Gilliom, of Berne, Ind., former president of that State and now trustee of the United Society, who conducted the devotional services.

Although the Mennonites are scattered all over the United States and many of the European countries, those attending this conference were principally from Kansas and Iowa.

Talks were made by various members present, showing that among the thirteen branches of Mennonites now existing there is a large field of work to be done especially through Christian Endeavor.

The chief reasons for Christian Endeavor's not having flourished as it should in this denomination were analyzed as follows:

1. Lack of information about Christian Endeavor among the church-leaders, who are mostly older men.
2. Lack of co-operation among the various branches of the denomination.
3. Failure on the part of the denomination to co-operate closely with the State and national organization of Christian Endeavor.

The leader showed that one of the largest Christian Endeavor societies in the United States is a Mennonite society of more than four hundred active members and an Intermediate society of one hundred and fifty members in the same church.

Rev. R. P. Anderson, of the United Society, was present, and gave a splendid talk on the spiritual life of the individual as it relates to his own denomination and Christian Endeavor.

The meeting was greatly enjoyed by all, and was dismissed with prayer.

The Congregational Rally

Close to five hundred Congregationalists gathered at Plymouth Church for the consideration of interests primarily denominational. The roll-call indicated that about eighty per cent came from Iowa.

Rev. Royal J. Montgomery, director of Congregational young people's work for Iowa, presided. Prayer was offered by Rev. Charles J. Christianson, of Grand Island, Neb. Several of the leaders present were then introduced.

A feature which proved to be popular was a series of four addresses by young people who are leaders in their home societies. Miss Cunningham, of the Waveland Church, Chicago, outlined the ways in which young people can relate themselves helpfully to the church school. Douglass Orr, of Lincoln, Neb., grandson of the greatly beloved Dr. T. O. Douglass, for twenty-five years superintendent of the Iowa Conference, showed by his treatment of the theme "Young People Sharing in the Programme of the Home Church" that both by study and by practice he was qualified to speak effectively.

Robert Goodwin, of Plymouth Church, Des Moines, one of the outstanding leaders in the Christian work of West High, spoke out of a fine background of experience on what young people can do toward shaping community standards. Miss Irene Dewey, of Ames, herself a Student Volunteer and a leader in Iowa State College Christian activities, set forth the guiding principles which a Christian should follow in choosing a life-work.

Rev. Ralph Harlow, of Smyrna, Turkey, gave some of the outstanding contributions which Congregational young people can make in the great missionary enterprise, emphasizing especially intellectual freedom in the building of faith.

Secretary Robert W. Gammon, of the Congregational Education Society, outlined some of the most significant forms of service possible for young people in the local church. He has a strong conviction that to the young people who loyally stand by the work of the home church should be given more glory than they generally receive. He appealed to the young people strongly to stand by their pastors.

Rev. Wayne L. Waters, of Des Moines, chairman of the Iowa Conference committee on religious education and young people's work, challenged the audience to the attainment of as great an enthusiasm for the Christian programme as they manifest in national patriotism. He also outlined some of the ways in which our young people are being built into the denominational programme, and assured them that our aim is to give them a still larger place.

Rev. Edward W. Cross, of Grinnell, always a favorite with Iowa young people, set forth the appeal of Christian life-service. Out of his own experience as a Christian minister he brought forth what seemed to him to be the most commanding elements of the appeal of the leadership of the Christian programme. It was all made doubly challenging by the evident joy of the speaker in his own service.

One of the most inspiring features of the rally was the message brought Dr. Clark on behalf of the United Society. Referring to the Congregational ancestry of himself and Mrs. Clark,

Des Moines Group

he went on to trace briefly the relationship of Congregationalism to the Christian Endeavor movement and to express the hope that his own denomination would find Christian Endeavor of still greater service in the years to come.

From across the sea came another great Congregationalist with a rousing indorsement of Christian Endeavor, the president of the British Christian Endeavor Union, Rev. Lionel Fletcher, one of the strongest of the Convention speakers, also, until recently, the pastor of the largest Congregational church in Britain. It was indeed a heartening word which he brought, especially in line with the evangelistic goals being established by the United Society.

The closing address was given by the leader of Congregational work among the colored people in home-missions areas, Rev. Harold M. Kingsley, of Cleveland, O. In spite of heat and the weariness resulting from a long programme, there was no disposition to leave until he had spoken his last word. With characteristic frankness and good humor he appealed for a square deal with the Negro, for sympathetic co-operation and for patience. There was no question that his audience was with him.

Rev. John Gonzales, of Kansas, pronounced the benediction.

The Congregational rally served to emphasize the fact that the churches are moving forward to a better day in their Christian Endeavor work. More and more it is being recognized that our young people are an asset and not a liability. To the conservation of these resources there is a challenge in a great Christian Endeavor history and enlarging opportunities.

Primitive Methodists

At the Primitive Methodist rally it was resolved:

First, That we express our disappointment at the small representation of Primitive Methodists at this Convention, and feel that it is a distinct loss to Primitive Methodism in general and to the individual in particular.

Second, Be it further resolved, That we urge every Primitive Methodist church in America to organize a Christian Endeavor society at once where there is none, and that every society already established do its utmost to extend its influence and usefulness, by adopting and seeking to bring to its final consummation the programme proposed by our worthy founder and president, Dr. Clark, the "Friends-of-Christ Campaign."

Third, It was further resolved that the general committee of the Primitive Methodist General Conference be asked to appoint a special committee to push forward this "Friends-of-Christ Campaign" in our churches.

Fourth, RESOLVED, That a copy of these resolutions be forwarded to *The Primitive Methodist Journal*, THE CHRISTIAN ENDEAVOR WORLD, and pastors of Primitive Methodist churches.

United Brethren

The United Brethren rally was held at the St. Andrew's United Brethren Church.

The one hundred and seventy-five delegates, from twelve States, were joined by two delegates representing the United Brethren Church, Old Constitution. This is the largest representation of United Brethren Christian Endeavorers ever in attendance at an International Convention.

Rev. O. T. Deever, general secretary of the department of young people's work of the denomination, presided. Rev. Leslie Whitesell, of Lexington, Ill., president of the Illinois United Brethren Conference Christian Endeavor Union, led the singing. Rev. G. W. Emerson, president of the Iowa United Brethren Conference Christian Endeavor Union and a member of the local entertaining committee of the Convention, made helpful suggestions for conserving the benefits of the Convention.

Rev. T. A. Tripp, of the Oklahoma Conference; Miss Pearl M. Parks, of Minnesota; Rev. J. D. Good, of Pennsylvania; Miss Myrtle Lefever, general Junior and Intermediate superintendent of the denomination; Rev. H. F. Shupe, D. D., editor of *The Watchword;* Rev. W. O. Jones, president of York College, York, Neb.; Dean C. E. Ashcroft, of York College; Rev. I. H. Mohler, of Porto Rico; and Secretary O. T. Deever made short addresses. Others announced their names and the positions in Christian Endeavor work.

One hundred and fifty of the Endeavorers lunched together in the basement of the church. At the luncheon strong resolutions were adopted commending the splendid work of the United Society of Christian Endeavor, emphasizing and heartily approving the new "Friends-of-Christ" campaign, and urging the necessity for greater efforts along Junior and Intermediate lines of work.

A fine spirit of fellowship prevailed, and all departed with a determination to push the cause with new vigor.

Lutherans

The Lutheran rally was held in St. John's Lutheran Church, of which Rev. A. B. Leamer is pastor, and Rev. I. W. Bingaman presided. Only about thirty were present, but all took part. Pennsylvania, Maryland, New Mexico, Texas, California, Illinois, and Missouri were represented. Rev. Mr. Bingaman responded to the pastor's well chosen words of welcome. Nearly all the societies are emphasizing mission work in some form. Some support missionaries; others do hospital work and also minister to the orphans and shut-ins; and others carry on fresh-air work. Rev. A. B. Knudsen, of Albuquerque, N. M., the pastor of the only English Lutheran church in New Mexico, spoke of conditions there. Members of his society hold responsible positions and take charge of the midweek prayer meeting. Rev. A. B. Knudsen, of Albuquerque, N. M., was chosen president for the rest of the year and Miss Clara Dohme, of Baltimore, Md., secretary and treasurer.

Methodist Protestants

Thirty-six delegates were present, representing societies in Connecticut, Illinois, Iowa, Kansas, Maryland, Missouri, New Jersey, and Ohio.

Rev. G. W. Haddaway, D. D., of Maryland, presided, and talked about "The Church of To-morrow."

A few minutes were spent in getting acquainted, the delegates arising by State groups and telling their names and the names of their home churches.

Rev. J. N. Link, of Maryland, talked about "Putting the Programme Across in the Rural Church."

Rev. E. A. Sexsmith, secretary of young people's work of the Methodist Protestant Church, spoke of the educational programme he is formulating, and laid stress on the fact that the young people's union of every conference in the Methodist Protestant church ought to have a summer institute.

It was an impressive moment when every delegate present, with right hand uplifted, took the pledge, "By the help of God we will help to put over this bigger programme."

An open discussion of denominational needs followed the address of the secretary.

Short talks were made by Rev. R. Underwood, of Harmony, Md., and Rev. Mr. Butterfield, of Osceola, Io.

The Churches of God

The conference was conducted by Rev. F. H. Snavely, Christian Endeavor secretary for the Churches of God of Ohio, in the absence of the denominational trustee, Rev. T. M. Funk.

The programme consisted of the following addresses: "Our Junior Work," by Miss Ella Martin, Shippensburg, Penn.; "Our Intermediate Work," by Mr. J. G. McDonald, Harrisburg, Penn.; "Our Senior Work," by Miss Eva McCauly, Fort Wayne, Ind.; "Our Graded Work," by Rev. F. H. Snavely, Smithville, O.; "Our Work till 1925," by Rev. C. C. Crisman, Martinsville, Ill.

The splendid addresses and the gratifying reports of increased activities, along with the increased attendance of Church of God delegates, caused the conference to adopt the following resolutions:

1. That our slogan of the last two years, "Every Church a Christian Endeavor Church," be our slogan for the next two years, with the addition of one word to make it read, "Every

Church a Graded Christian Endeavor Church." 2. That our goal of Church of God delegates to the next International Convention be a one-hundred-per-cent increase.

The conference concluded with get-acquainted greetings and a special luncheon for the group.

The Reformed Church in the United States

A splendid fellowship was enjoyed, and many worth while subjects were discussed, at the denominational rally of the Reformed Church in the United States. Greetings and expressions of regrets were sent to Miss Catherine A. Miller, the much loved Secretary of the Young People's Department, who was unable to be present because of illness. That Miss Miller is serving our young people well is indicated by the general acceptance of her plans and suggestions, and by her universal popularity on the field.

Rev. Gustav R. Poetter, Reading, Penn., gave an informing and inspiring talk on "Reformed What." He emphasized the fact that since the church has come to its present place and power, partly at least because of its interdenominational spirit and world vision, we are challenged to continue along those lines. He pointed out that this attitude is peculiarly favorable to the promotion and development of Christian Endeavor.

Rev. John S. Adam, Silver Run, Md., told in interesting fashion the story of the Children's Christian Education Foundation, and urged all churches to co-operate in the promotion of the plan.

Rev. T. L. Heffley, Lincoln, Neb., presented "The Way," emphasizing the value of the various departments and urging its general use.

Alvin J. Shartle, Treasurer and Publication Manager of the United Society of Christian Endeavor, Boston, presented "The Programme and Policy for Reformed Church Young People." He commended the work of Miss Miller and expressed satisfaction with the developing program of the Young People's Department. He also expressed the hope that soon a series of summer conferences for Reformed Young People would be established.

Clarence C. Hamilton, Field-Secretary of the United Society of Christian Endeavor and Field-Manager of THE CHRISTIAN ENDEAVOR WORLD pointed out the value of a greater denominational consciousness among our young people. He suggested the need of more denominational education, and challenged all present to see to it that their churches follow the plan of mission study this year; the Hungarian people in America to be studied this fall, and Japan after the first of the year. "Joy from Japan," a book by Miss Catherine Miller, just off the press, will prove a great asset to the workers.

Mr. Hamilton then presented the following subjects and led an informal discussion on each subject: "The Christian Home Friendship;" "Graded Christian Endeavor;" "Co-operation with

Other Agencies in the Church Having to Do with the Educational Programme;" and the "Friends of Christ Campaign" the new two-year programme of Christian Endeavor outlined by Dr. Clark.

Represented in the conference were one or more delegates from the following States: Iowa, Nebraska, Kansas, Ohio, District of Columbia, Maryland, Pennsylvania, Indiana, and Massachusetts.

A. M. E. AND A. M. E. ZION RALLY

The denominational conference under the auspices of the A. M. E. and A. M. E. Zion churches brought together a group of leaders in young people's work. The number attending the rally was augmented by colored delegates of the Baptist Church.

Professor Aaron Brown, General Secretary of Christian Endeavor A. M. E. Zion Church, presided, assisted by Rev. S. S. Morris, General Secretary of Christian Endeavor A. M. E. Church and an interesting programme was gone through.

At roll-call each delegate announced name and address, and quoted a verse of scripture.

Rev. J. F. Fisher delivered an address on "Young People and Missions, and Dr. M. E. Davis spoke on "Leadership Training." Mrs. Anna T. Owens spoke on "Young People and Denominational Co-operation," and "Methods and Goals" was the subject chosen by Professor Aaron Brown and Dr. S. S. Morris. Dr. T. J. Moppins spoke on "Young People and Amusements." Bishop A. J. Carey and Bishop L. W. Kyles also addressed the rally. Luncheon was served by the A. M. E. Zion Church (Kyles' Temple).

THE EVANGELICAL RALLY

More than one hundred persons attended the Evangelical rally which was held in the First Evangelical Church. This was the first gathering of the sort held since the organization of the united Church, which occurred in October, 1922. Rev. E. W. Praetorius, the General Secretary of the Young People's Work of the church, presided, and introduced the various speakers in a pleasing manner. Rev. C. H. Stuffacher, one of the missionary secretaries of the church, spoke on evangelism, pointing out the splendid opportunities which exist in connection with the plans of the General Managing Board. Mr. Stanley B. Vandersall, of the United Society of Christian Endeavor, described the "Friends of Christ" campaign and the relationship which the young people of the church may well have to this movement in Christian Endeavor. Rev. R. L. Karney told of the opportunities for denominational development. Other speakers included Miss Martha

Hake, a missionary under appointment to China, Miss Lottie Arnold, a teacher in the Kentucky Mission, and Rev. Thomas Evans.

Following the rally, a picture was taken on the steps of the capitol, and a social time and the noon day meal were enjoyed at the Capitol Cafeteria. The gathering was marked because of the establishment of many new friendships on the part of the representatives of the united branches of the church.

Presbyterian, U. S. A.

The Presbyterian, U. S. A., rally was held in the Central Congregational Church, with Rev. William Ralph Hall presiding. A large group of young people assembled and many pastors and leaders of young people's work were present.

The plans and programme of the New Friends of Christ Campaign were outlined and discussed in a striking way, bringing both information and inspiration to the audience.

After the rally luncheon was served in the church, which entertained the delegates right royally. A pleasant social time was spent, and a brief after-dinner programme was greatly enjoyed.

Chapter XIII

THE PARADE

Saturday Evening, July 7

We saw the great Christian Endeavor parade down Fifth Avenue, New York, two years ago. It was a magnificent affair, but the Christian Endeavor parade in Des Moines was every bit as interesting and impressive. It was a splendid exhibition of Christian Endeavor enthusiasm, inventiveness, beauty, and manliness. It was fully sixteen city blocks long, and we do not know how many thousands were in line, certainly ten thousand, very likely fifteen thousand. It was more varied even than the New York parade, and no more varied parade had been seen in the world before. Probably the Christian Endeavor parade in Portland, '25, will contain many new features, for the Endeavorers are endlessly skilful in devising pictorial appeals as well as appeals through the ear.

The lovely and elevated grounds surrounding Iowa's splendid capitol were covered with groups of Endeavorers in brilliant costumes, every one of them a delight with the gracefulness of youth and its exuberance of zest. The long line formed east of the capitol, marched around the south side, down Walnut Street into the heart of the city, crossed over to Locust Street, and eastward again to the Coliseum and across the bridge, disbanding on the eastern side of the river. Boy Scouts with poles guarded the street corners.

The long march was vocal with the ringing songs of the Endeavorers, brisk, sweet, joyous, sometimes patriotic, sometimes humorous, sometimes the great songs of the church.

The uniforms were simple but exceedingly charming and effective. There were the Connecticut girls attired in quaint blue and white checked dresses and big blue sunbonnets. The big New Jersey crowd, Mr. Sproull prominent among them, were brilliant with orange sweaters and coats, "N. J." carried on them in big black letters. The fine New York delegation swung along led by Father Knickerbocker, escorting an automobile that bore a young woman representing "Liberty Enlightening the World." Maryland wore black and orange caps, while Massachusetts was impressive with blue caps of Continental cut. Texas carried in the centre of its group five staffs bearing at the top five big red outline letters, T-E-X-A-S. The rest of the Southwestern union

—Oklahoma, Arizona, Wyoming, Utah, New Mexico, Texas—carried white sunshades with the Christian Endeavor monogram upon them. Colorado Endeavorers had interesting headbands: colORado printed on them, the OR making a peak.

It is especially interesting to know that Oklahoma headed the procession of States because it was first to complete its quota for preregistration to the Convention; and Utah, Arizona, and Wyoming followed because they also completed their quota, and in this regard these four southwestern States stand alone. All honor to their enterprise and zeal!

District of Columbia Endeavorers were accompanied by a capital Uncle Sam and a charming Columbia. The colored societies of the District bore a banner reminding us that "One is your Master, even Christ, and all ye are brethren." The goodly Pennsylvania company bore a great Keystone banner, and wore red and white bands with gold lettering. Virginia carried a big red banner, and all Dixie Endeavorers were distinguished by the big red fez which has become a tradition. "Hail, hail, the gang's all here" was a frequent song of this tuneful regiment.

California's fine company wore purple bands over white garments, with gorgeous paper hats representing the yellow California poppies. The Minnesota delegation were unique with the two great strings of fishes they carried and their banner: "The Home of Volstead. We're with him." They also had a banner, "10,000 lakes, 10,000 Endeavorers."

A Wisconsin banner asserted, "Wisconsin stands for law-enforcement." These Endeavorers wore bright red feathers on their heads. The Michigan crowd had big farm straw hats. The large Kansas delegation was brilliant with yellow hats and sunflowers on their coats, while they indulged in many cheers. Ohio's splendid crowd wore purple caps marked "C. E.," and carried staffs with long tassels of purple and yellow. Illinois was brightly led by a girl cornetist leading their singing. They wore red capes and carried big red balloons. Chicago had a notable delegation whose song was "Chicago will shine to-night."

"Missouri, the heart of the country" carried big red pasteboard hearts on sticks that lifted them over their heads. Indiana, Nebraska, Oregon,—how the marchers shone in the splendor of their Christian devotion! "Miss Portland," a beautiful young woman in a prettily decorated automobile, reminded us of our next meeting-place. A placard that touched the heart of every spectator promised us cool nights for sleep when we should get there.

The superb marching hosts of Iowa aroused great enthusiasm. "Horace Greeley meant Iowa" one banner read. "Ioway" was the favorite song, and went with a swing along the whole line. "Law not War" was a motto worn by many. The Des Moines Endeavorers wore blue and white caps. They marched by churches. There was a goodly group of Epworth Leaguers and

United Society Officers in the Lead

Christian Endeavor Parade

MINNESOTA DELEGATION

ILLINOIS APPROACHING

A Feature in the Parade

another of B. Y. P. U.'s. Many Junior Endeavorers marched proudly with Des Moines. A company of about twenty Endeavorers carried the banner, "The Youngest of the Bunch, organized July 1, 1923." Another society informed the spectators that they were only one year old. Still another announced that the advance registration of that society for the Convention was 320%. Other Endeavorers carried in their arms sheaves of wheat. Others carried wire arches which reached across the street, and many red and white ribbons fluttered from them. One banner read, "Des Moines, the City of CErtainties." Another read: "Can you pray? Join the Comrades of the Quiet Hour in daily devotion." A host of Des Moines Endeavorers spelled out "For Christ and the Church" in great capital letters cut out and borne aloft, one letter to a delegation, the motto thus strung out along an entire block. Two ancient buggies were driven along, bearing signs showing that they had been on the road, like Christian Endeavor, for forty-two years. Some of the Iowa Endeavorers carried great, full ears of corn fastened to red-and-white sticks.

The long procession was headed by a police escort. Then by World War veterans, most of them medalled men. Then by the Des Moines Convention Committee headed by Judge Utterback, then by Dr. and Mrs. Clark in an automobile, then by the United Society officers marching in a street-wide line, Landrith in the centre, the big man with the comically little sunshade. Then followed the ten thousand Endeavorers. There were inspiring bands at intervals, including the drum corps of the Oregon Post, American Legion, a band of the Salvation Army, and an interesting Negro band, "the Community Service Band." The delegation from Des Moines that closed the parade was a company of forty clad in bright red shirts. They were the Endeavorers that went to Chicago in 1915 and to New York in 1921, and who, we all hope, will be a bright feature of the parade to which now we all look forward, that will march through the streets of Portland in 1925.

Chapter XIV

THE LEAGUE OF NATIONS
Coliseum
Saturday Evening, July 7
Rev. Daniel A. Poling, D. D., Presiding

Kansas was in evidence—Kansas, "where the tall corn grows"—and many other States, in the Saturday evening meeting. Dr. Daniel A. Poling presided, the first part of the programme being in charge of Professor H. Augustine Smith.

First came a series of stereopticon pictures of the life of Christ, the audience singing familiar hymns connected with the story. Solo singing was also introduced while the pictures were on the screen. The pictures were reproduced from masterpieces of religious art found in the galleries of Europe and America, and were beautifully colored.

The first address was delivered by Rev. Ralph Harlow, from Smyrna, Syria, who has been on the firing-line in the turbulent Near East. He opened with a beautiful tribute to Christian Endeavor, to which he said he owed his inspiration and his vision of missionary work.

WAR, PEACE, AND THE NEAR EAST
By Ralph Harlow

Whether you will agree with what I say to-night or not, I am not sure. I ask that God be with me and that I may try not to please you but to please Him according to my conscience. The other day I was in New York City speaking in a fashionable hotel, and a woman asked me if I was a German spy because I had been advocating feeding the German children. Another day in Boston a man said I was a Britisher. I said that I didn't feel insulted at the remark for years ago my ancestors were, and I am proud of all the British blood I have inherited, but that I happened to be American born and bred.

In a certain charge during the war in which one of our battalions had paid heavily in life for a gain of a few yards, a young officer coming up over the field and seeing the dead and dying said, "What a pity that these men had to give their lives for these few yards of earth!"

A young officer who had been in that charge turned to him and said, "Not for these few yards of earth, but for every yard of earth in all the world that liberty might come, for that these men gave their lives."

Well, the war is over. Has liberty come to all the world? I have been through nineteen countries the past year, and I will say that liberty does not walk the streets of many of these countries. We of the Christian church have a peculiar right, it seems to me, to ask this question.

I am not going to apologize for being personal to-night. I have been out in the Near East, and God knows that we know what war is out there, war, and death, and massacre. I have stood on the streets of three cities and seen thousands taken out to massacre and death, little children from their mothers' arms. But I am not here to-night to talk of atrocities. I am here to raise this question: Can the followers of Jesus Christ participate again in war? Do we mean it when we speak of a warless world? And if I have changed my ideas somewhat since the day when I put on a uniform and sailed away to fight, I have reasons. In 1916 I was crossing the Atlantic Ocean. A man stepped up to me and said, "You are not a good American."

I said, "Why?"

He said, "Good Americans not only talk as neutrals but think as neutrals."

I traveled up and down the Bagdad Railroad day in and day out in those terrible days of 1915 and 1916. I remember riding for two days with a German major, and when I said to him, "Some day Germany will stand at the bar of the world's justice for this" — out of our window we could see an endless line of women and children, massacre, death, starvation, torture! I said, "Germany, a great Christian nation, stands by and watches it all."

He said, *"We do not intend to let anything stand between us and our military goal,"* and when I saw neutrality in our country change to force without limit, I was asked, a minister of the gospel of Jesus Christ and a missionary of His cross, to go out and tell of the atrocities I had seen in Asia Minor.

It was a devilish thing to ask a minister of Christ to stand before men with guns and try to inflame them, unless it means that those atrocities, those cruelties are to be forever ended.

On the walls of our barracks there was a motto set there by our government. Did I not learn it and repeat it to thousands of troops going into action? When I repeated it in Philadelphia the other day to a group of reporters, they laughed at me. I said, "Gentlemen, you did not laugh in 1917 when we were asked to go and kill and die."

At last, thank God, at last we sing:

"Their is no tribal liberty,
No beacon lighting just our shores,
No girding guarding but our doors;
The soul that led our fathers West
Turns back to free the world's oppressed.

"Allies, you have not called in vain,
We'll share your conflict and your pain.
Old Glory, through its stains and rents
Partakes of freedom's sacraments.
Last come, we will be last to stay
'Till Right has had her crowning day."

And we wrote it on our barracks walls, *"Last come, we will be last to stay till Right has had her crowning day."*

Soon after the war ended I was back in the struggle there in the Near East. Devastation, agony, untold starvation, three hundred Christian girls in Turkish harems in that district alone! Terror everywhere, and then one call, "America, God bless her!"

We appointed two commissions, the Harvard Commission, and the King-Crane Commission to investigate how we could help the Near East. They said, "America, come over and help us."

I stood in the streets of one city when seventeen thousand people were dragged out to massacre and death, and the little school was ruined, the teachers were dragged out and killed; and when, with my wife and little baby boy, I stood in the hell of it all, I said, "Can there be a God?"

And then I said, "Let us pray," and I knew there was a God. I came back to the cathedral there in 1919. There they were, a pitiful remnant that had come back. Would that you could have looked into their faces and heard their stories and known them as I knew them! That morning by candle light I said, "Never again need you go to sleep in terror, never again need you wake with the hands of those upon you who will seize your daughters and give them over to lust." I have stood on the streets of burning cities. I said to these people, "America has been asked to accept a responsibility in the Near East, and under God we will," and they broke into cheers. *My friends, the other day the Christians in that town were taken out and massacred in cold blood; and where was America?*

Then I began to ask myself what it was that we did, we Christians, in the war. God knows that when the next war comes I am going to stand for a warless world. When Russia collapsed and America came in to the war, the Russians said it must be for democracy. The Germans pasted on the sides of the freight cars and sent them all over Russia, thousands of posters, and one they used frequently was a picture of a room with a green table in it, and seated around it were a group of American financiers, and one of them, speaking to the others, was pointing to some figures on the blackboard and saying that Great Britain owed us so much, France owed us so much, Italy owed us so much, and that if we didn't go to war then we would lose our loans and be financially bankrupt.

I have learned that those great interests, which must always stand behind great governments to-day before there can be a war, are not interested in humanity as the church is, and I say it is time for the Church of the Lord Jesus Christ to make her voice heard. We are not afraid to die, but we are afraid that this world will become a world of hatred, when Christ came that it might be a world of peace.

And then there came the great hope in our hearts — the League of Nations. Shall I speak of it to-night? Mr. Harding has said that the League is as dead as slavery, *but nothing is dead that is alive in the heart of God, and I believe that the idea of the unity of the nations has been in the heart of God for a long, long time.*

In view of the great ideal for which Jesus Christ gave his life and shed his blood, that all men might be one, I don't believe that kings or presidents, though they may proclaim the League dead, can kill it, for the purposes of God are ultimately beyond defeat.

When I was in Washington the other day and said, "Can't we do something, something for humanity?" one of the men raised his hands and said "Mr. Harlow, there are seven million votes against your doing anything."

But when my friends cast their votes in the last election there was a speech our President made in Indianapolis in which he said (and it was broadcasted), "I give you my word of honor that when I am elected I will call together the best minds in America, and we will plan how we can call together the leaders of the nations to form an association of nations to work out the things for which the League stands and America stands."

In Chicago I sat by the side of Fred B. Smith. He is a great Christian statesman, and I heard him stand up there and tell the audience how as chairman of a committee sent by the Federal Council of Churches to Harding he said, "We want to vote for another party, because of the business conditions of our country, but do not want to disassociate our country from the great problems of the world." Mr. Harding replied, "I promise you, gentlemen, that if I am elected I will call together an association of nations which will stand in the life and humanity and the world for all those things which are fine in the League."

Now, what can we do in the future? We have done something, but what has been the result of what we have left undone? What happened at Lausanne? At Lausanne four great concessions were made. If the

Dr. O. T. Deever

Rev. Lionel B. Fletcher

Dr. H. L. Pickerill

Dr. A. B. Bowman

conference had been held in Flanders Fields or on Dead Man's Hill perhaps the concessions would not have been given. What were they?

The diplomats gave the right to the Turks to drive out all the remaining Christians, when women and children and girls between sixteen and thirty were not permitted to leave from any port. One hundred thousand Christian girls are slaves in Turkish harems. The diplomats gave permission to the Turks to keep in Asia Minor all the men between the ages of sixteen and sixty, the fathers, the brothers, to be put into the chain gang and die on the roads.

Turn to the reports of the Near East Relief. During the last few months I have been in hell. That is the Near East. I have seen the darkest evidence of man's inhumanity, crowds of five thousand, twenty thousand, fifty thousand cowering, frightened, cold, half-starved human beings.

One of my friends wrote me, "One hundred and eighty children died in my camp to-night."

I said to that German major that Germany would some day stand at the bar of the world's justice, but oh, where do we stand? Massacres, worse than those of 1915 and 1916, deportations more cruel than took place on the Bagdad Railroad, and the Christian nations squabbling while this is going on!

I believe if America had accepted responsibility in the League of Nations the Turks would not be in a position to advance their selfish ambitions which may plunge us into war, another hell. America has done nobly. We have given seventy-five millions of dollars through the Near East Relief. Thirteen thousand orphan children to-night as they bend over their little bowls of bread and milk, thank God for America, and I thank God for America, too. We of the church have not refused our moral mandate in these lands. I have been in China and India and Africa. I have been to Europe, and wherever I went, there I have found the representatives of the church of Christ not with bombs or swords, but with open schools, with hospitals, your missionaries, your ambassadors, holding a mandate for Christ in the life of the nations of the world. You men and women can stand behind that battle line.

If you could go into the streets of Europe and see the thousands of girls in black, with their pinched faces, and learn about the heavy burden of taxation, and see the endless row of crosses! There are 2,500,000 young men in Europe to-day still on beds of pain. Dare we keep aloof from all that? We must give to the Near East what we can.

I do not believe we have learned from the war that the Lord does not bring the things that we thought, in our day, and that with poison gas and bombshells the followers of Christ must only betray themselves into the hands of sinners who will use them for their own means; and when at last it is all over they will laugh at them and say, "Don't trouble us with your talk about humanity."

What can you do? Poor little I; what can I do? The other day a painter came down from the mountains. He had lived all his childhood in the hills. He was an artist at heart, but he had never learned to paint. He painted his own little pictures up there. He came to Florence and stood before Titian's great canvas, and when he saw that picture he bowed his head and closed his eyes. He couldn't look at it for the glory of it; he didn't know that pictures were like that. When he thought of his own attempts at painting he bowed his head and looked up with a smile and said, "I, too, am an artist. I, too, am a painter." We stand before the Son of God and bow our heads, but oh, thank God, he has put into our hearts something divine which answers back, "I, too, am a child of God." Go ye into all the world and preach this gospel to every creature that there may be a warless world, that there may be a brotherhood between nations, that there may be justice in our industrial life, and that at last the kingdom of God may come in our midst.

It was a terrible speech, bristling with facts that do not get into the newspapers. And Mr. Harlow *knows*. He has seen the things he described. And God knows, if his indictment be true, as we believe it is, that our beloved nation will have to answer for its aloofness at the bar of the Eternal God.

Hon. Simeon D. Fess, the honored United States Senator for Ohio, followed with an eloquent and logical speech on the general theme of whether we can prevent war in the condition of the public mind the world over.

CAN WE PREVENT WAR?

By Senator Simeon D. Fess.

Mr. Chairman and ladies and gentlemen: I accepted the invitation to address you in the belief that this would be one of the most representative crowds, with the most militant ability to do good to the world, of any audience that I would be permitted to address this year. In thinking of what I might say that would be of most importance, I think it would be in order for me to make some observations on the general theme of whether we can prevent war under the present attitude of the public mind the world over. I want to make this statement now, without qualification, that causes of war exist, that causes of war are not likely to be prevented. They arise over disputes of rights. One nation claims that this is her right; another nation disputes it, and out of that double interpretation of rights, quarrels come and sometimes eventuates in war. I have no hope of preventing those causes; they will come up. You need no further statement from me than the recital of what is going on in the Near East. When you go further, realizing the disputes over minorities, and realize that the minority in one place is the majority in the other, you will recognize why the powers of the world have not taken a position on that question.

The situation to-day between Britain and France, the most delicate problem facing the world at this hour, is a question of dispute over right, and the student of this subject is bound to be fair to Britain and is bound to be fair to France. The entente is broken, broken over an economic difference. Were it a racial difference or a religious difference or a political difference it wouldn't be acute, but being an economic difference you can see at once the very seriousness of the strained relations.

Britain has eighty per cent overseas commerce while one-fifth only is domestic agriculture. France has eighty per cent agriculture while only one-fifth overseas commerce. Britain's unemployment problem, which to-day sees nearly one and a half million men out of employment five years after the war is over, is the most serious problem that she has had in the last score of years; and she thinks the only way it can be solved is for a revival of the producing and consuming powers of the great countries that have been somewhat depleted in their productive power by the war. So Britain takes one view; and France sees the other side of the picture, and takes the other view. Economically these nations are going in different directions; one is going towards the rebuilding of markets; the other towards the security of her home situation. I am not inclined to criticize Britain for her position, and neither can I fail to sympathize with France for her position. What the outcome will be I do not know. No one knows; but the prayer is going up the world over that these nations may continue to be friends.

And you see our own country now disputing a right. I doubt whether there is a citizen within sound of my voice that would question the right of America to enforce the decree of the American law that has been declared constitutional by the highest tribunal of the land, and yet foreign nations constantly permit themselves openly to violate the American decree that this nation must be a sober nation. And while we are undertaking to enforce the law not only within our boundaries, but also beyond or within the three-mile limit, which is our right, other countries are questioning the right. I don't believe there is any one here who does not say that the United States is not only justified, but that she *must* enforce the law.

Ladies and gentlemen, I am going to speak frankly when I say that the United States is going to enforce that law if it takes the army and navy to do it.

Again, causes of war grow out of policies. Britain's policy in Mesopotamia is not assented to by all countries. France's policy in Morocco is in dispute. Japan's policy in China does not meet with approbation. The policy of the United States in regard to America, namely the Monroe Doctrine, is not accepted in Europe. We have never gone to war in defence of that policy, but we *might* go to war in defence of it. We have come very near doing it. It was announced in '23; it was reaffirmed in '26; it was reaffirmed in the Treaty of Grenada in '46; it was reaffirmed again in a treaty in '50. At the close of the Civil War, after France had sent an army at the head of which was Maximilian, who was placed at the head of the French Empire in Mexico, we pleaded as a government with France not to violate the Monroe Doctrine in that way. The pleadings were not listened to.

When the war closed Phil Sheridan at the head of fifty thousand of the best seasoned troops in the world was sent to the Mexican border. France was asked to withdraw. She did withdraw, and war was averted, but suppose France had not withdrawn! Our army would have crossed the border, and you know what would have been the result.

In 1887 when Grover Cleveland was President, Britain was in dispute with Venezuela. We asked Britain to arbitrate. Lord Salisbury, listening to the quotation we offered from the Monroe Doctrine, made this statement, which, by the way, is true: "The Monroe Doctrine is not international law, no matter how brilliant the statesman that announced it, or powerful the nation that backed it." That came from Lord Salisbury, the Prime Minister of Britain.

Cleveland immediately sent a special message to Congress to authorize the appointment of a commission to make the survey, and then asked the power of Congress to enforce the findings of that survey. That was leading to war. When Salisbury saw that over a dispute down in South America, two wings of the Anglo-Saxon people might go to war, he submitted the dispute to arbitration. You recall that under Roosevelt, when Germany sent two warships to Venezuela with orders to take two ports and hold the ports until sufficient revenue was collected to pay the debt that Venezuela owed Germany, President Roosevelt said: "If you can take two ports, you can take all the ports. If you can hold the ports until a debt in dispute is paid to your satisfaction, then you can hold them indefinitely," for under conditions like that the Monroe Doctrine was broken down. He asked the German government to submit the matter to the Hague Conference. The German government stated that it was not a subject of arbitration and closed negotiations suddenly. Then Roosevelt gave them forty-eight hours to withdraw those warships from those waters, and when after twenty-four hours had elapsed, the German government represented to the President that it was impossible, physically, to withdraw those warships in forty-eight hours, Roosevelt snapped back and said, "You haven't got forty-eight hours; you have only twenty-four hours left." Then the German government agreed to submit the dispute to arbitration, and it went to the Hague Conference.

This was our attitude, not on a right, but on a policy. This indicates that this very moment wars grow out of disputes, over rights, and wars grow out of the furtherance of policies, and as they do now they likely will in the future.

Not seeing the way to prevent these causes coming up, I think the Christian people of the world ought to look for some method by which at least, recognizing the persistence of wars, we might use our good offices to prevent their occurrence even though the causes appear.

America has stood in the forefront of effort to prevent war. She has tried every conceivable means known up to date as substantial preventatives of war. Conciliation and mediation have been a plan favored by America. Right now America is waiting for a suggestion from both France and Britain that America's good offices might be welcome to find an adjustment between those two mighty countries in the Old World. But conciliation and mediation can never be applied without being first welcome by both of the nations in dispute.

Mediation is temporary. Mediation is contingent. There isn't any assurance that nations in dispute will welcome mediatory power, so that other methods are necessary The United States has stood in the forefront of arbitration. Arbitration is better than mediation, but arbitration is weak; it is faulty; it falls far short. Arbitration is temporary. When arbitration has rendered a decision the arbitrators are dismissed, and there is no longer an arbitrating body to sit upon disputes until a new one is selected. Arbitration is also always partial; it is never impartial. An arbitrator is never a judge; an arbitrator is always a negotiator; he is always an advocate; he is always a special pleader. If we are in dispute with a nation, and we agree to submit the dispute to arbitration we appoint our arbitrator. The nation with which we are in dispute appoints her arbitrator, then the two nations will agree on an umpire. The umpire is supposed to be neutral, and the dispute is always settled by the umpire.

That is why Salisbury refused to submit in 1887. He used this expression that disputes are always settled by an umpire, and the umpire is always an alien, never friendly.

Now, ladies and gentlemen, hear me. America has made a hundred and thirteen treaties of arbitration. America has prevented war in not less than sixteen' specific cases of arbitration, and no one will say that when a nation prevents a war it is not commendable, for war is a negative. Wars are never constructive, never positive. Wars do not give us permanent and abiding results. Wars do not settle disputes; wars leave bitterness, wrangling, and the dispute has to be adjusted later on. If anybody is in doubt, cast your eye across the ocean to-day and then ask the question whether war settles a dispute, and with that in view, anything that America can do to-day that will prevent war is positive achievement, for when war is once prevented you are cultivating a habit of mind towards peace as against war. If we can get into the habit of preventing wars, we can ultimately create a habit of thought that will be the guiding sentiment of the civilization of our time.

In 1899 America took the lead in a great conference. That was the first Hague Conference called by the Czar of Russia. In the twenty-six nations that sat under that roof, America, as you would expect, took the leading part. Our representative was the distinguished Dr. Andrew D. White, ex-president of Cornell University, and at the time, our ambassador to Germany. He it was who suggested three conventions in this first Hague Conference. It was he who proposed the settlement of international disputes by a court of arbitral justice, and when the convention finally proceeded and abandoned any hope of final action, Andrew D. White, at the close of the convention, made a passionate appeal that the convention do not adjourn until it passed a motion to seek to settle international disputes by some method that is better than war. The result of that passionate appeal was the board of arbitration known as the Hague Tribunal. That was American in origination.

Then, later, the first subject of dispute ever submitted to that Tribunal was our dispute with Mexico, because we wanted to show that our practice was in accordance with our theory; and the first great dispute that was submitted to this Tribunal was that submitted by Germany in dispute with Venezuela under the inspiration of the President of the United States.

The home of this Tribunal is the palace of peace built and endowed by an American citizen, and in that home still meets the old Hague Tribunal.

The second Hague conference was not called until some years later. Now, ladies and gentlemen, the American President instructed our Secretary of State, who was none other than Elihu Root, probably the greatest international mind alive, to-day, to instruct the American delegate in that

Rev. W. A. MacTaggart

Dr. A. B. Kendall

Hon. Simeon D. Fess, LL.D.
(*See address in Chapter xiv.*)

second conference not to stand for the old board of arbitration but to substitute for it a court of justice, to be made up not of negotiators and special pleaders, but of judges who would base their decisions on justice and equity. Mr. Choate, our representative, following the instructions of his government, proposed the court that is now known as the international court, in 1907.

This conference, unlike the first conference, which was represented by twenty-six states, was represented by forty-six states, and the definite result that came out of it was the court of justice. The conference provided for the number of judges, for the tenure of office, for compensation, but the one thing, unfortunately, that they did not provide for—because a dispute came up—was *the method of selecting the judges.* Like the first conference, which did not finish its work, but awaited a second conference to complete it, this conference adjourned with the suggestion that a third conference be called at which time the unfinished work of the second would be taken up. But see what happened. That was in 1907. The very next year the Near East went into the storms of war, and in three years the second Balkan War was on, and within one year, three years after that, the World War was on, and the third conference was never called. It was not because people didn't want it, but because it is difficult to hold a conference of peace in the presence of nations involved in war.

In 1918 and 1919 at the conference of the commission at Versailles, one of the things that was uppermost in the minds of those commissioners was whether there is a way by which wars, if they can't be prevented, may be lessened. A suggestion was made,—it was referred to by the prior speaker. I regret that the major emphasis was placed upon the League of Nations rather than upon the court. Nobody would question that any peace conference that would meet after the World War would discuss the proposal of reviving the world court that had been recommended and all but completed in the second Hague Conference of 1907. Whatever dispute arose over the League of Nations there was no dispute over whether the world court ought to be instituted. I regret that instead of the emphasis being placed upon the court it was placed upon the League which, of course, immediately struck a division in our own country. There had been no division on the world court. All political parties were for it.

The political party to which I happen to belong put into its national platform as early as 1904 a pronouncement favoring the idea of settling disputes by specific methods rather than by war. They repeated it in the platform of 1913. They again repeated it in a specific recommendation for a world court in 1916. While that political organization did not pronounce in favor of the League in 1920, but withheld its pronouncements, it did pronounce in its platform in favor of the world court. The court has been the result of the fourteenth article of the League of Nations.

It was the fourteenth article that authorized the appointment of a commission to recommend a plan for the organization of the world court. You were requested to loan to that commission Elihu Root, and, of course, America was delighted to send Mr. Root to sit upon this inquiry commission. And don't overlook the fact that the draft statute out of this commission that provided for the court was written by Elihu Root, an American citizen, and statesman.

It went back from this commission to the council of the League. The council made two or three minor amendments, then sent it to individual nations for ratification or rejection. Fifty-four nations ratified it, so far as I know. So far as I know no nation voted to reject it. It then went into operation two years ago.

America was then given another tribute. The Council of the League asked the United States whether they would be permitted to appoint John Bassett Moore, who had been counselor of the State Department first under Taft, and second under Wilson, and who at the time of his appointment was the Professor of international law in Columbia University, and we were very glad to allow John Bassett Moore to take a permanent position on this court of eleven judges with four deputies, so that in case a judge is absent, you can have one of the deputies sit in his place. The court therefore is represented by eleven men.

Don't misunderstand. John Bassett Moore does not represent the United States on that court, any more than Howard Taft, the Chief Justice of the United States, living in Ohio, represents Ohio on the Supreme Bench. No judge of the Supreme Court represents any State. Judges of the Supreme Court represent the United States, and no State,—otherwise nine states would have representation and the balance of them would have none.

We must not make the mistake of thinking that only the eleven nations which have judges appointed on the world court are represented. That is a mistake. These judges are the representatives of the nations that will submit their differences to the court. That is one point that seems to be overlooked constantly when we discuss this question. The United States has a citizen on the court, but he is not a representative of the United States; and the man who comes from Britain is not a representative of Britain. In other words, the differentiation is this: *these are judges*. They are *not* negotiators. They don't make agreements. They come to decisions. They look into the justice of the two sides in dispute, and undertake to settle it on that basis. That is the distinction between the proposed court and the board of arbitration that it is to supersede.

Now, there is objection to the court. Men say you can't adhere to this court unless you enter the League of Nations. Thas is absurd. There isn't anything to that at all. The League of Nations has started some movements that will have the commendation of the world. They are undertaking to suppress traffic in women and children in the world. They asked the United States whether we would be represented on that commission. The United States said: "Your movement is a great movement, and whatever we can do in an advisory capacity we will be glad to do. We will be glad to throw our influence in the suppression of this traffic." Therefore Miss Abbott of the Labor Department of Washington sits upon that commission as the consultative individual. Does that put us in the League, because we are assisting in some work that the League is putting forth? Certainly it does not.

The League is undertaking to suppress traffic in opium and poisonous drugs. We have gone to the extent of even sending the Chairman of the Foreign Relations Committee of the House to Europe to make an investigation on the subject, and have allowed a representative to be on the commission in a consultative manner, because the work is a great work and ought to be fostered.

The League of Nations is undertaking to prevent epidemics. They have taken their cue from the marvelous work against Yellow Fever by the late Dr. Gorgas. Such a movement as that appeals to the world. They asked us whether we would give our influence.

The court is open to us. We can submit anything. Anything! We can submit anything with any nation, if the other nation will agree to the court, and they will listen. The judges will sit upon it. We don't need to adhere to the court in order to use it, but in the name of common decency, if we believe in the efficiency of an effort to lessen the chances of war, and if we can't remove causes, then we might at last submit our disputes to some agency that may prevent war; if we think that is right, why should we not give our moral and financial support to the movement? That is the question.

It costs money to keep this court. Our nation is wondrously wealthy, and if we think that is a good thing we ought to support it and we ought not to only support it from the rostrum but from the treasury of the United States.

Now I speak, ladies and gentlemen, as a responsible Senator. There is a dispute on the subject. I can't see myself why our nation in the face of our record in mediation and conciliation and in arbitration and in our treaties and in what we have achieved and how we have stood for this as a substitute of the old arbitration, cannot give its undivided support to the world court.

And as a Senator who does his own thinking and who takes the dictation of no man or any group of men, I propose to use my influence to see that the Senate does ratify adherence to the programme.

America is in a wonderful position to-night. She is the leader of the world. She has the most magnificent record so far as I know of any nation in the world. Only in this country could you have accomplished what was accomplished in that Arms Conference where seven conventions were agreed upon, and not a single negative vote cast against any one. "Only in America," said a famous French delegate, "could you do it. It couldn't be done in our section of the world. We have rivalries, disputes, suspicions, and unanimity of decision seems impossible." When Arthur Balfour left our shores, he said: "Up to this time we have always counted ourselves equal, but no longer. America leads the world to-day."

So, ladies and gentlemen, America stands on vantage ground, and what America is, and what she will be is not in our acreage, is not in our minds, is not in our transportations, not in our wealth, but what America is, and what she will be, lies in the type of manhood and womanhood we produce.

Then followed a series of motion pictures shown by the Portland, Ore., delegation, pictures giving the Convention a most alluring impression of the city and State where the 1925 Convention will be held.

Chapter XV.

THE SUNDAY AFTERNOON MEETING AT THE FAIR-GROUNDS

SUNDAY, JULY 8

Rev. Ira Landrith, D. D., Presiding

The most spectacular meeting of the Convention, one of the most magnificent meetings Christian Endeavor has ever held, was that on the Iowa State fair grounds on Sunday afternoon. These grounds are very spacious, and are beautified by many splendid trees. There is a great covered grand stand, one of the largest in the entire country, with uncovered wings seating several thousand more. An audience of uncounted thousands gathered here, crowding the grand stand, filling the space in front of it, and filling automobiles in the big field beyond. In front was the speaker's stand, fitted up with the wonderful device that carries every word spoken at the centre to the uttermost listener in the field. The many thousands gave perfect attention, as if they were all condensed into a little room ten by ten. It was one of the most impressive of all Endeavor meetings.

The irrepressible Endeavorers sang their vigorous songs, led by a cornet. It was most interesting to see "C. E. will shine" carried out by about four thousand in a bunch going down with the sun while another four thousand rose with the moon. After a noble concert by the Argonne Post band of the American Legion, Rev. Earl E. Harper, of Massachusetts, an especially skilful and successful song-leader, led a song service that was at the same time bright and spiritually impressive, closed with an earnest prayer by the leader. One feature was the singing of "America," followed by the salute of the flag by the enormous crowd.

The arrival of Bryan was the signal for a tremendous demonstration, showing the honor and affection that millions of Americans cherish for this noble Christian statesman.

The chairman of the afternoon was Dr. Landrith, who, after a brief prayer by Dr. Poling, introduced Rev. James Kelly, of Scotland, remarking that all over America a cordial welcome awaits any man with that name, as he will find a kinsman on every corner.

IMPRESSIONS OF EUROPE

By Rev. James Kelly

Former President of the British Christian Endeavor Union

I have been asked to speak to you this afternoon concerning one or two impressions and interpretations following upon a recent visit which I have just made to Central and Eastern Europe. No one can visit the Continent of Europe these days without receiving many vivid and interesting impressions, but a just interpretation of those impressions will require thought, knowledge of history, knowledge of life, and above all intelligent sympathy. In the course of my time I traveled something like five thousand miles through Holland and Belgium and Germany and Czechoslovakia, Jugo-Slavia, Austria Hungary, Italy, and France. Traveling on the Continent to-day is not to be measured by miles. In the course of our traveling we crossed no fewer than seventeen frontiers, and we were subjected to at least twenty-four pass and personal examinations. Impressions have borne in upon me.

The first is the state of privation and distress to which the middle-classes, especially in Austria and Germany, have been reduced. In both these countries there is undoubtedly the greatest distress, particularly in Austria, which is suffering even more than Germany. I saw underfed children, impoverished working men, and a destitute middle-class reduced to the dire straits of want and misery. Milk, butter, and cheese are luxuries and are obtainable only by the rich. All those who had money saved or lived on their investments or had fixed incomes, see the money disappear, and they are reduced from comfort to starvation.

In Vienna there are forty thousand homeless families. Some of these families are living in unused trucks or vans near the railroad station, and many of them are scattered over the city. I met at dinner one day a company of lecturers and professors from the University and Technical College of Vienna, at what is known as the Professors Club. For something like twenty months at least, nearly one hundred of these men have been supplied with the one solid meal in the day through the American Relief Administration. The food is supplied by the Administration, and each individual or recipient pays an amount equal to two cents in your money for service, and that helps to lift the whole proposition above the level of charity.

I saw much of the relief work that is being carried on in Eastern Europe, but of all the scenes I witnessed this was to me the most pathetic.

A scholar of great eminence told me that all he wore had been given him. He had the highest degrees that three great universities could confer. Many of these men, like most of the pastors of the country, are trying to exist on salaries ranging from five to fifteen dollars per month.

A rent restriction-act prevents in Austria the raising of rents, and these remain at the pre-war figure, which is a mere fraction of the former value. It may cost a landlord, I was told, more to repair a single broken electric light than he receives in rent in one year. Orphanages, relief centres, and the like can only exist largely through the aid of America, and I want to assure you this afternoon that the name America is beautiful in the minds of many people who would have starved without help.

There are twelve thousand students in Vienna and seventy per cent must work for their living, while at their studies. The common way of earning a pittance is by doing errands, doing menial work for shop-keepers or something of that kind. Only a few months ago Austria was regarded as tottering to an imminent doom, but thanks to that loan which was successfully floated through the League of Nations, a loan to which America contributed so liberally, she is now beginning to pick up. When one recalls these facts it is not surprising to gather the impression that an attitude of pessimism is settling down on the best minds of Central Europe.

The second impression born in on me is that there can be no security for any country until the public opinion of Europe is right. Everywhere there is bitterness and malice and hatred and jealousy.

In dealing with the relations of France with Germany and of Germany with France, every newspaper in Germany shows a spirit of deep hatred of their western enemy, which seems to have entered into the very marrow of the nation. This passionate hate is laying a sure foundation of calamity for the future. We British people are given a kind of aloofness approaching isolation in the German's way of regarding us. The difference the German finds between us and France is one of spirit and mind. In Germany's opinion we may be inequitable in our policy towards Germany, but to a far greater degree than France we allow ourselves to be guided by far-sightedness, by the spirit of justice, and to be influenced by the principle of the Golden Rule, to live and let live. Germany looks upon this country still with great suspicion; she cannot believe that all the efforts that are being put forth in the interests of suffering humanity are from an altruistic point of view, and one greatly deplores the spirit that is to be found practically everywhere, not only there but in these other countries, that spirit of suspicion and malice and jealousy.

The Austria of to-day is but a tiny state, Roman Catholic in religion. The economic situation occupies the minds of all, and the heart is full of bitterness at having lost so much territory, while envious eyes are cast on Hungary and Czechoslovakia. Hungary is very greatly reduced as a result of the war, and her condition is far from happy. Economic distress and dread of revolutionary movements occupy the minds of the men. Budapest suffered seriously during the periods of the communistic ascendency and the Roumanian occupation, and to-day there is undoubtedly a desire on the part of the people for a stable government, which takes the form of a desire for a return of the monarchy, but not for a Hapsburg restoration. Extreme poverty appears in the cities, and the mood of the people is represented in the army of suicides.

In France there are large areas of territory devastated and thousands of her homes desolated. She won the admiration of the world by heroic endurance, but to-day the spirit of antagonism is everywhere manifest, and seeds of malice and hardness of heart are being sown, which, if not removed, will bring a deadly harvest in a future generation.

In Italy it was feared some time ago that the country would be a prey to disaster, liable to uprisings and mobs, and it was threatened even with revolution, but there arose a strong man, Senor Mussolini, the leader of the Fascisti movement, a man who bound the people together in a band of national unity and prevented disaster; yet one found there the spirit of envy, the spirit of animosity and ill-will and suspicion on many hands. Again I say there is no security for any country until the public opinion of Europe is changed. A change of heart is absolutely necessary before there can be any true and lasting peace, and that change can only be brought about by the principles of peace; for politicians in all lands are gambling, governments are scheming for commercial advantages, and the press hides the truth from the people.

In Czechoslovakia I found things a little different from most of the other countries. A great movement has been created away from the Church of Rome. The Czech Brethren Church claims a gain of no fewer than sixty thousand new members within the last four years, and the Czech-Slovak Church, served by ex-priests of the Roman Communion, retains much of the Catholic ritual and claims as many as one million adherents. These have receded from Rome and are indifferent to the Pope's decree of excommunication pronounced against them. There is probably no other country in Europe where the appeal of the gospel is meeting to-day with such an immediate response as among those people for whom John Huss is a national hero and where his memory is a living force.

It may interest you to know briefly what led up to the revolution and thereafter the reformation. First of all it had come to be recognized that the papacy was at the back of Austria, and was using Austria as a means to crush Protestantism. Certainly the action of the party during the war was openly on the side of tyranny represented by the Central Powers. Thirdly, the people came to see that the Roman Church was misusing religion, degrading it for political and selfish purposes, and that she had no interest in the spiritual life. Fourthly, it was recognized that the Church had no sympathy with the oppressed.

For centuries the Bohemians had demanded freedom to realize their own splendid ideals of humanity in action. They had cherished notions of humanity and a true brotherhood, but every effort they had made to set up Christian democracy had been crushed by the hand of Austria at the bidding of the Pope, and under all the friction of these years of papal oppression the memory of the words of John Huss kept alive the ideal. When the war was drawing to its close the doom of the Roman Catholic Church in Bohemia was sealed. It was a memorable day on the 28th of October, 1918, when the Czech people finally threw off the Austrian yoke.

It was a bloodless revolution. Austria tried to make it otherwise, but she was not successful, and so the Republic of Czechoslovakia was created by the union of Bohemia, Moravia, Slovakia, and part of Silesia.

The President of the new Republic, Professor Masaryk, formerly occupant of the Chair of Sociology in Prague University, is a Protestant statesman who had been scorned, cursed, condemned, and sentenced to death by the Austrian government as a traitor, a man whose life had been one romance of adventure and magnificent adherence to an ideal, and who has been one of the instruments of the institution of the Republic.

During the short interview I had with President Masaryk I was privileged to find that he was a man who stood for the best and highest ideals of his race, and while striving for complete national unity, he and his government seek to allow the largest liberty to racial and religious minorities in the land, and cultivate a genuine friendship with surrounding peoples.

The third impression borne in on me is that unless there is a new spirit created throughout the whole of Europe there is going to be nothing possible but another war. If the nations continue to be selfish and arrogant, what is the inevitable result? Nothing but the application of the principles of the Gospel of Jesus Christ will save Europe to-day and lead the world to its home in God.

Europe, men and women, holds the key to the solution of the problem of world-wide peace, and you and I, followers of the Prince of peace, must help to bring about this new condition. To begin with let me say we must alter our policy. We must lay aside the instruments of slaughter. It is horrible to think that in these days, after six years of bloody war, men are scheming whereby they can invent machines so that, if another war should come, they could pour down hell upon the earth; and yet such men exist to-day on the Continent of Europe. We must lay aside our instruments of slaughter. No nation has ever yet made peace a part of its policy. What we have called peace has been merely an interval between wars. Every nation has had her War Department. No nation has yet had a peace department.

Never in the history of any nation has the half of one per cent of the revenue been devoted to peace. Not until God Almighty allowed us to be shattered and blasted on the battlefields of Europe did men seriously wake up to ask themselves whether these complex and ever-recurring questions could only be blindly settled by the brutality of war, or whether there was not a better means of arriving at justice and recognizing human brotherhood.

I have heard politicians say on both sides of the Atlantic that the world has been made safe for Democracy through the overthrow of the Central Powers. I am not so sure about that. But what I am concerned about is that Democracy should be made safe for the world, and to make this possible patriotism is not enough, brotherhood is not enough, humanity is not enough. The Christian programme is absolutely essential to national and international progress, because the spiritual ideals which alone guarantee true spiritual progress need a Christian democracy to keep them alive. A passion for righteousness is the moral minimum with which national and international life can be safeguarded. As Christian people, particularly in this land and in Great Britain, we have got in these days to look out on men and things through the eyes of Jesus Christ; as Christian people we must cultivate the international mind; we must pray for the international heart; we must develop the international conscience; we must look out upon humanity as a family and build up in ourselves the grace and virtues which we know are indispensable in the home, the virtues of trust and forbearance and mutual good-will.

Brotherhood is the thing for which the world has been made. Sometimes I hear it said that Christianity has failed. Nay, verily, Christianity has not failed; civilization has failed, but Christianity has never been given a chance. There is enough moral dynamite in the teaching of the Sermon on the Mount, were it practised, to blow to pieces the tyrannies that curse the world. Christianity has not failed, Jesus Christ stands to-day on the water's edge of this troubled era of ours. He holds in His hand a key for every heart, a message for every soul, a solution for every problem. He is still the same, yesterday, to-day and forever, and to this weary, war-worn, sin-stricken world He is saying, "Come unto Me, all ye that labor and are heavy laden and I will give you rest and peace."

Men and women, the world is dying to-night for the lack of a great moral adventure, and why should not the church cast aside un-Christian caution and embark on what would be the greatest of all crusades? The world cries out to-night not for civilization, not for education, not for social reform. *The world cries out for peace*; it cries out for Christ, and unless the church gives real constructive leadership, and is sufficiently influential in the so-called Christian nations to create the sentiment which will make possible international peace, we need not be surprised if humanity in despair, turns elsewhere for moral leadership. Beneath all the chaos and turmoil of our time is this irresistible divine purpose which is forcing the present generation to give its brain to the problem of the oneness of humanity.

Now, what is our particular part of the programme? As the Young People's Society of Christian Endeavor, what is our particular part of the programme in relation to international and national progress?

I hold it is to mobilize the moral insight of the youth of to-day through the collective emotion of ideals. Youth has the sensitiveness and the imagination, the passion, the faith, and the initiative, the dynamic force, and the daring which must be matched against this hour of priceless privilege; if the world is to be saved from the horrors of war, boys and girls, our youths and maidens, must be taught the way of peace.

Therein lies the whole solution. We have not succeeded in the past. Shall we succeed in the future? Our highest hope is in our Sunday school, our Bible classes, our Christian Endeavor societies. The young people of this generation must be taught this fundamental truth of Christianity, and in bright, joyous service to others, bring in the bright new day.

A few Sunday evenings ago I stood in the centre of a great cemetery in France, I think for the third or fourth time, one of those great acres sacred to God and liberty and freedom, and as I stood in the centre of that great cemetery it seemed to me there were buried there representatives from nearly every country in the world. Here lay great groups of American and Canadian boys sleeping side by side. Here were men who had come from Australia and from New Zealand. Here were men who came from Austria and Germany and France. Here were men who came from Britain, and there they were, all asleep in that great cemetery. And as I drew near to the centre of the cemetery to pause for a moment in front of a great rough cross that had been erected there, I noticed that the setting sun on the western hill was casting the shadow of the cross over the whole cemetery, and it spoke its own silent message to me. The shadow of the cross was covering the representatives of those countries who had died to set us free. Men and women, God has taught us that He loves all men, black and white, brown and yellow, bound and free, and that we should think

A Portion of the Sunday Afternoon Meeting at the Fair Grounds

great things about Him, and thus it behooves us to be greater in our faith, in our hopes, and in our aims.

I beseech you to-night to dedicate your manhood and your womanhood to the service of God and humanity, and help to banish from the face of the earth this great curse, that the day may soon come when the knowledge of the Lord shall cover the earth as the waters cover the sea, and when throughout the length and breadth of the whole wide world, Jesus shall reign "Where'er the Sun doth its successive journeys run."

Dr. Landrith made a vigorous plea for a good collection, which resulted in a very fine and helpful offering. One tin pan had a horseshoe in it, whether placed there for luck by the bearer or by some contributor we do not know. Then Dr. Landrith wittily introduced "the only man in America for whom so vast an audience would gather on such a hot July day," and the great event, a speech by Bryan, was on.

Mr. Bryan sat on a table, facing the disks of the voice-amplifier. He took this position because of a sore foot, and Dr. Landrith took pains to state that in all the years Bryan has been before the country he has never developed a sore head, which is certainly true.

The address showed Bryan at his splendid best.

THE "ALLS" OF JESUS

By Hon. William Jennings Bryan

I am greatly pleased to be here to-day. I have been attending national meetings of this great society for many years. I think the first one was at Minneapolis in 1908, and the last one in New York two years ago. I was at the State meeting of this organization in the city of Miami last month, and I have attended the local meeting in many places, because I regard it as one of the greatest of the Christian organizations in the world. It is worth going a long way to catch the inspiration which such a meeting gives, and it is worth traveling a long distance to commune again with the saintly man of God who has rendered incalculable service to the world by organizing and leading for now over forty years this great religious society.

My subject for this afternoon is in line with the programme outlined for the next two years. A special appeal has been made to you and through you to the Christian world for greater personal devotion and evangelism, and you have set the mark at an increase of fifty per cent in the Christian churches in the next two years. I did not know until I arrived here that the attention of the delegates was focused on this programme. I could not have stated my own view and my own desires better than you have stated them, for I believe it is the need of the world and the only salvation of the world. I want, therefore, to ask you to consider three questions.

First, does the world need a religious revival; second, are there those who can lead the world in such a religious revival; and, third, is there a message that can revive the world? I might state it a little differently. Is the harvest ripe, are the reapers ready, and will the sickle cut?

These three questions can be answered in the affirmative. I believe the world never needed Christ more than it needs Him to-day. We have just come out of the war, and that war has demonstrated conclusively the impotency of every other method suggested to save the world. You have listened to this splendid address of our brother from across the sea. He has traveled through the stricken countries of Europe, has gathered information, and I think he has rightly estimated the great need, the one essential thing, and that is to get back to God and to God's word and to

God's Son. They have demonstrated that force and fear can never bring the world peace. Peace can not grow upon this tree. They have written the history of the world in letters of blood because they have attempted to terrorize the world into peace. It was a great lie; many believed it, many were deluded. Why should anybody be deluded further? There is only one peace remedy, and that is the substitution of love for force. There is only one basis upon which to build peace, and that is brotherhood and the spirit of co-operation. And the one word that they need to learn in Europe, and we need to learn it here, is forgiveness, and not retaliation and revenge. For more than a generation they were balancing powers. They had been warned by far-sighted statesmen. John Bright, that great leader of peace, not more than half a century ago warned them that rivalry in armaments, the worship of the scimiter, could lead to nothing but war. But they would not listen. Under the devil's leadership, and carrying the devil's burden, they have marched the great civilized nations up to the verge of the bottomless pit.

We look back upon the war and we find that thirty millions of human lives were lost, that three hundred millions of dollars worth of property created by the brain and the toil of man was destroyed, and that the debts of the world were six times as great when the last gun was fired as when the war began. There is no hope for the world except in peace, and there is no hope of peace except in world disarmament, and there is no hope for world disarmament until the nations can join in that international anthem that startled the shepherds of Bethlehem, and must some day be the song of all the world.

The world needs Christianity, it needs Christ. It needs Him as a Savior, it needs Him as a teacher; and in this country we need a revival. In this country, my friends, we have gigantic problems to meet, and there is nothing else that will meet them and solve them except the gospel of the meek and lowly Nazarene.

Looking at the antagonism between labor and capital, I am not exaggerating when I say that never since our nation was born was the situation in industry as grave as it is now, and never since Christ was born was it as grave in the world as it is now. What is the difficulty? Class consciousness. We have never had as many individuals in the labor group and in the capitalistic group class conscious as we have to-day. And by class conscious we mean that they think in terms of class and not in terms of the whole country or in terms of humanity. These classes are getting wider and wider apart, and the feeling is increasing; and there is nothing that will speak peace in the industrial world save the gospel of the church which believes in God, who created both employer and employee.

Here is a nation of a hundred million of people; twenty-nine per cent of them live upon the farms, and out here in the greatest State among the forty-eight, I want to say to you that agriculture was never so depressed or oppressed as it is to-day. The farmers are in worse condition than they have been before in thirty years, if ever before. Thirty years ago the farmers were burning their corn because they could not get enough for it to buy coal; they were buying upon the same level that they sold. To-day they sell on a pre-war level and buy on a level thirty per cent higher than the level on which they sell. The farmers to-day can not hope to buy more than two-thirds as much with the products of their farms as they did before the war, and that means that they must either use less, or they must gradually drift into bankruptcy. The farmers are being driven from the farms. There are more than a million fewer persons on farms than a year ago.

Now, my friends, what is the trouble? I think the only trouble is injustice, and injustice is merely the outgrowth of a lack of brotherhood. We have never had organized greed in this country as we have it to-day, and there is nothing that is going to save our country from increasing injustice and increasing dissension except the spirit of Christ in the hearts of the people, manifested not only in the conduct of the individual but in the laws of the nation.

What else do we have? We have organized lawlessness in this country. We have a great element, of course it is but a minority, a small minority, but it is an organized and persistent minority that defies law and encourages violation. We have won the greatest moral victory that was ever won by the ballot since man began to vote—we have prohibition, and there will be no turning back or weakening of the law. But, my friends, while that is true, this opposition to law enforcement, this attempt to bring back a curse that has been driven forever from under the American flag is diverting attention from other questions, and we have to fight to keep what we have and to preserve this bulwark erected around the homes of the land when it ought to be a settled question with our people free to take up the greater problems that confront us along other lines.

There is work to be done. Have we any organization that can be enlisted in this work? Yes, all our churches must be, and all our Sunday schools, our Y. M. C. A. with its nine thousand organizations throughout the world, over half of them in this country; we must have our Young Women's Christian Association, we must have our Knights of Columbus, we must have every organization of every denomination that seeks to protect the youth of the land from the dangers that assail them. But among them all I know of no organization that has more power and, therefore, upon which rests greater responsibility than the Christian Endeavor society. Three million members in the United States, over four million in the world! If you would understand the magnitude of this great army, just remember that it is larger than the army raised by the United States to do its part in the world's biggest war. I am looking to this organization whose very name suggests activity, Christian Endeavor; Christianity can not live without work. In the word endeavor you have expressed an essential condition of existence, and with the splendid leadership that you have had, and God grant it may be long continued, you have never been more militant than to-day, you have never had a larger programme before you than now, you have never been more sorely needed in all your life than at this present moment.

Now, my friends, if the harvest is ripe and if the reapers are ready, have you something with which to do the work? I suggested that the third question is whether the sickle is sharp. It is necessary to have machinery with which to do the work. Have we a sickle that is sharp? Turn to Hebrews, fourth chapter, twelfth verse, and what do you read? "The word of God is quick, and powerful, and sharper than any two-edged sword." It is the word of God. That is our weapon; that is our implement, and all we need to harvest the crop; all that we need for the use of these splendid reapers is the word of God. May I now take from that one word of God and place emphasis upon it? When a minister takes a text from the Bible, he doesn't expect to improve his text. A preacher who would expect to put into his sermon anything better than the Bible text upon which he builds it, would not be fit to preach. All that he can hope to do is to make you understand the text better, to feel it more deeply and apply it more constantly. And so my purpose this afternoon is to take one word and burn it into your minds and hearts so you will never read that word again without feeling a greater interest in it than you did before you came to-day; it is one of the smallest words in the Bible, it is the word "all," a-l-l, and while it is one of the smallest words it is one of the biggest words in the Bible.

I want to show you how Christ used the word "all." I take the word "all" eight times as Christ used it in three passages. The first you will find in Matthew. We are told that a lawyer came to Christ and tempting him asked, "Which is the great commandment of the law?" And Christ took the commandments that relate to man's duty to God and compressed them into one, and proclaimed as the first and great commandment, "Thou shall love the Lord thy God with *all* thy heart and with *all* thy soul and with *all* thy mind." Here the word "all" is used three times. In another gospel it is used four times, adding the word "strength"—with all thy strength. He could not have used any other word. The whole history of religion would have been different, or there would have been no history of religion to write, if Christ had said, "Thou shall love the Lord thy God with *nearly all* thy heart and with *most* of thy soul, and a *part* of thy mind." If we do not love God with all the heart, then there is something else in the heart besides the love of God. There is a divided allegiance, there is no singleness of purpose, there is a continual conflict between love of God that fills a part, and love of something else that fills another part.

In the story of the rich young man we find that that very point was stressed. This young man came to Christ. The Bible says he came running, and, kneeling, he expressed a desire to follow Christ. But Christ noticed that there was one thing in his heart besides love of Him. Aye, something that was even greater than the love of Christ, and so He put him to the test; and he couldn't stand the test; he went away sorrowing because he had great possessions. He loved his possessions more than he loved Christ. There must be a completeness, a wholeness of this love, and besides, my friends, unless the heart is full it can not overflow. *There is nothing in the human heart that can help others.* The only thing we can give to others that will help them is love of God that overflows from our hearts.

I think the most fascinating thing in nature is a spring. I never saw a spring until I was twenty-two. But it has never been out of my mind since then. To me it is the best representative of a Christian life, as a stagnant pool best represents a selfish life. A stagnant pool! Why that just receives the water that flows from the sloping sides around, but a stagnant pool gives forth nothing, and it finally becomes a centre of disease and death; it is the most repulsive thing in the world except a human life that is built upon the same plane. But what about a living spring that just pours forth all the time of that which is refreshing and invigorating? It asks nothing in return, and a living spring is the most inspiring thing in the world except a human life that is built upon this plane. And why is a spring a spring? Have you ever asked yourself the difference between a stagnant pool and a living spring? A spring is a spring just because it is connected with a source that is higher than it is. A spring is not itself at all; it is just a place where the water from above finds an outlet; and I can not better describe one of the great purposes that Christ had in coming, at least one of the greatest results of His coming, than to say that Christ connects a human being with the Heavenly Father and makes a connection so vital that man becomes the means through which the goodness of God pours out to the world.

Now, my friends, these alls are so numerous that I have not time to take up each one and emphasize it, but I am going to stop just a moment on the "all" that I regard as most important at the present day. Take "all thy mind."

You may cultivate a boy's mind, you may give him all the learning you can, but if his heart goes wrong, his mind goes with it. I need not tell you that in all our penitentiaries there are men splendidly educated, but their hearts went wrong. A few weeks ago at Springfield, Ohio, a banker was sent to the penitentiary for nineteen years. He had stolen a million dollars, and spent it gambling on the market. Was he an ignorant man? No. An ignorant man can't steal that much. If a man wants to steal a great deal he has got to be educated, for unless you are educated you won't be trusted with money. This man was well educated, enough to be trusted with a million, and he stole it. Now he is wearing stripes.

Another effect of mind worship is that we are putting those who train the mind above those who train the heart. I believe one of the first things we have to do is to restore the ministry to its rightful place. I believe that every Christian should insist that the man who deals with eternal things shall not be shoved off the walk by the one who deals merely in temporal things.

The science of how to live is the most important of all the sciences. Christianity is the greatest friend of education. But Christianity lays emphasis upon the science of how to live, and to show you the relative importance let me use this illustration. We want all our children to learn all the truth that there is. We want them to know philosophy, and we want them to know science; we want them to know how far the stars are apart, and the age of the rocks; but the Christian understands that as between geology and the science of how to live, it is more important to know the science of how to live. It is more important that we shall know the rock of ages than that we shall know the age of the rocks if we can't know both.

It is all well to know how far the stars are apart, but it is better to know Him in whose hands are the stars, and who separates them one from the other. So, my friends, we mustn't let them mislead us. The mind must be devoted to God, the mind must be subservient to God, the fear of God is the beginning of wisdom and there is no other beginning to wisdom.

I now come to the second group. In the first group of "alls" we are told of the completeness of the love that God demands of us. We can't do His work unless our love of God is a whole-hearted, whole-souled, whole-minded love of God, but if we have qualified ourselves to be His representatives, His messengers, it is worth while to know whether His gospel is as complete as the love that is required. I invite your attention, therefore, to the concluding verses of the last chapter of Matthew. After Christ's crucifixion, after Christ's resurrection, He gave to His church the greatest commission that was ever given to any organization. He said, "All power in heaven and in earth is given into my hands," not some power, but *all* power. Then he sent his disciples out to make converts of *all* nations, not of some nations, but of *all* nations, and He told them to teach *all* the things that He had commanded, not some of the things, but all of them, and He concluded with that wonderful promise, "Lo, I am with you always, even unto the end of the world."

Here is a gospel for every human being, here is a code of morality that is to last for all time, and here we have back of these a Christ with all power in His hands, and He has promised to be with us *always*. Christ for all and forever! There is no limitation placed upon our gospel, and here again no other word less comprehensive than "all" would have been sufficient. If there is to be a day after which Christ's gospel will not be sufficient, it is not what we have been led to suppose it is; but here we have it said that it is to last always, and it is to be for everybody. — not a living soul in all the world is beyond the reach of Christ's salvation, and everything that He taught is worth being taught.

Then there is another "all"; it is in the concluding verse of the eleventh chapter of Matthew. "Come unto me, all ye that labor and are heavy laden." That "all" gives us the universality of Christ's call. Who would dare to shear from it one atom of its wideness, who would dare to put restriction on Christ's call to the world? He said, "Take my yoke upon you and learn of me. My yoke is easy and my burden is light." The yoke is the symbol of service. I used an illustration once that I thought was original, but very often we use illustrations that we think original and then we find somebody else has used the same thing. I said in one of my speeches on this subject that if you will travel through this land you will have difficulty in finding a single steer that is six years old that hasn't a yoke on its neck; for the farmers will tell you that when a steer is four years old the sooner you fatten him and kill him the more profit you will get out of him. The longer he lives after four the less money you make on him and, therefore, the only steers that live are those that wear the yoke.

I thought this was a good illustration, but I used it in Virginia one day, and when I was through a friend came up. He said, "That is a good illustration, but I saw what I think is better"; and then he told me his illustration that he had read, and I thought it was better too. I think you will remember it better. It was this: Two oxen came in from work one evening and one of them said to the other, "I am tired of this work, and I am not going out to-morrow." So this lazy ox just loafed around the barnyard, and the industrious ox went out as usual. And when the industrious ox returned in the evening the lazy ox said, "Did the master say anything about me?"

The industrious ox said, "No, he didn't say a word."

The lazy ox said, "I will just stay around the barnyard to-morrow also." The second evening when the industrious ox came back the lazy ox said, "Did he say anything about me to-day?"

The industrious ox said, "Not exactly," and the lazy ox pricked up his ears and said, "Exactly? What *did* he say?"

"Well," said the other ox, "he didn't mention your name, but he did say that he was going by the butcher's shop to-morrow."

Now, my friends, the yoke is a thing that people seem to dislike. Sometimes we find objection very early in life to what they call a yoke. Take the parental yoke. How many young people, girls as well as boys, have tired of the parental yoke?

The Bible tells us of a case. I think it is the most beautiful story ever written. It is the story of the prodigal son. There was a young man who tired of the parental yoke. I couldn't say just when he asked for his portion, but if I were guessing I would say it was very soon after he became legally of age. He had been looking forward to the time, he had counted the years until he could be rid of the yoke, and then he counted the months, and then he counted the weeks, and then he counted the days, and I can hear him say, "Only five more, only four more days, and three more, only two more, and then to-morrow and I shall be rid of this yoke." Finally the day came, and he went to his father and said, "I want my portion." He had his plans all made and the poor father couldn't protect him any longer. He loved him, he would have saved him, he would have aided him by his advice, but he was powerless; so he gave him his portion, and the boy went out to have a good time, and he had a good time as the boys describe it. He had lots of friends, too. There are people who know by instinct when a rich boy gets his money, and they stick to him closer than a brother. They would be with him at night, and they would enjoy headaches together in the morning. But what a time they had!

And they stayed with him until the money was all gone and then they went also, for these boys who know when a rich man's son gets his money also know when it is gone. Then he had to work, and he wasn't in such good condition to work as he was before he had wasted his substance in riotous living. Then he had to take the best work he could get, and the best wasn't good, and finally he came to the worst, for feeding swine was not the same in those days as it is in Iowa on these splendid farms. It was the lowest and most degraded work there was. Then he had time to think. He had no time to think when the boys were there, they were too busy at night in revelry, and they didn't feel like thinking the next morning; but when his money was gone and his friends were gone, and he had nothing but hogs for companions, he had time to think, and then he came to himself. He said that wonderful thing: "I will arise and go to my father," and then he prepared the speech that he was to make to his father. I guess he never prepared many speeches before, but he wanted to get this one down exactly. He said, "I am not going to ask him to be a son again. No, I haven't any right to that, I will just ask him to let me be a hired man, for the hired men in my father's house have bread enough and to spare."

He arose and started back, and all the way he was rehearsing that speech, and he was wondering what impression it would make on the father. He had no idea of what the father had been thinking. He didn't know that the father had been lying awake at night more than he had, and the father was making a speech up, too. The father was thinking, "If he comes back, what shall I say to him?" The father had his speech all ready, and, then, just let the women stand aside for a moment, aren't you glad that there is a story in the Bible that tells about the father's love?

Well, as the boy was hurrying back home rehearsing his speech the father saw him, and saw him afar off, and he ran out to meet him. The son tried to make his speech, but it wasn't fair to the son to take all the time, the father had a right to some time to make a speech, too. So when the son began to tell his father, the father stopped him and told the son how glad he was to have him back, and then the father took him to the house and he hunted up the best robe, and then he got the fatted calf, and he invited in his friends, and they made merry and welcomed him.

My friends, have you thought of the contrast between the rich young man and the prodigal son? Here was a rich young man with a blameless life, but he lacked one thing, and that was that he wasn't willing to follow Christ, and what became of him? He came into the light for a moment and then he disappeared and the last thing you see of the rich young man is his back as he retires into obscurity and is not mentioned again. But here was a spendthrift; he had disgraced the family name, he had done all the sinning a boy could do, but he repented and he was sorry and he was forgiven. When we leave the prodigal son he is happy with his friends and the father is shouting, "My son that was dead is alive again," and all this is to tell us how happy the Father is when the wanderer comes home.

What other word but "all" could be used to emphasize the universality of Christ's call?

Now, friends, just let me recapitulate. Here we have the word "all," describing the extent, the wholeness, the completeness, of that love that we must give to God before we are in position to go out and do His work; and then we have the largeness and the wholeness and the completeness of the work that we are to do, that we are to carry, "all" that Christ said to "all" people everywhere, and keep carrying it always with Christ back of us "all" the time. And then we must let the world know that there isn't anybody anywhere that Christ doesn't desire to save, and we must extend his gospel to "all" who labor and are heavy laden, and bear His yoke, that is easy, and His burden, that is light, and we can offer these to every soul that suffers and to every community that is rent assunder with dissension and a world that is weary of war.

What a glorious gospel we have, what a wonderful opportunity for the Christian Endeavor society to join the militant hosts of God to carry Christ's message to all the world that we may hasten the day when His Kingdom shall come and His Will be done on earth as it is in heaven.

A prayer and benediction by Dr. Clark closed the most successful outdoor meeting in the history of Christian Endeavor. The tremendous audience stayed to the end, though the heat was terrific, and everybody was happy, inspired, and satisfied.

Chapter XVI.

SUNDAY EVENING AT THE FAIR-GROUNDS

The Fairgrounds, Sunday Evening, July 8.
Rev. Francis E. Clark, D. D., Presiding

The music of the band called the delegates again to their places for the short praise service before the evening session at the fairgrounds.

Rev. Abram E. Cory, D. D., was the first speaker.

THE QUEST FOR GOD
By Rev. Abram E. Cory, D. D.

The daily papers to-day are sounding the note of God. The question that surges in upon us is, "Are we bringing to the man in the street who has that uppermost thought of God, an interpretation of God, or are we living such a narrow life in God ourselves that he passes us by and says that he finds no interpretation of God with us? Listen to me carefully in this statement. Let us present indeed rightfully the Bible, but let us remember that the Bible is not God. It is the word of God. It is the way to God.

I went to a doctor a little while ago, and he took out of his case a book on Materia Medica. He did not take this book and eat it, but out of the book he got a prescription, and said, "If you will take this, it will help you."

Not long ago I was driving through the wonderful hills of North Carolina. In my hand was a road-map. I decided I would follow Route 10, Route 75, and Route 55. When I decided that I would follow those numbers on the guide posts, little did I know the glory of the sunsets, of the wonderful foliage, of the glorious views that there were to meet me. It was only a map that led the way.

Let us realize, friends, that we may have the Bible and not have God. It is said of Robert Ingersoll that he could repeat the whole New Testament, but he missed his Christ; he missed God. You say to me, you Endeavorers, "I know this book, or that book, or all the books of the Bible." I ask you in your knowing of them, is it mechanical, or have you discovered the road-map that leads you to a personal, definite, real experience in God?

Oh, how many gospels are being urged in upon us to-day! the economic gospel, the social gospel, the cultural gospel, the intellectual gospel, perhaps all good in their emphasis! But I was reminded of God when with a friend of mine I went through the railroad yards of Chicago. I was utterly confused at the sidetracks and the switches that were about me everywhere. There seemed to be cars here, and cars there, and roads beyond. Finally the man in the signal tower signalled to us, and we stepped off the track that we were walking on. He said: "The switches are closed now. Everything is ready. They are making way for the Overland Limited." Let us emphasize this definiteness. No matter how great we are socially or intellectually, let us be sure, my friends, that the Overland Limited is not sidetracked. The one thing we want is this: How shall men discover God? The Overland Limited to God is this, "Philip, if you have seen me, you have seen the Father." Have we enough of Jesus Christ in us that men looking upon us and the Christ in us say, "We have seen God in him."

Fred Stone was once in one of our western cities, snowbound on the western prairies. For something to read he picked up the Bible,—that great clown of the American stage. He began to read, and he saw Jesus Christ. Stone had that uppermost desire for God in his mind as does the man in the street, and what was the result? When he came to that verse, "Philip, if you have seen me you have seen the Father," Stone said "Why, I know God, for I can understand that man of Galilee that walked and talked among men and saved men by His divine power."

Friends, if a great marching army shall have limitations, restrictions, and negatives, it will, indeed, go to defeat. I can see that the Jews committed two great crimes. They crucified Christ, but they committed a greater crime than that. They put their formalism, their negative life, their definitions before the work of Jesus Christ. Jesus said, "I have come that ye might have life and that ye might have it more abundantly."

So, friends, I glory in the rapid development of this great State. But I am remembering that old battle chief out in the Philippine Islands, who when a man was telling him, "Why, in America we have this; in America we have that; in America we have the other thing," responded: "You think to be better off is to be better?" I say to you to be better off is not to be better. We must realize to-day, friends, that Christ is offering us the abundant life. Let us not be praying for power. The power is here. Let us pray that we may have the courage to make the connection.

Some one has said that life is a problem. Life is not a problem. *Life is a power*, if we are connected with Jesus Christ our Lord. I am saying to you to-night that your usefulness, young people, as you go back home, should be your attitude toward life. Do you have the attitude of Sinclair Lewis in Main Street, that cynical attitude, that attitude of analysis, or that glorious attitude of Mrs. Wiggs of the cabbage patch? What we need to-day, friends, is a life that makes us want to share the experiences of the world. When that great founder of the Salvation Army went down into the London slums, somebody said to him, "Mr. Booth, why do you go down into the London Slums?" He said, "I hunger for hell." Most of us are hungering for Heaven. I wonder how many of us to-night hunger for hell, in order that Jesus Christ may live in us, through us, and by us, that the world may be saved.

The standards of life have been the standards of power and the standards of wealth. A few days before Dr. Sheldon, the great missionary of Tibet, started for Tibet to be martyred, I saw him standing with one of the richest men in the world; and as this man without money, with only a great passion for God, told this rich man goodbye, the rich man turned with wet eyes and said to me, "Mr. Cory, he is one of the richest men in the world." And it is true, friends. Referring to the man who said that he had never done anything worth while for God without being scared to death. I am wondering how many of us have ever been scared to death. Young people, I think we talk too much about God's call to us. I believe, friends, the important thing is not God's call to you but your call to him, as Paul said, "Lord, what wilt thou have me do?" And he could say later, "I was not disobedient unto the heavenly vision." Why has God called such unexpected men? Why did he call a street-car conductor to preach to the hosts of the world? Why was Moody called as he was called? I have no doubt that God called many a city preacher and many an able man, but the reason that Moody was called *was that Moody called to God*. Why was it, friends, that he called a prisoner out of the prison of New York? Because Jerry McCawley called to God through Jesus Christ. When God was going to pick a man to break the shackles of the slave trade, why did He not take some of the powerful men of the earth? I will tell you why. He called, but Livingstone down yonder in the jungles of Africa was calling back to God.

As you go home, the question is not, "How is God calling me," the question to you, friends, you young men and women, is, "How are you calling to God? What are you saying to him in this hour?"

We come from great churches, many of us, but most of us come, as Dr. Frank Crane calls it, from the little church on Main Street. Somebody from some little town in Iowa, Missouri, or Kansas says, "What can I do?" Frank Crane said, "Who made America dry? The newspapers? The politicians? No. The great city churches? No. It was the little church on Main Street that put America dry." Who is going to bring law enforcement? Who is going to bring world peace? Who is going to bring economic justice? Who is going to bring this great revival of religion and the saving of souls that our honored President called us to the other night? You young men and women, you in that little church on Main Street.

One day in Moscow I went into one of those great churches. In that church there was a great bell. A friend of mine said, "You ought to hear that bell." Finally he called to a young man who came forward. That young man had something in his hands which I at first thought was a stick, but I could not see how he could reach the bell up there many hundred feet above him. That young Russian came out and stood under the very centre of that bell. Then he lifted the flute, for that was what he had, to his lips and he sounded the flute. At first there was no answer. Then he stopped for a second or two and sounded the flute again. Finally from out of the great metallic heart of that bell came beautiful notes that linger in my soul to-day.

My friends, God is here. God is ready, but he is waiting for us to place the flute of devotion, the flute of confession, the flute of obedience, the flute of absolute abandonment, to our lips, and if we will sound it He will answer. Then we can answer the call for God in the mind of the man in the street.

One of the marked indications of the favor of God upon the Christian Endeavor movement is the men and women He has brought to the front as secretaries and leaders in the different departments. My mind goes back to the early days, and I remember many whom God has particularly blessed, men of hearts, men of intellect, but above all men of heart. I think of John Willis Baer. You remember how fascinating was his appearance upon the platform, and how he often stirred our hearts. And William Shaw, I would like to pause for just a moment as we think of Shaw. I am sure he is thinking and praying for us to-night. And Clarence Eberman, field-secretary, who died in the Canadian Rockies while on one of his pilgrimages for Christian Endeavor. And we are wonderfully blessed now in the personnel of the society. I will not speak of these men, because they are here, and because I do not need to, for you know them. One of them is going to speak to us to-night. The man who is going to speak to us to-night we admire, we love, we honor, the Associate President of the United Society of Christian Endeavor, Daniel Poling.

THE GREATEST FACT IN HISTORY

By Rev. Daniel A. Poling, D. D.

Associate President of the United Society of Christian Endeavor

Christianity is the greatest fact of history, greater than creation, greater than discovery, greater than invention, greater than government. Creation is bringing into existence that which did not before exist. Creation is first, save only the Creator, who is always greater than His word.

Christianity is the supreme expression of the creative mind and will. Discovery is a making known, as in art or science, or in the natural world. Christianity is a making new, the recreating of the souls of men, the ways of the institutions, and the spirit of human relationships.

Invention is devising in the mechanical world that which was not known before. Christianity has to do with the minds and the spirits of the inventors. It becomes the supreme expression of their minds and souls, even as it becomes the summum bonum of us all. Government is control, regulation, authority, as in the home, the state. Christianity has to do with subjects, controls governments, because it dictates the expressions of the conscience.

Christianity is the greatest fact of history, Christian Endeavorers, because of its promises. In my father's old library was a set of books entitled, "Thirty Thousand Promises," and every promise was taken from between the pages that stand after Genesis and before the closing words of the Revelation, promises covering every human need, promises meeting every legitimate human desire, thirty thousand promises. Every circumstance of suffering, every necessity of temptation is covered in one great promise, "As is thy need, so shalt thy strength be."*

Years ago a young man carrying the colors of his Alma Mater on a college overall, with the finish of a grilling race less than thirty yards away, was suddenly taken by a muscular seizure known at one time or another by practically every athlete. He discovered himself going rapidly out of hand. He faced the overwhelming thought that after having practically won his race, after having won not only his race, but the meet of the afternoon, through no fault of his own he was about to fall and fail of completing his task. Then there flashed into his mind that promise, "As is thy need, so shalt thy strength be." He prayed not for victory, only to be able to do his best. And on that promise, Christian Endeavorers, gathering himself together, he launched his failing body into space and crossed the tape, winner of the race.

"As is thy need, so shalt thy strength be." The widow gathers her fatherless children beneath its shelter and the dying turn their failing eyes toward its unfailing beacon. The tempted gather from it strength with which to meet their dearest sin. "As is thy need, so shalt thy strength be."

Other religions have promises, too, but I do not imagine that we will find any follower of Mohammed or Buddha or Confucius standing successfully in debate with a follower of the Galilean, at this point. "As is thy need, so shalt thy strength be," perfect strength, perfect health, and the perfecting of good.

Christianity is the greatest fact of history because of the contribution it has made to society as well as to the individual. Judge every tree by its fruit. I think that sometimes we as Christians have failed at this point that we have been unwilling to judge every tree by its fruit. Perhaps the stern school of persecution in which the early church was trained caused men to deal with sternness when they came into power. It behooves us all to put into application the homely philosophy of the simple verse:

> "There is so much bad in the best of us
> And so much good in the worst of us,
> That it doesn't behoove any of us
> To say anything much about the rest of us."

Christianity strengthens herself in the expression of her followers when she recognizes the fact that institutions and agencies not directly related to her programme have made a vast contribution to human good. Indeed, it is when we thus appreciate and when we thus evaluate that we gather a truer perspective with which to measure our own faith and with

---

*FOOTNOTE: Dr. Poling is obviously paraphrasing the text, which reads: "And as thy days so shall thy strength be."

which to treasure that which God through Jesus Christ has done for us. For Christianity has not only made her direct contributions to man. Christianity has refined and perfected all other contributions that have been worth while.

There may be a difference of opinion, but in the humble judgment of the speaker the supreme contribution of Christianity to man is the sense of the divine in man. When Jesus said, "Ye are the temple of the Holy Ghost," He gave the right about face to civilization. Ye, not the altar in the inmost sanctuary, ye are the holy of holies: Then did He lift a babe, child of the humblest toiler, above the diadem of state, then did He set in motion influences that were to bring to pass a day when the thorn in the heel of a barefoot boy would be of vaster importance than the trappings of a prince, and when the hours of toil and the wage for women and children would be a more vital concern with governments than the protection of temporal wealth.

Everything that sets itself against personality, Jesus Christ has arrayed Christianity against. Everything that pollutes the human mind, that degrades the human heart, that spoils the immortal soul, Jesus Christ has called His followers to go out to destroy. With hospitals and institutions of learning, with programmes of healing and plans of mercy, He has called us to this war to bring to pass the day when the kingdoms of the earth shall have become the kingdom of our Lord and Saviour Jesus Christ. The most intrepid missionary adventurers and the bravest reformers that the Christian church has inspired and led, have followed in the train of Him who said, "Love thy neighbor as thyself."

Slavery died because it violated human personality, the personality of the slave-driver as well as that of the slave. Dueling was outlawed because it degraded personality. Prohibition could not have come to be had it not been for the fact that the beverage traffic in intoxicating liquors raised the brute and destroyed personality. Organized vice will be removed because it leaves a red blotch of shame upon human personality. And war, red-handed and colossal destroyer, will some day pass from the stage of human action, because it moves against the Divine impersonality, because it leaves its dead twice upon the planes of battle, once in the fair-eyed sons who had just begun to live, and once sealed forever in the laws of potential fatherhood it has destroyed, once in generations that can never be. Yea, this into which God has poured Himself, this which is His supreme expression, the supreme expression of His creative mind and love and will, this which as God Himself is deathless, can never die, this is Christianity's supreme contribution to man. Not in altars, not in shrines, not in temples, not in works of art, but in a child, a babe, a maiden, a lad, a man, a woman, genius or toiler, worker or captain of trade, within it God dwells. "Thou art the Holy of holies."

Christianity is the greatest fact of history because of its authority. The religion of Jesus Christ is the religion of supreme authority. It is the ultimate authority. That word is not a pleasant word in these days. We turn from it; we shrug our shoulders to shake off its restrictions. But, Christian Endeavorers, until we learn to know what the implications of the word are, you will be late on the street and early into trouble. Our courts will continue to be publicity agencies for stories of shame in the life of the American home. Statesmanship will continue to be rather the football of scheming politicians and will fall short of the purposes of the fathers of the nation who knelt about the table in the room where later they signed the Declaration of Independence, and called upon the Captain of the nations of the earth to give guidance and direction to this new adventure in liberty.

The religion of Jesus Christ is the religion of supreme authority. We have here the divorcement of the church and state. But, in the words of former Associate Justice Brewer of the United States Supreme Court, this is a Christian nation, and only in proportion as the principles and the Spirit of Jesus Christ become regnant in the lives of the people may we hope to survive the disasters that have come to all similar adventures in freedom.

I have no desire to-night to speak of the things that have so largely commanded our attention in the days immediately preceding this, as we have addressed ourselves to the great social and industrial problems that are essentially the Christianities of the American people. They remain. They will remain. The eight-hour day is yet in the offing. The enforcement of prohibition has not yet been fully accomplished, but I am especially concerned with the question, "How may we, the Christian Endeavorers of the church, address ourselves successfully to the tasks?" We have declared our intentions. We have made plain our purposes. Where is the plan that offers hope? Where is the trail up which the legions now may march?

Christianity is the greatest fact of history, because Christianity has an answer for that question. Other religions have made their contribution to the happiness and culture of man, have raised walls of beautiful cities, have stretched wide the boundaries of empires, have furthered man's ambitions, have filled his coffers, yea, and have answered the imperial cry of his mind for light, light, more light! Have fed his soul, fed it with husks, perhaps! But, Christian Endeavorers, Christianity alone has been able to answer that cry, that cry for light, more light, because Christianity alone has Jesus Christ in His fullness of love and power, and, in the last analysis, this is the reason why Christianity is the greatest fact in history.

Are we discouraged? Are we pessimistic? Are we troubled beyond reason of that which we have seen and heard and felt?

> "Oh Captain! say the night is black with thunder,
> The ship is tossing in the waves' wild will;
> The foaming white-caps hiss and slip from under;
> The mighty engine's throbbing heart is still.
>
> "Where are we drifting in this night of error?
> Hysteric pilots wrangle at the wheel,
> With rudder gone, into the glooming terror,
> The great ship rushes on uneven keel!
>
> "'Oh, ye of little faith, am I not able'
> (I hear my Captain's answer brave and strong),
> 'When every anchor slips her faithless cable,
> To guide the ship that I have kept so long?
>
> "'The little pilots, at each others' railing,
> Soon fall asleep and all their strife forget;
> But I who sets the fleets of time to sailing
> Have thy great nation in my guidance yet.'"

And let me say to-night, Christian Endeavorers, that in my humble opinion, the supreme and immediate task of the church of God, and our supreme and immediate task as militant children of the church of God, is the task of presenting Jesus Christ, not only as a Saviour of the institutions of our society, but more specifically, more particularly, as the Saviour of the individual and the State.

We have talked about the new world. We have talked about the new social order to-night. But, Christian Endeavorers and friends of the church, there will be no new world without new world-builders, and man is yet dead in trespasses and in sin until he becomes new in Jesus Christ.

The message of this convention in the harvest time, in the fullness of the season, is the message of evangelism. Go out to the people; tell the glad story, the good news. Make plain the gospel plan and gather all the nations to His mind. He is the only sufficient Savior, and except we believe in Him and practise Him we cannot survive.

And do you recall that when Jesus Christ left His plan of campaign to His followers, the plan that was to abide until the Heavens roll up as a scroll, He said, "And I, if I be lifted up from the earth, will draw all men unto me." Never before in history were words so amazing spoken by a leader: "I, if I be lifted up from the earth will draw all men unto me." But that spirit survived, where power failed, that spirit sent the first missionaries of the cross toward earth's last frontiers, that spirit set the signal fires of the Pentecostal upper room. That spirit held the gaze of Stephen when through showering stones he turned his face toward the opening heavens and cried out for forgiveness for his murderers. That spirit thrashed Saul of Tarsus with lightnings and thrust him forth to be the first great field-marshal of the Lord's advance. That spirit conquered Rome as Attila or Hannibal never conquered it. It made out of the heathen coliseum a Christian church. It set up by the Golden Horn a spiritual empire more potent and extensive than the temporal throne of Constantine. "I will draw all men unto me." It marched before the cross of St. Augustine. It came first for Savonarola. It led the Ironsides of Cromwell. It eased the seas about the prow of the Half Moon. It calmed the waves that washed the decks of the Mayflower. It opened the wilderness to the circuit riders of our church, Charles Wesley, Zinzendorf, Luther, David Livingstone, followed in the train of His never-dying spirit, and presently the waste places of the earth, dead in superstition and sin, blossomed with the flowers of salvation. They swung Him up 'twixt earth and sky. They nailed Him to a slave's cross and with the first breath of His "It is finished," began the disintegration of the Roman Empire. They fed His followers to the lions, lions starved for the occasion, and that bloody sand became the seed ground of His church. They chained His Book, only to discover that they had released His word. And then came high success, and men took on His name in easy fashion and cloaked their real selves behind loud professions, but His cause stood fast. It survived prosperity. It survived the leaderships of captains who forgot the passion of His cause as they followed in the train of earthly monarchs. And to-day, with perilous times behind, and yet weightier events before, rises an irresistible tide in the affairs of civilization bearing man forward, lifting him upward and on.

In all history there is not another spectacle like this, an empire without a capital, a conqueror without an army, a king without a sword. The fact is proof that love is the greatest thing in the world, and its only answer is God.

It was a war day in Winnipeg. I stood with friends in the great station of the Canadian Pacific Railway. It was after Vimy Ridge, two months, and men were coming back with sightless eyes and limbless bodies. We watched them borne through on stretchers, men no longer fit for cannon fodder. And then I saw a sight that until all the flowers of memory fade and die I will never forget. Two lads came through the gate, one with the telltale and darkened glasses of the blind above his sightless eyes, and with an awful scar upon his face. He leaned upon a crutch that took the place of a limb that he had left on the other side. The other chap was strong and alert, with no visible mark upon his body save for the hollows in his cheeks and the flame of fever in his youthful eyes that turned impatiently to the left and right. Women were about the entrance. From the group one woman tore herself free. She threw herself upon the lad, who seemed to have something of the strength with which he marched away. She took him to her heart. She lost her fingers in his hair. She covered his face with her kisses. My eye centred on that group of home-coming gladness. Suddenly I saw the boy disengage himself, press his mother back and turn as with a passion of fear to the blind lad who had been with him.

The sightless fellow had not moved from his place, quite forlorn he stood, quite alone. There had been for him no home-coming party. Now, the other fellow with his finger pointing toward him cried, and I can hear his voice to-night, "Mother, he did it. He did it." And the mother left her son standing as though she had lost him, took the blind and forlorn soldier to her heart and *lost her fingers in his hair*, kissed him as another woman might have kissed him had she been there.

This was the tale. It was at Vimy Ridge. The one lad stunned by shell shock was laying in the open. The other went out to bring him back, and an explosion made him sightless, gave him the wound below his hip that left him presently with only one leg. But with the passion of an iron will he gripped his buddy and turned toward the trench. He crawled through ages of agony back to safety. He did it!

Christian Endeavorers, to-night that is the message that I bring to you. Christianity is the greatest fact of history, because Jesus Christ did it; because He saved men in His body, in His life, in His death, in His resurrection, in His everlasting life. He did it.

"Go preach, the kingdom is at hand,
The Kingdom's at the gate,
Go tell the news in every land,
He comes for whom ye wait.

"He comes with lightnings and in wrath;
He follows down the sea;
He sweeps the barriers from His path
To set the captives free.

"He comes with laughter in His eyes,
Soft as the yellow dews;
And hungry children hush their cries,
To shout the glad good news.

"He comes, He comes, with healing balm
For all the hurts of men;
He comes, He comes with hope and calm
Where all the wars have been.

"Sound, trumpet sound, in golden flood,
His reign that shall not cease;
He comes to make of all one blood,
Triumphant Prince of Peace!"

After a brief prayer Dr. Poling asked that any that felt God's call to confession or the declaration of a great purpose would stand in the dusk in the vast crowd. One verse of "Alas, and did my Saviour bleed?" followed the appeal.

CHAPTER XVII

CHRISTIAN ENDEAVOR FIELD SECRETARIES

PLYMOUTH CONGREGATIONAL CHURCH, MONDAY, JULY 9.

Clarence C. Hamilton Presiding

Monday morning there was a special meeting for those States that had not held conventions. At this meeting a splendid group of State field-secretaries were present and spoke. C. C. Hamilton, field-secretary of the United Society, was the leader and fittingly introduced his brothers and sisters of the Christian Endeavor road.

In some ways this was a remarkable meeting, for it showed the fine calibre of the men and women who have risen to leadership in Christian Endeavor, a splendid group, able, eloquent, earnest secretaries who have intimate knowledge of all aspects of Christian Endeavor. It was a delight to listen to them.

PRISON CHRISTIAN ENDEAVOR

MISS GEORGIA DUNN

Kentucky's Field-Secretary

The first thing we want to know is why we do prison work. The humanitarian motive, though that is a high one, will break down, for after we have done our best for these people some of them will turn against us. The thief will return to his thieving, and the murderer will return to his killing, but when we go into the work with the motive of pleasing the Master and doing something for Him, we know He is unchangeable and whatever they do He is the same, and the blessings will come.

Now, the method. There is opportunity for plenty of jail work. We haven't been doing much in Kentucky. But officers are getting on the track of the moonshiner, and the jails are filling up, not because there is more lawlessness, but because we are going after it more. This is the order of jail Christian Endeavor service: first, a devotional service, songs, hymns, prayers, Scripture, and if you can get a speaker to make a short speech, have that speech. Have a little personal work if you can depend on some one to do that work. This is no place for a worker who has not proved to be a consecrated worker.

These men like the old hymns, like "Nearer, My God to Thee." We had a man who heard those songs in Lexington when I was there in college, and he said, "I haven't been to Sunday school for twenty years. When I get out I am going back to those old songs." How they do love "God Will Take Care of You"!

If your prison is in politics, as they are in many places, be sure you get some one who has influence with the authorities to go with you

The Pennsylvania Delegation

and introduce you to the superintendent of the institution. See that you are properly introduced and that the superintendent understands he will be reported if things do not go along smoothly, and then see to it that your part of the work goes along smoothly, too. Don't let anybody ever break a single prison rule.

Get your chaplain and some faithful friends who may be among the guards of the prisoners to help you select the leaders that you are going to put at the head of your Christian Endeavor society in the prison, that is if you are going to organize in your State prison. Don't undertake to organize until you have proved yourself there. Go down for a simple devotional service before you say anything about it. Let them know that you are coming to do them good. Get a committee appointed; they know who the best men are, and they will be glad to point them out and give them a chance; and then we organize almost as we do on the outside. This committee appoints officers. We used to let the prisoners elect their own officers, but they have some politicians, and they used them with deadly effect, so we had to appoint our committee and they take care of it. You will have your president, vice-president, secretary and treasurer, and there will be committees that look after the social and amusement part, the prayer meeting and the music. I am surprised at some of the committees that they invent. These committeemen will take the greatest pride and delight in doing their committee work.

On Thanksgiving last year we took four hundred and thirty-two cakes to Frankfort Reformatory, and each man got a huge slice of real Central Kentucky cake. At Easter time at Eddyville we had seventy-five cakes for the four hundred and eighty men there, and they were the happiest men we ever had. Next year on Christian Endeavor's birthday we are going to send cakes to Eddyville.

We have had some men come out of the prison at Frankfort with hands stained with their brothers' blood and go back to preach the gospel in the places they made life miserable before.

Last Fall as I was going down into the mountains of Kentucky I had to ride eleven miles, for at the other end of the line there was a society of one hundred and twenty members whose president was a man who caught a vision of service in Frankfort six years before, and he had so proven himself that the people of that village had come to the conclusion that he was guiltless of the charge brought against him. And there are many cases like this.

CHRISTIAN ENDEAVOR IN THE CITY CHURCH

Harold Singer

Oklahoma's Field-Secretary

As we think of Christian Endeavor we sometimes wonder whether the organization of Christian Endeavor will work in the large city church, and if it works, whether it will reach a great number of the young people. We are having come into the programme of Christian Endeavor to-day the idea of the graded system, and as we apply the graded system of Christian Endeavor to our city church, no matter how large the church, we find that Christian Endeavor is meeting the need in the church, and I think that is the first thing we have got to take into consideration: the need, and see if Christian Endeavor will meet that need.

I talked with a director of religious education in a big church and he told me there was great need for leaders in the church. He couldn't find any one to head a real Junior Christian Endeavor society; for some time they had been without a Junior society—for over a year—for they could not find any one willing to give their time to that work.

From the standpoint of leadership they needed the organization of Christian Endeavor that trains leaders for the church.

Last January they organized in that church, a Christian Endeavor society for every group or grade they had in the Sunday school, and as they started out that system on the first Sunday in January it was interesting to watch the increase in the number of folks attending the Christian Endeavor society of that church.

Under the old system of three societies they had something like seventy-five attend Christian Endeavor organization. Now they have eight Christian Endeavor societies, six grades, but eight societies, having two Juniors and two Junior high school or intermediate groups from fourteen to eighteen years of age. They have a membership of one hundred and ninety, with an average attendance of one hundred and sixty-eight.

I think to work the Christian Endeavor organization, the graded system, in our city churches or any other sized churches, it is well to get the groups together, as these folks meet together a half-hour before the regular Christian Endeavor meeting each Sunday night, for a little sing-sing.

As to organization, they have a Christian Endeavor Council, consisting of the presidents of the two older societies, the superintendents of the younger societies, the Juniors and Intermediate and high school folks. This Council gets together once a month, and there in that body the leaders from the different societies map out the programme for all those organizations.

The folks that should be in certain societies are put there by this Council, and so they work the graded society, the graded organization; they promote the members from time to time so that they are keeping their grading regular, as it should be.

I think it is necessary, also, to get the folks together regularly as executive committees. The first Monday night in each month they come together as an executive committee. The executive committees of all the societies come together in a little banquet, and then they go to their different rooms and have their executive committee meetings.

Here we have a proposition of applying the organization of Christian Endeavor to the city church. The need is there; Christian Endeavor will meet that need. We just have to set up the machinery so it will meet the need in the most efficient way.

CHRISTIAN ENDEAVOR AND THE QUIET HOUR

RUSSELL J. BLAIR

Field-Secretary for Massachusetts

I am not thinking this morning specifically of the Quiet Hours we have at our State conventions, and our International conventions, or any other group meetings where we come together in large numbers, but I am thinking this morning of the Quiet Hour we have as individuals, the Quiet Hour covenant that thousands and thousands of young people have taken, individually, in their own lives, as they are coming in the early hours of the morning to spend just a few moments in quiet communion with their Heavenly Father.

I am thinking that I might say to folks who ask me why Christian Endeavor is the vital force that it is to-day: Christian Endeavor has prospered in these days that have gone by, and is prospering in this present day, because there are thousands upon thousands, yea millions upon millions of folks who have gone through the ranks of Christian Endeavor, who are in the ranks of Christian Endeavor to-day, who are glad to spend a few moments in communion with their Heavenly Father, asking that His blessing might be on their lives, that His blessing might be on the organization which we love and whose name we bear, asking that His plans might be carried out in the lives of the young people. Christian Endeavor is what it is to-day because we have believed in prayer. Christian Endeavor is what it is to-day because young people all down through the forty-two years of the history of the movement has been willing to spend time in quiet prayer. How are we ever going to know what Christ wants us to do, how are we going to find His plan for our lives, unless we are willing to give to Him the opportunity of speaking to us in that quiet way? We must be willing to allow Him the privilege of telling us whatsoever it is that He would have us do. We repeat our pledge time after time, "Trusting in the Lord Jesus Christ for strength, I promise Him that I will strive to do whatever He would like to have me do." Now, how will we know what that "whatever" means unless we do give Him the opportunity of speaking definitely to us and through us to the other folks that we are coming in contact with?

I have found that the things that would worry me most weigh down more heavily the day I forget to keep that pledge. We all forget from time to time, but, young folks, and comrades of the Quiet Hour, we need to take a new courage; we need to have a new thought in our mind and resolve definitely that we will have those few moments in quiet communion. Our days will be brighter; our work will be lighter; we will be able to do things in a better way.

Then, too, there is another thought that has been running through my mind lately. Some of our young folks seem to have the wrong conception; they seem to think that after they have spent fifteen minutes in prayer their duties and obligations have all been met, and there is nothing further to do. Folks, we need to be in touch with God for more than just the fifteen minutes that we spend in our Quiet Hour. Splendid and fine as it is to start the day out in that way, how much more we need our Heavenly Father to be with us all through the day, to be with us at the noon hour, to be with us through the afternoon hours in our business, in our play, in any work that we have to do, having Him with us, not being afraid to take to Him the perplexing things that come up in our lives, not being afraid to tell Him the joyful things we have in our lives, but all through the day being in close touch with Him, by communing with Him.

It is not always necessary to get down on your knees to pray. It is not always necessary to be in church to pray. It is not always necessary to be in the quietness of your room to pray, but we can pray wherever we are. We can be in touch with Him by our thoughts going up to Him and by His thoughts and His wishes for our lives coming down to us.

We are to give some specific and definite ways of working these different departments that we have. I hardly think it is necessary for me to say that we should have a Quiet Hour superintendent in every union. We should have a Quiet Hour when our folks have the privilege of getting together and talking over their problems. We should have prayer services, and in all things we should be emphasizing that prayer is the power that ties us up to God. Prayer is the method by which we come in touch with Him. May we make more of our Quiet Hour. May our Quiet Hour mean more to us because it is our individual opportunity of coming in touch with our Heavenly Father.

THE TENTH LEGION

HERBERT HICKS

Field-Secretary of the Connecticut Union

I am wondering how many of you are enrolled as members of the Tenth Legion? I know what some of you are going to say. You are going to say, "What difference does it make?" It doesn't really make a great deal of difference, if you are giving a tenth of your income to the Lord, whether your name is on the record or not. We don't urge it except for one reason, and that is simply the fact that adding your name to the thousands who are so enrolled is an encouragement to the young people who are starting. It is enrollment between you and God really, and not between you and the United Society, and so the enrollment is meant to help others and not merely to swell the numbers enrolled.

I am wondering if the incomes of those thousands that met yesterday were taken and added together, and one-tenth taken, how much more the Lord could do through us and through our gifts than He actually is doing! And when we multiply that by the other thousands of Christians throughout the world, I am wondering what the storehouse of the Lord would contain!

I just want to make a definite suggestion, and that is this: first, from a personal standpoint if you have not yet enrolled, take it to the Lord, don't decide on the ground of what I say or what any one else in this convention says, but between you and Jesus Christ make your decision whether or not you ought to be giving that tenth to Him; and then not only enroll yourself, but carry back to your society and to your union some sort of germ of a definite plan so that you shall set before your union and set before your society, as a goal, as many State unions, many county unions, many local unions and societies have set before us in times past, a definite percentage of your membership enrolled as members of the Tenth Legion within a given length of time.

We must have a definite goal, and we must have some definite way of reaching it, and that means to place upon the shoulders of one individual of upon the shoulders of one committee the need of this, and of working out plans for carrying it out, presenting it from time to time in the most attractive way, presenting it so that the young men and young women will feel in their lives and in their hearts the impulse to enroll as members of the Tenth Legion, and thus increase the amount which can be used in the Lord's service in this world.

COMMUNITY CHRISTIAN ENDEAVOR

Ernest Davies

Field-Secretary of the Colorado Union

I have in mind several societies, one in particular, that are putting over a real community programme. They are taking the church programme once a month. I know one society in Denver that is going out into the suburbs every Sunday and putting over a community programme. One Endeavorer takes the pulpit and preaches a sermon, another Endeavorer acts as superintendent of the Sunday school, another Endeavorer leads the singing, another Endeavorer plays the piano, and all of that is done by one society, and they do that every Sunday. They are absolutely taking over this mission out there, and handling it in fine style.

I was up there just a few months ago and organized them into a community society, and it happened that some of the older folks were there. They hadn't any idea of a Community Endeavor before; they thought it was necessary to have a Christian Endeavor society in one church and another in another.

It seems to me that a Community Christian Endeavor society has to have a real programme in order to put it over. This you can do as an individual society in the community, or you can do it as a community society, but it seems to me there is a plenty of work for each committee to do. For instance, the prayer-meeting committee can hold outdoor services. You can hold these services after a rousing song service and a good gospel message, and then ask the people to get up and give testimonies. It might touch some soul that just stopped to listen to the talk, and win them.

Then there is the lookout committee. There is a real job for the lookout committee to co-operate in putting over any evangelistic meetings that might be in town. I was in one town a short time ago, and after I arrived I found they were having an evangelistic meeting. The young people had planned a rally for us that evening. Immediately we called it off and all went over to the evangelistic meeting, and it meant a great deal to us. We need to get the inspiration of evangelistic meetings now and then. We can back up an evangelistic meeting in our own town in every way; we can see that the ushers are supplied; we can see that the books are distributed, and then we can organize and promote a church census. One society is putting over a census in a town where they have divided the town into sections, and each Endeavorer is taking a certain section and calling at the houses and finding out how many young people there are there, and if they are attending any church or any Christian Endeavor society.

Then there is the social committee. The social committee has a programme to put over. We can go right into the community and organize the children's play, and have Saturday afternoon as a time when we can help these folks really to learn how to play. It is surprising how few children really know how to play, and that is a real job that we can put over as a Community Endeavor. We can also organize community athletic contests. It seems to me there is a fine job for us.

Ofttimes we do our church work on too small a scale. If we were in business, and had any money at stake, we would do it on a larger scale; advertise it, put it in the papers, put posters all over the street corners, and pass small hand bills around announcing that we are going to have a big missionary meeting in our church on Sunday night. There are many ways of putting over a community programme in the town.

If you are trying to carry on your work as a small society, and there are other societies in your town, I would urge that you try to get them together. You will have to work that in very close co-operation with your pastor and your boards, but it can be done, and I know that every one of us, trusting in the Lord, Jesus Christ for strength in carrying on this work, can do a great work for our Master.

FLOATING CHRISTIAN ENDEAVOR

REV. C. E. HETZLER

Field-Secretary for Pennsylvania

I am going to take as a sample from which to speak, the Philadelphia Christian Endeavor Union in our own State, which is doing perhaps the greatest floating Endeavor work in all the country. Now the question may arise, as it did with me before I was acquainted with it, just what floating Christian Endeavor is. It is Christian Endeavor in activity among those who go down to sea. That is about as briefly as I can put it.

I want to say, before I speak of the floating Endeavor work, that it is very fortunate for the Philadelphia Christian Endeavor Union that they were able to hook up with the Seamen's Church Institute in Philadelphia. Some thirty or forty years ago I believe there was a church built on a raft which floated around there in the harbor, and that was the seamen's church. That burned, but now they have a building at 201 South Walnut Street where they are carrying on what is practically a Y. M. C. A. for the men who go and come on the sea. There they can get beds for twenty-five or thirty cents—nice, clean beds. It would just do you good to visit that place to see how nice and clean they keep it. There they get meals for a very small sum; there they have all kinds of reading, everything that would go with a Y. M. C. A., and so it was the great fortune of the Philadelphia Christian Endeavor to connect with the Seamen's Church Institute in their work, and while the Seamen's Church Institute carries on what we might call Y. M. C. A. work among seafaring folks, the religious work on board ships is delegated to the Christian Endeavorers of the city.

Rev. Mr. Tressler is the superintendent of that department for the State. Now the religious work on the boats, as I say, is delegated to the Endeavorers, and the eight branches of the Philadelphia Christian Endeavor Union are each one responsible for their section of the seventy miles of the city's water-front. They have three services a week; each branch does not have three services, but that is what they aim at—Sunday morning, Sunday afternoon, and Tuesday evening, two hours at each time. The Endeavorers go on board the ships and visit the seamen, going to their cabins, and if it is bad weather they meet in the dining-room, and if it is good weather they hold their religious services on deck. Ten to twenty-five Endeavorers go out in a bunch.

It was interesting to me when I visited this work to talk to one Englishman who very emphatically stated that the best treatment they got in any port was in the ports on this side of the water where this work is being done. This Englishman took us into his little room and said, "I am not a Christian, but I am not the meanest man in the world, I don't shut the door on them when they come in and read the Bible." He took out a nice Bible and showed it to us with a great deal of pride.

[Mr. Hetzler showed the audience a "comfort-bag," such as Endeavorers give in large numbers to sailors. He told what such bags contain.]

We furnish a little folder with needles and safety pins, and here is another little pin cushion. Here is a spool of black thread, a piece of beeswax, two spools of darning cotton—black and white—and a little roll of wrapping tissue for wrapping sores. Then there is a small jar of vaseline for any little cuts and bruises that they may receive. Here is a sack of buttons of various kinds. A Testament goes in every comfort bag that is given out to any of the seamen. Here is a pair of scissors, and if you want to see some real awkwardness, go down and see them use those things. Here is a thimble; I suppose it would be interesting to see them use that. Here is a little bag of emery, for the salt water makes their needles rust, and whenever they want to sew they jab them into that a little bit and it grinds the rust off. Here is another spool of thread.

These boys and girls in the Philadelphia branch unions are going out carrying the gospel, preaching and teaching; they have hundreds of meetings and thousands of sailors go to these meetings and enjoy them.

CHAIRMAN HAMILTON: Let's have the names of some of the ports where some of this work is being done.

. . . The following names were given: San Pedro, San Francisco, San Diego, Vallejo, Cal.; Bellingham, Wash.; Portland, Or.; Chicago, Ill.

RURAL CHRISTIAN ENDEAVOR

Madilene Carter

Field-Secretary for Kansas

We really have some fine rural Christian Endeavor societies out in Kansas. I will admit that it is hard to work rural Christian Endeavor in some districts. I will admit that Christian Endeavor societies are started in some of our rural districts, and that they die out and must be started over again; but just because two of the four trees I planted this spring died is no reason why we can't have some trees in our back yard. We will start over again next fall and put in two more, and they may grow to be larger and better because they had to be planted in the fall instead of the spring. So if you folks have let Christian Endeavor die out in some of your districts, dig your hole a little deeper, and give it a little more water, and start your Christian Endeavor society over again, and it may grow to be bigger and better than some of those you started years ago.

One day I went to a rural community. I wondered where they were going to find any people for this picnic they had invited me to, and after a while they came across the prairie on their ponies to a little house for the picnic. It was a little house of two or three rooms. They called me in after the meal was over to talk to them. Out of a group of sixteen people there was only one who had ever heard of Christian Endeavor before. They organized a Christian Endeavor society that afternoon, and all this winter I have been thinking of those people as they have been meeting on Sunday afternoons in a rural schoolhouse, some of them coming six or seven miles across the prairie on their ponies, some of them walking, and they had to carry their own fuel because the school district would not furnish fuel for a Christian Endeavor meeting.

I could take you into the southeastern part of the state where we have many rural Christian Endeavor societies. Here is a town which is merely a wide place in the road. Years ago there used to be churches there. The two churches there have been combined and there is a united society. Out of that has come one of the best district workers in the State of Kansas. He can go into any district of his State, and the pastor will gladly step out of his pulpit and give him a chance to bring the message of Jesus Christ, because of the wonderful work he has done. Let me tell you that he lives six miles from a railroad, and when he calls a Christian Endeavor meeting he has to walk that six miles or ride his pony. When it was too cold to take his pony, because he wouldn't leave it standing in the cold, he walked the six miles because he believed in Christian Endeavor. Are you carrying Christian Endeavor to your rural districts? You don't have to have a church or even a schoolhouse to have a Christian Endeavor society. You have your young people; you can gather them together. They have nothing else in some of the rural districts. They have no social life except social life of a kind you wouldn't want them to have, and they need the Christian Endeavor. You can come in with a Christian Endeavor society and clean up the whole social life of a community. I have seen communities where even the picture shows closed up when the Christian Endeavor societies held a social or a business meeting. The basketball games have to be put off because the young people are in Christian Endeavor.

In one church nine young people of the society are in training for full-time service for their Master, because of what Christian Endeavor did in that little rural church. Down in a little town of six hundred inhabitants, in Kansas, they have four Christian Endeavor societies. You need Christian Endeavor graded just as you do in your big churches, and one of those Christian Endeavor societies out of the four caught the vision of doing work for their Master, and they threw out as a challenge to the other Friends societies in the United States that they would raise one thousand dollars for missions in their little society of forty members. They not only made the challenge, but they raised that money, and there is a thousand dollars more for the work being done for Jesus Christ by the Friends Missionary Society than there would have been if the church had not believed in graded Christian Endeavor.

Because you live in a city, don't think you have nothing to do with rural Christian Endeavor. The folks who have had training in the local churches ought to go to the rural districts and carry the message of Jesus Christ to the young people there.

One of our Christian Endeavor societies caught the vision in one of our conventions and started out to organize a Christian Endeavor society. They went into a little mining town where the young people had had no advantages along church lines at all. Some of them had never been in a

Sunday school, and it was impossible to start Christian Endeavor there, but they did start a Sunday school.

They gathered together the children of these miners in a little dirty schoolhouse, and week after week taught them about Jesus Christ. One Sunday morning when they came down they found the schoolhouse empty. That was unusual, for those children and those young people were so eager they were always there long before the workers reached the town, and they sat there a few minutes and waited.

Presently the door opened and in came a little bit of a girl and she was crying. She said, "Our little baby died yesterday. The children are all up at our house, and my mother sent me down to get you folks. She wants you to come up and conduct the funeral services."

They said, "We can't go. You should get a minister. We don't know how to do it."

She said, "No minister ever comes to us. You folks came and told us about Jesus, and my mother wants you up there." So they went. They didn't know just what to do, but they went up there to the house and they found a crowd of miners waiting for them, and they conducted a little service. Then they drove seven miles to the cemetery and buried that little baby. When they told me about it I said, "How could you do it? How could you do it?" And they said, "We took this pledge: 'Trusting in the Lord, Jesus Christ, for strength, I promise Him that I will strive to do whatever He would have me do,' and that seemed to be in that *'whatever.'*"

CHRISTIAN ENDEAVOR FRESH-AIR WORK

FREDERICK L. MINTEL

Field-Secretary for New Jersey

There are four countries of our State that are definitely organized along the lines of fresh-air activity.

I want to show you, in the few minutes I have, how easy it is to get an important work of this kind under way. You can start with nothing. I am going to speak more particularly of the work in Union County. Not because it is the largest work, but because it is the county with which I have been most closely associated. It was my privilege about twelve years ago to be one of the original committee appointed by the Union County Christian Endeavor Union to look into the feasibility of launching some phase of fresh-air work. We had nothing to work with. We had nothing with the exception of the committee appointed. We thought at the time that it would be necessary for us to go to our near neighbor, New York City, for the poor people. We did not believe that in our city we had the kind of guests that we were hoping to entertain in connection with this fresh-air work, so in the first two or three years we did go to New York City and through some of the agencies there secured some small newsboys whom we took out to the mountain sections of Jersey, and pitched a few tents there, and tried to carry in that very primitive way some fresh-air work.

Then, later, some of the Endeavorers felt we ought to limit the work to our own county, and we went on an investigation tour of the county, especially in the larger cities of Elizabeth and Plainfield, and discovered cases of real poverty that were just as destitute as those we were in touch with in New York City. And we also found that the real problem was among the mothers and babies especially, more so than the boys who were allowed to romp about in the city streets, and perhaps in some of the nearby fields, and play, and get the fresh-air they needed.

And so we changed the entire policy of our camp, and instead of just taking the boys, we decided to appeal more particularly to the mothers, and to the babies. That made it necessary, of course, for us to have some sort of a permanent camp. You will see it would not be possible for us to entertain these folks in the tents we used for the boys; so we purchased four acres of land up in a beautiful spot in the mountains in New Jersey, and there we put up some rude structures which were suitable for our work for the first two or three years. But the demands became so great it was necessary for us to enlarge our work, and, without taking you through each succeeding year, I want to give you a picture of the camp we have to-day, and it is only twelve years old. To-day we own thirty-eight acres of land. We are entertaining throughout the season about five hundred guests. Our buildings are modern and were built within the last two or three years to meet our particular needs. The board-walks leading from one building to another are enclosed; they are all sheltered. Our big combination dining-hall and kitchen are all screened in, making a delightful place for the folks we take out there. The idea is that we give each guest a two weeks' vacation.

We have four shifts a year, operating through the months of July and August. Each gets a two weeks' vacation, all expenses paid, both to the camp and back home, and through the co-operation of some of the ladies of our church, we are able to send them back home with better clothing than they wore when they came to the camp. Now that is just the work of Union County.

Essex County is one of the oldest, if not the oldest county engaged in this work, and I believe it has the largest camp in the United States. Essex County entertains between twelve and fifteen hundred guests each season. They have splendid equipment at a new place called New Fernwood out in the mountain regions, and they are doing a most magnificent work. Three of our camps are located in the mountains, one of them down in the southern part of the State in Camden County.

Hudson County entertains about three hundred, Union County about four hundred, and Camden County about three hundred, during the season. So you see that we are taking care of close to twenty-five hundred people during those two months of July and August.

The Sunday morning service is what we call the preaching service and that is conducted by some of the leaders of the county organization. We have our Sunday school in the afternoon at each of the camps, and some Christian Endeavor society is responsible for the Sunday-afternoon Sunday school.

The only people connected with the camps who are paid (and then a very small sum) are the matrons and the cooks. There is a great deal of volunteer service on the part of Endeavorers in the counties, and many of them give a great deal of their time and a great deal of their money in the promotion of the work.

Frequently we take to the camps an entire family, families ranging from four to seven, and sometimes eight members, and many of the mothers have told us that never before have they had a vacation, and had privileges they enjoyed at the camp. You will be interested to know how much some of these societies are raising for the fresh-air work. Some raise each season upwards of five hundred, six hundred and seven hundred dollars.

ESSENTIALS OF A SUCCESSFUL PRAYER MEETING

BERT G. JONES

Field-Secretary for Arkansas, Mississippi, and Tennessee

I think that the greatest need in all Christian Endeavor prayer meetings to-day is a real definite purpose. Every Christian Endeavor prayer meeting should be planned with a definite purpose in view.

The second essential is prayer. We must remember that the greatest power, the greatest asset that we as Endeavorers have is the power of prayer, and in our prayer meetings we should take full advantage of this God-given privilege.

Another essential is preparation. We cannot put over a successful prayer meeting unless this meeting is planned carefully and planned well ahead of time, so that the monthly meeting of the Christian Endeavor prayer meeting committee, with the four or five leaders for that particular month, carefully prepares the meeting.

Another essential I think is punctuality, and this is where lots of Christian Endeavor societies over in Europe fall down. Let's get and keep the habit, for there is nothing in the world that will take the life and the interest out of a Christian Endeavor prayer meeting more than sitting down and waiting for tardy members to arrive.

We don't stress enough the importance of music in our meetings. We should be very, very careful about the selection of our songs. Some of us have had cases of the misuse of music in our Christian Endeavor activities. Let's plan carefully; also let's use the music in our prayer meetings to develop the talents of our own young people, in order that they may be trained to use them in the service of the Master.

Then another essential is participation. We must endeavor to use each of our members as far as possible to take some part in our meetings, aside from the singing. One reason why young people who are experienced in Christian Endeavor refuse to take part is downright laziness. We should try to train our Endeavorers to study the topics well ahead of time, and the best way I know is to use "The Endeavorer's Daily Companion," "The Christian Endeavor World," and our denominational papers. We must live more closely to the ideals of our Christian Endeavor pledge if we are going to put over successfully Christian Endeavor prayer meetings.

The last thing I am going to mention is personal responsibility, personal responsibility of each individual member. We are sometimes inclined to place the responsibility of the success of a meeting upon the leader or upon the prayer-meeting committee. We must realize that each one has a definite responsibility towards the success of our Christian Endeavor gatherings.

Chapter XVIII

PRACTICAL ENDEAVOR PROBLEMS

Coliseum, Monday Afternoon, July 9

Paul C. Brown Presiding

A splendid audience came together in the Coliseum on Monday afternoon. It was most inspiring to see the fidelity of the Endeavorers to the Convention in spite of the intense heat. The meeting opened with a practical lesson in singing, conducted effectively by Mr. Harper.

The ever-popular Paul Brown was roundly applauded as he came forward to conduct the session, first saying a word about the new campaign of Christian Endeavor for the next two years.

The campaign subject is before us this afternoon. Perhaps there is nothing that interests the average delegate and the union leaders more than the question of what is next in the Christian Endeavor programme for the coming two years. You will notice as the programme proceeds this afternoon that about all that needs to be said on the subject of our new tasks for the two years will be outlined in one fashion or another by these various men and women representing the field force of Christian Endeavor and the United Society of Christian Endeavor.

The programme begins with E. P. Gates, general secretary of the United Society, and "The New Campaign" is the topic. Explanatory, more or less, of his first remarks will be the other portions of the programme.

Secretary Gates: We have had a good many campaigns in Christian Endeavor. Something new is launched at every International Convention, but I believe from the bottom of my heart that we have here in these suggested activities for your Christian Endeavor society the best statement of the things a Christian Endeavor society ought to do than we have ever had in any campaign. The details of it are here.

We are asking you to take this campaign back to your own church and society; change it if you want to, so as to make it adaptable to local conditions, but put over something tremendously big for Christian Endeavor during these next two years.

Footnote: The debate that follows was of course, arranged beforehand. It looked serious, however, until the audience "caught on."

Mr. Charles F. Evans: (Chattanooga, Tenn.): May I interrupt you a moment. I just got hold of one of these sheets.

Chairman Brown: I beg your pardon, Mr. Evans. I am presiding here this afternoon and the subject isn't sheets. Furthermore, we have one speaker, and it is courtesy that he be not interrupted.

Secretary Gates: That is all right, Paul. If Mr. Evans has anything to say, any objection to this campaign, I would like to have him say it. Won't you come up here where the rest can see you? This convention is as free as air. We are glad to have you express your opinions. I don't want anybody to go away and say that anything was forced on you. If there is anything you don't like about this campaign, say so.

Mr. Evans: Perhaps I should apologize to Mr. Brown for the interruption, but I have a feeling that we ought to give this some very definite consideration. The truth of the matter is, I am fed up—

Secretary Gates (interrupting): You look it.

Mr. Evans: On campaigns, not on food. I have a feeling that our States and sections ought to be allowed to make their own campaigns. I see here in the first part of it, for instance, graded Christian Endeavor, then it talks about the three grades, and it talks about the "Al-um-ni" Council.

Secretary Gates: Where do you come from anyhow? What section of the country do you come from that you don't know what an Alumni Council is? Don't you know the biggest thing in Christian Endeavor is the Alumni plan these days, and that we are organizing Alumni Councils all over the country, and an Alumni Council organized in your church would look after the work of the young people and help them put over a programme?

Mr. Evans: We need those young people in our societies; we don't want them out on something else.

Secretary Gates: We are not graduating the young people out of the societies; what we are doing is taking the folks that have been in your society for forty years and putting them into an Alumni Council so as to give the young people a chance.

Mr. Evans: How is the average society to take this programme and digest it?

Secretary Gates: Digest it, yes.

Mr. Harold Singer: Mr. Chairman.

Chairman Brown: There is an interesting debate going on up here, you may have your turn in a minute.

Mr. Singer: I would like to get into that debate. If it is going to be a scrap, I would like to get into it. I come from a little State out here called Oklahoma. (They all take off their coats.)

Chairman Brown: This new intruder's name is Singer. We will now have a solo.

Mr. Singer: It will be a solo if these fellows don't agree with me. I sort of agree with this fellow here (Mr. Evans). I don't believe all of this programme is going to work.

SECRETARY GATES: What is the matter with it? There is nothing the matter with this campaign.

MR. SINGER: Listen.

SECRETARY GATES: I am listening.

MR. SINGER: I want you to turn over to the middle here. Now under No. 3, you say "Leadership Training."

SECRETARY GATES: Yes, study-classes. Don't you know that California last year had over twelve thousand young people enrolled in study classes?

MR. EVANS: There is too much work.

SECRETARY GATES: What do you think a Christian Endeavor society is for, anyway? Do you think we are just running a young people's prayer meeting on Sunday evening?

MR. EVANS: You are asking too much.

MR. SINGER: The high school folks don't get study-classes.

SECRETARY GATES: I will leave it to Paul Brown if they don't get any study-classes in California.

CHAIRMAN BROWN: They are in the habit of study already, and they make the best students.

MR. EVANS: They are studying in school all the time, and they say they can't do any more.

CHAIRMAN BROWN: Why, they are the ones that learn easiest; they are the ones that have the best chance at it. Why, you can count on them all the time. The older ones get too lazy to study.

SECRETARY GATES: The trouble with you fellows is you have the idea that you have to do this whole campaign at once.

MR. SINGER: You have it all here.

SECRETARY GATES: That's all right; when you go up to Hotel Savery, you don't have to eat everything on the bill of fare just because it is there. The idea of this thing is that it is on the cafeteria plan, and you pick out the things that will help your Christian Endeavor society, and you work those particular things. You have two years to put the whole campaign across.

MR. SINGER: Come back to this here.

SECRETARY GATES: I am coming back. I have to go a long way back to find you, though.

MR. SINGER: Graded Christian Endeavor! How in the world are you ever going to promote anything like that in most of our churches?

SECRETARY GATES: What State do you come from?

MR. SINGER: The best State in the union. How in the world are you going to put six or seven Christian Endeavor societies in a little one-room church?

SECRETARY GATES: We are not going to put any more in than the church needs.

MR. EVANS: I am interested in one statement. What did you say about not working it all at once?

SECRETARY GATES: You go through and take one thing at a

time. You do that thing and then you take up something else and do that, then at the end of the two years your society has done something besides having a meeting on Sunday evening. You are organizing an Alumni Council that will stay organized, and you won't have to organize it every day. You are going to put over a recreational campaign. You don't have to keep on campaigning for two years for any one of these things. The idea is, here is something for every one in your society to do.

MR. EVANS: I am anxious to know what the pastor will think about this.

SECRETARY GATES: Suppose you go and ask him. I am glad to find somebody that has a real interest in the preacher. The idea of this campaign is to make the Christian Endeavor society more useful to its own church and pastor.

MR. EVANS: Then it hasn't been outlined simply to promote Christian Endeavor.

SECRETARY GATES: It is for the purpose of helping the pastor and the local church. A Christian Endeavor society isn't a Christian Endeavor society unless it is boosting its own pastor, standing behind him, and not too far behind.

MR. EVANS: That sounds like something there. Maybe we didn't give it enough consideration.

SECRETARY GATES: I would like you boys, if you are willing, to sit here on the platform for a little while and listen while some of the other folks on the programme this afternoon explain some of these things.

MR. EVANS: Sure, we will do it. Fine, fine. I congratulate you.

CHAIRMAN BROWN: Well, we won anyhow.

Next we will have something on the subject of the Junior society, "Why Have a Junior Society?" by Mr. F. D. G. Walker.

JUNIOR SOCIETIES

BY F. D. G. WALKER

Statistics show us to-day that the vast majority of those who are converted are converted at the age of twelve, and we can well afford, if we can have only one society in a church, to disband the Senior society and have a Junior, if we haven't leadership enough to have both societies.

In your Christian Endeavor Society back home you have said, "Trusting in the Lord Jesus Christ for strength, I promise Him that I will strive to do whatever He would like to have me do," and I dare you to go back and say that pledge again, renew it to Him, and not think that He doesn't want you or wouldn't like to have you start a Junior Christian Endeavor society in your church.

I would like to use an illustration that you will find in the New Testament. It is familiar to many of you. I have used it before, but I would like to leave it with you to-day as your challenge. It is the story of the little apothecary shop in the old country of Palestine; it was not like the ordinary drugstore of to-day, the kind I have had the privilege of serving in, with everything in the window from an alarm clock to a ham sandwich. Mary came around with her long black robes around her; lifting the latch she walked in, and she saw the old gentleman of the apothecary shop standing behind the counter. He had a long flowing beard and a skull-cap on top of his head. Stepping up he asked if there was something she would like to have. What do you suppose she wanted? She wanted perfume. The old gentleman reached up and brought down a jar. "Here is one that is worth about twenty-five cents." Mary said, "Sir, haven't you something just a little better?" The old gentleman took down another one. "Here is one at fifty cents that we sell a great deal of. Our very best trade uses it. It is the greatest seller we have." Mary said, "Sir, haven't you something just a little better?" He reached up to the shelf and brought down the best thing he had. "Here is one that is worth a dollar; our very best trade uses it. If you don't like it, bring back the empty bottle and we will give you back your money." Mary said, "Sir, haven't you something a little better?" The old gentleman a little out of humor walked back into the old dusty, musty prescription case and reaching down he brought out a little box of ointment, about the size of a twenty-five cent mentholatum jar. He paraded up the aisle and said, "Lady, here is the finest thing on the market to-day, but it is worth three hundred dollars," little dreaming that Mary would ever be interested. Mary didn't gasp and say, "That is too much, I didn't want anything so expensive." She looked at him and said, "Sir, it is none too good for my Master. Wrap it up and I will take it home," and she took it home and broke that alabaster box at the feet of Jesus, and the perfume of it has been spreading through these nineteen hundred years, and will continue to spread so long as time shall last, for it is said wherever this story be told it shall be told in memorial of her.

I challenge you Christian Endeavorers to-day who are without a Junior society in your church to go back home and break the alabaster box of your love for the Master by making a sacrifice that I know will cost you something in starting a Junior society, not only to train the young people, but to hold them to the church of Jesus Christ, the greatest job in your church or mine to-day.

CHAIRMAN BROWN: Mamie Gene Cole is going to tell us the "How to Have a Junior Society."

JUNIOR SOCIETIES

By MAMIE GENE COLE

MAMIE GENE COLE: My friends, we are building wonderful buildings that cannot be built with hands; we are building human characters, and it is up to the Junior Endeavorers of this country and of the world to see to it that the Christian Endeavor movement lives on through.

The first thing to do in organizing a society is to get the permission of the pastor to have such an organization, to show him that Junior Christian Endeavor will help to train the members for his church. Then we can go to the Senior society and show them that if they would insure Christian Endeavor for the next forty years they must invest in boys and girls by having a Junior Christian Endeavor society. And then we must show them that we must have the proper leadership, for unless you have the proper leadership it is better to have no society. In looking for your leader, the first thing that you want to look for is consecration, because without consecration she or he can do nothing for you or for Christ.

The next thing to look for in your leader is personality, the personality that will be attractive to boys and girls.

The next thing to look for in your Junior superintendent is her willingness to work. Some people seem to have the idea that all the Junior superintendent has to do is to meet with the boys and girls on Sunday afternoon. I say to you that the Junior superintendent who is not living Christian Endeavor seven days a week and twenty-four hours a day is not a real Junior superintendent. The superintendent must be willing to study, to work, because if you think you can interest Twentieth Century boys and girls with Eighteenth Century methods, just try it. Our Junior superintendent must keep abreast of times, she must know what is going on in the public school, she must know what is going on in the church, in the Sunday school, in the community, and in the world, and she must tie up Christian Endeavor to life, because we are preparing our boys and girls for life.

One person cannot conduct a Junior society. We must have assistants. I would like to call them counselors, and they must come from the Senior and Intermediate societies. If I were going to organize a society in your church, I would not ask for one person, I would ask for four people to work with that society.

First, you need some one to care for the missionary work. The Junior society that is not teaching denominational missions is not a real Christian Endeavor society.

And then we need some one person to be responsible for the social life of the boys and girls, to help plan the socials, to plan the social-service work for the society and to care for outside activities. Then it seems to me that we need one person to care for the music of the society, then to follow in line with the programme, that our music may be part of our worship service.

Then we need some one person to look after the hand work of the society, the expression work, because unless that handwork is tied up to the society, there is no use in handwork in the society, so we need some one person to care for that, since we cannot have it in our regular Christian Endeavor programme.

A Group of Endeavorers on the Banks of the Des Moines River

Then comes the organization of the society. If you are going to organize a society, go to your Sunday school, enlist the interest of the Sunday-school superintendent, the teachers, and the pupils. Announce your meeting, and do not call it an organization meeting, because it will not be an organization meeting, it is just a meeting to talk things over. We want all the boys and girls to come and invite the parents to come and see what we are going to do. At that meeting you simply want to put before your people what Junior Christian Endeavor really is. You will present the pledge; you may at first present just the preparatory member's pledge, but you want to show those boys and girls that to be an active Christian Endeavorer they must take the Christian Endeavor pledge. Then on the next Sunday the boys and girls who bring back the pledge, signed (it must be signed by the parent also), will be the active members of that society, and you will plan one month's work. Do not elect your officers at that time, simply appoint temporary officers, and at the end of a month you may appoint a nominating committee to meet with the superintendent to elect the officers for your society.

CHAIRMAN BROWN: The next subject is "Why Have an Intermediate Society?" by Miss Madilene Carter.

INTERMEDIATES

MADILENE CARTER

MADILENE CARTER: The Intermediate societies are for the boys and girls thirteen to fifteen years old. That is the age when they are the most active, and they ought to be active for Jesus Christ. They are too old for a Junior society, they would spoil these Junior societies, and for every one that you hold in the Junior society up to that age as a leader, you lose ten or a dozen that ought to be in service of some kind. They are too young for a Senior society; they will spoil the Senior society. Now I know, because I did my best at that age to spoil as good a Senior society as there ever was out in the state of Kansas. Fortunately, I didn't succeed. Besides, at the Intermediate age young people need a superintendent. They are anxious to work, but they do need lots of direction. They are at the age when the social instinct is just developing and they want to be together; they are either going to be together in an Intermediate society or they are going to be together outside of the church.

Pardon me for giving you an illustration. Not many months ago in one county convention there came twelve from a society. Six of these are very much older than I am. One of them was chairman of the prayer-meeting committee, and he told me that those boys and girls thirteen and fourteen years old were too young to know how to pray or talk in Christian Endeavor; and the boys and girls came to me and said, "They won't let us pray, they won't let us talk." They needed an Intermediate society in that church, and they have one now, and they have got the group of boys and girls that used to be outside of the church.

The boys and girls thirteen and fourteen years old can do more to win the other boys and girls for Jesus Christ than you and I can do. Why not let them do it?

Most of our church organizations for the boys and girls at that age are either for just boys or just girls. I will leave it to you folks if you don't think that the boys and girls of that age like to be together inside the church as well as outside the church. It takes an Intermediate society to mix the groups and train them for service for Jesus Christ.

CHAIRMAN BROWN: The next speaker is E. F. Huppertz, who will speak on "How Have an Intermediate Society?"

INTERMEDIATES

BY E. F. HUPPERTZ

E. F. HUPPERTZ: My experience is that you cannot get an Intermediate society to do anything unless they want to do it. They are a peculiar group. If you give a vision and an idea, they will work their heads off. These teen age boys and girls are the greatest workers in the world, and they would rather be on the right side of a question than on the wrong side.

If you find that you are going to have a difficult time in making the ages of twelve to eighteen mix, you might try our plan. Down in Texas we have a six-society plan, and in that way we have two ages for the Intermediate; one of them embraces the high school age—in other words, we have the Intermediates from thirteen to fifteen, and then from sixteen to eighteen. These young people work better that way, because somehow or other when they get to be sixteen years old nowadays they are grown up, and they don't like to play with the kids, as they call the twelve to fifteen year olders.

My advice to you is that if you have a group in your church today of the Intermediate age, don't call it a Senior society, call it an Intermediate society. These young people want recognition, and if you recognize them in the right sort of way you will find they will produce results, and they will bring forth from that group not only the leaders of the to-morrow, but missionaries and preachers and full-time workers.

Send this young group to district conventions. If you have no Intermediate society, send the boys and girls to district conventions or State conventions, or even better to one of these big International Conventions, and let them get a vision of this great task; and let them go out and find a superintendent, and they will find him.

CHAIRMAN BROWN: I would suggest, in connection with the organization of any of these societies, and particularly of an Intermediate society, that we do not look to a large group for the organization but be content to organize with a few, just a little group of dead-in-earnest people who are willing to take the principles of Christian Endeavor and the pledge and the plans and work and go forward on that basis.

CHAIRMAN BROWN: We will have a message from Mr. Carroll M. Wright, field-secretary for Maryland and Delaware, on "An Alumni Council for Every Church."

ALUMNI COUNCILS

By Carroll M. Wright

Just about the middle of last month, I think it was, a young friend of mine graduated from Cornell University. They had wonderful commencement exercises up there. I think there are about eight colleges or so in connection with that university, and during the commencement exercises the graduates from the different colleges sat in their own groups; there were seven or eight hundred graduates this year from Cornell. There were so many graduates that they didn't attempt to pass out the diplomas the afternoon that they had the graduating exercises. The students had to go back to the different colleges and have the deans hand them out after the services were over, but that wasn't the biggest thing I found out about the graduation exercise. The biggest thing about it was the reunions of the different classes, the classes of former years. I found that all of the dormitories of Cornell were turned over to these former graduates, these former students of this great university; I found that those former students were up there doing all sorts of service.

I find that a large part of the success of Cornell University is due to former students, the Alumni of Cornell. We have got a great big university here, our university for Christ and the Church; we have got colleges all over this country; we are having reunions, but I wonder how many of the former Endeavorers are boosting the present-day Endeavorers as we should be boosting them. We are not dressing them up in uniforms and putting dates on them or anything like that; too many of us are just letting them take their own course, unfortunately. We are not helping them, we are not encouraging them as we should be. I found that these Alumni of Cornell had different chapters in the large cities and other places, and they get together there in addition to their class reunions in graduation week; they get together in these different local chapters, and there they boost their university, they work for their university among the young people of their different communities trying to get students for the university. I am wondering if we couldn't do things like that in our Christian

Endeavor movement? I don't think that we advertise Christian Endeavor enough among our young people, I don't think we older folks take enough interest in it sometimes. One way I think we can help is to have our local alumni chapters or Alumni Councils in every church. That is one way that we can help to promote Christian Endeavor in our churches.

There is a wonderful programme for our Alumni Councils to put on if they will. Just recently there came to my knowledge the activities of a couple of Alumni Councils in Wilmington, Del. One of the very active Christian Endeavor pastors over there had his brand new Alumni Council of seventy-five members meet him one night after prayer service. He presented to this Council a list of people in the church and community who could not get out to church—shut ins. He asked the Alumni Council if they wouldn't take care of them, going to their homes, taking a bit of sunshine into their homes, and holding Christian Endeavor prayer meetings in their homes; and that Alumni Council is doing that kind of work. Another alumni council has been taking over the mid-week prayer service for a large church in that city.

In presenting the Alumni idea to my folks I tell them that one of the biggest things they can do is to put on a complete educational programme for the young people of the church, to organize and conduct study-classes of all kinds, and get behind the Endeavorers in lots of different ways. You just get some of these leaflets, "What an Alumni Council Can Do," by Rev. Robert P. Anderson. I think you will find about twenty-nine different things that they can do to help the local pastor and the local church.

CHAIRMAN BROWN: Continuation now of the alumni subject turns to "The Alumni Fellowship at Its Best," by Frank L. Freet.

ALUMNI FELLOWSHIPS

BY FRANK L. FREET

FRANK L. FREET, field-secretary for Ohio: An Alumni Fellowship, if it is going to amount to anything at all, must accomplish three definite purposes.

I believe, first, if a Fellowship is to amount to anything at all, it must be an opportunity for fellowship for former Endeavorers. I am quite certain that each one of our Alumni Fellowships, which is the organization of the Alumni in a community, either a city, or a country, or a district, if we are to have any programme that will interest them at all, must give them an opportunity occasionally to have the same kind of fellowship as alumni as they used to have active Endeavorers.

Second, it should serve, be a service agency. I want to call your attention to a few of the things which an Alumni Fellowship can really help to work out. For instance, an Alumni Fellowship can help the Alumni Councils increase loyalty to the church, can help the pastor, can, in the second place, help in grading Endeavor, for the great problem, as I have heard it this afternoon, is to find leadership; and the group that can find the leaders is that Alumni Fellowship that meets together occasionally in the union, the city, the district.

A lot of us criticize our young people and say that they don't support the denominational enterprises as they should, when a good many have not been taught what the denomination stands for. The old Endeavorers are folks who have become the elders and deacons and stewards of the church, and they know what denomination means, and they can help their young people find out. They can help them by showing them how to do recruiting work, and by teaching them how to be faithful to Christian Endeavor fundamentals.

Finally, an alumni fellowship to be worth while must not only provide fellowship and serve, but it must be a supporting agency, it must help support the local work financially, and it must support the United Society too, it must support the world-work of Christian Endeavor as well.

May I bring you one thought for the service of support. You will always in your Fellowship gain greater financial support if you have a specific objective. The reason why the Cleveland No. 1 Fellowship raises so much money for Christian Endeavor is because it provides specific support in the name of Daniel A. Poling. You can do the same thing that we pastors do. We try to have our churches give their money to specific stations in the foreign field and home field; and I am asking to-day that you go back to your Fellowships and have them determine that they shall raise a certain amount this coming year for the work in Czecho-slovakia or Germany or Korea or some other nation. Have a specific objective.

CHAIRMAN BROWN: Our next subject is "The Alumni Loving-Cup and How it May be Won," by Stanley B. Vandersall.

ALUMNI LOVING-CUP

By Stanley B. Vandersall

STANLEY B. VANDERSALL, Alumni Superintendent of the United Society: Four years ago at the Buffalo Conference in August, 1919, comparatively few people knew what the alumni idea was or how it was operating. Two years ago at the New York Convention there was held a great alumni banquet and there was given a fine demonstration of alumni interest and support, and the growing intelligence of the rank and file of Endeavordom concerning the alumni work.

In 1923 at Des Moines we remember that we have been four

years and a little more in talking and thinking and promoting alumni service. We are still in the period of education.

The two addresses which have been given, one describing the Alumni Council in the local church, the other talking about the Alumni Fellowship in the local union, have described admirably some of the operations of these two alumni organizations. It remains for all of us together to give more thought and more attention and more promotion to the cause of the alumni where we live. This beautiful loving-cup has recently been given by Mr. and Mrs. Fred R. Ball, of Cleveland, Ohio, for the purpose of encouraging alumni organization and development in the United States. It is proposed that this beautiful loving-cup shall be competed for by many State unions, through their Alumni Departments, the State union which makes the best showing in alumni promotion and development in the course of a year shall be awarded this beautiful cup, not for permanent possession but to hold for one year, or until one state wins it three times. In that case it becomes permanent property. Each year the name of the successful State will be engraved on the cup. The idea in this alumni contest for the cup is that there shall be a genuine all-around promotion of alumni service in the state, that the two alumni organizations—the council and the fellowship—shall actually be organized and operated. Any state union, then, through its Alumni Department, may enter its alumni record. The cup will be awarded each year by an impartial committee chosen from the Board of Trustees of the United Society. Since this campaign is pretty largely on a proportionate basis, each State union will have a fair chance in striving for this beautiful recognition one year hence.

CHAIRMAN BROWN: Just now we will hear a message that was not received this morning, a message from Rev. J. B. Gleason on "College Christian Endeavor."

COLLEGE ENDEAVOR

By J. B. GLEASON

REV. J. B. GLEASON, field-secretary for Wisconsin: I will try and tell you how we reached young men and young women of the University of Wisconsin.

First of all, we tried to appeal to the social instincts of the students. They came there, and many of them wanted to belong to the fraternities and to the sororities and to other clubs and lodges, because they believed in sociability. What was the church to do? It was our business to reach them for the church and to hold them for Jesus Christ; so we put on a campaign, what we call a unit system of calling. Many of those young people, freshmen—some of them just about as green as grass—coming there for the first time, were homesick. We call on them; we have a unit system made up of about thirty young people, and we call on every student that comes there of our own Baptist societies. The other University Endeavorers do likewise. We have in the fall a great college social, and we invite them to that and get acquainted with them, and then a personal letter is sent to them from the pastor.

We have hikes, dinners at Thanksgiving and Christmas, and a lunch Sunday afternoons before the devotional meeting. We are adapting our Christian Endeavor programme to the needs of a college student. These young people want to be fed spiritually. Many of them come there from no churches, and practically without any belief, and it is our business to win them to the church. They study biology, zoology, study geology, and so they must find out the relationship of Christianity to the great problems of life. Hence we put on what we call a monthly programme of intelligent study, and we have a leading professor who is a Christian man—by the way, we have scores of professors at the University of Wisconsin that are teaching Bible classes and are doing a wonderful work for Christ and His church—who talks in our society; then we gather our leaders together in what we call a normal school, and those normal-school young people study the problem for the month. One topic is "Reconstruction of Religion," and topics of that nature. Then we give what we call the freedom of expression, and that appeals to those young lawyers and engineers, to be able to get up in their own free way and express themselves for Jesus Christ.

We have something like a hundred Chinese and Japanese students, and we invite them to a foreign-student banquet, and our boys of the Christian Endeavor society meet them and take them to the banquet to get them acquainted with American ways.

Then we have what we call the gospel-team expression, a coeducational team. We send out men and women together, going to communities and for three days putting on real constructive evangelistic campaigns. They go there on Friday night and have the fathers, mothers, sons, and daughters together in a banquet; on Saturday they teach those country young people how to play games, and on Sunday they have them in the Sunday school and in the young people's societies, and finally at night they put on a real decision meeting, and I know we have had numbers of young people get up and decide for Jesus Christ and for His Kingdom.

CHAIRMAN BROWN: Mr. E. F. Huppertz will tell about Graded Christian Endeavor.

GRADED ENDEAVOR

By E. F. HUPPERTZ

MR. E. F. HUPPERTZ, field-secretary of the Texas Union: In the first place you know the ordinary grading of Christian Endeavor is seven to fourteen for Juniors, fifteen to eighteen for

Intermediates, and from eighteen up is the Young People's society.

Down in Texas in the larger churches we have tried the six-society plan, and the ages are this way: from seven to eleven, Junior; from twelve to fourteen, Intermediate; from fifteen to seventeen, Senior; from eighteen to twenty-four, Young People's society; and from twenty-four to thirty-five or forty the Fellowship society. We call it the fellowship society; you don't have to call it that. We just call it that because the original church that used the six-society idea called it that, a society in which the mothers, fathers, and the older people met.

You have tried same grading in your Sunday school; why not have it for Christian Endeavor. I think by having this greater Christian Endeavor idea it will work out more satisfactorily than the three-society plan. I am not speaking against this plan, for that is the one the smaller church will have to continue to use; but the six-society plan can be used very effectively in a larger church.

CHAIRMAN BROWN: Now we are to have a message from Harry C. Allan on the subject of "Leadership Training."

LEADERSHIP TRAINING

By HARRY C. ALLAN

HARRY C. ALLAN, field-secretary for California: The general line of efficiency is rising in all departments of life. There isn't a department of the business world to-day but is making larger demands upon its employees than it did a few years ago, and the Christian church, if it is to keep pace with general events, must also better train men and women to carry on the work of the church. The greatest amount of the work of the church will yet be done by volunteer service. There will be a larger staff of those who are giving their entire time to it and have received special training, but there is need for even those who serve in a voluntary capacity to fit themselves to serve more adequately than they have ever served before, and Christian Endeavor is the training-school of the church. That is an acknowledged fact. If we look over the past forty-two years of the history of our Christian churches we find that those persons who have risen to positions of leadership have very largely received their training through Christian Endeavor.

I was talking recently with a director of religious education for a section of our State representing one of our great denominations, and he showed me a programme that he had outlined for the religious education of the church, a rather comprehensive one, and he said to me, "I want you to understand that in this programme I have prepared I have not given a lesser place, but rather a larger place to Christian Endeavor, because I am counting upon it to be the training-school of the church."

During the past two years in the Foursquare Campaign, one of the features has been leadership-training. For a number of years mission-study classes are really a part of our programme. No Christian Endeavor society should be content to go through the year without at least one mission-study class, and I should prefer two study classes, one on home missions and one on foreign missions.

The programme for the next two years is going to emphasize evangelism. Now zeal alone will not accomplish it; zeal plus knowledge will equip you with the spirit of God to perform the work that is expected of us as Christian evangelists, and, therefore, in your leadership training make provision for personal-work study classes.

I suggest that you might use in your individual societies some of the books that have been put out by the United Society of Christian Endeavor concerning some of the fundamentals of Christian Endeavor, some of the principles upon which their main committees in Christian Endeavor operate. These are some of the things that our Christian Endeavor societies should do.

CHAIRMAN BROWN: May I now introduce to you Mr. Frank Lowe, Jr., who will speak on "Vocational Guidance."

VOCATIONAL GUIDANCE
By FRANK LOWE, JR.

MR. FRANK LOWE, JR.: Any human enterprise requires guidance for success. This is true of governments and armies; it is true with societies and schools; it is true in industry and in commerce; it is also true in the field where young people are making their vocational choice.

Vocational guidance undertakes to help young people get information about their requirements in the different callings, about the drawbacks and the satisfactions and human qualities desirable for success in the different vocations in which one may engage. It undertakes, in addition to giving them information, to give them experience through tryout courses and through visiting factories and becoming acquainted with workmen, and interviewing those who are engaged in the profession. It undertakes to help them find employment, and after they have found employment it follows them up and helps them get advancement in the work they have undertaken.

Vocational guidance does not mean dictation; it does not mean limitation of any human being in the work he will undertake. It simply means the encouragement of young people in finding the things for which they are fit. Vocational guidance believes that all work that is legitimate may be Christian.

You may be interested in hearing the proposed preliminary

Christian Endeavor vocational guidance pledge. It reads something like this: Believing that all legitimate vocations may be Christian, and that one ought to serve where he is best fitted, or where obligations seemingly unavoidable may have placed him, therefore, trusting in the Lord Jesus Christ for strength I commit my whole life, whatever my life career may be, to His guidance and to His spirit; but feeling myself especially concerned about the callings of the missionary and the full-time lay worker, I promise for one year to make a definite study of religious vocations, of my personal fitness, and the advisability of my enlistment, and to the end that I may make a wise investment of my life in service, I promise during that period first, to make my decision a matter of constant prayer; second, to read available literature; third, to take council of my family and pastor; fourth, to correspond with my denominational or other agencies, and finally to try out my capacity wherever possible."

CHAIRMAN BROWN: The subject of Carlton M. Sherwood's address is "Christian Endeavor Publicity."

PUBLICITY

BY CARLTON M. SHERWOOD

CARLTON M. SHERWOOD, field-secretary for New York: This is the day of advertising, the day of all days. Men are more and more considering the matter of publicity. There are many good causes that suffer because they have not learned how to tell the folks throughout the world their real values. So this afternoon I would suggest to you folks that you may know a great deal about Christian Endeavor, that you may believe a great deal in Christian Endeavor, that you may have a great heart interest in your own Christian Endeavor society and in your own Christian Endeavor union, and yet you may fail to achieve the largest measures of success for your Christian Endeavor society, because you have not efficiently carried forward a programme of advertising Christian Endeavor.

We can advertise Christian Endeavor to the young people by announcement in the church services. We can advertise Christian Endeavor through the Sunday School. Two societies in the city of Ithaca, where Cornell University is situated, every fall put on a splendid social for the incoming students that they might bring them in touch with the other young people in the Christian Endeavor societies and thereby bring a contact which will be carried through in a larger spiritual way.

We can advertise Christian Endeavor in the church. I believe sometimes that many of our pastors in their lives are not altogether acquainted with the Christian Endeavor activities and programmes of their own young people's society, let alone the larger union activity, simply because the young people have failed to tell the preacher just what they are doing, to make their own pastor acquainted with the various things of their own programme. Tell your preacher you can do many other things in the church. Every once in a while we run into a Christian Endeavor society that somehow or other is just the tag end of the church programme. I talked to one of the leading elders of a large Presbyterian church not many months ago. I said, "Have you a Christian Endeavor Society in your church?" He said to me, "Why, I think so. We used to have one. Yes, I am pretty sure we do, but maybe we don't. I don't know."

We need constantly to keep before the whole church what the young people's society stands for, what it means in the life of the church and exactly what it is doing, and I give it to you folks this afternoon that if the whole church, all of the members of the entire church, appreciate what some of our Christian Endeavor societies are doing, we would have an even finer support from the church than we have had before.

CHAIRMAN BROWN: The next is the indispensable Clarence Hamilton.

THE CHRISTIAN ENDEAVOR WORLD

By C. C. HAMILTON

CLARENCE HAMILTON, field-secretary of the United Society and field-manager of "The Christian Endeavor World": Those of you who know me well know the thing I am going to mention as indispensable in putting over a successful Friends for Christ Campaign. You know that I am going to say that you must have the official organ of the Christian Endeavor movement, "The Christian Endeavor World."

I was up in Michigan some time ago at a convention, and I told the folks up there in that convention that we have a slogan, "The Christian Endeavor World in Every Christian Endeavor Home." After the session a bright-faced high-school girl came to me and said, "Mr. Hamilton, we are interested in what you said about 'The Christian Endeavor World,' but it did not concern our society."

I said, "I regret that it did not, but it may have concerned some of the other societies here."

She said, "You know we take the paper."

I said, "That is fine. Who takes the paper?"

"*We* do."

"*Who* takes the paper?"

"Mr. Hamilton, I said *we* take the paper."

I said, "You have said it twice now, but I don't understand you. I am going to ask you again. *Who* takes the paper?"

She said, "We get a copy for our Christian Endeavor Society." I had just been talking for ten or twenty minutes about

"The Christian Endeavor World" *in every Christian Endeavor home.* We want every society to have it, of course. We would that every society might subscribe for a copy for the Sunday school, and for the pastor, that he might keep in touch with the movement. The programme of Christian Endeavor will never go over in its full possibilities until we have "The Christian Endeavor World" more largely represented in the homes of our young people. One of the things that is essential absolutely in the Friends for Christ Campaign is that a greater number of our young people take the paper. One reason you should have "The Christian Endeavor World" is that you may receive the weekly message from Dr. Clark, the founder of the Christian Endeavor movement. In "The Christian Endeavor World" every week you get a message from our genial and much loved Mr. Gates. He will have a Secretary's Corner, where he will outline definite, helpful suggestions for the promotion of the campaign.

Do you want the news of the campaign? That is gathered from the far corners of the earth by the editor of the paper, Prof. Amos R. Wells, our much beloved editor. You need that news of the campaign for its many helpful suggestions and its inspiration. We need the message given in special articles that will be printed in regard to the campaign. They will be written by men like Dr. John Timothy Stone, Dr. Foulkes and other great leaders.

In addition to that, twelve of the outstanding men of the world will be asked to write special articles in connection with the campaign. We know you want these articles that you may keep in touch with the campaign and lend yourselves most effectively to its promotion.

CHAIRMAN BROWN: Chaplain Ramsden, who is the Army and Navy Superintendent of the United Society, will give the closing address.

ARMY AND NAVY ENDEAVOR

BY CHAPLAIN S. C. RAMSDEN

REV. S. C. RAMSDEN: The object of the Army and Navy Christian Endeavor Department is to foster the moral and religious life of the sons of our country, who for a time are serving in the United States Army, Navy, and Marine Corps.

For some years isolated work for men in the army and navy has been done by local societies of Christian Endeavor, or at times by city Christian Endeavor unions. Here, as in other fields of work, "in union there is strength." The writer, finding Christian Endeavor so useful in carrying on work for the men of his regiment, noticed occasional reports in *The Christian Endeavor World* of similar work being done in both the army and the navy. Correspondence naturally followed, and gradually there came a vision of a larger field of usefulness for Christian Endeavor if these various efforts for the welfare of the soldiers, sailors, and marines could be brought together for the developing of plans and interchange of ideas. The growth of the movement was such that in October, 1915, the United Society of Christian Endeavor created the Army and Navy Department of Christian Endeavor, to give recognition to the work and make possible greater opportunity for development.

As best results can be secured only by systematic, organized effort, it is the desire that each State Christian Endeavor union adopt the Army and Navy Department among its State activities, and also elect a State superintendent who shall have charge of this department. The State superintendent of this work will endeavor to have a chairman of army and navy work in each district or city union, that young men who enlist in the service may be followed from their home towns and churches to the place where they may be stationed for duty.

State superintendents should note the location of military posts and naval stations within their State borders, and strive to promote the religious welfare of the men at these places, always, of course, working through the army or navy chaplain, if one is located there.

State superintendents can also foster the State pride of Endeavorers in vessels named after their State, cities within the State, and individuals native to the State. Virtually every State in the Union has a battle-ship named after it.

Much information for State superintendents can be obtained by writing to the Superintendent of Documents, Washington, D. C., enclosing twenty-five cents for copies of "Army List and Directory," fifteen cents, and "Navy and Marine Corps List and Directory," ten cents. The first-named publication contains the list of regiments, locations, names, and addresses of army chaplains, information on different branches of army service, and other facts of interest. The second-named publication includes names of vessels of the navy, naval stations, names and addresses of naval chaplains, etc.

The War and Navy departments each have chaplains to provide for the social, educational, and religious life of the men in the service, and local societies would do well to communicate with these chaplains and assist them whenever and wherever possible. Much help was given the writer by the St. Paul, Minn., Endeavorers and the Galveston, Tex., Endeavorers when he was on duty with his regiment near these cities. Local societies may assist in organizing Christian Endeavor societies among the men at these stations. Cause these societies to become a part of the city union, or seek to have these men individually unite with the local societies.

The Endeavorers of the Atlantic and Pacific Coast States, which are carrying on this work in the navy, find the load, financial and otherwise, almost more than they can carry, because of the number of naval vessels constantly in port or within reach. Herein lies the opportunity for the inland States, not only to help relieve this burden, but to take upon themselves the work properly belonging to them.

The Texas Endeavorers, when our troops were on the Mexican border, found an immense field of possibilities which they could only barely touch. Not only did they have their own State troops on duty on the border, but practically all National Guard troops as well. How much might have been done if the Endeavorers of other States had regarded the young men of the regiments going from their States as their especial charges, and co-operated with Texas Christian Endeavorers by sending Testaments, "housewives" (needles, thread, buttons, etc.), magazines and small games, such as checkers and dominoes, thus making the lives of these young men on duty on the Mexican border more comfortable.

Floating Christian Endeavor in Great Britain has done a wonderful work since the outbreak of the war. Up to October, 1916, no fewer than 107,860 hand-written letters had been sent to soldiers and sailors, in addition to 87,492 printed letters; also 22,414 copies of *The Christian Endeavor Times;* 85,436 neddle-cases had been sent to sailors, and 5,716 letters to workers and relatives of soldiers. Thousands of pillow text-cards had also been distributed in hospitals, countless numbers of gospel tracts, magazines, and periodicals were sent to naval and merchant ships, and 100,000 Gospel portions and thousands of Testaments were given to outward-bound sailors on troop-ships.

Chapter XIX

CHAPTER OF ADDRESSES

Junior Endeavor Complementary to Home and School
By Miss Leila Gerry

Our concern in the topic, "Junior Endeavor complementary to Home and School" presents us with a condition of peculiar nature. It is true that a child's life could be of that three-fold type indicated by home, school, and church. It is true that these segments could be complementary one to the other in greater or less degree. But how to produce an evenly balanced swing of the pendulum that each part of the child's life may be developed equally and fully, yet not overdone, seems to be a question well worth our consideration. What is there to do? Must each, the home, the school, and the church attempt to develop all sides of the child life, or can there be a division of duties? Shall the church throw on the school all training-instruction, thereby adding to the burden already made huge by the change in our homes? Shall the home shirk all responsibility for religious and secular teaching?

The home used to be the centre of everything. The boys and girls, even in the days of our grandparents, knew whether or not the wool in their clothing was standard, and the processes of manufacture necessary to its becoming a garment. The home was also responsible for the fundamental knowledge known as the three R's. Children sent to the early schools were sent home unless they could handle the first steps in reading and number. In fact it was from some of these home schools where the mother in instructing her children discovered her gift of teaching and that some of our later schools sprung. And so the school centred in the home. Religion also centred in the home. We had the family altar, grace before meals, the reading of the Bible from cover to cover, the catechism, and many other definite forms of religious training and instruction. Thus we can picture to ourselves the definite all-around training that the home undertook, and the youth prospered by, in later life.

But now our pendulum has swung and our home with it. New economic conditions have changed the responsibilities of the home, and the training once brought about by necessity now becomes forgotten in the strife of the new organization. The majority of homes have dropped all religious training and have shifted the responsibility of the State.

Let us now examine how the shifted burden is being cared for. In doing so we first look at the school. In 1642 Massachusetts enacted one of the first school laws, and by this law it became the duty of the State to see that each child received an education. The home was fined if neglect of this law was manifest. No schools were provided for, so it was still in great part a home problem. The instruction was required principally for religious purposes that the child might learn to read the Scriptures. Church and school were here united in carrying to a further degree the training both secular and religious which the home had started. It was not until after the Revolutionary War that schools at public expense were accepted. The three R's were still paramount.

Now note the schools of to-day. Besides the fundamentals as we

know them Miss Elizabeth Hall, Assistant Superintendent of Minneapolis schools, gives us eight main issues that the schools are striving to do.
1. To promote health of the children.
2. To give every child a chance, bright or slow.
3. To make the three R's even more important than in the old days.
4. To form good habits in the children.
5. To teach them to enjoy life.
6. To give every child with a gift a chance to develop it.
7. To aid the child's development socially as well as mentally.
8. To make him a good citizen.

In this broad programme we note many new things for which the state has been forced to assume responsibility. First we see a more definite Health programme.

Domestic Science, or more broadly, as it is now known, Home Economics, is another field in which the school is caring for the future race. This covers the preparation and serving of foods, the management of the home, the care of children, home nursing, the manufacture of clothing and those arts which make our American home the basis of a true democracy. The pity is that many of these courses are not required for boys as well as girls, since it surely is as important to learn how to be a father as how to be an ideal mother.

The boys however were the concern of the State and nation when our comparatively new Industrial and Vocational educational programme was formed. The boy who in the old home learned to build a building because of a real need for that particular structure, now has no opportunity (in our cities especially) to learn this art. The schools have taken it over. Federal aid is given directly for the training of teachers and for salaries of teachers skilled in this form of teaching. Girls are also being trained to learn the arts of home making from a trade standpoint sufficiently well that in the period between school days and married life a living wage might be earned.

With this vocational education comes the vast work being done in vocational guidance. The Junior High has developed partly as a try-out period that the youth may earlier find his place in the world and thereby train himself towards that end. The guidance programme in itself a delicate non-measurable piece of work is in its infancy, and it is difficult to determine its scope and possibilities.

Children of all classes and beliefs are gathered together in our public schools, and a real public opinion is formed from results of general discussion. Pupils take definite and active part in leading such discussions and are apt and ready to go to sources for information to sustain their opinions. Citizenship according to Miss Ella Probst classifies itself into points which are carried out practically and definitely in some of the schools. Here are the points mentioned:
1. Civic responsibility.
2. Large group consciousness.
3. Submission to group opinion.
4. Obedience to law, respect for authority.
5. Loyalty, patriotism.
6. Truthfulness, honesty.
7. High moral standards, reverence, religion.
8. Care of private and public property.
9. Recognition and selection of good leaders.
10. Self-reliance, initiative.
11. Thrift, self-support.
12. Courtesy, kindness, generosity.
13. Health, cleanliness.
14. Appreciation of wholesome and helpful forms of recreation.

These clearly show how broad a field commands the attention of the schools.

And now may we look at the force of the public school of to-day in connection with many of the big projects attempted. The Red Cross drive, Liberty loan drives, prevention of cruelty to animals, and many other such

Dr. O. F. Gilliom

Rev. Dirk Lay, D.D.

Duncan B. Curry

movements, have found their large returns in the schools. Our prohibition of to-day is credited to the temperance pledges signed twenty years ago.

The question then arises does the school completely cover the needs of home and church? No! All of us will truly say that no machine-made child will possess what family love can give, nor have we seen any definite religious programme outlined in our curriculum. Many are urging even that this be given to the school. As an instructor I question the advisability of this. The school is now brightened with its complexity. The school is a thing separate from the church, as far as definite religious theory is concerned in this land of freedom of religious belief. Why ask the school to take it? Why not make the church through definite religious instruction assume its rightful place in our complementary picture? Is there in our land not quantities of work needed here. A religious programme not to cover activities of the home or school but working along with their special activities would give the all-around idea of home, school, and church working together for child and nation! But the pendulum must not swing too far in any of the three directions else the child suffers. We are not building schools to take the place of homes, nor are we urging church schools to cover work done by the school. Check each programme, adjust and correlate, above all, keeping in mind that it is not beautiful, building and equipment, reputation and advertisement which makes your progress, but the *need* of a child and in that child the need of a nation viewed from your particular angle of Junior Christian Endeavor complementary to home, church, and school.

Youth of the Church

By Adeline Goddard

The leaders of youth between the ages of twelve and twenty-four must come to realize the importance of the development of the four-fold life. Every church must offer to her youth a chance to grow as Jesus grew.

We find that the church loses a large percentage of the adolescents, the percent being much larger among the boys than the girls, due to two facts. First, the average church has made no provision for that group; second, the lack of knowledge of the characteristics that control this particular group.

One outstanding need to-day is adult responsibility and supervision of the youth of the church and a better knowledge of their needs.

First consider the three general divisions of the youth of the church. The organic, covering the ages, approximately, twelve to fourteen, that period of rapid physical growth; then comes that group fifteen to seventeen, which is more or less controlled by the emotional; then the third group, known as the intellectual group, eighteen to twenty-four, when the mind is alert to reception.

It will be well for us to think of some of the characteristics of these ages.

We have mentioned the rapid physical growth, then comes that individualism that seems to possess a youth as he slips out of childhood, the time when he comes to think things through for himself.

The social instincts awaken, the one time when leaders can help to direct the right relationship of young people to each other and the world. This is a period of conversion and conviction.

Records show that before graded lessons were introduced in the Sunday schools, the largest percent coming into the church during a given period was from fifteen to seventeen years, coming in on the emotional wave.

It seems to me that one characteristic of the youth lightly overlooked is the criminal period. Court records tell us that England's greatest crime record is from fifteen to seventeen years. We need only to look up the records of our own country to be convinced of our great responsibility. In a recent article an Old Judge stated that when a youth went wrong under the age of 'twenty it was a sign that some one had failed in the past.

Then last, but not least by any means that characteristic of doubt and perplexity which is so prevalent in youth. Catch our young people up, take them from the home life, church life, and well known friends, take them away to college in an entirely new life, many times to some great university where Christian influence is not strong. Small wonder they come back without the religion of our Lord and Savior Jesus Christ.

These are days when great hopes and ambitions are manifested, and it is left to us as leaders to help the youth realize their ambitions.

If you do not have a real heart sympathy for this group, if you are not willing to give of your best and be a real friend and hero you will never be able to lead the youth of the church up and out to a great field of usefulness and service.

Mr. Shartle

What I am on this platform for this afternoon is to talk about us, and by "us" I mean "Christian Endeavor." When I stop talking about "us," I am very sure I shall be dead. When God put it in the heart of Rev. Francis E. Clark to organize the first Christian Endeavor Society, he did not think of making a world-wide organization, but of meeting the requirements of Williston Congregational Church. But Christian Endeavor has grown and with it has grown a whole literature.

Dr. Clark gave to us, some years ago, this splendid book entitled "The Christian Endeavor Manual," a wonderful book that may be used regularly in every county, local, and State union. It gives all the information so necessary to make your union a success.

At Sagamore Beach, Mass., there is a little patch of ground that Dr. Clark calls his farm. He raises apples at a dollar each, tomatoes at fifty cents, strawberries at about twenty-five cents each, and the result is that you see Dr. Clark on the platform of this convention in the full vigor and strength of his manhood, due to the fact that while he is scratching that little plot of ground on Sagamore Beach raising fruit and vegetables at a high cost of production, he is regaining his strength and vigor. He has written the book entitled "The Gospel of Out-of-Doors," a splendid book that tells us of the old farm house and the little plot of ground at Sagamore Beach.

Again, Dr. Clark wrote a book entitled "Christ and the young people," a delightful book for young people, setting before them the ideal life of Christ, and what young people might do.

Some years ago Dr. Clark while traveling in foreign lands followed in the footsteps of St. Paul. At the close of that tour he wrote a wonderful book entitled, "In the Footsteps of St. Paul," a helpful and inspiring book for Bible students.

There are Americans, naturalized and native-born, who will call the average Italian a "dago," yet the native-born American citizen has neglected to help the future American citizen to meet the needs of his adopted America and to be the real kind of American citizen. Dr. Clark writes for us a book entitled "Our Italian Fellow-Citizen." Becoming an American citizen is quite a problem sometimes to the man who has left his home in foreign lands, and, consequently, this book will help us to better understand and help him in the work of Americanization.

Dr. Clark wrote the book entitled "The Charm of Scandinavia." This, too, will be a wonderful help to the folks who are present here today, because Dr. Clark gives us a splendid description of what we may find in Copenhagen, and other places in Scandinavia.

Finally, we have the masterpiece, "Memories of Many Men in Many Lands," Dr. Clark's autobiography, a book of 704 pages, containing 117 illustrations, and 65 chapters. It gives to us the life-work of Dr. Clark, and a sketch of world-wide Christian Endeavor.

Please remember that no matter what you do in Christian Endeavor, or how faithful you are, you will not know how to do it efficiently unless you take some of the literature and learn to know how. You may be willing, but if you don't know how, you lack the efficiency so necessary to make your society the kind of an organization God intended it to be.

FOUNDATION PRINCIPLES OF CHRISTIAN ENDEAVOR

THREE LECTURES BY
Rev. William Ralph Hall

LECTURE I.
The Right Foundation for the Individual Endeavorer

Christian Endeavor has high personal ideals. You may compare the ideals of other organizations in the church, and all the religions of all the world, and I am confident that through nearly a half century of experience, Christian Endeavor has proved itself an organization of high personal ideals.

As a text, may I suggest John 4.34: "My meat is to do the will of Him that sent me, and to accomplish His work." I ask you this afternoon to consider seven sub-divisions of these personal ideals that are ours. We will consider these essentials. Let us remember that there are many things good in themselves that cannot be listed as essentials.

First: A Clear and a Definite and a Practical Purpose

A clear and a definite and a practical purpose is one of the foundation elements in Christian Endeavor. It is a life in which Jesus Christ is supreme, not one in which he has a small place, not one to which he comes in times of difficulty, in times of serious problems, in times of sorrow, but a Christ who dominates our entire life. We have expressed that high ideal for our lives in the Christian Endeavor pledge. The exact phraseology of the pledge is not a foundation principle; there are at least four forms, there are others available; but there must be at the heart of the pledge the spirit of devotion to Jesus Christ. The spirit and not the letter is the thing that makes our covenant one of our high personal ideals. Young people have come into the society not realizing what was the content, the purpose, the sweep, the breadth of that pledge as they signed it. It is one of the rocks of granite in the high personal ideals of Christian Endeavor. You go back as leaders, magnify that pledge, for let me assure you that you can lift that pledge in your society life as high as you will to live it in the spirit of true devotion to your Lord and to your Master.

You would rise in your might against those who would trail our flag in the dust. Yet I am sincere when I express it as my judgment that there are many societies that have never protested when society members trailed the covenant, "Trusting in the Lord Jesus Christ for strength," and "throughout my whole life I will endeavor to lead a Christian life," in the dust. It is a foundation principle; let us lift it high.

Second: A Broadened and Deepened Spiritual Life

A broadened and deepened spiritual life is necessary if we would develop spiritual lives. Throughout the ages they have told us that we must keep in close personal touch with our personal living Lord and Savior, that we must go to the Guide-book of life to grow; to grow we must be fed. There are those who feel toward their spiritual growth very much like we feel toward our experience of learning to walk—a few weeks of blundering and falling and then we are on our feet for our whole life. You are not thinking very much to-day, as you move back and forth, on the process of walking; you have settled that for life. You cannot settle, in a short period of time, the matter of your spiritual sustenance and the development of your spiritual life. It is a growth. You can't learn once for all to be a spiritual factor in the Kingdom; it is the achievement of a lifetime and it is one of the rocks in the granite foundation of Christian Endeavor. Study the Bible, take time for prayer. Make the Quiet Hour a part of each day, when we talk with Him, when we listen to His voice, and when we get our spiritual strength.

Third: *A Training in Devotional Leadership.*

The third principle that we face is the expression of the devotional ideals of our life in prayer, in testimony, in the leadership of a meeting, in those things that make for the success of the Sunday evening devotional meeting. You grow as you take a place in the ship there. Others grow as they see you take your part there, and you must go forward year by year.

High schools have just closed in America. Several millions of young people are on their vacations; thousands of them received their diplomas, graduating from the school; others passed just one grade higher. I know the young lady, a fine girl in her social life, whose mother had told her a thousand times in the course of the school year, "Daughter, I wish you would give a little more thought, a little more care to the lessons, to the work of your high school," but she passed it by and said, "Mother, I have not failed so far, I guess I have got nerve enough to see it through and I'll cram when the exams come," and she did. But there came the day when the credits were given out and in one subject she utterly failed. She will be required to take it over again, and so far as her grade goes she has not passed. She came home to her mother and her face told the story; there was not the joy of achievement there and the mother, sympathetic, looked into her face and said, "But, Elizabeth, did you fail?" Yes, she had failed.

But I see as I look out upon the thousands of Endeavorers, those who have never achieved the grade higher year after year, but who in repeating the Bible verse, those who in reading the clipping, those who in taking the question, have stayed in that realm called the first grade or the second grade in Christian Endeavor throughout the years, and I say you have dishonored your Lord far more than this girl dishonored herself or her family when she failed in her grade.

Will you go back to your societies realizing that the rock in the foundation of testimony and prayer and expression is a rock that is one of the foundation elements? There must be growth and you must rise on stepping stones of your dead self to higher things.

Fourth: *Executive Training and Leadership.*

The fourth element in the foundation principles concerning high ideals of the individual Endeavorer has to do with the personal leadership in the executive work of our great organization. I find that for each professional leader in our great church, the minister, the assistant minister, the paid worker, etc., there must be back of him to help him do his work, at least forty to fifty volunteers. I believe that in this great crowd of young people we have a great many who are going to take up some walk in life to which Christian leadership will be a voluntary task. You will add it to your profession; it will not be your life work. Take it as sincerely as those take it who claim it as their life work.

You must realize that experience is the great teacher, and I am convinced after these years of contact with young people that nearly ninety per cent of our constructive, devoted, effective leadership is consecration to the task and the gift of time and talent and energy, and but one-tenth is what we call talent for leadership.

The society of which you are a part waits to-day on leadership. If it is a society of power, then I know that it has good leaders. If it is a society struggling to keep alive, then I know that the Lord has not deserted you, that you have deserted your Lord in the realm of constructive leadership.

Fifth: A Larger Vision of the Christian Programme and World Needs.

The fifth element in our foundation principles for the individual is the vision, the clear vision, the far vision. I call upon you to have Christian field glasses, the glasses that you will put to your eyes and see out into the field where your eyes have never seen. You must see and recognize that there is a world brotherhood and to understand it you must give yourself to thoughtful study.

Can you hear China's call, the call of India, the call of South America, the call of the world across the seas to you to-day? Not very well, possibly not at all unless with the field glasses of a devoted Christian you have looked out through the mission study class, through the missionary meeting, through the stereopticon lecture, through the missionary story into that field of beauty, but particularly a field of challenge to you who are followers of your Lord, and I can only leave the ideal with you. Bible study helps to clarify your vision; stewardship gives you the clear eye to discern your stewardship responsibilities before your God. Your great denominational history stirs your blood and puts iron in your frame to carry forward the light that they have lifted up that it may go forward in the programme of God. Get hold of your Christian field glasses for God; there is a fundamental element in the broad vision that can come to you only through the printed page, the study class and the meeting where you received added information.

Sixth: Individual Christian Service.

Let us take the sixth element in our foundation principles,—personal service. You heard the ringing call of Dr. Clark last night as he said that the charm and the great achievement of soul winning has not lost its place, that there are still tens upon tens of thousands who are waiting for the personal word on the part of the followers of the Lord to lead them to the foot of the cross. Are you speaking that personal word that brings young people into the society membership, are you speaking that quiet personal word that encourages the one who falteringly has prayed to pray again? There is the help, the strength for that one who fumbled and stumbled in a testimony to rise one step higher the next time if you by your personal word of encouragement will help. Yes, in the words you speak as an individual there is the personal service. I am keeping in the background now that service which we do unitedly. I am thinking of the service that you do personally. Some of us are willing to stand together in the society and speak and cheer and work for the Kingdom, but we so often fail to stand in practical ways and speak in definite ways for our personal Lord to those 'round about us.

Seventh: A Christian Example in All Life's Relationships.

I would that I could take all the time that is mine to speak on the last, the seventh point. Christian example in all life's relationships— in home, school, office, social life, etc. I know that it isn't hard for you to reveal Jesus Christ in some of your relationships. I know that it isn't difficult for you to reveal Jesus Christ if you can say to him, "Lord, I will reveal Thee here, but in these other relationships I claim the right to do as I please and to live the life that I please and to reveal the example that I please." But Christian Endeavor has high personal ideals that include all life's relationships, and you dare not leave one out: so I just place with you the challenge of the Christian example in the home. Thank God for your home, but thank God more for the strength of the Christian character that makes it possible for you to manifest Him in the words you speak, in the service that you render, in the burden that you bear for mother and for father and for those 'round about you and in the share of the load that in the face of your responsibility before God you carry because you love Him and because you know you are a richer, finer Christian because you do it.

But you must go outside the circle of the home, and I know that there are many here who face in the course of the year the testing of the school room, and I know that it is severe testing, it is the testing that takes iron and Christian iron in your blood to stand. There will come the test of the quizz and the temptation of the friend who urges you to do the thing that you know, down deep in your life, will injure your character, that will make you a smaller Christian rather than a larger Christian. Out in the school life I ask you to build on the granite rock of the Christian principle for which Christian Endeavor stands. Put Christ on the throne, have high ideals in your school life.

As I close our discussion on these personal ideals, I would bring to you the words of another, a pal of mine in seminary, who in his life was the most buoyant, the most virile, the most active, the most humorous sort of a fellow who knew all the joys of life, and yet down deep in his heart had the largest place of all for his Christ and his King, who laid down his life in the great struggle in India for his God in the influenza epidemic and whose words have echoed back and back again across this continent in those few lines called "My Creed."

> "I would be true for there are those who trust me;
> I would be pure for there are those who care.
> I would be strong for there is much to suffer;
> I would be brave for there is much to dare.

> "I would be friend of all, the foe, the friendless,
> I would be giving and forget my gift.
> I would be humble for I know my weakness,
> I would look up and laugh and love and lift."

Would you?

LECTURE II.

Christian Endeavor Unites Young People in a Training School for Kingdom Leadership.

By Rev. William Ralph Hall

Christian Endeavor unites young people in a training school for Kingdom leadership, not just for self-satisfaction, not for the pride of an organization that achieves, but unites them for Kingdom leadership, and I ask you to think of the verse in First Corinthians 3:9, "We are laborers together with God."

First, United—Built Together—for Kingdom Leadership.

First, we are built together for Kingdom leadership in an organization that ties the group of young people together with a very definite purpose.

Keep in mind, if you please, that we are talking about essentials, not attempting methods. There are many ways by which we may carry out these ideas that we are putting into the foundation. We are trying to find the things that are really essential.

We must not lose sight of the fact that our organization is a training school. We are binding people together that they may work together. It is one thing to do as you want in your individual life as you go along life's pathway; it is an entirely different thing to be a good team-worker. It means self-sacrifice. It means surrendering to the highest ideals of the group. It means submerging yourself in obedience to the largest interest, the highest purpose, of all concerned. Team-work is far above individual ability. One may be a genius and not be a team-worker. Our organizations succeed only when we work together, are united in training, united likewise in service. To make things clearer, as far as the organization goes, we lay down our constitution, and yet I find young people's societies that never set up a constitution. They think that does not matter.

If they have a meeting on Sunday evening and some people take part and there is no outstanding reason for criticising, they have gone far enough. Let me put it into your minds at the very beginning that one of the foundation principles of the organization is that we shall go higher and higher in our efficiency day in and day out, week in and week out, until we have achieved the greatest possible success. It is not sufficient that we shall have an organization that is above criticism. It is not sufficient that we shall get some things done. Our challenge is to unite people to do the best and to render the largest possible service in Kingdom building.

Let us realize the power of our constitution, let us be familiar with it, let us make it our chart, and add to it the challenge we have in our pledge.

Second: An Organization Christ-Centred and Church-Centred.

Emblazoned on the walls and in the store windows and in the station and in the different places of this city you find these words: "For Christ and the Church." They are not put there for the sake of beauty; they stand as the ideals of the Christian Endeavor organization of the past and, just as definitely, as the ideals of to-day. This organization is Christ-centred. It exists to build the Kingdom, nothing else. It exists to make our Lord and Savior the personal Lord and Savior of mankind. It is Church-centred. That does not mean that there is no organization existing in the little schoolhouse where no organization would exist in the name of Christ unless Christian Endeavor placed it there. It does not mean that we should eliminate the organizations that are in reformatories and prisons and schools and other places where the church as such does not exist, but the Christian Endeavor society in your church is a concrete part of the individual church of which you are a part.

I realize that sometimes there are organizations that live so much within themselves that they almost build a wall about themselves and in the life of the church they are not great rocks in the foundation but they are units quite apart from the foundation. Christian Endeavor societies are criticised sometimes. Remember, young people's societies, that criticism can never come back on those who founded the organization and placed above it the motto: "For Christ and the Church." Criticism can never come back on those State officers in the unions and other officials who have proclaimed again and a thousand times again the words, "For Christ and the Church."

Criticism comes especially when down in the local society some leaders have failed to remember that there is a definite obligation to the church, that Christian Endeavor is Christ-centred and is Church-centred. We are a part of the church to which we belong, in whose rooms we meet, to which we should give service. Let us remember that second element as we go back and emphasize it as one of the principles that we must not overlook.

Third: Uniting Young People of Mutual Interests in Fellowship and Service.

Uniting young people, those of mutual interests, those who fellowship together, and uniting them for service. Another phrase we so often use is, "The organization of the young people, by young people, for young people." That does not mean that we draw an age line and those who have passed the line called young people shall not have part in it; but it does mean very definitely that the supreme purpose of this organization is to reach and to develop and to train young people.

Therefore, it is a standard in societies in general that young people shall hold office, not one person hold it year after year. Somebody came to me one day in a conference and said, "How long do you think a Christian Endeavor president should hold office?"

I said, "There is no hard and fast rule. I am opposed to the plan of changing presidents every six months; I do not oppose the plan of having an election every six months, for sometimes it is a very fine opportunity to get rid of a president who in six months has revealed his inefficiency, but one who is efficient can always be re-elected to serve a year."

The person responded, "Well, I have been president of our society about seven years. Don't you think it is about time to change?"

"Yes," I said, "it was time to change five or six years ago."

There are few organizations throughout the country that carry out the plan of repeatedly re-electing the presidents. Sometimes it seems necessary. Our officers are young people. They are inexperienced. They are in a training school. Let's realize that!

Young people lead the meetings. Oh, I know they can't give such finished talks as older people, but it is a training school, and they must do the talking and do the leading.

But then where shall we have the adult? I believe in having the adult in the organization. I would put the adult in the organization very much in the same place that you put the coach in the football game or in the basketball game, or in some place like that. When the great game is called on the gridiron the rule is that the coach shall not cross the line. All he is able to do must find expression through that team of men out there in their football togs fighting for victory.

The catch type of leadership, the one who counsels, who is sympathetic, the one who advises, the one who gives help to the young people as they look out upon a field sometimes unknown and in which they have had little experience, is the right kind of leadership in my opinion. I believe we need sympathetic, kindly leaders in our organization who will take the place of the coach. I think we never need that one who shall try to run the society or assume the leadership place. "Of young people, for young people and by young people" is one of our granite blocks in the foundation of our organization.

Fourth: Holding Regular Meetings for Devotional and Educational Development.

Then we recognize, fourth, that in the devotional meetings and in our study classes and educational programmes that we are constantly developing workers there for devotional and educational leadership. I hardly need discuss this. The devotional meeting seems to be one of the constant factors.

Sometimes we ought to be ashamed for being so little prepared to meet the responsibility. Sometimes we should feel chagrined for using its opportunities so feebly, letting the opportunities slip by. But let me right now put it down in the foundation principles that it is one of the rocks, it is one of the things upon which we must build. We must make the most of it for let us recognize that it, to the outside world in a very definite way, is often the measure of our organization.

It is the scale by which outsiders weigh us, the rule by which they measure us. I was down in one of the Southern States one time and I slipped into a Christian Endeavor society where I was to speak in the evening. I was unknown. It was in the Fall and college was just opening. A row of young men, seven of them, sat just behind me in this meeting. I guess they did not know that I was a stranger like themselves. They were silent throughout the whole meeting. It was a very poor meeting. The leader was not prepared; I know, for the leader said so. No one need have said it; an explanation was unnecessary. The members of the society were unprepared. They said so in some cases. They revealed it very clearly in others. There were college students present who had come from societies in their home towns. This was their first meeting and their first Sunday in the new college town.

I slipped out the door with them and heard them talking about the meeting. "Never again," was the heart of the conversation. I wish I could have stayed by to see if they lived up to their promise, for they were resolved within themselves to leave that organization alone. That Sunday evening meeting of one hour was the scale by which the organization was weighed. It was the measuring rod by which the young people were measured. It is a foundation principle; it is a rock on which we build and old as it is, commonplace as it is, I plead with you that you shall make these devotional meetings of great spiritual power, meetings of the finest training for everybody, not just for a few. Work definitely to reach every member in the society and reveal such fine spirit and give such fine testimony and thoughtful discussion and enter so heartily into the worship that those who come will say to themselves, "My life has been enriched; I am finer, I am bigger, and I shall strengthen my spiritual life by coming again and again to this devotional meeting."

Fifth: Promoting Organization, Efficiency and Society Extension.

Business meetings and committee meetings are at the centre of this item. Do I need to remind you that here is one of the weak places in our society life? Oh, it is hard to get good business meetings and while we are not fearful of the hard things, some of us are just plain quitters. I will suggest a method to you that may help you. I know a bank that has a large board of directors. That board of directors is called to meet at eleven o'clock sharp on every Monday throughout the entire year except the month of August. These great business men found it a little difficult to come around at eleven o'clock on Monday morning, every Monday of their lives. A few officers of the bank considered the matter seriously and thoughtfully, then this is the way they solved their problem. They promised there would be a little envelope on the table in front of every chair on Monday—every single Monday of the year and in that envelope there would be a twenty-dollar gold-piece for each member who came. The attendance increased three hundred per cent in one month. Try it on your business meetings. I don't know where you will get your twenty-dollar gold pieces, but I know it will work. I would come myself.

You cannot build the Kingdom in your business meetings on twenty-dollar gold pieces. The bank may, but, nevertheless, you must just as definitely and just as effectively handle those business meetings and those committee meetings so they will challenge young people. These must be regular, they must be continuous throughout the months. I will not say absolutely every month, but I am saying that the life of a society will not rise to a place of power where you do not have constructive business meetings, where you do not have thoughtful committee meetings. Let's build that rock in our foundation.

Sixth: Supporting Local Church and Denomination.

The sixth point has to do with our relationship to our denomination. I would like to take a minute or two to caution you of a false note that is often sounded. There are those who say it is impossible for young people to be loyal to their denominations and be loyal to the inter-denominational fellowship of Christian Endeavor. I believe it is not true. I have been in the college life and seminary life and I am kept in close touch with hundreds of young people, and I have never found the place in high school or university where a man would not be loyal to his class because he could not be loyal to that and the university also. I find he is loyal to his class, but when the great university team comes out for one of the big games, he forgets his class. He sits with the crowd anywhere and cheers with them all for the university. It is not a divided loyalty; it is just a little larger loyalty. Find out the plans of your denomination when you return, and be loyal.

Seventh: Meeting Youth's Social Needs Wholesomely.

The seventh point has to do with the social life of the young people. I think I need not magnify that, but I do find a suggestion now and then in the minds of leaders of societies indicating that young people have too much sociability and their time is all taken up going here and there, but I say unto you that that does not solve the problem. Is the sociability that they have the wholesome, fine, well-balanced sociability that you can provide for your society group and for your community? Build into the foundation of your society life a wholesome, well-balanced, challenging, joyous programme.

LECTURE III.

The Right Foundation of Christian Endeavor Service for Others.

By Rev. William Ralph Hall

The subject to-day is "The Right Foundation of Christian Endeavor Service for Others."

Christan Endeavor commands young people to bear fruit. "Ye did not choose me, but I chose you and appointed you that ye should go and bear fruit."—John 15:16.

Chosen to go and bear fruit? Can we do it constructively? Can we do it in such a way as to bear an abundant harvest? Certainly we can.

I shall never forget the enthusiasm that was manifested in the voice and the features of a society president one day when I asked what his service programme was, and when he got the understanding of my question he said, "Yes, yes, we have a service programme, we take care of the meeting in the old folks' home every year on the Thursday before Christmas." One hour and five or ten minutes on the part of a society of sixty-five members. There was no definite plan. There was one thing written into the programme, and only one.

First: A Service Standard or Service Goal for Each Organization.

First have a definite plan, and as we think of our definite plan we must choose the field of service. There are a thousand doors open; we cannot enter all. Therefore, we as an organization must give ourselves thoughtfully to seeking out the field into which we shall enter to serve for our Lord and Master. We must divide the task. No one may do it all. There is no particular merit and very little glory in achievement in Christian Endeavor if that achievement be the result of one or two people who have given generously even to the point of tremendous sacrifice, for we are united as young people, serving for God among young people, and it must be a service that shall command us all, with our talents, with our energies, with our capabilities. It is not an achievement to command a few, we must command all.

That programme must find expression throughout the entire year. God forbid that we should do one or two things and glory in our achievement and idle during the rest of the year. Our programme must be definite, it must be comprehensive, it must take in the entire society, it must cover the entire year.

Second: Practical Service for the Local Church.

Let us begin at home and render service in our local church. I know that it is difficult some times in the large church where we have private secretaries and stenographers and assistant pastors and parish workers to find the task that seems particularly to help the pastor personally, but I commend to every society some plan whereby you render a very definite service to the pastor personally as the representative of your church. I asked a group of young people to name me one service that they had rendered in the months past in the name of the church definitely for the pastor, and I had a number of hands raised immediately, and in asking for the first answer it came without hesitation, "I attend the regular services." That is fine, but that is not service for your pastor, that is your training. You may honor him, he may rejoice in your attendance, but let us recognize in the foundation principles of our individual life we go to church, we stay by those services to develop our lives, not as a piece of service for our minister. I know a society that assumes the entire responsibility for the church calendar, and the pastor says that there is no service in the church that relieves him of so much anxiety. There are calls upon the sick, upon the new comers in the neighborhood, upon the shut-ins, and the absentees. You can not do it all; do something. There is the canvass sometimes in the interest of the church when the pastor needs helpers. I leave it to you to find not many tasks but one or two regularly that you can do within the circle of your home church in the name of your pastor.

Then I ask that you shall consider your church in the broader aspect, not the denomination, your church. It may be that you are helping to equip that church, meeting some very definite needs, a piano, some equipment somewhere else. I cannot begin to discuss the many ways, but find the way, lay down the plan whereby regularly you contribute some definite service to the church to which you are a part.

Third: Practical Service in the Community.

Our third challenge is the practical service in the community. It may be very distinctly related to our church; it may be very remotely related to our church; certainly it ought to be in the interests of the Kingdom of our Lord, Jesus Christ who would lift every life in every community just as high as possible and bring that life just as far as is possible in personal touch with Jesus Christ, our Lord and Master. I do not know what you may find to do, but I am confident that there is no community in the length and breadth of this great land of ours in which you are unable to find a task worthy of our talent and our energies. It may be in a hospital, an almshouse, a prison, and orphanage, a home for incurables. It may be that you will hold regular devotional meetings in some philanthropic institution. Do not confine your service entirely to that. Those in institutions enjoy the sociability of life, some of the pleasant things of life, and in some respects they get so little.. Take to them the entertainment, the joy of socialists, and some of those little things that are within the circles of practical service and are not devotional meetings.

And so you serve your community, but there is another field ofttimes presented—the mission. It may be for the sons and daughters of those born across the seas, but it is a great challenge, a work for boys, a work for girls, or young people. It may be a class in English, or any one of a thousand things. Now, let me caution you again; you may not enter all of these and bear fruit successfully; you must choose your fields.

I look back with keen pleasure to the hospital in which I served during my college career, and our society was a large one. Our hospital committee was large, and the service rendered in that institution was a service of seven days a week, all through the school year. We visited the wards, we wrote letters for those who undergoing operation were amazed to find that they could not even write a note home to tell the people what had happened. Some days we would go back to find the little white cot vacant where we sat some days before to write the quiet letter home. We would turn to the nurse with that inquiring look, and without word of mouth she would give us that look that would make it very clear to us that that life had gone. We thanked God that before it went we had served in His name just a little by the white cot in the hospital ward.

There are thousands of ways you may serve in your community.

Have one programme and stay by it with such faithfulness that the institution knows you are dependable, and can never say that you made a good beginning but in three months the whole thing went to pieces. We have called down criticisms upon our heads because we have made fairly good beginnings and because we have not stayed by. I commend to you in the name of our common Lord and Master a programme in the community where you stay by to the end, giving of time and of energy to the building of the Kingdom.

Fourth: Gifts in Time and Money to Kingdom Extension.

The fourth item is the matter of gifts of time and energy to Kingdom extension. Christian Endeavor around the world. Dr. Clark appealed to us in his first address to recognize the marvelous value of a dollar with the American stamp upon it in the great mission fields that are calling for help, and I know just how possible it would be for us to send all that they need if we would make just a reasonable sacrifice.

About two years ago I sat with the salesman of a great chocolate manufacturing company that sells chocolate bars by the thousands upon thousands to the American people. I was considering setting up a little summer stand in a summer conference of 250 people, and I said to him, "What is your basis of figuring the amount of candy that you would place upon a sale table at an institution like this?" He gave me these rather startling figures: 250 people in the same place for seven days would normally purchase and consume 3,500 bars—five-cent size—of milk chocolate, totaling $175. They would, in addition, consume in money value twice as much for cool drinks and ice cream—$350. I tested him out on the ten cents per individual per day basis and he was short the mark. It only takes half a page of paper and a little figuring to realize that on the slightest margin of sacrifice we could start a small flood tide of gold to the great world that waits upon our giving. I frankly ask you, as a denominational leader, one who believes in denominational loyalty, one who hears the cry of a denominational mission board constantly, I appeal to you with thoughtful balance of your benevolences to keep in your mind and heart the great needs and make a sacrificial gift to those who so need help for the world extension in the name of our great organization, Christian Endeavor, and for Christ and the Church.

Fifth: Gifts of Life to Full Time Service.

And when we hasten to our fifth point, and hear the call, "Who will go for us?" and the answer, "Here am I; send me." The response to the call to full time service is a gift, a tremendous gift, and let me, with very thoughtful judgment, confess to you that we have not begun to call into full time service the number who would willingly accept the challenge if we make the great needs known. The greatest asset of our Lord and Master to-day, second only to a consecrated, devoted life, is a knowledge of the world's great needs.

One of our large Presbyterian churches of over 1,500 members has for years held a splendid record for evangelism and for additions in church membership, but in the last fifteen years there has gone out from that church only one single soul into the ministry of the Lord, Jesus Christ, and not one soul into the mission field. And why? Too busy to magnify it, too busy to tell the story, too busy to make the world's needs known, that is all. And then I look at the fields down in the heart of Tennessee, the little church on a knoll in a quiet place that never has been famous for its numbers, for the salary it paid its ministers, but in more than fifty years of life and service has sent more than fifty souls out into the ministry and the mission field. And Why? Because in the days of the nation's great need for Christian leadership that church set its goal, namely, "one man in full time service for God every year of our ministry," and they have more than succeeded. There is a great field and we need to set definite goals; know the story of the great task before us and tell it again and again and again to our young people.

Sixth: Sharing the Denomination's Tasks.

Our sixth item is the same story, only it is related to our church family, that is all. And you ought to understand the challenge of your own church. The denomination counts on you; it plans its great programme across the seas depending upon your gifts; it plans its work under the flag, depending upon your gifts. Will you fail them? As I said yesterday, there is no divided loyalty in the life of that one who gives definitely, earnestly, with real consecration to the task of his church, and at the same time gives a portion of that which God hath given to him for the great extension work of Christian Endeavor or other work. And our task, then, is to share the responsibility of our church family in the way in which they expect us to share it.

Seventh: Participation in Interdenominational Fellowship.

Are we willing to say that of the time I have, the energy I have, the leadership I have, I will go out into a county union or a district union, or a State union and I will take a task this year and be a loyal, hard working officer to carry the organization forward?

I know that in some cases pastors complain about young people going out into such union work, saying that leadership is taken away from our young people. May I ask all those who have this thought to consider this. When there comes out of the rank and file of the individual church that young person who says, "I will go for God to China," do we give that life with joy? Do we not do a very similar thing in many respects when out of our group of leaders we take one or two and we dedicate them for a year, possibly two years, to an extension work, a missionary work in the name of our union? I am sure that union work usually makes strong leaders of them; sometimes it takes them out of a broader field. We will fill the ranks of leadership if we build solidly on these principles that we have been discussing.

Let us enlarge our vision; let us raise up leaders and let us have a definite, comprehensive service programme, and so I come to the conclusion of our three lectures on foundation principles. I, you, stand at the centre of the first. The society is at the centre of the second series of foundation principles, and the world is the open field of service for the third, and let us not neglect one of the three. All three go together in the building of our lives and our organization and the building of our Kingdom.

Chapter XX.

RELIGIOUS EDUCATION

Excerpts from Conference Led by Walter D. Howell
Thursday Morning, July 5

The meeting convened at St. Paul's Episcopal Church at nine o'clock, and was called to order by the leader, Mr. Walter D. Howell. He said:
Religious education is a phrase that is being used very frequently these days. It is not a phrase that stands for something new in the church. It stands for a gathering together of a lot of the things we had for a long time, not only gathering them together but lining them up and so relating them that they become a recognizable and definite part of the church's work. We mean the educational part of the church's work when we speak of religious education. We mean Sunday school, Christian Endeavor, missionary education, Camp Fire Girls, Boy Scouts, and all kinds of clubs for young people. We mean pastors' catechetical classes, we mean the newer forms of week-day religious instructon, we mean various types of supplementary educational work of which the Sunday school usually is the backbone in the individual church programme. There are some new things emerging into the programme of religious education, but we are still retaining most of the old things, but instead of leaving them to run each by itself in any direction that it gets enthusiastic about heading for, without attempting to co-ordinate their programme, we are trying to get religious education thought of by individual churches as a unit, into which different organizations fit with their policies and programmes and the service they can perform. That is very rough. I am not at all desirous of being philosophical or comprehensive in this class. What I want to be is practical and see just clearly enough so we can be concrete.
May we consider now the national situation which calls for a stronger programme? Statistics say that there are twelve million boys and girls of Protestant parentage between six and eighteen years of age in our country outside of every Sunday school and, of course, of church membership. That twelve million figure covers the age of grade school

and high school approximately, beginning with six and closing with seventeen, and it includes only the children of Protestant or nominally Protestant parents. Twelve million boys and girls not touched regularly by any Sunday school, and therefore not getting any definite or organized religious education anywhere! Where else could they get it? Is it likely that parents would be teaching religion to children in the home if those children are not in Sunday school?

The other statistics quoted with reference to religious education are different. Let's not get confused about it. It says there are probably about twenty-seven million young people under twenty-five years of age in this country to-day who are out of all touch with any form of religious instruction. What is the difference between those two figures? Twenty-seven million takes everybody, Catholic, Protestant, agnostic—no faith at all, and it runs from birth through the twenty-fourth year, while the twelve million figure starts with six and stops at seventeen. This last figure is staggering, is it not?

What Do We Do For Our Children and Young People?

The first thing is the Sunday school. We have at last got to the point, and we were long in getting there, where the average church considers itself not in good standing if it does not have a Sunday school. Some of you can remember when that could not be made a general statement. A good many churches still question about the permanent value of the Sunday school, still centring on adult discussion meetings and adult devotional services and leaving the educational side of the church's work for children and young people almost untouched. It is only fair to parallel that statement with the statement that must go along with it, that when that was the case there was a great deal more attention to religious instruction in the family by the parent in the home than there is now, since the Sunday school has been given a permanent place in the average Protestant church.

What are we doing outside of the Sunday school for the religious education of our children and young people in the average churches of the country? Will you answer? What else do we have besides the programme of the Sunday school which is definitely planned as an educational force for children and young people in the church?

The following suggestions were given: Daily Bible School, Week-day Class, Missionary Field, Boy Scouts, Camp Fire Girls, Special Periodicals, Colleges.

CHAIRMAN HOWELL: Colleges, some one says. That is advanced education and it comes to the favored few. We are thinking now of the thing that centres in the individual church.

We will stop with that, and some of you are questioning, as I am, I am sure, how many of these things we would have to rule out if we were going to consider the average Protestant church, the *average* Protestant church.

The Sunday school with some kind of a programme and a young people's society, either Christian Endeavor or some other name, with some kind of a programme and some sort of missionary education organization and programme and some sort of auxiliary clubs of one sort or another, mostly leisure-time programmes for boys and girls at certain ages, perhaps it would be fair to say you find in the religious education programme operating right now in the majority of our Protestant churches. All right, we agree, I think, that the religious education programme of the average Protestant church to-day centres in its Sunday school. That is the big thing in religious education in Protestantism in our churches to-day, for a number of years past. A great many feel that the Sunday school will continue to be the principal factor in the religious education programme of the individual church. Whatever may happen about that certainly it is at the present time. Therefore, it becomes helpful to us in our consideration to understand clearly that what Sunday school is accomplishing, how nearly it is reaching what might be considered a fair objective to set. We have been emphasizing the Sunday school far beyond anything else in our religious education propaganda as Protestant churches, have we not?

We are organized denominational and interdenominational bodies to further the Sunday school. We have considered the Sunday school in countless thousands of conferences here, there and everywhere, all over our land. The permanent educational boards and agencies of our denominations got behind the Sunday school, promoted it, and tried to put it on a definitely educational basis, and to increase its efficiency. We have had teachers' training, the graded movement; we have had a wonderful amount of time and thought and prayer put on improved curriculum. We have borne down on official boards everywhere until we have raised the Sunday school, and thinking of the church immeasurably in the last twenty years, yet some of us know what a short distance after all we seem to have traveled.

The best statistics we can get (and here, of course, we admit an inevitable degree of inaccuracy), which were handed to us by the religious education survey under the Interchurch World Movement and carried on under others, say that the average situation is about this: *One-half the members of the Sunday school present one-half the time.*

Now, I am of the opinion that it is fair to say if you would eliminate the adult on your Sunday school rolls and consider only those from the beginners on up to twenty-four, you

They are from Texas

would get a larger percentage than that. A great many of the absentees are reported on the adult-class books, but it would not go much higher than that, even if you eliminated the adults. What are we doing for those folks in the Sunday school? We are, of course, centring our attention in the instruction programme. Sunday school is chiefly to teach Christianity and Christian living. Some might disagree with that assertion. We will not quibble about it here, but I am sure we will all agree with it approximately, the chief business of the Sunday school. Character building through the teaching process and the study process is the chief business of the Sunday school. At any rate that is what we give the most of the Sunday school's time to.

What is the average teaching period when the classes are with their teachers, studying and being instructed in the average Sunday school of the country? Somebody says twenty minutes; another person says forty. Well, theoretically, thirty minutes. You go and ask the Sunday school superintendent anywhere in this country, and ninety-nine out of a hundred will say thirty minutes. That is the theory. Of course, the teachers will tell you something different. They will be more likety to say twenty.

Now, that other thirty minutes is religious education theoretically again. It may not be at all. It may be a hodge-podge that you could not by any stretch call educational or devotional because the devotional spirit is not felt nor developed. We are not here to criticize details just now. Theoretically, all of the hour is religious education, but it is not religious instruction which is one of the elements we are considering just now, the instruction programme.

What we do for the average Protestant boy and girl in our country to-day is to give them thirty minutes a week of religious instruction in the Sunday school, as far as *instruction* is concerned. Now, where else may that boy or girl be getting definite religious instruction besides that thirty minutes in the Sunday school?

What percentage would you say of the homes of your church are giving definite religious instruction to their children?

Five, ten and fifteen per cent were suggested.

CHAIRMAN HOWELL: May I give you this statement from the Presbyterian Religious Educational Board? Our Board conducted a quiet investigation and check-up on this matter, and then we were obliged to go out to our constituency with this statement (we wish we didn't have to make it but we feel we must; we think it is a conservative statement): in at least sixty-five per cent of the Presbyterian church members' homes of our country to-day, the Bible is almost never opened. We checked up with pastor after pastor who said that was too conservative. It is true for more than sixty-five per cent of the folks in our congregation, no doubt.

Christian Endeavor folks and other young people in the home use the Bible under the Quiet Hour plan, a great many of them, for a time. A great many of them quit after they have done it for a time, but it is fair to say that an astonishingly encouraging number of them keep it up, that they open that Bible in the privacy of their own rooms, usually as a matter of personal devotion.

That is self-instruction, but it is not religious instruction for the younger children growing up in the home. That is limited to the individual; they don't even get the influence of seeing their older brothers and sisters turning to God's Book on a week-day. They don't know it is going on in most cases.

We ought to have the religious instruction of the Sunday school in that thirty minutes on Sunday supplemented tremendously by religious instruction in the home, and I wonder if the church is not somewhat to blame, and the Sunday school people and the Christian Endeavor people and all the rest of us specialized religious educators are not to blame. I wonder if in the promotion of the Sunday school and other organizations we have not taken the emphasis off of the home as a factor in religious education until it has been easy for the parent to conclude that the church is now doing so much more for the boy or girl than it did when he or she was young that it is not necessary for the parent to assume responsibility for the religious education or instruction of the children in the home.

It matters not how many gaps we fill up in the specialized programme in our churches to-day, the church will never be able to give an adequate religious instruction to the children of the family without the co-operation of the families themselves.

Every parent inevitably is teaching religion to his children, therefore the Sunday school can never adequately take the place of religious instruction in the home or any other church organization. Oh, they can do wonders with the proper co-operation of the parents in the home, but without the co-operation of the parents we must accept the definite handicap always in our work.

God starts the building of character in the family, and the contact with parents and brother and sister in that little circle in the home. The Christian church is organized like that, it is the organization of families, believers, and their children. The family element must enter into any adequate religious education programme. We do very little in the home; we have thirty minutes a week in the Sunday school. We have half the attendance one-half of the time with the Sunday school open fifty-two Sundays in the year; at least four Sundays the lesson is not taught at all. You get down to a very low number of hours per year, but we won't go as low as we might justifiably. We will say now that the average child is present forty Sundays a year when the lesson is taught; thirty minutes a Sunday gives twenty hours a year. That is a liberal allowance for the religious instruction in the Sunday school, and that is the centre we say, that is the main factor in the religious education programme.

What is the value of that other thirty minutes or forty minutes in the Sunday school, that thirty or forty minutes that is occupied by something else besides the teaching and studying the lesson? Of course, it has some value. You can give it full value and figure an hour of religious education. I think you will follow me now as I distinguish between instruction and education. Give it all religious educational value, an hour and a quarter a week. That is worth something in religious education in the Sunday school and the child is there forty Sundays a year; that gives us forty hours.

What is the educational efficiency of the Sunday school at present? Immediately somebody says, "trained teachers." Of course, the overwhelming majority of our teachers in Sunday school attempting to teach religion are without training in the art or science of teaching, or with very little. Thoughtful Sunday school teachers who are also public-school teachers testify it is harder to teach the Bible, harder to teach religion than most of the subjects they get in the grade schools, and a great many they get in the high school. If it is, then certainly we need training there as much, at least, if not more, than we need it in general education work. Untrained teachers! What are some of the other things to contend with? Lack of continuity in the teaching work. If you are a public school teacher teaching grade school subjects, how would you like to teach a subject for thirty minutes on Monday morning and then not touch it again until the next Monday morning, when you would teach it for thirty minutes more, and then wait a week before you touched it again?

And then the multitude of other handicaps! The distractions constantly against educational efficiency in the teaching hour. It is only within the last few years that we began to build our church building with any reference to the needs of children and young people. I know what the statistics are for mine. After all these years of emphasis on the educational work of the church, after denominational and interdenominational spending of thousands and thousands of dollars and having hundreds of full-time workers to promote the Sunday school idea the Presbyterian U. S. A. Churches of America, about one-half of them, still have not more than two rooms in their buildings, and a lot of one room places are included in the two-room count. There is a little alcove where they try to sqeeze in what they call a primary class.

There are some ways to test the results of Sunday school work with young people who have been in the Sunday school through beginners' primary, Junior, Intermediate Department and got up to the age we will say of seventeen or eighteen, and are ready to go away to college or out of high school and into employment.

Some of you know Dr. Robinson. He used to be teacher of Bible in a rather strong college in the Eastern States. He had the custom of giving a little test examination on the Bible to freshman students who entered his Bible courses each year.

Remember, now, that I will quote you no answer from anybody who has not been in Sunday school for at least six years and most of them for eight or nine. Some of you have heard these before, but they occur to me just now.

"What can you say about Job?"

And an eighteen-year-old young lady who had been in Sunday school from a child, wrote this: "Job is a small town in Palestine not far from Jerusalem."

"Who was Pontius Pilate?"

A seventeen-year-old young man out of the Presbyterian church wrote this: "That is the ancient name for an inland body of water in the Holy Land now called the Dead Sea."

"Who were the Philistines?"

An eighteen-year-old girl writes this: "They were a narrow-minded religious sect in Jerusalem sometimes called publicans and sinners."

I won't go farther with Dr. Robinson's list. I wish I could think he had an exceptional experience.

I happen to know that Dr. Robinson's experience is not an exceptional one; I have tested that. I have tried it in two Sunday schools where I was superintendent.

If you want to test the educational efficiency, try this test. Some Sunday get the teachers of the classes in which are scholars from seventeen to twenty years of age to pick out two of their good scholars and give them to you. Take that group into a room by themselves. See that the Bibles and Quarterlies are removed, hand each one of them a list of ten simple questions about Bible facts and ask them to write a brief answer to each one of those ten, and you stay there to see that they have no opportunity to consult each other.

You are not interested in who made the answers. Don't ask them to put their names on the tests. I have never been able to discover any ten questions so simple that seventeen to twenty-year-old young people out of our Sunday school would not make an appalling percentage of errors when faced with a written test.

"Name the town in which Jesus Christ was born."

Would you think any child could be in Sunday school one year or through a single Christmas exercise without being able to name the town?

This gets the largest percentage of correct answers.

I sometimes ask this: "Name six of Christ's twelve disciples."

I wouldn't ask you to do it, the Northern Baptist Convention, or any other denominational groups to name all the twelve, because many of them are obscure, but is it not fair to say there are six that were closest to Christ, six personalities who outside of that of Jesus Christ Himself are the personalities most often referred to in the story of the four gospels and the Acts. Those six names are what I ask for. Three-fourths can name six correctly, but almost every one has to get in Judas for the sixth. Twenty-five per cent cannot name six disciples. Some start out, "Matthew, Mark, John," and then try to find the others. A great many put in Paul as one of the disciples of Christ, and a number will drag in Timothy or somebody else.

Here is another one: "State in a few sentences what you recall about David."

I thought he was a fairly prominent Bible character and a young man, an elder's son, not a weak-minded boy, just thoughtless, just careless, that is all, who had been in Sunday school from the Primary Department since he was seven years of age until he was eighteen, wrote this answer: "David was a young Jew who was kidnapped by Arabs because they wanted his coat of many colors. They took him down to Egypt where he became king of the country. David wrote the Book of Proverbs and had a good friend named Joshua."

Now, perhaps you do not realize that in a standard daily Vacational Bible School, meeting five mornings a week for the summer vacation, you can give the boys and girls in your church as much religious instruction as they get in the Sunday school for an entire year. You can double that twenty hours of instruction easily by the standard Daily Vacational Bible School programme.

Three hundred communities and more that we know about in the United States to-day are operating in addition to their Sunday school work in their Protestant churches, some of them, some kind of week-day Bible classes, and those week-day Bible classes are hooked up with some kind of public co-operation with the public schools of that community, some of them slightly related to the public school programme, some of them thoroughly related, at least a hundred and fifty of them getting the public school time to teach the Bible, scholars excused from public school at least one hour a week on request of their parents to go into a church or somewhere and be taught the Bible.

What are the essential elements in a well-rounded programme of religious education? Religious educators everywhere are well agreed about that. They use different language, they may name things differently, but analyze it all and you will find this is a wide-spread agreement that the three essential elements of religious education are worship, instruction and expression.

The Christian Endeavor society was designed to be and is still in the overwhelming majority of cases, a school; but it is not the same kind of a school as the Sunday school. If Christian Endeavor has any place at all in the religious training of the church, it is there on the word expression. *It is a school of expression; it is not a school of instruction; it is a school of worship.* I don't mean it is secondary in importance, but in the amount of time and attention given to worship. I do not say that expression is more important than worship or that worship does not come first. It does. If any organization has a right to permanent existence in your church it ought to have a specific purpose it can work out better than any other organization in your church.

But what we are on now is the lack of appreciation in many churches that expression is necessary at all in religious education. The idea that if young people go to church and listen to the pastor, get the worship value that there is in the devotional service that makes up our Sunday morning and evening service, if they are given some attention by the parents in the home, the admonition of the Lord and spiritual life is developed in that way, and then in addition to that if they go into the Sunday school and get the instruction and what little expressional value the Sunday school in its modern way can put into the service of worship or opening exercise or devotional the Sunday school can give them, it is enough.

Unless your Sunday school is different from the average Sunday school I think you will admit there is little opportunity for definite training and expression. How do you get training and expression? You get training and expression by doing something yourself. You can't get it by listening to somebody else do it.

Now we come to this question: "Can the Christian Endeavor Plan Give the Best Expressional Training?" and you will notice it says *"can."*

In most of the churches most of the people are more interested in what the adults are doing and what the church is accomplishing through its adults than they are in what the church is trying to do for its young people. So the Christian Endeavor plan that is operating in a given church just now may be different in a number of respects from the real genuine

Christian Endeavor plan, the plan which Francis E. Clark started and which his successors are maintaining and promoting everywhere. Let us consider that plan and see if we can understand it. What is the real Christian Endeavor plan and what are the possibilities that come out of it?

In the first place the Christian Endeavor plan is flexible; it is not fixed. It is capable of a number of modifications and adaptations and changes. It has always been flexible. If you read the first piece of Christian Endeavor literature Francis E. Clark ever issued, you will find that statement, that Christian Endeavor principles are fixed but that Christian Endeavor plans and methods of applying those principles and working out those principles are flexible.

You don't have to have something in Christian Endeavor a lot of folks think you do. It is a flexible organization. That is one of its chief characteristics and a characteristic that is largely unappreciated and misunderstood.

Secondly, it is self-dependent. That is the Christian Endeavor members of the society depend on themselves very largely, and not upon teachers or others. The plan is to challenge the young people to do the things themselves, to learn to do the things by trying to do them, to learn to speak about religion by trying to speak about religion, to learn to pray by trying to pray, to learn to do good work for the church by trying to do good work for the church, and all those things.

Put the work up to the young people themselves, but they are not left without guidance in the real Christian Endeavor plan. They always have adult guidance which is not leadership, but guidance. The Senior society, sometimes called the Young People's society does not have adult supervision; it does not centre around a superintendent or teacher, it centres around its own officers except for the guidance which all the organizations of the church have, the guidance of the pastor and official board of the church.

I am giving you the plan as I understand it; some of you Christian Endeavor folks may not understand it like I do. The principle of the thing is that it is self-dependent, that it believes in learning by doing, not learning by studying nor learning through watching or listening. That is not the Christian Endeavor job. It does that kind of learning by listening, watching and hearing, of course, but that is not what it was organized for.

Then Christian Endeavor has some fixed principles, and I doubt if any organization would receive your O. K. as an expressional training school if it did not have fixed principles.

They are exceedingly fundamental and surely far-reaching. They have not changed since first enunciated forty-two years ago. I am giving you Dr. Clark's own list, his minimum list, but he says it is comprehensive and includes all the things into which you might break up these principles.

First, a confession of Jesus Christ. The Christian Endeavor plan involves at some time in the Christian Endeavor training—it may not be at the start—a willingness to be openly regarded as a follower of Jesus Christ.

Second, there is service for Jesus Christ. They are to get training through service. Here comes the expressional element clearly and strongly, not to go to attend meetings, to listen or to be taught lessons, but to go to the meetings definitely to learn how to give a personal service to Jesus Christ.

Third, loyalty to the church from its inception to the present day. Over and over and over countless times Christian Endeavor has sounded forth this principle. The Christian Endeavor society is not a separate organization; it is an integral part of the church. It is within the church, not apart from it. The only authority that any Christian Endeavor society has over it is the authority that its own church designates. No Christian Endeavor union or officer of a Christian Endeavor union, county, district, State, or national has a thread of authority over that society anywhere.

Now, that is the plan. Maybe the plan does not work just now in your community. I have been in some where they had it upstairs and downstairs and they were about as separate as the upstairs is from the downstairs. That is not the Christian Endeavor plan. It came about in that church because the old people didn't know that Christian Endeavor ought to be a part of the church. That is the principle.

The last is fellowship with Christ's people. In other words, Christian Endeavor says, "My own church, my own denomination, my church, my pastor, always, never any other ahead of it."

But Christian Endeavor does not say, "My church first, last, and all the time," because Christian Endeavor does not believe that Jesus Christ says or teaches that, neither does Christian Endeavor say, "Fellowship with every other church and all other people." It says, "Fellowship with all other churches and members and all other young people who believe that Jesus Christ is the divine Son of God and therefore come within the evangelical family."

If you get those principles in you have a right to call your society a Christian Endeavor society. It is built on the Christian Endeavor plan. It is true that there are some practices, some methods, some forms of organization that have proved in the majority of cases to work better than others, that are very common in Christian Endeavor, but they are not essentials. They may be taken out, one or more of them, from Christian Endeavor. They may be modified, changed or greatly varied. You still have a Christian Endeavor society for young people.

Another characteristic is that its membership is voluntary.

It is not automatic or involuntary. The person who goes into a Christian Endeavor society makes up his own mind to do that. The average boy or girl goes to Sunday school because his father or mother makes up his or her mind that the boy or girl shall go. That is not true of Christian Endeavor.

It is true you cannot have a genuine Christian Endeavor society unless somehow or other, not necessarily by a pledge, —it may be by a statement of standard or some other method, —you have held up before those who are members of a society the idea of a personal responsibility between you and God, that you recognize that you covenant with Him, and that He covenants with you.

Does any one want to make a comment or raise a question or anything that has gone before about the characteristics of Christian Endeavor as an organization within the church?

MR. PAUL BROWN: I want to say I believe absolutely the time is coming when we must have adult supervision under the church authority for the Senior society as well as the younger groups.

CHAIRMAN HOWELL: All right. This seems to be a question largely up to the individual church organization. I don't suppose the question itself is proper for us to discuss here. I didn't know, really, that the time had come when we needed a plan for Senior societies; I do know that there are high school societies masquerading as Senior. I didn't know we had come to the time when societies made up largely of people eighteen years of age or over had to have adult supervision over them other than the pastor and the church official board. Somebody will have to tell me on that if it is so. If that is so then you can abandon a great deal of the personal initiative and the sense of responsibility and the development of individual service powers which have been discussed here.

MR. CURRIE: If Christian Endeavor is to fill its rightful place in this programme it is just as essential that there should be a superintendent of Christian Endeavor work in the church represented on the official board as a supervisor of the Sunday school.

RELIGIOUS EDUCATION

Excerpts from Conference Led by Walter D. Howell

Friday Morning, July 6, 1923

Religious educational leaders in all denominations are pretty well agreed that the three essential elements of an adequate programme of religious education for childhood and youth are worship, instruction, and expression. We are agreed that the Sunday school as at present operated in the great majority of cases can fairly be evaluated as an energy which gives the worship element in part and majors on the instruction element, that its chief job is religious *instruction*. We also see that the Young People's society of the Christian Endeavor type gives the worship element in part and majors on *expression*, that its chief job is expression. In the Sunday school you have partial attention to worship, a little incidental expression and a great deal of religious instruction.

The Christian Endeavor society, properly organized, and maintained on the true Christian Endeavor plan, gives the worship element, incidental instruction (very little of it), and majors on expressional training. Now, then, we are facing the question: "Is that arrangement adequate for young people?" Of course, we need the supplementary missionary instruction in specialized organizations, the supplementary physical and mental training for boys and girls of the teen age given by Boy scouts, Camp-Fire Girls, or what not, the pastors' catechetical classes, week-day religious instruction, etc., all of which build around and centre in the major organizations for young people's religious education, the Sunday school and the Young People's society.

The question we are now facing is: "Can the present division of worship, instruction, and expression elements in religious education between the two major organizations, the Sunday school and the graded Christian Endeavor societies furnish the best and most comprehensive plan for the religious education of childhood and youth in the church? Can the Christian Endeavor plan give the best expressional training for youth in our churches?" That is the question we are facing, and under that we are considering the other suggested plans which would either eliminate Christian Endeavor or modify it in some way. What are the other suggested plans?

Just at the close of our meeting yesterday we came to the expanded Sunday school idea as an alternative plan which is being urged in some quarters. Why can't we do it all in Sunday school? Why can't the Sunday school as a single organization provide adequate worship training, adequate instruction, adequate expressional training for all the children and young people of the church? We are then at that point, and the question we are here to discuss just now is: "What shall we put between 'Sunday school' and 'Christian Endeavor?'" Shall we put the abbreviation vs, which means *versus?* Is it Sunday school against Christian Endeavor, or the Christian Endeavor against the Sunday school? Or shall we put in the word "and"? In other words does a unified programme of religious education for the church mean the correlation of existing organizations or the elimination of some existing organizations and the merging of their constituency into another organization?

One suggested plan is an expanded Sunday school with

a programme on Sunday and a programme through the week, providing adequately for worship, instruction, and expression for the childhood and youth of the church. Now, what is your honest opinion of the adequacy of that plan? Will an expanded Sunday school with such a programme be practical? Will it meet the need for a comprehensive, unified, properly related programme of religious education for the young people of our churches?

May I suggest to you, first, the possibility that eliminating a Young People's society and saying we will provide expressional training in an expressional session for all young people under the Sunday school will not necessarily secure expressional training for all those who receive instruction in the Sunday school? There are very few persons who claim that it is possible in one continuous session of the Sunday school on Sunday, without adjournment, to give adequate attention to devotions, instruction, and expressional training.

It is suggested that the Sunday school have a second session either on Sunday or some other day of the week where it will major on expressional training, retaining the present Sunday school session for devotions and teaching, majoring on worship and instruction, just as it does now.

Now, then, my question is: "Suppose the Sunday school does that, will it get in that expressional session at the second hour all the folks who get instruction in the first session at the regular Sunday school hour, just because it is all under the Sunday school, everybody belongs to both, and everybody is expected to go to both?"

Here is the suggestion that is made: "Christian Endeavor only gets a small percentage of the young people in the Sunday school. They *all* need the expressional training. Why not give it to them *all?* Why limit expressional training to a selected group of young people who are more earnest, more ambitious, than the others, more consecrated, and so are willing to join the Christian Endeavor society with its rigid standards of membership and take that training? Why not throw it open to everybody in the Sunday school classes? We will do that by putting it all under the Sunday school, not calling it anything different at all, just saying when they join classes in the Intermediate or Young People's Department of the Sunday school, "This has two sessions for you, one session on Sunday morning or Sunday afternoon, and another on Sunday evening. You come to both. We do one thing for you in the morning and another in the evening. You need both. When you become a member of this class you are expected to attend both sessions."

It seems to me that those who thus argue forget that you will never be able to get as many people to go to church four times on Sunday as three times. You will never get as many three times as two times, and you will never get as many people to go twice as once. No matter what you call it, in my judgment, no matter what the overhead organization is, you cannot hope to get a one hundred per cent attendance of young people at two sessions on Sunday under any plan at all. There will be more who will be willing to go once than twice, more who will go Sunday morning than Sunday evening; or, the other way around, there will be more Sunday evening and not so many Sunday morning.

May we close this point? The all-Sunday school plan will not give expressional training to all those who receive the instruction. Therefore, it will not be a successful substitute plan.

The second point I would like to make is that the all-Sunday school plan will have in it a diminishing place for expressional training, a diminishing attention to expressional training. That is almost inevitable. If you merge in the Sunday school the Christian Endeavor society and its programme, it will have a place in the religious education programme of the church as compared with the place of instruction and worship training about comparable to these little chairs and these big chairs. It will come out in the little end of the horn. Expressional training will have a diminishing attention in the religious education work of the church which attempts to do everything, worship, instruction, and expressional training under one organization. The folks who will be at the head of that organization will be the folks who have been trained in the Sunday school, the chief job of which is to give instruction in an atmosphere of worship. That is the thing they have been giving their lives to and which they will continue to give their major attention, in spite of honest effort to change.

A good many of them do not see the value of expressional training, do not appreciate it, and I would not say that without immediately adding that a good many Christian Endeavor folks do not see that expressional training without adequate instruction paralleling it will not do at all. There is a woeful lack of appreciation of what real religious education is in its comprehensive sense, even among some of the district, State, and union leaders. You will admit that readily. One of the things we need to do is to know religious education, not just our own end of it, but all of it and how our part fits in.

Let's go to the next point, which is that this all-Sunday school plan, in all instances I know about, makes membership in the expressional organization automatic. You do not decide to join the expressional section yourself. You do not take upon yourself any personal obligation. You do not assent to any standard goals or objectives. You just join a Sunday school class, say you are willing to have your name put on the roll and to come and hear the lesson taught, to participate in the exercises of that Sunday school. Then they tell you that thereby you become a member of an expressional meeting or group or second session of the Young People's Department; that it has a separate meeting at some other time and that you are supposed to come and take part in it.

Do you see the loss of any of our present values by throwing out membership conditions and voluntary assumption of certain responsibilities and *automatically* making young people members of an expressional training school in the Christian church?

If I am sure of anything about the Christian Endeavor plan as it affected my own life and the lives of scores of young people contemporary with me, I am sure of this thing: that the sense of individual personal responsibility for helping make that thing go did more to develop initiative, and to carry me towards leadership than anything else I got in my church experience. The fact that I could not depend on a teacher, as there was no teacher to depend on, the fact that I could not shove off my particular responsibility on any other member of the society and be honest and conscientious about it, was uppermost in my mind. I, as an individual, assumed a certain individual responsibility, voluntarily, and my entrance into that society was conditioned on my assumption of that personal, individual responsibility for my part of that work, and I faced that question and said it would be hard.

Any plan of automatic membership under which the individual is not faced with any such definite obligation to try to do his part, in which the teachers of Sunday school classes are still the central focussing points, are still the ones who are there to be leaned upon whenever any one feels any inclination to lean, any sort of an automatic membership seems to me to lose a great deal.

The next thing I want to speak of is the difficulty in getting loyalty. Young people do get off the track, pull themselves away from the church, and regard themselves as two separate organizations. Some of the time, and perhaps all the time, the older folks are trying to prevent this, and are trying to deal wisely with the young people, but usually that is not the case. Usually when the young people get to drifting away from the church there has been too little recognition, too little attention, too litte sympathic support by the leaders of the church.

Now, this point, the difficulty of getting loyalty, we will not discuss long. It is a minor point. You can see what I mean. Here is Christian Endeavor with a wealth of tradition behind it, centred in its members, with an atmosphere and a slogan and a challenge to young people that has meant something in the lives of thousands of young people for many years. You can be loyal to Christian Endeavor with its motto, "For Christ and the Church." Is there not difficulty in getting that same *esprit de corps,* that sense of loyalty to something that is ours, when that something is just "the expressional session of the church school," or is just "the second meeting of the Young People's Department of the church school?"

May I call your attention to the fact that it is possible to argue, at least, that a second session of the young people of the Sunday school with an expressional programme is just Christian Endeavor under another name? There may be some advantages in eliminating the name, trying to convince the young people that they are not in two organizations, but in one. But you have not put in a new plan. When you do that you are admitting that the thing that needs to be done is the thing that Christian Endeavor has been doing for forty-two years; wherever it has been genuine Christian Endeavor.

May I bring before you this, which to my mind is one of the vital questions we must face as we consider these alternative plans. If we insist that no alternative plan that has so far been presented would justify the elimination of Christian Endeavor by its marked advantages, I think we must decide what the national policy shall be on this question. Is Christian Endeavor an *inclusive* society for *all* young people of the proper age in the church, or is it a *selective* society for *some* of the young people of the proper age in the church? Which is it going to be? Is it possible for it to be both, or to be neither?

It is possible to claim that Christian Endeavor is a selective organization, a kind of normal training school for leadership; that you can't expect to get all the young people in the Sunday school to join; but that those young people who are more interested, more earnest, and more truly consecrated, and who probably have the greatest potential qualities of leadership, will gravitate toward the Christian Endeavor society. That it is worth while even if you have twenty-five such young people in your Christian Endeavor society out of a hundred of the same age in the Sunday school. That if you only have twenty-five, it is worth while to give them the kind of leadership training and spiritual development, enlarged vision and greater capacity for service that the Christian Endeavor Training School will give them, and just do as much as you can for the other seventy-five people in the Sunday school. But don't be too greatly discouraged if you don't get them into the Christian Endeavor society, because it really is a *selective* training school.

Here is the other possible claim:—Christian Endeavor is a society for **all** young people in the church. It is a flexible organization and you can make it do anything that an all-

Sunday school plan would do. It is an inclusive society. It is for all young people, and you can so modify it that you can take in all. All will be willing to come in under a modified arrangement. You can still make it a Christian Endeavor society.

I am inclined to think some of the criticism we face and some of the confusion about Christian Endeavor policies manifested by educational leaders whose vision, knowledge, and capacity should command our respect, centres in this situation. Do we know what we are? Are we settled in our own minds as to whether the legitimate appeal of Christian Endeavor for a place in the religious education programme in the modern church is the appeal of a selective training school for some of the young people, or the appeal of an inclusive training school for all the young people? Or can it be made an organization which is inclusive for all young people and still retain the values of a selective, specialized training school for a part of the young people's group in the church?

No policy for the whole church with regard to religious education can satisfy which does not endeavor to give to every young person as much expressional training as the church can get him to take. Certainly no church ought to be satisfied with a religious education programme or organization plan for young people that does not do everything that could possibly be done to get expressional training for every young person who can be persuaded to take it. Let's take our stand squarely on that. If we do not meet the issue in a constructive way, we must not object to the Sunday school putting into its programme what expressional elements it can get without sacrificing the instructional elements. We have got to demonstrate we can give expressional training to as large a percentage of the young people of the church under the Christian Endeavor plan as under any other plan, or else we must be satisfied for the church to give some expressional training to the folks we do not get into Christian Endeavor.

There has been in my mind for some time the possibility of operating Christian Endeavor as an inclusive expressional training school into which all young people of proper age in the church will enter, and, at the same time, reserving for Christian Endeavor the very marked advantages of a selective intensive training programme. I have seen the possibility of doing it by adding a third classification of members, with a name which may or may not be the one that has just been suggested:—*affiliated members.** We have two classes of memberships now. Why not add a third class, entrance to which would be automatic, while the associate and active memberships retain their present standards? Everybody who

---

*NOTE: This class of membership has for years been recommended by the United Society of Christian Endeavor in the Model Constitution.

joins a Sunday school in the Junior, Intermediate, or Young People's Department becomes an affiliated member of either the Junior, Intermediate, or Senior society of Christian Endeavor and is so informed. It is explained to him that his affiliated membership does not carry full responsibilities in the Christian Endeavor society, but opens to him the privileges of meetings, socials, and activities, and he is asked to consider at once, and definitely, whether he would find it worth while to assume some of the responsibilities. It may be explained to him in a leaflet that is given him or a piece of printed matter, written in an interesting way, that there are two other classes of membership; that no one is going to try to force him into either; both are open to him, and if he wants to, after considering the conditions of active membership, he can move from affiliated to active by an act of his own will and an assumption of responsibilities and an assent to standards such as are connected with the active membership. But if he is not ready for that, there is an intermediate stage that he can voluntarily assume —he can become an associate member now, if he will. If he is not ready to do either, he remains in the affiliated.

Is this relationship sufficient to lead towards full membership in such a way that we would get a larger per cent of the Sunday school folks into the regular membership, either associate or active, of the Christian Endeavor society than we get now, where there is no direct plan of affiliation between the Christian Endeavor society and the Sunday school?

We are thinking of this plan as an alternative for the all Sunday-school plan. If the church agrees on the all Sunday-school plan or this kind of correlation plan, the church is behind it. We are not contemplating a situation now which is parallel to the situation many of us face, where all the Christian Endeavor propaganda has to be done by members of the Christian Endeavor society, where all the effort to take membership in the Christian Endeavor society comes from those already in the society.

We are talking now about a church plan of religious education upon which the whole church agrees which comprehends all the necessary elements of worship instruction and expression which the whole church will support, which the Sunday school will promote as a part of its plan or rather as a part of the church's plan, to which it is loyal and for which it is responsible, which the Christian Endeavor will promote on its side, not as its plan, but as the church plan, a correlated plan in which the Sunday school has its part and for which the Christian Endeavor as well as the Sunday school stands. That is the idea behind the plea for an expanded Sunday school, for an all-Sunday school idea, that it becomes a religious education programme. This plan is designed to be an all-church plan, not a Christian Endeavor plan with merely a polite request that the Sunday school teachers would please help these folks. But the Board, through its council of religious education or cabinet, or whatever the overhead educational organization is in the church would stand, or all of this plan, for the Sunday school part of it and the Christian Endeavor part of it, and would back everywhere this idea that membership in the Sunday school carried with it membership also in the Christian Endeavor society, although it was only the lowest classification of membership, and it would work vice versa. You could not, under this plan, take somebody in as a member of the Christian Endeavor society and not have him enrolled in some Sunday school class unless he were individually accepted for some reason which the church would accept as a good reason, some physical condition or some conflicting of time which would prevent their coming at the Sunday school hour, or something of that kind.

If this plan is wrong, is it not fair to say that the whole Sunday school plan is wrong? I can't escape that conclusion myself. We cannot say that the whole Sunday school plan is the only plan which offers the possibility of bringing the great majority of our young people into close contact with expressional training, to put it mildly. It is not necessary to eliminate Christian Endeavor and carry the automatic membership from one section to the other Sunday school plan. This, at least, will do the same thing the expanded plan will do. If this is open to too many dangers and is not right, then the all-inclusive plan will not work for expressional training, that is for thorough expressional training, and we ought to settle back on the position that you can give instruction to everybody you get in your Sunday school in a worshipful atmosphere, but that to go ahead and give intensive, thorough expressional training to those folks is not practical; that you can only do that for part of them, which is to say, as an illustration, that you can get all your folks into the class-rooms in chemistry, but you can't take them all into the laboratory; you can get all the folks to study the text-book, but not all to do the field work; you can get them all to do the principles and theory of the thing, but can't get all to practice applying them.

I don't like to say that. It is a weakness. It may be a condition which we can only change by a slow and gradual process, but I believe if that is true we ought to change it as fast as we can. One of the troubles with us educational folks is that we refuse to use educational methods in our work. We might put in a director of religious education for two or three years, then change and have a gap for a year or two, or oblige the director of religious education to follow the pastor's educational policy, then change the pastor. The new one may have a different educational policy and you are required to shift to that.

We want to do something in a big hurry, have a series of intensive courses or institutes, and we are going to get the whole proposition taken care of by short cuts. Over and over again we refuse to follow the educational process in educational work.

I believe we all understand that this is between the Sunday school and the Christian Endeavor society. Our biggest problem is to reconcile the place of this form of expressional training. After all, I suppose it is fair to say that it is possible, at least, to conceive of a plan whereby all the instructional elements of the religious educational programme centre in the Sunday school, no matter where they expand to; or, still better, that they centre in one department of the church school, while all the expressional elements centre under the Christian Endeavor plan and the auxiliary. I am not recommending it. I say that it is along the line of thinking of some folks. There are big questions under the question of a correlated programme for the entire church which we are not touching here. The only point I am anxious for now is that nobody gets the idea that we want to head up everything educationally in the church, Sunday school, and Christian Endeavor.

May I suggest a thought or two about what eliminating the Young People's society would bring about? If you eliminate the Young People's society, the interdenominational organization of Young People's societies, what may follow from the standpoint of the churches? One thing that we must set up all over this country is Denominational Young People's conventions, each denomination with a convention for its young people which majors in expressional matters. There would be little hope of getting it done if the whole matter went over under the Sunday school; it would be done in a half-hearted way. You know what happened in the Baptist church. The B. Y. P. U. has no separate conventions with a possible exception of an occasional one in one or two States. The B. Y. P. U. conventions are tacked on to its Sunday school conventions, as an annex, as an appendix, and they do come out at the little end of the horn. I know what I am talking about, for I worked in the Baptist church for four years. I am afraid it would follow that the expressional side of religious education would come as an overhead matter, a matter of overhead consideration and administration and would be given the time left after the other elements of denominational religious education had been given attention. That may not be true with some of the strong denominations or the Young People's societies where they have a fine set-up, but it ought to be considered clear through. It would mean the denominational Young People's society specialized and paid for by the denominations in the given territories to take the place of the Christian Endeavor field-secretaries of the present. Not every denomination would welcome such an addition to its budget expense. Some might be happy to add it. It would mean an attempted combination of Sunday school promotion. I mean the promotion of the other elements of the programme and the expressional elements of the programme, the teachers in the Sunday school, the children's different superintendents, and the Young People's different superintendents would be asked to carry along with that promotion of expressional training of young people outside of the Sunday school hours.

This is what would happen. We would come out on the expressional training proposition at the little end of the horn. Then if there were objection, as I imagine there would be in some quarters, to an interdenominational overhead for training work in our churches that would not disappear but you would transfer from one interdenominational overhead organization to another. In other words, the Sunday School Council would take over what the United Society of Christian Endeavor now attempts to do. You would not have overhead supervision in the hands of the denominations entirely. I think we ought to face the question that the denominations may request a re-organization of the United Society of Christian Endeavor and its auxiliary State organization on somewhat the same basis of the re-organization of the interdenominational Sunday school organization, so that the denominations will be more directly represented in the administration of the United Society of Christian Endeavor and its auxiliaries.

I rather think that would be somewhat easy to accomplish. I am afraid we are in a more difficult position now than we might be had we done that long ago. As Christian Endeavor specialists we bear in mind carefully the fact that ninety-nine out of every one hundred societies that bear the Christian Endeavor name are bound by their own Christian Endeavor pledge, that their first responsibility is to the church to which they belong that they recognize when they adopt the model constitution of Christian Endeavor that the only authority over them, the only organization that has the slightest right to tell them what to do is the church and the denomination to which they belong. I say simply that Christian Endeavor specialists must be more careful than ever before on that point; but eliminating the Young People's society and its overhead organization, denominational and interdenominational, would mean the assumption by the denominations or the interdenominational Sunday School Council of considerable extra expense and machinery, or us trying to get along without additional experience or machinery, or very little. The whole cause of expressional training would immediately suffer to a very alarming degree. Then, finally, eliminating the Young People's society, if you do it suddenly, will bring about a veritable young people's revolution in our churches. It will not be done with the consent of the young people all over the country. If you go through the process of getting it accomplished slowly, you are going to lose momentum and are going to be under some handicaps that are very real and that we will not have time to discuss now.

We must spend the rest of the time on some possibilities of increasing the educational efficiency of Christian Endeavor. If we cannot do that, I doubt whether we have a very clear right to insist that Christian Endeavor is entitled to a permanent place in a modern, progressive, up-to-date, carefully balanced, well-supervised church programme of religious education for which the whole church is responsible and to which the whole church gives its support.

Christian Endeavor needs better grading than we are getting in some places. Roughly, its grading ought to approximate the modern grading of the Sunday school, not absolutely the same, but very close to it, and the grading ought to be maintained not just theoretically.

All over this country there are Senior Christian Endeavor societies which have almost no Seniors in them. They are made up of people of high school age, yet they are operating under the Senior plan with no superintendent, high school students attempting to run a plan that was never meant for high school folks, but intended for young people of eighteen years of age and up. We are losing educational efficiency, for we are allowing that sort of a situation.

We ought then to have regular promotion and the church ought to take enough interest in its Christian Endeavor work to help the Christian Endeavor officers make regular promotion from one grade to another. Educational efficiency means regular grading. Educational efficiency means steady operation in all grades, not having a Junior society for two years and none for three, because you can't find anybody for superintendent; not having an Intermediate society part of the time and none part of the time, unless you have no people of high school age in your Sunday school, but a steady maintenance with the support of the whole church behind it, just as there is a steady maintenance of Sunday-school work with the support of the whole church behind it. Adequate supervision is one of the greatest educational needs of the Christian Endeavor. I don't think, personally, we ought to have a superintendent of the Senior Christian Endeavor society, so named and appointed, who is expected to be present at every meeting of the Senior Christian Endeavor society, to meet with the executive committee every time they meet, to carry the general responsibility for supervising the work of all committees in that Senior society. I do think an advisor is a fine thing to have for that society. Each of the age groups ought to have superintendents with definitely recognized responsibilities and to have authority, to some extent, which they exercise when nothing else will do. An Intermediate department will get off the track if you don't have that kind of superintendency clothed with some degree of authority in connection with the work.

Educational efficiency calls for that overhead educational direction which centres in a church committee of religious education and council, or a cabinet of some sort which considers the religious educational needs and the religious educational policies for all age groups in that church, worship, instruction and expressional instruction, a body which achieves correlation, in other words, and unification in the educational programme of the church. That body needs to have responsible Christian Endeavor representatives, and that body needs to assume as a part of its responsible overhead general educational direction of the Christian Endeavor society.

Educational efficiency in Christian Endeavor means that whether the church initiates coördination or correlation or not, it is to the interest of the Christian Endeavor society to do all it can to achieve coördination of its programme and its activities with the other educational work of the church through the different organizations. It ought to be the effort of every Christian Endeavor society to find a way to build its programme in coöperation with the Sunday-school department of the same age, with the missionary organization, appealing to the children and the youth of the same ages, with the Boy Scouts and the Camp-Fire Girls, and other auxiliary organizations.

No Christian Endeavor society ought to be content to build its own programme without any definite consultation with the leaders of other organizations. You ought to start a movement for getting all educational organizations in the church to build their programmes co-operatively, then in consultation to operate them that way. A Christian Endeavor society ought always to consider itself a part of the whole educational system. It ought to be just as much your concern that those who are getting expressional training in the Christian Endeavor society should be at the same time getting adequate religious instruction, adequate training in worship through regular attendance at the Church teaching service on Sunday, regular attendance at the Sunday school, and regular participation in the specialized missionary organization.

Educational efficiency in Christian Endeavor demands that there be intelligence on the part of the Christian Endeavor leaders and officers with reference to the other elements in the programme. How to bring those elements to bear upon the education and training of the members of your society and the curriculum question is a debatable question.

What do we need to do about Christian Endeavor curricula in order to get increased educational efficiency? The Christian Endeavor topics are not handed down by the United Society of

Christian Endeavor, the churches, and other societies. There is in existence an Interdenominational Young People's Commission which selects these topics. On that Commission are the officially appointed, employed representatives of the denominations, not only Christian Endeavor but the B. Y. P. U., the Epworth League, and the Luther League. They meet once a year* and select these topics which become the official topics for Christian Endeavor, the Epworth League, and other societies on that commission. The Young People's Society, especially in your denomination, has had a place. The topics are interdenominational topics selected according to age. The organization represents not only the interdenominational United Society but every one of the constituent denominations wanting to be represented and sending its representative. But there is a debate on this question. There are those who take the position that a correlated curriculum as between the Sunday school and Christian Endeavor, or among the Sunday-school and the Week Day Bible School and Christian Endeavor is educational advancement.

I promised you I would have for distribution a few copies of the Presbyterian U. S. A. Young People's Quarterly offered as an alternative to the present Sunday-school lesson. For the eighteen to twenty-four age group each quarterly contains a Sunday-school lesson for that age group and also a correlated topic for the Young People's Society of Christian Endeavor, closely related to the Sunday-school lesson in the morning, issued in two series, one for Sunday school, using the uniform lesson, one for Sunday school using the departmental graded system. Other denominations have done that or are to do it very soon, so that, at least, you have the choice of which side of this question you will stand on, whether you will go ahead with an uncorrelated topic for your Christian Endeavor meeting, or whether you will take a topic correlated with the Sunday school. You can do either one without being disloyal to your denomination or to the Christian Endeavor.

As to the point of topics, it is fair to say that the United Society experimented years ago with this plan and had its Christian Endeavor topics three Sundays a month, leaving out the missionary meetings correlated with the Sunday-school lesson. All the lessons were uniform. It was tried out, and Professor Wells testifies it did not work. The young people did not want to rehash on Sunday night what they had had on Sunday morning. The correlation there may have been too close. It may have been considering the same thing under a different heading Sunday night than the heading you gave it Sunday morning.

At any rate, the thing we need to do educationally is to decide what our policy will be. By correlating the curricula of the Sun-

---

*NOTE: The Commission has a topics committee which holds at least two meetings annually and prepares the topics for submission to the Commission.

day school and the Christian Endeavor Society you can draw them together and increase the educational efficiency of both. There is in some denominations, including my own, a movement to give a correlated curriculum. The Sunday school has an experiment that is called the three-hour a week plan in some denominations, and it is operating successfully in a number of cases. The young person goes to class, studies a lesson based on the pages of the Bible, majors on the instructional and informational elements in the contents of that Bible passage. The same person goes to the proper department of the Sunday school on Sunday and studies that same passage, or a closely related passage, majoring on the devotional and spiritual values of that Bible passage. Then he goes to a Christian Endeavor society and studies, rather talks about and voices his expression, upon a topic that is very closely related to the two lessons preceding, one on a week day and one on Sunday. This three hour a week plan is having such a great degree of success that the attention of pastors and directors of religious education everywhere is being called to it.

We must be carefully directed on this problem of a correlated curriculum for young people and children in the religious educational plan. We must have a larger degree of church recognition for the Christian Endeavor work. If the young people are left to themselves without encouragement, recognition, or support, without being made to feel they are an important part, the religious education machinery of that church will not achieve the fullest educational efficiency which they might have if everybody were boosting for them, if everybody were sympathetic with them, and if the church as a church were making them understand that the future of this church depends very largely on how well they do in their Christian Endeavor society. Unless you meet the Sunday school by supplementing its instruction adequately with your expressional training, unless you so help the Sunday school with our young people as to turn out well-rounded and completely equipped leaders for the Church in the future, we shall not have the leadership that we need. The Sunday school can't do it. We are depending on you just as we are depending on them. We intend to help you as we help them, and unless there is that kind of a situation in the church, we must continue to suffer as we are suffering now in many churches from a lack of educational efficiency in the Christian Endeavor society. In other words, it is not up to the religious educator to stand off here and criticize Christian Endeavor and say, "Let's do away with it, because it is not educational." It is not up to him to say that until the church with which that Christian Endeavor society is affiliated has given that Christian Endeavor work such a place in its programme and such a degree of recognized support as to make it reasonable to acquire educational efficiency.

Chapter XXI.

RESOLUTIONS PRESENTED AT VARIOUS SESSIONS OF THE CONVENTION AND HEARTILY ADOPTED

Christian Endeavor

The Young People's societies of Christian Endeavor of North America, in convention assembled in Des Moines, Io., and representing a constantly enlarging movement with more than four million members and some sixteen million Alumni in every part of the world, reaffirm their principles of fellowship and co-operation with all who love and serve our one Lord and Master.

We deplore, as do all Christians, unnecessary divisions in the Protestant church, and the dreadful turmoils of the mutually hostile and war-torn nations of the world.

We offer the broad principles, practices, and covenant of the society as common denominators for all evangelical churches. Since the society is now found to a greater or lesser extent in all such denominations, since it is the only young people's religious society in many of them, and since more than forty years of service have tried and proved the obsolute loyalty of the societies to their own churches, the Convention respectfully asks why its name as well as its principles should not be universally adopted by evangelical churches.

The movement levies no taxes and demands no dues. It has no central headquarters with authority over any society, but only national bureaus of information. More and more it is promoting interdenominational harmony and co-operation among young people, as well as international good feeling.

The Convention believes that in all fairness the name should go with the principles and methods, and the principles with the name, "Christian Endeavor."

We trust that all who truly desire interdenominational fellowship and Christian unity of purpose will see in this organization for the young a God-given agency to these ends.

The Place of Christian Endeavor in the Educational Programme of the Church

Christian Endeavor rejoices in the growing interest of the churches in matters of religious education and especially the religious education of the young. Much of this interest owes its inception and its progress to Christian Endeavor. Our society extends a fraternal hand to all other agencies of religious education, and will gladly co-operate in all denominational programmes to this end, contributing its time-tried methods and its interdenominational fellowship and enthusiasm. Christian Endeavor has a place with the Sunday school in every plan of religious education. It is perfectly flexible, and is ready to adopt all plans of proved value. It seeks to supplant no other organization, but works with all under the banner of Christ and the church.

Others

In its service activities Christian Endeavor gladly aligns itself with all organizations that are working for the uplift of humanity. It sympathizes with efforts to care for and protect orphans and neglected children, with efforts to protect dumb animals from cruel treatment and to give them that measure of help which they need, with efforts to relieve the distress of peoples of other lands, famine-stricken peoples, war-impoverished peoples, or fugitives driven from their ancestral homes.

Christian Fellowship

The incoming tide of immigration is a challenge to Christian Endeavor to Americanize the stranger. We have among us groups of foreign-speaking peoples for whom real missionary work may be done right here at home. We believe that Endeavorers should get in touch with such groups and show them the spirit of the real America, a spirit of friendliness and helpful service.

To this end we submit the following lines of service: First, an educational campaign which will include the distribution of citizenship literature by Endeavorers. To create interest in work for foreign-speaking peoples in our midst we suggest the presentation of this subject at Christian Endeavor conferences and rallies.

Second, we suggest that our unions may undertake an investigation to discover how Endeavorers may co-operate in practical ways with other organizations that engage in civic betterment work. We suggest that Endeavorers study the duties of public officials, and perhaps carry out, or help to carry out, city or rural surveys, as well as assist in the work of social settlements.

Third, we suggest that Endeavorers form study-classes to study the Constitution of the United States.

We urge upon Endeavorers everywhere their duties as citizens, their duty to know the facts about State and Federal Government, and to lend their energetic support, not only to the support of the laws of the land, but also to all agencies that make for wise and sane citizenship.

Fellowship among Races

Christian Endeavor is a world-wide training-school in fellowship. Interdenominational Christian Endeavor unions have become established in every land. The organization stands for interdenominational, international, and interracial fellowship—for a Christian brotherhood that will safeguard a world peace.

Our interracial fellowship, whether black, red, brown, yellow, or white, is in this twentieth century one of mutual helpfulness, and the organization of young people of all tongues is a mighty agency for bringing about a better understanding among the peoples of the earth, and so a mighty agency for international and interracial good will.

The Golden Rule in Industry

We rejoice to see a growing spirit of partnership between employer and employee, and an increasing desire on all hands to follow in business relationships the spirit of the Golden Rule. We rejoice in the development of conscience in industry, and in the fact that to-day less than ever before in history does either employer or employee wish to stand on the opposite side of any labor question than that on which they honestly believe Jesus Christ would stand, were He among us. We believe that the law of brotherhood and love and generous dealing alone contains the solution of labor problems. Christian Endeavor stands for this law. It teaches no economic theory, but seeks to make grow in the hearts of men the kindliness of Jesus Christ. Standing on the Golden Rule it urges generous and full service on the part of the worker, and on the part of the employer a reward that will mean not merely a living-wage, but comfort and the ability to save for the future. We believe that only that specific code of economic programme can live and endure which is fertilized by the laws of Christ, and one of the biggest tasks of the Christian Endeavor movement is to bring the spirit of these laws to the youth of to-day, that the men of to-morrow may translate them into a programme of constructive action.

The Eight-Hour Day

Unrest and open warfare in industry constitute a distinct challenge to Christianity. Jesus Christ is for the individual and for the institutions of society the only sufficient Saviour. We believe that the application of His spirit and principles to the problems and controversies of commerce and trade will promote good will and establish peace.

We commend those who are acting as pathfinders of a new and Christian social order. Particularly do we commend such organizations as the Colorado Fuel and Iron Company and the International Harvester Company for their demonstration of the practicability of the eight-hour day, the shop committee, and the wisdom of the participation of workers in direction and control.

The twelve-hour day, the seven-day week, the espionage system, and autocratic control are relics of an industrial absolutism;

where they still continue, they are a menace to the American home, the Christian church, and free government; they remain as feudal evils that Christian civilization ought long since to have outlawed. Because of them the church is often unjustly measured by the working world. For vast numbers they stand as barriers in the road to Americanization. They promote unrest and make for bitterness. They are not good for a nation.

We pledge our best efforts under the wise leadership of our churches to bring them to an end.

Prohibition and Law-Enforcement

Prohibition has vindicated itself. In spite of great handicaps its benign effects are now apparent in the steadily declining death-rate as revealed in the bulletins of life-insurance companies, in the 74-per-cent decrease in drink cases with their attendant problems coming to charity organizations, and in the growing moral tone of our community life.

The great cities of our far-reaching coast-lines and wide-extending international boundaries present serious difficulties in law-enforcement, and cannot now be expected to reflect the prohibition sentiment of the nation. For some time to come they will continue to deceive themselves and our visitors from other lands who would rejoice in the repudiation of national prohibition.

Even these vast cosmopolitan communities record unmistakable benefits accruing from the closing of saloons and bars, benefits that will increase steadily with the strengthening of the spirit and agencies of law-enforcement.

For the bootlegger we have only slightly less condemnation than for his patron. The latter, from the standpoint of individual morality, is essentially the worse, while in citizenship he is a greater menace. Striking at one, he slashes all. He gives heart to every evil-doer, and by the measure of his influence weakens the protecting wall that surrounds his life, his liberty, and his temporal goods.

In law-enforcement the supreme issue of the hour joins. The forces of nullification are active and determined. They have united powerful interests at home and abroad to embarrass public officials, to break the morale of conscientious enforcing agents, and to discourage public sentiment. They have found a spokesman in the governor of a great State.

We declare here that State righteousness is greater than States' rights, and that no State has rights which prohibition does not strengthen. We stand for liberty under law. We pledge ourselves anew to the Constitution of the United States. We commend the President for his repeated statements in support of the Eighteenth Amendment and the Volstead Act.

Speaking for four million enrolled young people, citizen and citizen-to-be, we further declare that no candidate for public office, and that no political party, failing to make such unequivocal commitment has the right to expect or will receive our support and votes.

We believe that total abstinence is the only consistent attitude for a Christian, and that the agitation for a modification of the Volstead Act to legalize light wines and beers is a subterfuge and blind; those who advocate it now were but a short time since the stalwart defence of the open saloon and the liquor traffic. It is a dishonest issue.

As the ultimate solution of the liquor problem for this nation was national prohibition, for which Christian Endeavor declared in 1911 with its militant slogan, "A Saloonless Nation by 1920," so the ultimate solution of the problem for all nations is world-wide prohibition. We here reaffirm our declaration of 1919 for "a saloonless world," and pledge the full strength of our movement to the achievement of this high goal.

A Warless World

Representatives of the Christian Endeavor societies of North America, realizing that they have Endeavor comrades in all lands beneath the sun, are naturally interested in every worthy international movement that brings the peoples of the world together in co-operative friendship.

In harmony with the declaration of the churches of all denominations to which they belong they rejoice in the effort of President Harding to bring the United States to the support of the World Court of Arbitration.

They appreciate the splendid forward step taken by President Harding and Secretary Hughes, two of our honorary Alumni, in calling and bringing to a successful issue the Washington Conference for the Limitation of Armaments, the longest step yet taken toward the final goal of world-wide peace.

While not minimizing or ignoring conscientious differences of opinion, as patriots and Christians, and as representatives of the young people who would have to bear the brunt of another war, should it ever come, we desire to give our support to all wise measures of co-operation among the nations that tend to bring about eventually a warless world.

CHAPTER XXII.

ON THE MOUNTAIN TOP

COLISEUM, MONDAY EVENING, JULY 9

Rev. Francis E. Clark, D.D. Presiding

The last meeting of every International Christian Endeavor Convention is, at the beginning, a noisy one, and this final meeting was no exception to the rule. It was a hot evening, following a merciless day; and a hot day following other days of mounting heat. Yet the great crowd of delegates came up to the closing session as full of "pep" as they had been on the opening night. They were happy. They had found that Des Moines Endeavorers are delightful hosts. Everywhere they had met with courtesy and kindness. And now, as they came to the end of their visit, their spirits overflowed in song and rhythmic cheer.

Kansas had a large crowd, probably the largest Kansas delegation to an International Convention in many years. The young people stood on their chairs, a Kansas banner in the centre of the group, while they intoned a monotone chant which gradually gathered impetus, until at the end it blossomed into a wild and vigorous yell.

Iowa's main delegation was in the gallery, and kept things moving merrily by singing their State chorus. One feature was the way that they rhythmically beat their hands upon their knees, clapped their hands, and then raised their arms above their heads to the words, "Iowa — that's where the tall corn grows."

Maryland, few compared with Iowa's host, took up Iowa's challenge, and sang with spirit a song the last line of which rang (the delegates pointing toward the Iowa group), "Iowa — that's where the sweet girls grow."

Missouri had a cornetist, and the shouts of the great delegation made the very roof ring. The young people made capital out of the fame of Missouri mules, for they sang Iowa's tune, but closed it, as they made suggestive mules' ears with their hands, with the words, "That's where the mule hee-haws." Ohio's large delegation was also in evidence, while the Wisconsin delegates with their red feathers attracted attention.

Under the leadership of Professor Alfred Smith the Convention chorus, a well-balanced group of five hundred singers, led the delegates in a fine service of worship. The opening part was

"Jesus, the Light of the World," Gounod's "Send out thy light."

The congregation, led by Rev. Earl E. Harper, took part in responsive reading and in singing between the choir's musical numbers. "The Heart's True Home" was the second chorus by the choir, Gounod's "Though poor be thy chamber." The third part was "Jesus, all names above," the choir singing with splendid effect, the "Hallelujah Chorus" from Handel's "Messiah."

Rev. Mr. Morris, secretary of the Allen League of Christian Endeavor, representing several thousands of Negro societies, led in prayer. After this three Pima Christian Endeavor Indians were introduced to the gathering, receiving great applause.

Judge Hubert Utterback briefly presented the members of the Convention committee, which had covered itself with glory by the way in which it organized the hospitality of Des Moines and carried smilingly the burden of multitudinous arrangements.

What a splendid group! None finer anywhere! We should like to mention every one, for none of them should be missed, but lack of space forbids. There was Roy Smith, who organized fifty groups of four-minute speakers who visited the societies and told the story of the coming Convention; Alfred Smith, music director, and Alma L. Garber, chairman of the music committee, who enlisted 640 persons for the Convention choir; and so on through a long list of efficient workers who richly deserved the applause that they received from grateful visitors.

The B. Y. P. U. of Des Moines and the Epworth Leagues and Luther Leagues were represented on the committee and gave unstinted service.

General Secretary Gates conducted the ceremony of presenting to representatives of the winning States the honor banners promised those States that first reached their Convention registration goals. Oklahoma, Wyoming, Arizona, and Utah were the happy States, and the banners were handed to them by Southwestern Secretary W. Roy Breg. Gold Christian Endeavor medals were also presented to the presidents and secretaries of these States, and another medal to Mr. Breg, who has done valiant things for Christian Endeavor in the Southwest.

Secretary Gates offered a hearty resolution of thanks to the local committee, the press, ministers, mayor, police, and business men of Des Moines, and to all others, including the management of the fairgrounds, who had helped to make the Convention the glorious success it was.

An interesting feature was the presentation by Dr. Clark of three banners, offered by the All-South union to the States in Dixie that showed the best Junior, Intermediate, and Senior Christian Endeavor work. The Senior banner went to Florida, and was given to Mrs. Karl Lehmann; the Intermediate banner went to old Virginia; and the Junior banner to North Carolina. The Dixie delegation greeted the announcement with their spirited song,

"Hail, hail, the gang's all here,
All the way from Dixie land."

Dr. Clark then introduced Amos R. Wells, editor of "The Christian Endeavor World," who proceeded to read his poem, "Christian Endeavor Possibilities."

CHRISTIAN ENDEAVOR POSSIBILITIES

By Amos R. Wells, Litt. D.

You have read how the prophet Joel, the Minor Prophet of old,
Foretold the days of the Saviour in words revealing and bold:
"Your young men then shall see visions, your old men then shall dream dreams."
And I, who am young in spirit but growing oldish, it seems,
Yes, I, who am named for a prophet, and a Minor Prophet as well,
I too have a dream and a vision that I am eager to tell.
A vision of Christian Endeavor, a dream of the coming days
When the youth of the world will be wondrous beyond my power to praise,
When down in the valleys of purpose the young will scorn to remain,
But the heights of splendid achievement the hero lives will attain;
When rid of the curse of the easy good they will dare the difficult best,
Their souls by the far ideal entranced and ennobled and blest.

And first I dream of their bodies. I see them swinging along
Bright with the glow of the morning, and strong as the trees are strong;
Their bodies the home of the Spirit where He may live without shame,
Not held in a rickety hovel, not cramped in a narrow frame.
They have made it their Christian Endeavor to banish hindering ills:
They run the ways of the meadows, they leap to the tops of the hills,
Their muscles are massively molded, their blood is invincibly pure,
Their backs are stout for the burdens, their feet are winged and sure.
Gay with the happy alertness that vigor maintains and endows,
They have added health to their pledges and written strength in their vows.
And thus of a new endeavor I dare a venturous dream,
A pedestal for the statue, and engine for the steam,
A body for the spirit, its tool for noble task,
This shall Endeavor offer, for this the ages ask.

And I see another vision, a dream of the coming years
When the minds of youth shall be widened to match with their broad careers,
When the lure of the truer learning shall seize them and hold them fast,
When their reading shall scorn the bubbles and seek for the things that last.
I dream of a new endeavor that dedicates minds to Christ,
That delves in the wisdom of ages, unstinted and all unpriced,
That makes a library sacred with hopes and aims divine,
That crowns a day with a chapter and lights an hour with a line.
Then the youth will save their minutes for precious and timeless things,
For words with purpose and power, for thoughts with beauty and wings.
They will count them over and over as misers count their gold,
And share them with one another as the happiest news is told.
So thus of a mental endeavor I cherish a dream elate,
Of studies led by ideals, of colleges consecrate,
Of thinking stirred by religion and religion deepened by thought,
Till the best of the past is captured and into the future wrought.

I will tell of another vision that shimmers before my eyes,
A dream of home endeavor all kindly and strong and wise,
A dream of a household heaven that does not care to roam,
"For Christ and the Church" no less, but also "For Christ and the Home."
I see the youth of the future, with planning and with prayer,
Take thought for the blessed home life and the joy of dear ones there.
I see them meeting in council, planning to cheer the old,
Planning to lighten their labors with furtherance manifold,
Planning homes joyful with labor, the work of a day in the day,
Homes all vibrant with singing and sunny with fruitful play.
Thou of all Christian households the sacred and glorious Head,
Smile on our home endeavors and let them be happily sped,
Till the "church that is in our house" has become the portal of love
Of the "house not made with hands," our home in the heavens above.

And still the visions continue, and still they splendidly grow,
The service of youth expanding, for they love their Saviour so.
To the churches I see them crowding with eager voices and hearts,
Ready for humblest labor, ready to play their parts.
I see them seek for the service that needs the most to be done,
I see them lifting the burdens that others carelessly shun,
I see them hunting assignments that others have shortly refused,
I see them glad to be busy and oh, so proud to be used!
More than a word in their pledges and more than a word on the tongue,
How has their promise, "Whatever," sunk in the souls of the young!
Happy the churches that own them and blessedly dare to employ
All of their freshness and fervor, all of their vigor and joy!
I dream of a church endeavor outreaching and bold and free,
Better than all the best that Endeavor has ventured to be,
For the world has not yet discovered the blessedly fruitful truth,
That the church that is nearest to Christ is the church that is closest to youth.

Still farther my venturesome visions pulse out in their trust and hope,
Since what can confine the spirit of youth and narrow its ultimate scope?
For youth are the world and the heavens, for youth are the land and the sea,
The harvest of all the past and the dreams of the years to be.
So out of their homes and their churches I see the Endeavorers go,
Their lances levelled at wrongs, their hands outreaching to woe.
I see them sweeping the alleys, I see them lighting the town,
I see them planting flowers and tearing the billboards down,
I see them cleansing the movies and the dance debauch as well,
I see them driving the last saloon to the depths of the farthest hell.
I see them lifting the press to the height of the Christian plane,
I see them driving from trade the pitiless greed of gain.
I see them filling the halls of state with gallant souls and true,
Wise to know what needs to be done and firm to carry it through.
I see them stretching brotherly hands to sundered nations afar,
I see them healing with balm of love the awful disease of war.
And best of all in the Saviour's eyes I see them pleading for Him,
Keeping alight their witness lamps that never grow smoky nor dim,
Bringing their own to the Master's feet, bringing their neighbors and friends,
Sending their mission proxies far to the wide earth's gloomiest ends,
Praying and giving and going until from the Northern to Southern Pole
The gospel has come to the farthest man and spoken to every soul.

A vision of Christian Endeavor, a dream of the coming days
When the youth of the world will be wondrous beyond my power to praise,
When down in the valleys of purpose the young will scorn to remain,
But the heights of splendid achievement their hero lives will attain;

On the Banks of the Des Moines River

When rid of the curse of the easy good they will dare the difficult best,
Their souls by the far ideal entranced and ennobled and blest.
For the level reach of Endeavor is pleasant to plod along,
But the mountain summits beckon the feet that are true and strong.
On the hills of God are our banners afloat with the challenging breeze:
Up through the aisles of the forests, up and above the trees,
Up where the path is steepest, up where the rocks are bare,
Up where the shards are sharpest, up in the tingling air,
Up where the beckoning banners on the wind of the Spirit are blown,
And find at the top of the mountain the King, and the Crown, and the Throne!

Then more banners! Mr. C. C. Hamilton, who directed THE CHRISTIAN ENDEAVOR WORLD campaign, told of the contests between groups of States to reach the quotas of subscriptions assigned to them, and the contests of individuals in the States to win a free round trip to the Des Moines Convention. There were five groups of contesting States, and one person in each group won a free trip. The winners were C. Raymond Vosburgh, Easton, Penn.; Donald Pierson, Geneva, Kan.; Miss Jean Milner, Oklahoma City, Okla.; John Purdum, Nampa, Ida.; Miss Vera Thomas, Birmingham, Ala.; and they received a great ovation when they came to the platform. Some of the contests were very close. Jean Milner, of Oklahoma City, who won in her group, was only two subscriptions ahead of the contestant in the State of Washington; and the Washington contestant was only three and one-half subscriptions ahead of Maryland, the third in the race.

Junior banners were given to the winning States in *The Junior Christian Endeavor World* campaign. Three of these banners were made — and the workmanship was exquisite — in China and two in Japan, the Endeavorers in these countries taking pleasure in doing their bit to encourage American brethren. Pennsylvania, New Jersey, Maryland, New Hampshire, and North Carolina are the winning States.

International Christian Endeavor Conventions generally close with a purpose and consecration service, and such a service of consecration was impressively led by Dr. Clark.

CLOSING MESSAGE

PRESIDENT CLARK

I have but a few words to say to you, my dear friends, before we pronounce the closing benediction, but surely it is time for us to lift up our hearts in thanksgiving to Almighty God for the mercies of these past days. So far as I know, in spite of the intense heat which has rarely if ever been equalled in any of our conventions, there have been no prostrations, no serious ones, at least. I have heard of no serious illness, though at such conventions as this very often the hospitals have been full in such a season as we have passed through.

But, thank God that during all these crowded sessions, during all these late evening sessions, during all these days which have been so strenuous for many of you, up early and late, God has preserved the lives of every one. He has allowed no accident to happen on the part of those who have travelled tens of thousands of miles, and in the aggregate hundreds of thousands of miles to attend this convention. Here we are, happy and contented, going home, I believe, well in body and better in spiritual health than ever before.

Oh, thank God for all these blessings, but surely these blessings bring with them a responsibility, an opportunity. If some friend had given you ten thousand dollars and said to you, "Now you can keep part of this for yourself, you can have a thousand dollars for yourself, but I want you to give the rest of it away, I want you to remember the great causes of the day, the cause of peace, the cause of missions, the cause of the Near East, for instance, the cause of Juniors, I am sure you would not take it all for yourself. You would not have put it into the bank when you got home and said that it was all yours to use as you pleased. You would have done your best to use the money the friend had given you for the glory and honor of God.

But, friends, He has given you something. This Convention must mean something to many of you. You have had spiritual gifts during many of these days that you never had before. You have had an uplift you never realized in the past. You have drawn nearer to God, I believe, in these Quiet Hours which have been overcrowded over and over again as never you did in the past. Oh, what are you going to do with these gifts that God has given you? Are you going to hoard them, use them just for yourself, just to make your own life a little happier and brighter? I do not believe it; I hope you are going home with the gift, with an opportunity, with a responsibility, which you never had before. Share these gifts with others. Give to others what you have gained here.

Go to your home and your great societies or your little societies, among your Juniors, in your different unions, throughout the land and these countries that are represented, Canada and Mexico, go everywhere in all these forty-eight States and all the provinces and carry the blessings you have heard and received here. If you do not you will be derelict to your duty. You will have had something given you not for yourself alone but for a great many others. Why, there are millions of Endeavorers here in America who would rejoice to come here. They could not come because of good reasons, financial reasons, family reasons, care of little children. There are a thousand causes that have kept them away, but you, a comparatively few picked men and women, have come here. God has given you the opportunity which He has denied to millions of others throughout the country. Oh, then remember what God would have you do. Use not your spiritual wealth for yourself alone. Do not try to hoard it. Do not seek your own happiness. You will lose it if you do. If you give it away, if you share it with others, you will keep it as long as you live.

As you go home to your echo meetings in your own societies and in your unions, as you tell them about these addresses and about the social part, the gladness of our social gatherings, our fellowship, why just remember that long list of denominations that held their rallies day before yesterday, or was it yesterday? Thirty-seven different denominations are represented here, and remember that when you go home.

This fellowship, this communion one with the other, these new acquaintances you have met, these old acquaintances with whom you have shaken hands and whom you will rejoice to meet once more, these blessings of fellowship have been given you to share, take them home with you and tell them about them, inspire them with the enthusiasm you have had here.

I cannot go on. You know what blessing has come to you. Take it home with you and share it with every one whom you can possibly reach during the two years to come, and then come back to the Convention in Portland, Oregon. When you do you will come with more spiritual power than ever before, to make that not simply a duplicate, a replica of this meeting, but one with still greater power, greater energy, greater devotion and greater prospects for advance for the Lord we love. Take home the message of evangelism, the message of personal devotion to Jesus Christ, and in your own society do not look for some great big meeting, but use your own society. Get fifty per cent of your active members during the last two years as converted members of the Church of Jesus Christ to which you belong. That is the challenge that has been given you over and over again. Do not forget it. Do not fail to share your blessings with others, and gain not a banner, it is well enough to have banners, but oh, how much better it is in spiritual life, in souls for Jesus Christ to show what we have done, and yet I am not making slight of these banners. Every one of the banners is earned; every one of them means service. Every one of them means real devotion to Jesus Christ, but if you don't get a banner, get a soul.

And now, friends, in the last few minutes shall we unite in a very brief meeting of consecration to God? May I ask every one to stay during the next ten minutes or so? Please do not interrupt or move around.

One feature of Christian Endeavor is the consecration meeting. Every month we are expected to have it. Every month the roll is called to see that those who have promised are present and ready to confess their love for God. This has been one of the great things of Christian Endeavor, one of the things that has declared our purpose, during all these forty-two years. In the first society there was a consecration meeting and that has been a distinctive, important, and necessary feature of our movement ever since. You can't all express yourselves. I should be glad if every one here could state his purpose. That is not possible, but will you unite with me in a purpose meeting, in a consecration service in heart devotion to Him who hath loved us and given Himself for us? I am sure you will.

ADJOURNMENT

Then the song which closes with its sweetly solemn strains all our Christian Endeavor Conventions, "God be with you till we meet again," was softly sung, the benediction was pronounced by Dr. Clark, and the great Des Moines Convention was over.

It was a Convention of rare power. The speakers were men of wonderful spiritual insight. Seldom has any Convention drawn such immense crowds to the morning Quiet Hour services. The churches — three of them — could not house the throng. All through, the delegates stuck to business. There were no distractions, no recreations even. It was a Convention of work.

The effects are sure to be great and lasting. This Convention will change the current of many lives. It has brought high vision to thousands. It has shown our youth the source of power. It has made hearts tender with sympathy, and it has steeled the wills of thousands to fight iniquity.

God was in it all, and Christ was glorified.

So in the warm evening the multitude dispersed, some to go to their home places, near or far, and some to see America's wonderland in the Yellowstone Park, in Pike's Peak, and in Glacier Park. May God be with them all!

GLEANINGS

I believe that being decent in politics is as religious as being devout in prayer meeting.—*Dr. Ira Landrith.*

Any righteous cause is as sure to win as the sun is sure to rise tomorrow morning.—*Wayne B. Wheeler.*

God made America out of the blood of all the world so that we should be interested in all mankind.—*Dr. Ira Landrith.*

"Special music at this time by the audience," was one of Secretary Gates' announcements. "The ushers will pass the plates. Make as much of a noise as you can."

Cradle-roll Christian Endeavorers had a representative two and a half months old, who appeared at some of the sessions and seems to be in training for a field-secretary's position.

A passenger on a train in talking with a Dixie delegate without knowing him to be an Endeavorer spoke of the excursionists in a critical way. The steward of the dining-car overheard, and expressed himself to this effect: "I don't want any speaking disrespectfully of Christian Endeavorers in my car. They are the only convention crowd that I care to have travel with us. Other convention crowds are finding fault about everything, but they are pleasant and courteous."

Rev. William Ralph Hall told a story coming from a Philadelphia rabbi. A Jewish merchant had been most unfortunate in venture after venture. Just as he was unpacking his Christmas goods in hope of making good some of his losses he was dismayed to see a new store close to his opened by a Mr. Goldstein. Suddenly there appeared the Christmas fairy offering to give the despairing man one wish he might make, but adding that she should give Goldstein just twice as much. "I tell you what I wish," was the answer after some hesitation. "I wish I was half dead. That will get Goldstein." Mr. Hall thought that his audience were probably two-thirds dead without any fairies after the strain of several days in the heat.

Overheard in a hotel lobby: From her, various emphatic complaints about her room. From the excursion manager: "Oh, come now! Keep sweet! Look on the bright side! Smile, smile, smile! Why, I laugh every time I look in the mirror." *From her:* "Oh, but you see, *I* am not a monkey!"

The trustee meeting was attended by sixty-seven members, one of the most largely attended meetings of its history.

The Convention badge was of celluloid, and was very pleasing. Yellow, red, and white were the colors. Across the top was a beautifully drawn ear of corn. From it hung the badge, bearing the C. E. monogram, a picture of a bright wheat-field with a harvester at work, and the motto, "The Harvest Time is Here." This, with the name of the Convention, the place, and the date, makes one of the most interesting and significant of Christian Endeavor's many badges.

One of the most interesting sights of the Convention, which, however, few saw, was the nimble work of the young women who operated a stenotype machine. This is a machine which is operated like a typewriter; is, in fact, a form of typewriter; but its keyboard is so arranged that half a dozen or more letters can be struck at once, and an expert writer can easily follow the most rapid speaker. Moreover, the machine operates quite silently. A very large part of the Convention report was captured by this machine.

Some of the delegates remarked the physical similarity between Wayne B. Wheeler, the great prohibition advocate, and former General Secretary William Shaw. The men are of about the same size, and in action they are equally vigorous, equally fiery, and equally eloquent. Both are masters of facts, with fine ability to marshal them and drive them home to the hearts of the audience.

Dr. Reiner's illustration of unselfishness, the prayer of the young woman who said, "O Lord, I am not asking anything for myself, but I do wish you would give Mamma a son-in-law."

The "Amens" at the close of the hymns conducted by Professor Smith produced a beautiful effect, the first loud, the second very soft, and both reverently prolonged.

The amplifier produced a really startling effect as one stood in the streets outside the Coliseum, for it was as if the speaker within stood at one's elbow, and the words were actually louder, as the writer can testify, on the street far away from the speakers than they were on the platform only ten feet away from the speaker.

Mr. A. G. Fegert, of Chicago, visiting Rev. John Timothy Stone, D.D., in his room in the hotel, found him reading the Bible. Dr. Stone told him that he made it a rule to read *one book of the Bible a day* — not a chapter, be it noted — during his summer vacation, and that it was in this quiet study of the Word of God, up in the mountains, that he found sermon material for all the year. Dr. Stone is one of the busiest pastors in the country. Last year he delivered fifty-one commencement addresses, besides countless other talks. It is interesting to know that he draws from the inexhaustible fountain of the word of God the spiritual nourishment that makes possible so splendid and fruitful a ministry.

Hundreds were disappointed when on the second morning of the Convention they went to hear Rev. Lionel Fletcher in his second Quiet Hour service at 8 A. M., for by that hour the large Central Christian Church was filled by a great host of Endeavorers eager to hear the message on soul-winning. Fortunately the crowd was able to find quarters in nearby churches where other speakers were conducting services.

Rev. Frank Lowe, Jr., author of "Religious Vocations," who last January resigned his position as associate pastor of the Church of Christ (Disciples), New York City, has just taken the degree of doctor of Philosophy, Columbia University. Mr. Lowe has returned to his home in St. Louis, Mo.

The delegates to the Des Moines Convention came for business. No Convention programme has been so strenuous as this, every moment of every one of the five and a half days being fully occupied, and in no Convention have the conferences been so well attended. Each day fourteen conferences were held, each lasting three hours, a period of intensive study and discussion that proved exceedingly helpful.

One morning at breakfast in the headquarters hotel the delegates found perched on the edge of their tumblers cleverly made grasshoppers with wings of blue tissue paper. The mouths of the insects were made by means of a little daub of sealing-wax, the bodies of peanuts. On each plate was a card cut in the shape of a note of music, the following message being printed on the head of the note. This, presumably, was the grasshoppers' note. The message read:

>Here we all sit like birds on your water-glass,
>   On your water-glass;
>   ,On your water-glass;
>Here we all sit like birds on your water-glass,
>   Waiting for something to happen.
>
>*Chorus.*
>
>Whose gwine make something happen?
>Whose gwine make something happen?
>'We all Junior workers are here for to say,
>   Are here for to say,
>   Are here for to say,
>We Junior workers are here for to say,
>We're gwine make some things happen.

Eight vigorous electric fans, placed around the Coliseum auditorium, helped to moderate the fierce heat that reigned through most of the Convention.

One could see the emotional effect of the great choral service Thursday evening in the Coliseum. While the splendid audience was singing "All hail the power of Jesus' name," one could see delegates here and there, lifted out of themselves, with clinched fist beating time, evidently following with great feeling the thought, "Crown Him Lord of all."

Hon. Frederick A. Wallis, Commissioner of Correction of New York

City, and a new president of the New York State Christian Endeavor Union, sent the following message:

"I have been entertaining a lingering hope that circumstances would at the last moment permit my attending the great Convention, but to-night suddenly the last vestige of hope has gone. No one knows my keen disappointment. However, as the new president of the New York State Christian Endeavor Union I will have the opportunity to promote Christian Endeavor in the Empire State this year. Watch us! My cordial and heartiest greetings to the Convention, and especially Dr. Clark and the Committee of Arrangements.

(Signed): "FREDERICK A. WALLIS."

The Exhibits

Up-stairs in the splendid building of the Des Moines public library were a large number of booths containing some delightful and profitable State Christian Endeavor exhibits. There was a remarkable miniature village of India made by the Moravian Juniors of West Salem, Ill. Ohio's booth had some fine Christian Endeavor posters. There was an extensive and most alluring show of photographs of Oregon scenery. Texas had a superb showing of 51,232 inches of Christian Endeavor publicity — a vast volume. The special feature of the Southwestern union was a miniature oil-well and derrick. New York sent interesting Christian Endeavor photographs. California's show was especially strong in Christian Endeavor posters; that of Kansas, in banners. Kentucky exhibited admirable work by prison Endeavorers. In the extensive exhibit of the Des Moines union, we noted a photograph of "the only entire girls' cabinet," that of 1918-1919. There was also a good Intermediate exhibit, and booths fitted up by New Jersey, Pennsylvania, and Missouri.

It Is Portland, '25

The trustees met on Thursday noon to decide upon the Convention meeting-place for two years hence. In 1921 Portland, Ore., was a strong competitor with Des Moines for the 1923 Convention. It yielded gracefully to the vote of the trustees at that time, and continued its invitation. Portland's claims were finely presented by ex-president Robinson, of the Oregon union, who emphasized not only the adequate financial guarantees, but the marvellous physical advantages of Oregon and Portland, and the spiritual gains the Endeavorers would reap from a Convention there and the great stimulus to Christian Endeavor on the Pacific Coast that such a Convention would bring. The vote of the trustees was unanimous and enthusiastic, and Miss Elaine Cooper, the present president of the Oregon union, thanked the trustees in a happy little speech. For the next two years Portland, Ore., will be the cynosure of all Christian Endeavor eyes.

Vesper Services at Fairgrounds

Scattered here and there over the great fairground enclosure groups of Endeavorers from several States held vesper services between the afternoon and evening sessions. The sun was sinking, a red ball of fire, into the haze of the west as the young people gathered around their leaders and listened to quiet talks on spiritual themes. They took part, too, in sentence prayers, as they do in their Christian Endeavor meetings, and their earnestness was abundantly apparent. In the hush of the evening hour they drew near to God, lifting the soul beyond the staggering beauties of a world bathed in glory to the Creator and Father of all. These group meetings perhaps helped to tune aright the mass-meeting that followed.

The editors write shorthand, and well remember their struggles to keep up with glib speakers whom they were trying to report verbatim. They gazed with interest and admiration at the young lady who was reporting the speeches on the wonderful machine called the stenotype. Silently operating a keyboard at which she never looked, her fingers moved with self-possessed sureness and amazing slowness, while the long ribbon marked with mysterious letters spun out on the floor.

Several of the conferences, which were held in churches and church halls, were literally crowded out. The conference on prayer-meeting methods packed the hall assigned to it, and overflowed; there was nothing to do but command an exodus, and the host of young people marched to the First Baptist Church, whose floor and gallery they filled. Mr. Walter D. Howell's conference on the place of Christian Endeavor in religious education found its quarters too cramped and moved to more adequate accommodations. Other conferences, like Mrs. Gates's on social-committee work, worried along, although the rooms were far too small for the crowds that attended them.

In Des Moines Churches

Probably never before has so thorough a distribution of Convention speakers been made on Convention Sunday among the churches of the entertaining city as was made at Des Moines.

Baptist churches heard Dr. Montgomery, Dr. MacTaggart, Dr. Reiner, Rev. George Moore, and Rev. Earl E. Harper.

To Christian churches went Rev. Dirk Lay, Rev. Glen MacRae, Rev. E. A. Sexsmith, Secretary Sherwood, Dr. Kendall, Rev. John Hardcastle, Rev. James Wray, Secretary Harry Allan.

Congregational churches listened to Dr. Landrith, Dr. Frank Lowe, Jr., President Brownell of the Pennsylvania union, Dr. Poling, Mr. Walter D. Howell, Dr. Cleaveland, and Secretary Blair.

Lutheran churches were served by Dr. I. W. Bingaman, Mr. William Ralph Hall, Dr. Duryee, Dr. Kirkpatrick, Rev. H. L. Streich.

Addresses in Methodist churches were given by Chaplain Ramsden, Secretary Hetzler, Rev. Lionel Fletcher, Dr. Amos R. Wells, Secretary F. P. Wilson, Rev. H. L. Pickerill, Dr. Gammon, Chaplain Hoffman, Secretary Paul Brown, Secretary Bert Jones, and A. J. Shartle.

To Presbyterian churches went Rev. James Kelly, Secretary Hicks, Secretary Gleason, Rev. F. A. Mattox, Rev. J. B. Good, Superintendent Vandersall, Rev. James DeForest Murch, Dr. Preston.

United Presbyterian churches heard Rev. P. I. Mohler, Dr. Deever, Dr. Shupe, and Rev. I. Moyer Hershey.

To churches of still other denominations went Rev. James A. Cosby, Dr. Bowman, Rev. G. W. Haddaway, Secretary Evans, Secretary Freet, Dr. Carpenter, Secretary Clarence C. Hamilton, Bishop Carey, Rev. S. S. Morris, Professor Aaron Brown, Dr. W. W. Matthews, Dr. T. J. Moppins, and Rev. T. A. Tripp.

It was a grand mix-up, men seldom speaking in churches of their own denominations, and was a splendid illustration of Christian Endeavor fellowship.

INDEX

"Alls" of Jesus 169
Alumni Banquet, Luncheons 106
Challenge of the Times 83
Choral of the Ways 78
Christian Endeavor 256
Christian Endeavor, Foundation Principles of.. 219
Christian Endeavor, Place of, in Educational
    Programme 256
Christian Endeavor Possibilities (Poem) 263
Christian Endeavor, Substitutes for 102
Christian Endeavor, Worth and Mission of.... 130
Closing Message 265
CONFERENCES
Expert Endeavor, C. F. Evans............ 87
Religious Education, Walter D. Howell 87
Recreation Methods, Mrs. E. P. Gates....... 87
Missionary Education, Faye A. Steinmetz.... 88
Citizenship, D. A. Poling................ 90
Prayer-Meeting Methods, F. D. G. Walker..... 90
Religious Vocations, Frank Lowe, Jr. 91
Teaching Missions, W. M. Cleaveland 93
Union Work, C. C. Hamilton............... 93
Fine Arts in Religion, Augustine Smith 94
Intermediate Work, Frank Getty 95
Christian Leadership, H. L. Pickerill 95
Junior Methods, Mildreth Haggard.......... 112
Denominational Rallies 139
    United Brethren, 139; Friends, 139; Presbyterian, South, 140; United Presbyterian, 141; Disciples, 142; Christian, 142; Mennonites, 143; Congregational, 143; Primitive Methodists, 145; United Brethren, 146; Lutherans, 146; Methodist Protestant, 147; Churches of God, 147; Reformed Church in the U. S., 148; A. M. E. and A. M. E. Zion, 149; Evangelical, 149; Presbyterian, U. S. A., 150.
Denominations, Relation of Christian Endeavor
    to the 70
Duties of Majorities and Minorities under the
    Constitution 32
Education, Christian Endeavor and......... 63
Education, Comprehensive Programme of..... 74
Education, Religious 230, 241
Eight-Hour Day 258
Executive Committee, United Society....... 19
Europe, Impressions of................... 165
Fair-Grounds 164
Fellowship among Races................... 257
Fellowship, Christian 257
Friends of Christ Campaign............... 20
FIELD SECRETARIES' MEETING AND CHRISTIAN ENDEAVOR PROBLEMS
Prison Christian Endeavor................ 184
Christian Endeavor in the City Church..... 185
Christian Endeavor and the Quiet Hour..... 186

Tenth Legion 187
Community Christian Endeavor............. 188
Floating Christian Endeavor.............. 189
Rural Christian Endeavor................. 190
Christian Endeavor Fresh-Air Work 192
Essentials of a Successful Prayer Meeting.... 193
Junior Societies 198, 199
Intermediates 201, 202
Alumni Councils 203
Alumni Fellowships 204
Alumni Loving-Cup 205
College Endeavor 206
Graded Endeavor 207
Leadership Training 208
Vocational Guidance 209
Publicity 210
Christian Endeavor World 211
Army and Navy Endeavor 213
Gleanings 267
God, The Quest for 176
Golden Rule in Industry 138
Greatest Fact in History 178
Home, Christian Endeavor and the 64
Industry, Golden Rule in 255
Junior Endeavor Complementary to Home and
    School 215
Life-Work, Choosing a 66
Luncheons, Junior Workers' 108
    Intermediate Superintendents 108
    Experts 109
    Life-Work Recruits 109
Motive, the Master 79
Negro's Contribution to the Religious Life of
    America 127
New Campaign 195
Officers of United Society 18
Others 257
Pageant 122
Parade 151
Pima Indians 98
Pledge, the Backbone of Christian Endeavor.. 100
Prohibition 259
QUIET HOUR
The Sword and the Cup 37, 58
Friends of Jesus 37
Christ, the Saviour of the World 38
Sermon on the Mount 38
Your Call and Mine 42
How to Win Friends for Christ 46
Why This Waste? 59
The Great Crusade 61
To Live Is Christ 134
War, Can We Prevent 158
Warless World 260
War, Peace, and the Near East 154
World Peace, Christian Endeavor and 124
Youth of the Church 217

www.ingramcontent.com/pod-product-compliance
Lightning Source LLC
Chambersburg PA
CBHW051747040426
42446CB00007B/257